Chasing the Last Laugh

ALSO BY RICHARD ZACKS

Island of Vice
An Underground Education
History Laid Bare
The Pirate Hunter
The Pirate Coast

Chasing the Last Laugh

MARK TWAIN'S RAUCOUS AND REDEMPTIVE
ROUND-THE-WORLD COMEDY TOUR

Richard Zacks

DOUBLEDAY

NEW YORK LONDON TORONTO

SYDNEY AUCKLAND

Book design by Pei Loi Koay
Jacket design by Emily Mahon
Front-of-jacket image: Mark Twain, America's Best Humorist
by Joseph Ferdinand Keppler, c. 1885. Courtesy of the
Library of Congress, Washington, D.C.
Spine-of-jacket images: (top) Mark Twain on a ship deck, 1901 © AS400
DB / Corbis; (bottom) Lithograph by Edward Penfield. Courtesy of the
Library of Congress, Washington, D.C.

LIBRARY OF CONGRESS CATALOGING-IN-PUBLICATION DATA
Names: Zacks, Richard, author.
Title: Chasing the last laugh : Mark Twain's raucous and redemptive
round-the-world comedy tour / Richard Zacks.
Description: New York : Doubleday, 2016. | Includes bibliographical
references and index.
Identifiers: LCCN 2015036843 | ISBN 9780385536448 (hardcover) |
ISBN 9780385536455 (ebook)
Subjects: LCSH: Twain, Mark, 1835-1910—Travel. | Authors,
American—19th century—Biography. | BISAC: BIOGRAPHY &
AUTOBIOGRAPHY / Literary. | PERFORMING ARTS / Comedy. |
BIOGRAPHY & AUTOBIOGRAPHY / Historical.
Classification: LCC PS1334 .Z33 2016 | DDC 818/.409—dc23
LC record available at http://lccn.loc.gov/2015036843

MANUFACTURED IN THE UNITED STATES OF AMERICA

1 3 5 7 9 10 8 6 4 2

First Edition

To my inner circle: Kitty, Georgia, Ziggy and Kris

Contents

Chasing the Last Laugh

Prologue

I n February 1896, Mark Twain—pilot of the Mississippi River, whitewasher of American fences—was just about to board a tiny six-seat open railroad car in the Himalayan mountains in India. He was circling the world with his wife and daughter, entertaining English-speaking audiences because he needed to make a lot of money in a hurry to pay off debts from bad investments.

International celebrities get perks, but the following perk seems almost too amazing to be true. The British higher-ups at the Darjeeling Himalayan Railway—an engineering marvel designed to transport tea from the steep slopes—had decided to let him use thirty-five miles of track *as a personal roller coaster*. Chill winds off the majestic snowy peaks ruffled the famous bushy eyebrows. He told a handful of tea plantation owners that he was glad the blanket of clouds had cleared so that he could see the world's highest peaks because then he wouldn't have to lie about it. The night before, during his stage act, he had mentioned America's first president. "Think of it. George Washington could not lie," said Twain. "Grown person, you know—could *not* lie. Comes right out & *says* it. Seems to me I'd a known enough to keep *still* about an infirmity like that."

The views of far-off snowcapped Himalayan mountains were dazzling and the drops were unquestionably fatal. An elephant had recently splattered its enormous guts after slipping off the Hill Cart Road, which paralleled the tracks.

Twain gazed over the edge at the track falling down sharply and "corkscrewing in and out of crags and precipices, down, down, forever down."

No seat belts are mentioned in any narrative. The author *thought* he might have heard a story about a prior lieutenant governor's train jumping the track and hurling everyone off the mountainside. He shared the story. And even if that story wasn't true, that didn't mean that they were safe.

He was doing what many self-respecting fathers/husbands would do in this situation. He did his level best to scare his wife and daughter. "The car could really jump the track," he told Livy and Clara. "A pebble on the track, placed there by either accident or malice, at a sharp curve where one might strike it before the eye could discover it, could derail the car and fling it down into India."

Gravity would propel them downward; only a hand brake could slow them. They would race through four horizontal loops so steep that the train had to double back through tunnels. The Darjeeling Himalayan Express ran along slopes so nearly vertical that the engineers couldn't lay long winding curves but four times had to set the line in Z-shaped zigzags that required reversing directions. Twain and family would briefly be heading blindly backward and downward. To add to the thrill, the track was only two feet wide, which gave the six-foot-wide cars the sense of floating, not riding the rails.

By way of precaution, British officials sent another railcar ahead of Twain and his family.

> [The danger] was for Mr. Pugh, inspector of a division of the
> Indian police, in whose company and protection we had come
> from Calcutta. He had seen long service as an artillery officer, was
> less nervous than I was, and so he was to go ahead of us in a pilot
> hand-car with a Ghurka and another native; and the plan was that
> when we should see his car jump over a precipice we must put on
> our brake and send for another pilot. It was a good arrangement.

The family wrapped themselves in fur blankets and shot down the mountain. At "Agony Point," the curve radius was so tight that they truly expected to go flying. Halfway down, they rested, drinking Darjeeling tea at a mountainside chalet. They also saw a Tibetan dance play. They reboarded and plunged downward.

"For rousing, tingling, rapturous pleasure there is no holiday trip that approaches the bird-flight down the Himalayas in a hand-car," wrote Twain. "It has no fault, no blemish."

And he later judged that February day in India the single most enjoyable day of his entire yearlong, debt-paying trip.

———

The idea of Twain in India is discombobulating enough; the idea of Mississippi Mark telling purely American stories in the Himalayas is even more extraordinary. Robed priests squatted outside, spinning prayer wheels. Sherpa guides prepared for Everest treks. That weekend, Twain's wife, Livy, wrote to their fifteen-year-old daughter:

> Jean, darling, look on the map, and try to realize that we who belong to you are away up here in the Himalayas, on the border of Thibet. I cannot myself believe it can be true.

Twain, whom many pictured in a straw hat and corncob pipe, performed his stand-up routine onstage in a black evening suit. He never smiled. Never. Crowned king of deadpan. No props, no notes. He called it a "reading," but it was really the greatest hits from his best books. And he memorized the whole ninety-minute show. He selected choice morsels such as "The Celebrated Jumping Frog of Calaveras County" or "How I Escaped Being Killed in a Duel."

He tailored his material, paced it, pared it. He stood five feet, eight and a half inches tall, weighed 145 pounds, wore a size-seven shoe, and talked very s-l-o-w. S-l-o-w-e-r than that. His daughter and others called it a "drawl." It made the audiences listen carefully, and it let him go for long pauses and then surprise them.

Samuel L. Clemens, the living, breathing man who sometimes wrote and performed as "Mark Twain," was a wonderful hodgepodge of uplifting sentiment and bad habits, of flash mood swings, from temper tantrums to jokes; a fellow of stunning irreverence and of conventional yearnings for praise and wealth. He raced to judgment and often rued it; he avoided curse words in deference to his wife but created a spectacular genre of vitriol; he smoked two dozen cigars a day; he drank a hot Scotch most nights; he demonized his enemies and former business partners; he haloed only his closest friends and helpers; he embodied so many contradictory traits in such ample helpings—envy/generosity, suspiciousness/gullibility, loyalty/paranoia, arrogance/insecurity—that no one, not even he, could predict his moods.

Twain was an abysmal investor, an absolute magnet for con men and fool schemes. He was America's highest-paid author and one of America's biggest investment losers. "There are two times in a man's life when he should not speculate," he wrote around this time. "When he can't afford it and when he can."

During his yearlong trek, Twain would perform 122 nights in 71 different cities in Australia, New Zealand, India, South Africa, and North America; he would spend 98 nights at sea on steamships and almost 50 days ill from coughs, colds, boils, stomach illness. He would travel by rail, rickshaw, mule-drawn carriage, man-toted palanquin and elephant. And his sightseeing boat would veer near floating corpses in the Ganges, and Zulus would do war dances for him.

Amid moments of elation at the exotic travels, he would also sometimes be privately furious that financial losses had forced him to play the clown. He remarked that once audiences see you stand on your head, they expect you to stay in that position.

The famous author had turned sixty years old and had already written *Huck Finn* and *Tom Sawyer,* and had envisioned himself more in the role of lazy literary lion than as a "platform" joke teller; he had also expected to be basking in Rockefeller-style wealth, not trying to shovel his way out from shame.

The highest-paid writer in America had succeeded in losing his entire fortune and the fortune of his coal heiress wife through appalling investments. With no patience for details, he had repeatedly staked all with cock-eyed optimism and unrufflable self-delusion. He had encouraged others to follow him with the carny barker aplomb of Colonel Sellers of his novel *The Gilded Age.*

The author of *Innocents Abroad* had thought himself shrewd and savvy right up to the day that he lost it all and newspapers across America had proclaimed, "Mark Twain Fails." His heiress wife, Livy, seems to have felt the shame even more deeply than he did. "I have a perfect *horror* and heart-sickness over it," she wrote to her sister. "I cannot get away from the feeling that business failure means disgrace."

And what's so odd and wonderful (and forgotten) is that most of America, when it found out about Mark Twain's financial disaster, wound up loving him more for failing, and for being humiliated, and then for having the fortitude to scrape himself up and try to pay off his debts. Twain circled the globe—as he put it, raiding and pillaging—and he planned to talk his way out of hell and humiliation.

CHAPTER 1

Joys of Self-Publishing

Twain was a proud man, so he kept up a false front of success to all outsiders. In the summer of 1893, he was by reputation America's greatest humorist and a successful publisher who was married to an heiress. He ranked among the nation's highest-paid magazine writers and most prized after-dinner speakers. His life—on paper—marked a fabulous success story, from Hannibal to Hartford to the family's current address abroad in Paris.

Twain owned a publishing house; it was failing. His latest book, a contrived, almost slapstick novella, *The American Claimant*, hadn't sold well; his backlist, even including *Tom Sawyer* and *Huckleberry Finn*, was limping along, bringing in small change.

The publishing house owed money to bookbinders, paper suppliers, printers, owed rent for a plush office at 67 Fifth Avenue, at 14th Street; meanwhile, their list included underwhelming titles such as *Stories from the Rabbis* and *One Hundred Desserts* and *Tenting on the Plains* by General Custer's widow. Twain had invested heavily in a typesetter that had 18,000 moving parts but was supposed to revolutionize the printing industry.

Twain teetered on the brink of financial ruin. At first he blamed himself for numerous bad business decisions, but once he got that formality out of the way, he unleashed his sizable writing talents on blaming others.

He wrote in a private notebook his thoughts on the inventor James W. Paige, whom he had amply funded but who still had not delivered his invention. "[He] and I always meet on effusively affectionate terms; and yet he knows perfectly well that if I had his nuts in a steel-trap I would shut out all human succor and watch that trap till he died."

Twain and his wife owned their expensive home in Hartford, but they had run out of enough cash to live there in the style to which they were accustomed, with seven servants (a black butler, a gardener, cook, coachman, tutor and maids), and horses and an elegant carriage. They had moved out two years earlier, claiming Livy's health required a change of scenery, and they chose Europe, which sounds odd for financially strapped people, but it was cheaper than their Hartford high life. They chose self-exile over the public shame of a diminished lifestyle.

The beautiful mansion lay empty.

"I have never felt so desperate in my life, for I haven't got a penny to my name & Mrs. Clemens hasn't enough laid up with [her brother Charles] Langdon to keep us two months. . . . I do not sleep, these nights, for visions of the poor-house. . . . Everything does look blue, so dismally blue."

Twain's publishing house had started off magnificently in 1885. He had installed his former gofer, his niece's thirty-three-year-old husband, Charles L. Webster, to run it, even called it "Charles L. Webster & Co."— perhaps to insulate himself from blame. The quirky founding contract stipulated that Twain could "not be called upon" to perform any managerial or editorial duties but nonetheless would retain final approval of all new books.

The company's first two releases were *Adventures of Huckleberry Finn* and *The Personal Memoirs of Ulysses S. Grant*. One was a modest success; the other a record-breaking blockbuster.

Grant's memoirs set publishing records, with 600,000 volumes issued and nearly $400,000 ($12 million in today's dollars) paid to the Grant family. Twain had lured the former president away from a verbal agreement with *Century*, calling for the general to receive industry-standard royalties—10% of the cover price; Twain instead offered 70% of net profits (after printing expenses, etc.), which Twain promised—rightly— would turn out to be double the *Century* offer.

And, contrary to some reports, Twain did *not* write the memoirs. In fact, he was furious when Joseph Pulitzer's *New York World* charged that General Adam Badeau had ghostwritten many chapters as Grant lay dying from throat cancer. Twain dropped his threatened lawsuit, claiming he didn't want to give any free publicity to "that daily issue of unmedicated closet paper [*i.e., toilet paper*]."

The seeds of ruin, however, sprouted early. Sad-eyed, balding Webster failed to oversee the torrents of cash; a bookkeeper embezzled $25,000 (wound up in Sing Sing prison) and a Midwest book agent stole $30,000. These were huge sums in that era when a beer cost a nickel. The company signed up famed minister Henry Ward Beecher, but he died before he could complete his autobiography or his life of Christ. Civil War generals—Sheridan, Sherman, Winchester—lined up to repeat Grant's deluge of gold, but the public quickly tired of war memoirs.

The company pinned its hope on the pope, the immensely popular Leo XIII, whose face seemed to be everywhere, since his portrait accompanied an endorsement of Vin Mariani, a cocaine-laced wine. Webster traveled to Rome, landed the contract, and was knighted to the Order of the Golden Spur, with robes and a ceremonial sword. (Webster later found himself the only papal knight in Fredonia, New York.)

"[Twain] had no words in which to paint the magnificence of the project, or to forecast its colossal success," later recalled author-editor-friend William Dean Howells. It bombed, despite the unusual inclusion of two color chromolithographs of the pope. "We did not consider how often Catholics could not read," surmised Howells.

Twain replaced Webster with young Fred Hall, a stenographer with no publishing experience; he said he was replacing "guesswork" with "brains." But no one saw that the Library of American Literature was crushing the company under a mountain of debt.

Ironically, their biggest seller was destroying them. Salesmen had no trouble lining up tens of thousands of "subscription" orders for the eleven-volume collection. The well-respected editors Edmund Clarence Stedman and Ellen Mackay Hutchinson had skimmed the cream of Hawthorne, Melville, Longfellow, and the like to create a compendium of 1,207 authors, 2,671 selections, 303 full-page illustrations. More than half the nation still lived on farms and in small towns, and rural buyers, especially fond of ornate bindings, could achieve instant gentility and respectability with the purchase.

But the business plan had one crucial flaw. Customers had to pay only the *first* $3 monthly installment of the $33 cover price to receive the *entire set,* but it cost the company $13 to print, bind and ship, and another $12 in commission to the agents. The publisher was $22 in the red on every sale, and, as the economy soured, customers increasingly stopped paying installments. Delinquent payments ballooned from $28,862 in 1891 to $67,795 in 1892.

The office manager observed, Twain-like: "The faster installment orders came in, the faster our capital shrank, until our prosperity became embarrassing."

Twain himself called it a "lingering suicide."

———

What had begun as a quest by author Twain to receive a fair shake from publishers had spiraled into a nightmare. Now, instead of furnishing money, his venture, Charles L. Webster & Co., was sucking up cash. Twain deferred his royalties. Livy pumped in large sums, but the company eventually had to borrow from Harlem's Mount Morris Bank, itself on shaky ground because of a bad investment in the Chicago & Alton Railroad.

The whole country was reeling from the Panic of 1893, as the stock market had crashed in June and more than 16,000 businesses failed, and more than 2½ million men were unemployed. Credit was tight and fear great.

Twain tried to unload his publishing house on Harper & Bros. but failed. "I want to sell because I am not made for business," he wrote. "The worry of it makes me old & robs life of its zest."

Twain had one overriding fear: that in the chaos of his publishing house suddenly going under he might lose the copyrights to his own books, that *Huckleberry Finn* might wind up owned by a bank or a printer. "If they go, I am a beggar," he wrote on August 14, 1893, to the man running his publishing house.

On Monday, September 11, 1893, he learned that a Webster Company debt note for $8,000 ($240,000 today) would be coming due in one week. He had tapped out his ability to borrow from his depressed brother-in-law, who had recently cosigned $21,000 in Mount Morris Bank loans for them. Twain had no cash but was using his *Cosmopolitan* magazine fee for "The Esquimaux Maiden's Romance" to live on. He was saving more money by staying at the home of his friend Dr. Clarence Rice, throat surgeon to the Metropolitan Opera; the *Century*, America's most prestigious monthly, was so squeezed it had refused to pay Twain for his new novella *Pudd'nhead Wilson* until it started running in November. Fred Hall, who had stopped drawing a salary, was near broke and had already borrowed $15,000 ($450,000 today) for Webster & Co. from family friends, the Barrows.

(A quick note on historical dollar values; day laborers made *15 cents an hour;* a fine three-bedroom Manhattan apartment rented for $80 a month; economists suggest multiplying 1890s dollars by *thirty* to gain an approximate value in the early twenty-first century.)

A sudden failure could put the creditors in control, could open Twain to lawsuits by companies that might succeed in seizing his home and his books.

As Twain put it, "the billows of hell" began rolling over him. He didn't want to go to Hartford—where people would ask embarrassing questions about why the Clemens family had not returned after two years, but he forced himself.

Twain walked over to Grand Central Depot on Tuesday evening, and under the magnificent 200-yard glass dome covering the platforms boarded a train to Hartford. He did not go to his home on Farmington Avenue, his beautiful burnt-orange confection of turrets and balconies. He visited two wealthy Hartford businessmen, longtime friends, members of the informal Friday night billiards club, Edward M. Bunce and Henry C. Robinson. He wanted to borrow $5,000.

They turned him down. He sat in the parlor of lawyer Robinson—former mayor of Hartford, twice nominated for governor—with bank executive Bunce, and the trio brainstormed for an hour. They came to the conclusion that it was hopeless; Bunce had heard of a Chicago millionaire during this Panic of 1893 who had been turned down trying to raise $600,000 on prime real estate worth four times that amount. Robinson told Twain he couldn't borrow even $3,000 on his Farmington Avenue home, even though Twain claimed it was worth $170,000.

He later wrote to Livy: "My friends . . . they were not moved, not strongly interested, & I was ashamed that I went." And Twain spent the night at the Bunces' but informed Livy he had seen no one else in Hartford. She was obsessed with keeping their financial setbacks secret.

"The holy passion of Friendship is of so sweet & steady & loyal & enduring a nature that it will last through the whole lifetime if not asked to lend money." He had written those lines a year earlier as a Pudd'nhead Wilson maxim.

Twain—in those days of few telephones—sent a telegram to Livy's sister, Sue, saying, "I have no shame; the boat is sinking," and asked for $5,000. She said she didn't have the cash, and her banker informed her that her bonds were not negotiable in New York, but she traded a bond with her sister-in-law, Ida. She said if Twain telegraphed on Friday, she'd messenger the bond to him.

Twain and Hall walked the corridors of Wall Street, discreetly trying to find a loan. They failed. Hall told Twain that $5,000 from Sue wouldn't save them. They needed $8,000. Twain collapsed on the bed on Wednesday night at Dr. Rice's house, thinking he was a ruined man. With all the stress and travel, he had developed a deep, phlegmy hacking cough.

He was at the Webster offices Thursday when a messenger arrived from the plump, genial doctor. "[Dr. Rice] told me he had ventured to speak to a rich friend of his who was an admirer of mine about our straits," wrote Twain. "I was very glad."

Twain was told to send young Hall down to the gentleman's office at 26 Broadway, in the Standard Oil Building, the following afternoon with their account books. Apparently, the executive had absolutely loved *Roughing It,* Twain's tale of Nevada cowboys and silver mining mishaps; the executive had read it himself, then had read it aloud to his family.

Fred Hall showed up at 4 p.m. on Friday and in "six minutes" he had a check for $8,000 and their "worries were over"—temporarily.

———

Twain's new friend, worth about $50 million, was Henry Huttleston Rogers, a fifty-three-year-old vice president at Standard Oil and one of the wealthiest men in America. Their friendship would last to the very last days of each man's life; it would disturb some of Twain's literary brethren; many biographers would gloss over it.

Around this time, they met briefly in a drawing room at the Murray Hill Hotel. They even resembled each other, with Rogers being slightly taller but slender with ample mustache and bushy eyebrows. Rogers's piercing blue eyes were mesmerizing, and at times distracting, during tough negotiations.

The affinity between the two men was near instant. They would quickly discover that they shared a love of Twain's writing, of cigars, boxing matches, poker and especially billiards; both liked practical jokes, hated opera, had strong senses of humor, heavy on the sarcasm and vitriol. (Rogers kept his hidden except for a circle of close friends.)

One perceptive observer of both men thought their bond was actually anchored in a profound "mutual envy": Twain envied Rogers's financial prowess and his huge self-made fortune, and Rogers envied Twain's popularity and unbuttoned irreverence.

H.H. Rogers, three years younger than Twain, spent his childhood in maritime Fairhaven, Massachusetts, working his way up from grocery store delivery boy to making a fortune in the oil industry. The nineteenth-century oil boom, with wells first geysering in Pennsylvania, centered on supplying millions of gallons of *illuminating* oil to fill portable lamps in unelectrified cities and in rural America, replacing Civil War–era sperm-whale oil. The market also mushroomed for oil by-products such as varnish, paints, solvents, naphtha, long before the viscous black liquid was refined into automobile fuel.

H.H. Rogers over the weekend reviewed the Webster account books Hall had brought and by Monday had a more ambitious solution for Twain's dire cash shortage. He suggested selling the Library of American Literature and the subscription sales department to his son-in-law William Evarts Benjamin, a memorabilia dealer with a literary pedigree from his father, the poet Park Benjamin.

Why would the money-hemorrhaging Library of American Literature appeal to Rogers? There was $67,000 in *uncollected* subscriptions, 585 eleven-volume sets sitting in the warehouse, another 5,000 sets printed but unbound, printing plates, and a veteran sales force. Rogers and his son-in-law offered $50,000. Once the Panic ended and people could pay their bills, the property should rocket in value.

Twain was outraged by the price but didn't share his opinion with his very new acquaintance, Rogers. Instead he unleashed his fury that Monday on a respected Oxford-educated copy editor at the *Century* magazine who had dared to change his punctuation in *Pudd'nhead Wilson*. Twain wrote Livy: "I said I didn't care if he was an Archangel imported from Heaven, he couldn't puke his ignorant impudence over *my* punctuation." Twain restored his commas and semicolons the following day.

Twain and Hall didn't reject Rogers's offer outright, but they frantically tried to find a publisher willing to pay more or to buy the whole company. Hall also tried to negotiate a higher price. Both efforts failed as more scrutiny of the accounts reduced the deadbeat subscriptions to

$50,000, and Rogers would value these unguaranteed debts at only 50 cents on the dollar.

Twain blamed himself; he wrote Livy his regret over not realizing three years ago that Webster & Co. couldn't handle the expense of this gargantuan literary series. "A child should have seen it."

When his host Dr. Rice was called away to Chicago, Twain found himself "so lonesome . . . that he couldn't stand it," so he moved into a $1.50-a-night room at the Players Club, the artists' elegant Stanford White–designed all-male club on Gramercy Park. He said the manager gave him a "deliciously quiet" room on an upper floor with an "electric light over my pillow" which he liked exceedingly. "I am horribly home-sick," he wrote to his daughter Clara, "not for any *place*, but for the family."

Twain pondered the $50,000 offer and became increasingly desperate. Webster & Co. owed more than $100,000 (equivalent to $3 million today) to various printers, binders and banks, but it also owed $66,000 in unpaid loans to Livy, and Twain himself had left about $75,000 in royalties and unclaimed profits in the company. Selling the Library of American Literature would leave a shell of a company still burdened with massive debts.

———

He had another way out, but he didn't like it.

"Sometimes I seem to foresee that I have *got* to go on the dreadful platform again. If I must, I must—but nothing short of absolute necessity will drive me." By "platform," he meant standing up onstage to do his act. Despite his great talent at it, he claimed to loathe performing for money.

"He detested the thought of lecturing at all times of his life and yet, when actually on the stage, he almost always succeeded in electrifying himself to the point of pleasure," wrote his daughter Clara, reminiscing years later.

"It was not purely perdition for him, or rather it was perdition for only one-half of him, the author-half," wrote W. D. Howells, "for the actor-half it was paradise."

Twain hoped never to have to go, but he asked his wife if she would accompany him. Two weeks later, Hall and Twain accepted the $50,000 and tossed in furniture such as four rolltop desks and seven revolving chairs.

CHAPTER 2

Printing Mogul

For 400 years since Gutenberg, printers had repeated the tedious process of hand-setting loose pieces of type, inking them and printing pages—then collecting and sorting them and doing it over again, and again. Now, the race was on, among the likes of James W. Paige, Ottmar Mergenthaler, and Joseph C. Fowler, to invent a fast automated machine, with a simple keyboard, that would lay out lines of type. This quest marked the holy grail of nineteenth-century publishing; the inventor and his investors would become fabulously wealthy, selling the devices to tens of thousands of newspapers, magazines and book publishers.

Twain now hoped to lure H.H. Rogers—deal-making plutocrat—into backing James W. Paige, a man Twain once called "the Shakespeare of mechanical invention."

Twain had the opposite of the golden touch when it came to investing. He had passed on Alexander Graham Bell's telephone (despite having one of the first home phones in the nation) but had sunk $42,000 into an engraving process, Kaolotype, involving impressions in white china clay that would revolutionize illustrations. (It didn't.) He lost money on the New York Vaporizing Co., which was going to improve steam engines, handing the inventor $35 a week. "He visited me every few days to report progress and I early noticed by his breath and gait that he was spending 36 dollars a week on whisky, and I could never figure out where he got the other dollar." He lost at least $14,500 on a steam pulley (magnified to $32,000 in his autobiography). He also lost money the old-fashioned way by buying stocks and selling at the wrong time—buying Oregon Transcontinental Railroad at $78 a share, watching it climb to $98 and selling at $12 a share. "I . . . don't wish to ever look at a stock report again."

Twain, with his vast enthusiasms, never had any patience for the minutiae of business plans. His request during one investment:

"Let Marsh send me a statement—not one of those damned incomprehensible professional-technical debtor-&-creditor enigmas, which none but the gods & bookkeepers can make head or tail of, but a plain sensible *written-out* statement of the case, which Jean [*then age two years, thirteen days*] can understand."

————

About the only successful investment for Twain was something called the Mark Twain Scrapbook. He had actually invented it: a scrapbook with pages with strips of dried glue, which, when moistened, allowed the customer easily to paste in letters, articles and photos. If he hadn't partnered with a thief named Dan Slote, he would have reaped huge profits, but Slote went bankrupt at least twice and died before repaying a large loan.

Twain thought he knew printing, thought he knew a good investment when he saw it. Little Sammy Clemens had been a "printer's devil," his first job around age thirteen as an apprentice in Hannibal for the weekly *Missouri Courier*, picking, sorting, cleaning, inking pieces of type for room, board and two sets of clothes a year, hand-me-downs from the press owner. "I was only about half as big as [he was], consequently his shirts gave me the uncomfortable sense of living in a circus tent."

When Twain ran away from home, he lived by doing journeyman printing jobs in St. Louis and New York. Outside of writing, Twain mastered two professions in his lifetime: piloting a Mississippi riverboat and working in a printing office. He knew the job right down to reminiscing about how the candle they shoved in the letter *K* box always dripped wax onto the *D*'s, and how whenever the boss wasn't looking, Twain, instead of re-sorting used letters, would drop them all into the π box, with all the miscellaneous symbols.

On a Saturday in the late 1880s in Hartford, Twain was absolutely awed by how a mechanical device performed his former loathsome job. **"EUREKA!"** he wrote in thick bold letters in his notebook.

In one of his moon-shot mood swings, he gushed to his brother:

At 12:20 this afternoon, a line of movable types was spaced and justified by machinery for the first time in the history of the world! It was done automatically—instantly—perfectly.

. . . and so by long odds the most amazing and extraordinary invention ever born of the brain of man stands completed and perfect. Livy is downstairs celebrating.

. . . All the witnesses made written record of this immense historical birth . . . and also set down the hour and the minute. Nobody had drank anything, and yet everybody seemed drunk. Well—dizzy, stupefied, stunned.

All the other wonderful inventions of the human brain sink pretty nearly into commonplace contrasted with this . . . mechanical miracle. Telephones, telegraphs, locomotives, cotton gins, sewing machines, Babbage calculators, jacquard looms. . . . all mere toys, simplicities! The Paige Compositor marches alone and far in the lead of human inventions.

In two or three weeks, we shall work the stiffness out of her joints and have her performing as smoothly and softly as human muscles, and then we shall speak out the big secret and let the world come and gaze.

———

The "two or three weeks" kept rolling into two or three more weeks, then months.

The mechanical challenge was immense: to press one of the 108 letter/number/or symbol keys, send a small piece of type into line after line, and then afterwards return those pieces of type to the proper channels. Making the job much harder was "justifying" each line, that is, creating equal spaces between the words so the lines would end evenly.

An operator would set the length of the line for a book or newspaper column, then the machine would calculate the number of upcoming words that could fit comfortably in that line and insert the proper space dividers. Say the line was four inches wide and seven words could fit with a half inch left over; the machine would "know" that seven words needed six spaces and would divide the half inch by six and insert a $1/12$th-inch spacer between words. (This is why Twain thought the machine could "think.") All these spacers, some varying by only $5/1000$ths of an inch, also needed to be returned to the proper channels. It is not surprising the machine needed 18,000 movable parts.

Paige received his first typesetter patent in 1874; in two decades, he had run through *four sets* of backers. Twain first invested in 1880, when a Hartford jeweler with whom he played billiards offered him some stock. The inventor had his workshop at the massive Colt Firearms factory, along the Connecticut River, famous for miles around for its royal-blue-and-gold onion dome. Those backers ran out of money, and then Twain and Connecticut lawyer William Hamersley stepped in, with Twain signing a spectacularly naive contract that granted him profits only if he paid for *all expenses until the completion of the machine*.

The immensely complicated device was always one tweak from perfection. Twain had already written *The Gilded Age* in 1873 in collaboration with Charles Dudley Warner and had unknowingly foreshadowed the Paige typesetter.

And there in Kentucky, when [Colonel Sellers] raked up that old numskull that had been inventing away at a perpetual motion machine for twenty-two years, and Beriah Sellers saw at a glance where just one more little cog-wheel would settle the business, why I could see it as plain as day when he came in wild at midnight and hammered us out of bed and told the whole thing in a whisper with the doors bolted and the candle in an empty barrel.

Oceans of money in it—anybody could see that. But it did cost a deal to buy the old numskull out—and then when they put the new cog wheel in they'd overlooked something somewhere and it wasn't any use—the troublesome thing wouldn't go.

———

That was Paige in a nutshell, always one cogwheel away, or sometimes the cogwheel briefly seemed to pop into place, miraculously, seducing Twain all over again.

Twain, then earning solid royalties, spent up to $4,000 a month funding Paige—including the manufacturing, now at Pratt & Whitney; the drafting of the longest patent application in U.S. history (417 pages and 856 drawings); the Paige lifestyle that featured a beautiful "small, plump and well-formed" actress as mistress. The author funded the enterprise until he had squandered about $170,000 (about $5 million nowadays).

Paige then found a set of New York City backers, who because of Paige's factory location, called themselves the Connecticut Company; when they refused to pony up another penny, Paige—an enthusiastic hummingbird of a man—found a Midwest manufacturer, Towner K. Webster, to back him and build a custom factory in Chicago. In the Panic of 1893, that company also ran out of money. "What a talker he is," Twain once wrote of Paige. "He could persuade a fish to come out and take a walk with him."

————

Now H.H. Rogers, after discussing the Paige typesetter with several experts in the field who had witnessed exhibitions, decided that he would try to back it.

Paige, over two decades, had created a tangled mess of contradictory contracts assigning shares of profit and royalties per machine produced, and another mess with foreign rights. Twain, for instance, was convinced he still owned a "handsome" share of European sales.

Complicating matters, the main rival, the Mergenthaler Linotype, was already being used in the *New York Tribune* newsroom and dozens of other printing places nationwide. It could not match the Paige prototype for speed, but it was more trustworthy and had the advantage of actually being manufactured, refined and sold.

H.H. Rogers, with Twain's help, gathered the New York investors and the remaining Connecticut sponsors to meet in New York at the Murray Hill Hotel on December 4, 1893. In a daydreamy entry in his notebook that night, the author described himself as having a three-year option to decide whether to accept *a quarter million dollars in cash or a half million in stock*.

Rogers scheduled another meeting and schooled Twain on how to play a small con on the rest of the investors. He told Twain to inform them that Rogers was on the verge of backing out and Twain would need a guaranteed share bonus before trying to keep Rogers aboard. The ruse worked—even though Rogers never had any intention of leaving.

Twain described to Livy how much he enjoyed watching H.H. in action, negotiating to set up the brand-new $5 million Paige Compositor

Company that would supersede all previous companies. "Well, Livy darling, it is better than a circus . . . it was beautiful to see Mr. Rogers apply his probe & his bung-starter & remorselessly let the wind & the water from the so-called 'assets' of these companies."

Twain clearly enjoyed watching his Wall Street maestro flatten these men who had pummeled Twain. H.H. "sweetly and courteously . . . stripped away all the rubbish" and reduced the value of the "whole gaudy enterprise" from several million to $276,000. Then he said: "Gentlemen, I am prepared to listen to a proposition from you to furnish capital."

The room was silent. They eventually asked that their shares be valued at 50 cents on the dollar in the new company. H.H. announced they would take a break till the following morning. He told Twain the other side would be glad to get 12 cents, but he would offer 20 cents. He predicted they would have a hard time hiding how pleased they were.

Casual observers of Twain might find surprising his instant friendship with a notorious robber baron, nicknamed Hell Hound Rogers, but actually Twain savored the friendship of wealthy men, such as Andrew Carnegie and Stanford White; he sat in their boxes at prizefights; he teased them in ways few others dared.

On December 21, 1893, around 1 p.m., Twain and H.H. Rogers took a ferry across the Hudson and boarded the train at Penn Station (then in Jersey City) to set off on a whirlwind trip to Chicago to convince James W. Paige to forsake all previous claims and accept the terms of the new company.

They boarded the 2 p.m. "fast train," scheduled to reach Chicago in twenty-five hours, hurtling at more than thirty miles per hour. Their private car, attached at the end, featured a "darling back porch—railed, roofed and roomy." The two men had met three months earlier but had never spent extended periods of time together, beyond a negotiation or a dinner party.

Twain wrote Livy that although they had plenty of reading material, they talked almost constantly till midnight, both going and returning. Occasionally, the men would plot strategy for the upcoming negotiations. H.H. would muse aloud about deal points, and Twain reported his role was to pace, smoke and agree.

The car, on loan from a railroad executive, featured a sitting room, four overstuffed armchairs and two sofas that pulled out into beds, a dining area and also a bedroom. They ate canvasback duck for dinner, with claret and champagne served. A bit later Twain drank a hot scotch.

Around midnight, they discussed sleeping arrangements. Twain examined the bed and judged it much wider than the couches. He then judged himself a trifle wider than H.H. Rogers, so he claimed the bed.

———

H.H., elegant and even-keeled, met Paige, the effervescent temperamental inventor. It was no contest. Twain advised H.H. to remain low-key, which would prevent any confusing hysterics from Paige. As H.H. walked in, he overheard Paige's lawyer counseling Paige to accept "this golden opportunity—the best one by long odds you have ever had, & possibly the last one you will ever have, for you are bankrupt, deep in debt, without credit, & without a friend or a well-wisher in the world as far as I know."

Paige conceded every point until the topic came to cold cash. Besides the stocks, the deal offered him $5,000 a year in salary. He wanted $36,000 and money to pay his immediate debts. H.H. didn't budge, and he and Twain boarded the 5 p.m. "Limited" that same day back to New York. As Twain explained to Livy, "Paige is the only one who *can't* wait."

H.H.'s private carriage awaited them in Jersey City; they rode in comfort onto the ferry, and H.H. dropped Twain off at the Players Club. Both men expected Paige to cave. Twain sent a telegram to his family in Paris: "Merry Xmas! Promising progress made in Chicago."

Word arrived from Chicago that Paige was ready to sign, with just a few not-so-niggling demands: $7,000 up front, $7,200-a-year salary and the new company must assume two of his debts—$8,000 to Pratt & Whitney and $70,000 to a businessman in Hartford named Newton Case.

On the morning of December 28, Twain received a hopeful telegram that Paige was strongly leaning toward signing. In an exuberant mood that night, Twain attended a dinner party for a dozen people, including Mr. and Mrs. H.H. Rogers, at Dr. Rice's elegant townhouse near Gramercy Park. At 10 p.m., sixty people arrived and sat in camp chairs in the library. Twain, his back to the roaring fire in the fireplace, delivered "The Californian's Tale"—a plaintive story about a lonely prospector who can't wrap his mind around the tragedy that befell him when he lost his wife. A masterful storyteller who slipped into the voices of the characters, Twain mesmerized this audience for more than an hour. "Now I tell you it *was* a good time, & everybody said so, in the most outspoken way," he wrote Livy at 1:30 a.m. "I don't know *when* I have so enjoyed hearing myself talk."

Pudd'nhead Wilson was also running to raves in the *Century*.

The New Year, 1894, brought more of the waiting-for-Paige-to-surrender game; Paige would counteroffer, Rogers would reject; Twain would anguish.

Livy desperately missed "Youth" (her affectionate nickname for Twain) and implored him to come reunite with the family in Paris at the earliest possible moment, especially since both Livy and Susy were ill.

On January 12, H.H. Rogers's patience with Paige ran out. He sent a "courteous but firm" telegram, demanding a yes or no answer to their proposal.

On January 15, 1894, Paige agreed to sign. Twain discovered the telegram when he returned to his room at midnight. He played billiards in a fog for over an hour.

> I came up to my room & began to undress, & then, suddenly & without warning the realization burst upon me & overwhelmed me: I and mine, who were paupers an hour ago are rich now & our troubles are over! I walked the floor for half an hour in a storm of excitement. Once or twice I wanted to sit down & cry. You see, the intense strain of three months & a half of daily and nightly work & thought & hope & fear had been suddenly taken away, & the sense of release & delivery & joy knew no way to express itself.

It's no coincidence that Twain's next entry in his notebook was: "There are people who can do all fine & heroic things but one—keep from telling their happiness to the unhappy."

Paige finally signed on Wednesday, January 31. Twain sent a telegram to be placed on Livy's breakfast plate on Friday, February 2, 1894, the date of their twenty-fourth wedding anniversary. "Wedding-news: Our ship is safe in port. I sail the moment Rogers can spare me."

Livy replied: "We rejoice with you & congratulate you on your well-earned success."

CHAPTER 3

Safe Eggs and Broken Eggs

Twain in his notebook wrote a quote from his friend Andrew Carnegie: "Put all your eggs in one basket—& watch that basket."

He and Rogers had pinned Paige down, but Twain's troubles were not over. He increasingly worried that his faltering publishing company might undermine all his plans. What if Charles L. Webster & Co. collapsed and creditors seized all his assets, including his life-changing, fortune-making stock in the Paige typesetter?

Twain made a quick notation to ask lawyers about taking Webster into receivership; he also reminded himself to ask about converting the publishing company into a limited partnership or a corporation. Above all, he wanted to sell it, and the *Century* seemed quite interested if it could become the exclusive publisher of Mark Twain.

Twain's notebooks around this time seem buoyed by a renewed sense of playfulness. He was brimming with maxims: "Familiarity breeds contempt & children." "If you tell the truth, you don't have to remember anything." "Noise proves nothing. Often a hen who has merely laid an egg cackles as if she had laid an asteroid."

Invitations flooded in: he dined at the best homes; he attended a prizefight. He played billiards one night at H.H. Rogers's mansion on 57th Street, then attended a male-only artists' soiree at a photographer's studio till 4 a.m. with the likes of "electrician" Nikola Tesla (who had taken a famous photo of Twain) and journalist Richard Harding Davis, who sang Kipling's "Road to Mandalay," and the world's most famous French stage actor, Benoît-Constant Coquelin. (The actor imitated an Englishman trying to speak French. "It nearly killed the fifteen or twenty people who understood it.") Mario Ancona, head tenor at the Met, sang half a dozen songs; the handsome actor John Drew gave a tribute to Twain, who rewarded the crowd with a story.

Twain wrote very long letters every few days to his wife, and she must have tallied up his calendar of events. "Mamma, dear, *I* don't go every-where—I decline most things," he wrote Livy. "But there are plenty that I can't well get out of; I will remember what you say & not make my yarning too common." (Although Twain had a large repertoire of stories, he sometimes fell back on the same handful: stealing his first watermelon, the botched christening and the slave ghost story.)

Livy often feared that her husband might ignore some important tenet of polite society, such as properly thanking Rogers. So on February 14 she wrote from Paris directly to H.H.: "I intend that some of the things he says about you get to your ears." So she quoted Twain's letter to her.

Yes at two p.m. yesterday we were paupers and five minutes later
we were rich people. It is a miracle and a quite dramatic one.
And who achieved it for us? Who has saved us from separations,
unendurable toil on the platform, and public bankruptcy? *Henry Rogers*.

And he was the only man in America who both could and cheer-fully *would*. His name is music in my ear.

Assemble the family now and drink long life and happiness to
Henry Rogers.

———

Twain was especially pleased that Rogers never made him feel the weight of the obligation. The author was genuinely baffled when Rogers—a confident, direct man—suddenly grew tongue-tied when asking a favor for his ailing wife. Would Twain come up in ten days on Washington's birthday to help dedicate a new ornate Town Hall the Rogers family had built in Fairhaven, Massachusetts, a three-day trip?

He was as shy & diffident about it as if he were asking me to com-mit suicide; but said Mrs. Rogers was afraid it was asking too much of me & was sure she could never get up the courage to do it; so she had entreated him to do it for her. Think of that! Why, if they should ask me to swim the Atlantic I would at least try.

The dedication speech—despite minus-five-degree temperature—went off seamlessly. Twain was a master of this sort of public appearance. He said the marble-columned building would speak eloquently for at least 100 years; he was good for only forty.

Negotiations to sell Webster to *Century* were dragging along. Twain was already trying to sell some of his shares in Paige; he talked London theater manager Bram Stoker (future author of *Dracula*) into buying twenty shares on a slow-payment plan. But Twain needed cash. And Livy had a hard-and-fast rule that he must never accept gifts of money from anybody, especially not H.H. Rogers.

So Twain accepted the chance to perform with popular comic storyteller-versifier James Whitcomb Riley at Madison Square Garden: $250 for thirty minutes each night. Heavy snowfall on February 26 and 27 left the theater half full, which Twain always took as a personal insult. A third night was scheduled at Chickering Hall for March 3 and it sold out. He told of his first duel in Nevada, his knack for tormenting interviewers with contradictory facts, and then a ghost story. Some newspaper reviewers favored Riley, who recited his sentimental Civil War poem "Good-bye Jim." Twain berated himself for botching these performances; his timing was off. This fiasco just hardened him against having to mount the platform for money.

With that infusion of funds from H.H. Rogers, the Paige typesetter workshop in Chicago had reopened, with fifty-four men working under engineer Charles Davis. Paige had failed to display his machine at the World's Fair, but the goal was now to run a test at the *Chicago Herald* as soon as possible. Once the machine passed the test, selling stock would be easy.

Twain still stood at risk if Webster & Co. collapsed. But he had already booked passage on a steamship sailing March 7 to Southampton, and then on to France.

H.H. Rogers—one of the finest financial gamesmen of the era—came up with a solution, worthy of a man dubbed "The Artful Dodger" by the *Wall Street Journal* for his ability to avoid prosecution. Wall Street veteran Rogers recommended that Mark Twain immediately transfer *all of his assets,* including his book copyrights and his Paige stock, to his wife, Livy.

The maneuver would mark a classic hedge but also a fraudulent transfer. If Webster went under, creditors would find Twain had no assets. If Webster and Paige survived, the assets could be shifted back to Twain. No one would need to know that they had ever been moved.

On March 6, 1894, Samuel L. Clemens signed over broad power of attorney to Henry H. Rogers to handle all his business affairs. One John Flynn of Brooklyn notarized the signature. Two of H.H. Rogers's children accompanied Twain to the pier the following day. H.H. sent a cablegram to Paris allowing Twain to draw up to $1,000 in his name.

On March 9, 1894, H.H. Rogers, acting as attorney-in-fact, signed a tightly reasoned four-page legalese-laden document on Twain's behalf. It stated that Olivia L. Clemens had loaned her husband an unspecified sum to invest in the Paige typesetter and loaned Webster & Co. more than $70,000, with $65,146 in debt notes. It stated Olivia L. Clemens desired a "settlement" and that therefore Samuel L. Clemens does "hereby sell, assign, transfer and set over" all his "capital stock of the said Paige Compositor" and all future stock issues, also any patents, rental fees, sales of any typesetting, distributing or justifying devices . . . as well as all the "copy-rights upon the various books written by me" . . . and all dramatic rights. "I do further authorize, empower and direct each and every of the publishers of my books and stories to pay over to said Olivia L. Clemens all moneys due." He also granted her the right to sue in his name to recover moneys owed.

The document was signed by Rogers and witnessed by his executive assistant. Twain (via Rogers) had signed over everything of value he possessed to his wife.

———

Twain reached Paris on March 15, 1894, and reunited with his wife and two of his three daughters after six and a half months apart, the longest separation of their marriage. If a major objective of the Clemens family's self-exile to Europe was saving money, they made a curious hotel choice: the Brighton at 218 Rue de Rivoli, opposite the Tuileries Gardens, was a fine upscale hotel that served them meals in their suite of rooms.

Twain repeatedly mentioned regretting the scrimping and saving he inflicted on his family during this period. He also mentioned a family budget in Paris of $1,000 a month and European summer spa budget of $1,700 a month. Most Americans of that era would have loved to scrimp and save at that rate. Twain's brother Orion lived for years in Keokuk, Iowa, on $100 a month and was able to survive on $50 a month.

Medical bills and music lessons, carriage rides (since Livy rarely could walk 100 yards), meals (since she never cooked), a maid and a tutor boosted the family expenses, as did attending opera and theater. Livy was now undergoing expensive "electrical treatment" at one of Paris's premier clinics for her weak heart, nerves, gout. Technicians attached moistened sponges to deliver the tingling current to various body parts. She thought the treatment was helping.

Twain never begrudged her spending a single penny and always berated himself for any cutbacks she had to endure.

Livy had grown up quite wealthy and had inherited one third of a $1 million fortune in 1870, the first year of her marriage to Twain. Some of it was tied up in the now-beleaguered Langdon coal company, but some she had received in lump sums from various investments, such as $50,000 in 1882 when they built their Hartford home.

Youngest daughter, Jean, thirteen, was just starting to show signs of the erratic behavior that was later diagnosed as absence seizures and epilepsy.

Eldest daughter, Susy, was just celebrating her twenty-second birthday. Thin, excitable, often moody like her father, she suffered frequent illnesses, sometimes diagnosed as "neurasthenia" or "weak lungs." She fought her tendency toward introspection and listlessness. She wrote Clara that year:

> The world looks so attractive when one has something to do! I have written out a program of occupations for the future as follows:
> 1. Singing. 2. Acting. 3. Singing teaching. 4. Study of languages.
> 5. Guitar playing[.] 6. Possibly writing. That does tolerably well don't you think so? I take a cold sponge bath and do gymnastics every morning and am leading an altogether virtuous and exemplary life inspired by your example.

Precocious Susy back at age thirteen had written a biography of her father that is unfailingly perceptive. She asked why he didn't go to church every Sunday.

He told me the other day that he couldn't bear to hear anyone talk but himself, but that he could listen to himself for hours without getting tired, of course he said this in joke, but I've no [doubt] it was founded on truth.

She also, like her mother and both her sisters, hoped that "Papa" would be hailed as a *serious* writer. (He planned to resume writing his next book, *Personal Recollections of Joan of Arc,* that year.)

How I hate that name [Mark Twain]! I should like never to hear it again! My father should not be satisfied with it! He should not be known by it! He should show himself the great writer that he is, not merely a funny man. Funny! That's all the people see in him—a maker of funny speeches!

———

The greatest writer of American boyhood was surrounded by women who craved him to be a more literary, highbrow writer.

After just one week with his family in Paris, he received an urgent message from H.H. Rogers to return to attend to the problems of the Webster publishing company, which might need bankruptcy protection. Twain delayed two weeks, then left April 7 to return to the United States. Livy immediately wrote a letter imploring him to find some way to save his publishing company. She called their recent three weeks together "an angel's visit."

He reached New York on Saturday, April 14, just as the crisis was about to break. Twain's partner, Fred Hall, had rented out much of their swank Fifth Avenue office space to save money, but over the past few weeks, several creditors were clamoring to be paid immediately. As Twain put it, only the name of H.H. Rogers had kept them at bay. Rogers came to the Webster offices on Monday, April 16, and examined the accounts and wrote checks totaling $2,613.

Twain had Livy's words echoing in his head, and he implored Rogers to find some means to save the company.

Mount Morris Bank had two $5,000 loans coming due within a week and wanted to be paid in full. Rogers wanted the bank to roll over the loans so that only the 6% interest would be due.

Fred Hall contacted the bank's lawyer, Daniel Whitford, who had often stepped in to help Webster get a rollover. Hall approached Whitford, who said the best he could do was get the bank to loan an additional $1,000 at 6% to Webster & Co. if the company would pay the $10,000 in full. The bank had just elected a new board of directors and appointed a new president, a seventy-year-old millionaire art collector, William H. Payne. The new man wouldn't budge.

Twain said the bank was "crowding" H.H. Rogers, trying to bully him.

What no one knew for eight months, until the story broke in the newspapers in December, was that respectable Mount Morris Bank, in its beautiful Renaissance-style building on 125th Street, stood on the verge of collapse. The previous president had overinvested in Evansville & Terre Haute Railroad, which had plummeted and caused the bank to have insufficient capital. (The New York State bank examiner would discover the shortfall in July.) Payne, a very successful grain merchant trying to clean up the mess, demanded $10,000.

On the morning of April 18, Fred Hall came to H.H. Rogers's office at 26 Wall Street expecting to receive a check. Instead, he discovered that Twain and Rogers had secretly hired the firm of Stern & Rushmore to take the company into a form of bankruptcy. Hall, who was a one-third partner, was shocked; he pleaded. He was ignored. "[Hall] could hardly keep from crying" when he signed the official papers, Twain noted. "I half thought he would go off & drown himself." The stealth was key; a creditor could have sued for nonpayment and a judge could have frozen the assets of Webster; this way, Webster had more control.

Technically, Webster filed for "Assignment for Benefit of Creditors" under New York State law. (There was no federal bankruptcy law then; the United States Congress had allowed the bankruptcy law to lapse in 1878 and would not pass a new one until 1898.) H.H. Rogers chose a young lawyer at Stern & Rushmore (40 Wall Street), with the impressive name of Bainbridge Colby, to serve as assignee to handle assets and debits and forge a repayment plan.

In its most simplified form, modern United States bankruptcy law allows a judge/referee to set a reasonable percentage amount of the verified debts to be paid equally to the creditors, in exchange for the debtor getting a fresh start.

In contrast, the New York State law of "assignment" prevailing in 1894 was much less generous. Basically, the lawyer/assignee would assemble the creditors and suggest a settlement; each could vote to participate or not. The concept was that an orderly assessment of assets and fair distribution of payments would benefit all parties. No one would be favored.

None of them yet knew that Samuel L. Clemens, the only partner in Webster with any money, had already transferred *all his assets* to his wife. Fred Hall had $136 in his bank account.

The news of the Webster collapse broke loud. The front page of the *New York Tribune* proclaimed: FAILURE OF MARK TWAIN; *San Francisco Call:* MARK TWAIN FAILS; *Washington* [D.C.] *Times:* NO HUMOR HERE; *Brooklyn Eagle:* NO JOKE. Pulitzer's leviathan *New York World,* with a circulation of 500,000, announced MARK TWAIN'S ASSIGNMENT while the *New York Times* (with only a 15,000 circulation) stated MARK TWAIN'S COMPANY IN TROUBLE. The news, thanks to the telegraph, was immediately picked up nationwide: *Salt Lake Herald, Omaha Daily Bee, Los Angeles Herald,* to name a few.

His humiliation was very public. Mark Twain had enjoyed a spectacular literary career and was thought to be a shrewd, wealthy businessman. Reporters seemed baffled. "The assignment was a complete surprise," declared one newspaper. No one could quite make sense of it, especially since Fred Hall had told the Bradstreet financial agency in January that Mark Twain had $400,000 outside of the firm.

Twain was nabbed for a quick comment outside the Players Club. He told reporters he had other business investments and would survive this setback. The *New York Times* tracked down Bainbridge Colby, who pegged the firm's debts at about $80,000 and said he thought if the creditors would agree to wait for payment and allow the firm to continue, it could come close to paying the debts in full. He would present a plan.

He did point out: "Such property as Mr. Clemens has is, of course, liable for the co-partnership debts but I am unable to accurately state at present the extent of his personal property." When pressed, Colby declared: "I do not think he has very much."

The *Brooklyn Eagle* ran an op-ed piece:

Mark Twain's latest is not a joke. C.L. Webster . . . made an assignment, which is expected to carry all of Mr. Clemens' property with it. It is not yet known how much the creditors will get. A far larger

circle of readers, friends and admirers of the humorist will be concerned . . . that Mark himself is expected to have, indeed, already
has, nothing. It is another case of a shrewd and bright observer of
things missing a moral which he could readily have taught to other
people.

Livy was crushed by the news. A cablegram reached her in Paris on
Friday, April 19, then the following morning a squib appeared in an
international paper, *Galignani's Messenger*.

She wrote to her adopted sister, Susan L. Crane, in Elmira, New York,
that Mr. Rogers could find no other way out.

> But I have a perfect *horror* and heart-sickness over it. I cannot
> get away from the feeling that business failure means disgrace. I
> suppose it will always mean that to me. We have put a great deal
> of money into the concern, and perhaps there would have been
> nothing but to keep putting it in and losing it. We certainly now
> have not much to lose. We might have mortgaged the house; that
> was the only thing I could think of to do. Mr. Clemens felt that
> there would never be any end, and perhaps he was right. . . . Sue,
> if you were to see me you would see that I have grown old very fast
> during this last year. I have wrinkled. Most of the time I want to
> lie down and cry. Everything seems to me so impossible. I do not
> make things go very well, and I feel that my life is an absolute and
> irretrievable failure. Perhaps I am thankless, but I so often feel
> that I should like to give it up and die.

Twain privately claimed to be "relieved" by the "assignment" and said
that numerous friends told him it was a standard business procedure.
But he knew his wife would not be pleased. He dashed off upbeat letters,
which would take a week to ten days to reach Paris. "Well, dearheart, I
read everything the newspapers had to say about it yesterday on my way
to Hartford, & discovered not one unkind or unpleasant or fault-finding
remark," he wrote on Friday, April 20. "As I hadn't done anything to be
ashamed of, I wasn't ashamed; so I didn't avoid anybody but talked with
everybody I knew on the train."

In another letter, he reported to her that John Mackay, a silver mining and transatlantic cable multimillionaire, had paid a visit and told

him: "Don't let it disturb you, Sam—we all have to do it at one time or another; it's nothing to be ashamed of."

He reported Poultney Bigelow, a fellow writer often at the Players Club, handed him a check for $1,000, which he refused. His lecture agent, Major James B. Pond, immediately approached him to go out on tour. "I hope your business troubles will not break you down," wrote Pond. "It comes hard at this stage of the game but with your vigor of mind and body I cannot imagine a better equipped veteran for a hard fight." Twain also informed Livy that a stranger had offered to take up a dollar collection for them.

In Hartford, friends congratulated him for bearing misfortune well, but he told Livy they didn't realize how "blithe" he felt at having the business burdens lifted.

> Except when I think of you, dear heart—then I am not blithe;
> for I seem to see you grieving and ashamed, and dreading to look
> people in the face. . . . You only seem to see rout, retreat and dis-
> honored colors dragging in the dirt—whereas none of these things
> exist.

Livy had grown up in the rarefied atmosphere of the mansion of Jervis Langdon; he was a teetotaler, pious, a nonsmoker and non-blasphemer, a staunch abolitionist who personally helped slaves escape via the Underground Railroad. She never once witnessed her father's predatory practices that forced rival coal transporters out of business. Livy had a very idealized view of business conduct, and she would firmly hold her husband to it.

The time came for Bainbridge Colby, along with H.H. Rogers and Twain, to meet with the principal creditors and inform them that Twain had preemptively shifted all his assets to his wife. They were informed that he had done so because she was the company's largest creditor, having loaned it more than $70,000. In exchange, Olivia Clemens was relinquishing all claims. No record exists of the creditors' reaction except that three of the largest creditors—Mount Morris Bank ($29,500), the Barrows family ($15,000), and Thomas Russell, bookbinders ($5,000)—eventually filed lawsuits.

In bankruptcy law, Twain's behavior is known as giving preferential treatment to one creditor.

Livy, once she understood the situation, considered this extremely unfair to the other creditors and voiced her concern immediately. Twain replied: "Nobody finds the slightest fault with my paying you with all my property. There is nothing shady or improper about it. We make no concealment of it."

She was not convinced, and wanted to give the creditors their house, even though it was currently worth only a fraction of its value. She wanted Twain to sign away some book royalties.

My darling,

I note carefully everything you say in your [letter]. . . . I note it reverently & lovingly, honoring you & loving you for what you say & for the high position which you take. You can take no other position; I would not wish you to take any other, I could not bear to have you take any other. My own position must necessarily differ from yours in one or two details. My first duty is to you & the children—my second is to those others. I must protect you first— protect you against yourself.

On May 3, 1894, Twain and Colby met privately at 40 Wall Street with the new president of Mount Morris Bank, Payne, and the bank's lawyer, Daniel Whitford. H.H. counseled Twain to say little, be courteous, and avoid losing his temper. "Hard conditions," he later called them.

Twain privately believed that half of his $29,500 bank debt was "bogus," that the bank or Fred Hall had tricked him into signing what he thought were renewals of $15,000 but were actually a new set of loans for that same amount. Twain would work up a rage against the bank. "I shall be a very old person before I pay the bank any more than half of their claim unless it can be clearly shown that I *owe* more," he wrote Livy.

Fred Hall, fifteen years later, contended he had indeed alerted Twain, then in Europe, to each of the new loans, and he added the author often chose to ignore "commercial matters" and had an "extreme impatience of business details."

The bank president and lawyer were furious that one of the wealthiest authors in America claimed to have no assets. They wanted to cable Livy to demand the royalties from Twain's books for a specified period. Colby replied that the royalties were her property to be disposed as she saw fit, and he would not recommend gifting them to the bank. Twain recounted the—at times, ridiculous—bank meeting to his wife.

It was confoundedly difficult at first for me to be always saying "Mrs. Clemens's books," "Mrs. Clemens's copyrights," "Mrs. Clemens's type-setter stock," & so on, but it was necessary to do this, & I got the hang of it presently. I was even able to say with gravity, "My wife has two unfinished books, but I am not able to say when they will be completed or where she will elect to publish them when they are done."

Once Mr. Paine said: "Mr. Clemens, if you could let us have Puddnhead Wilson . . ."

"So far, as I know, she has formed no plans as to that book yet, Mr. Paine." He took the hint and corrected his phraseology.

Twain, sensing his wife's extreme distress, left abruptly for a brief visit in Europe, making his sixth weeklong crossing in the past twelve months. H.H. Rogers told Twain he could draw *unlimited* amounts on Rogers's name. Twain, knowing his wife's views on receiving charity, drew almost nothing.

His presence gave Livy the courage to answer her friends' sympathy letters. "Thank you for being glad that I have a separate fortune but unfortunately a good deal of my money has gone too," she wrote to one of her closest friends, Alice Hooker Day. "I will not write more about it except to say the two most important things, that there was nothing dishonourable about the failure, and that the debts will all be paid." She added: "Mr. Clemens believes the company will work [itself] out of debt, but if it does not we shall of course be responsible for the debts and in time pay them all."

Twain returned to recommence negotiations on keeping Webster in business. Twain first delivered his condolences to H.H., whose wife had died while he was in Europe. "Mr. Rogers tried to tell me about the last days of Mrs. Rogers this morning, but it was finally too hard for him & his voice broke & he could not go on." H.H. told Twain that the hardest times, now six weeks later, were the mornings. "Coming out of sleep he is expecting to see her," Twain wrote Livy, "and then comes the daily shock and the new realization." The author closed his letter fondly but morbidly: "Let us be spared this, my darling. May we die together."

The first business matter to tackle was *Pudd'nhead Wilson,* which was just ending a successful seven-month run in *Century.* Although the near–comic opera plot hinged on feuding twins and babies—one slave, one white—switched at birth, two characters riveted readers: the scheming slave mother Roxy and the seemingly simpleton lawyer, Wilson. The novella earned an extra dollop of fame because of the irresistible Pudd'nhead maxims that Americans began repeating, such as "Few things are harder to put up with than the annoyance of a good example."

The creditors wanted the earnings from *Pudd'nhead* book sales, but the current Webster partnership contract called for Twain to receive 90% of net profits, if Webster was allowed to stay in business and publish it. Squabbling began.

Rogers, who handled the negotiations, started off by stating Mrs. Clemens would allow Webster to publish *Pudd'nhead* if she received a 25% cover price royalty. (The industry standard was 10%.) The creditors balked. Twain said he would consider 20%. The two friends were enjoying playing some old-fashioned country hardball. In exchange for *Pudd'nhead* profits, they expected the creditors to promise not to sue or harass Twain for payment for one year.

Livy was not pleased.

> If I were over there I should probably ask 10% or 15%. What we want is to have those creditors get all their money out of Webster & Co. and surely we want to aid them all that is possible. Oh my darling we want those debts paid and we want to treat them all not only honestly but we want to help them in every possible way. It is money honestly owed and I cannot quite understand the tone which both you & Mr. Rogers seem to take—in fact I cannot understand it at all. You say Mr. Rogers has said some caustic and telling things to the creditors. (I do not know what your wording was) I should think it was the creditors place to say caustic things to us.

> My darling, I cannot have any thing done in my name that I should not approve. I feel that we owe those creditors not only the money but our most sincere apologies that we are not able to pay their bills when they fall due. When these bills are all paid, as they of course will be, I do not want the creditors to feel that we

have in any way acted sharply or unjustly or ungenerously with them. I want them to realize & know, that we had their interest at heart, more, much more than we had our own. . . . Do not for one moment [let] your sense of our need for money get advantage of your sense of justice & generosity. Dear sweet darling heart! . . . You will always consider at every proposition whether it is one that I would approve, will you not?

H.H. had strongly advised against making even a "moral" promise to pay everyone in full; he also opposed making *any* payment before concessions were wrung. He thought creditors should be hungry and grateful. Twain found himself caught between the sharp-dealing pragmatism of his friend, H.H., and his wife's high road of chivalry.

The two—wife and mogul—would battle over the conscience of Mark Twain. It's never a good idea to bet against the wife.

In a letter that crossed the Atlantic just as hers was arriving, Twain tried to justify himself by invoking her late father, Jervis Langdon.

Suppose father had been here in Mr. Rogers's place? Would he have advised me differently? Indeed, no. He would have said, "If you let your property fall into the hands of those creditors it will be rushed upon the market & *nobody* will get his due. If you keep it & handle it yourself everybody will get a hundred cents on the dollar."

My very dearest, I love you, I honor you, & I am not going to do a single dishonorable thing. I am not going to wrong anybody. If ever I should, I am not going to begin with *you*.

The Mount Morris Bank refused to allow Webster to continue on the terms offered. Negotiations stalled. Colby, following Twain's advice, took Mrs. Clemens's book, *Pudd'nhead*, to another publisher and sold it for a 12½% royalty. Ironically, the other publisher was Twain's original publisher, American Publishing Company of Hartford, which still controlled half of Twain's books. Back in the late 1860s Elisha Bliss had snookered Twain into relinquishing his copyright and accepting a paltry 5% rube royalty on *Innocents Abroad* and then later promised him 50% net profits on future books but never delivered.

Twain would later describe Elisha Bliss as "a tall, lean, skinny, yellow, toothless bald-headed, rat-eyed professional liar and scoundrel. . . . It is my belief that Bliss never did an honest thing in his life, when he had a chance to do a dishonest one."

That animosity had sparked Twain's adventure into the nightmare of self-publishing. Now, Elisha's son Frank Bliss controlled the company, and here was Twain signing back up. Twain knew that even though he had once been cheated into a lower royalty, the agents of American Publishing were very good at door-to-door subscription book sales.

H.H. and Twain did have an ulterior motive, as well; they hoped that doing business with American Publishing would enable Twain to regain his copyrights for key early books, *Innocents, Roughing It, A Tramp Abroad, Tom Sawyer* and *Gilded Age,* so that they could create a deluxe complete works with another publisher.

Twain also struck a deal with *Harper's* to serialize—anonymously— his new novel, *Personal Recollections of Joan of Arc,* for a hefty fee near $10,000. (He feared his "Mark Twain" comic moniker would prevent readers from taking the work seriously.)

Despite Livy's words, Twain was leaving again in August for Europe after basically stonewalling the creditors. He was hoping that he could land a big payday and surprise them all with full payment. That gamble, that hope, that "one basket of eggs," was his/her stock in the Paige typesetter, which was now set for a two-month trial run at the *Chicago Herald.*

CHAPTER 4

The Trials of Paige and Joan of Arc

Twain hit the beach at Normandy and went straight to his room. To avoid thinking about the two-month test of the typesetter, he threw himself into writing *Joan of Arc*.

His family expected this book to be his literary masterpiece that would forever vault him from "humorist" ranks; they cheered him through nightly readings in Etretat of his draft, weeping at Joan's setbacks, applauding her military victories. Livy to her dying day called *Joan* her husband's best work; he seesawed between choosing *Joan* or *Huck* depending on his mood and audience but ultimately chose *Joan*.

The Clemens family was staying near a sleepy fishing village at a remote inn, Chalet des Abris . . . "such an incredibly small coop that the family can't find room to sleep without hanging their legs out of the windows," he wrote Rogers. But Twain judged the air "superb and soothing and wholesome" and the isolation excellent for an author.

"This is a book which writes itself," he enthused. "I merely have to hold the pen." Twain handwrote a hefty 10,000 words in his schoolboy-clear script in the first week back, and 40,000 within a month. The seaside was proving a good summer retreat choice as the Clemens clan was enjoying that extremely rare experience of all family members being healthy at once.

Livy made a momentous decision. As Twain put it, his wife intended to undertake "house-keeping" in Paris in the fall to save money. This "house-keeping," it turns out, would not entail her doing any sweeping, washing or cooking. Livy planned on moving the family out of the Hotel Brighton, where they had all their meals served in their suite, and relocating them to a rental flat, where she would hire a maid, a butler and a cook. (She hoped to cut their budget by $200 a month.)

After lingering through September, the family boarded a train for the 140-mile trip to Paris, but only made it fifty-five miles to Rouen. Susy had started coughing, suddenly grew quite sick in the hotel room, with her fever soon spiking to 104. (Coincidentally, Rouen was the city where Joan of Arc died.)

The doctor diagnosed "congestion of the right lung." The family would remain at the Hotel d'Angleterre in Rouen for a week, which stretched to several weeks as Susy recuperated. (Twain's *Joan* notes had been shipped to Paris, so he drafted a long magazine article to refute a French writer who had claimed the superiority of French civilization over American; Twain planned on listing American nineteenth-century marvels of invention and was sorely tempted to include the Paige typesetter.)

While Livy spoon-fed Susy and placed moist compresses on her brow, Twain was chafing at the incarceration; he poured some of his creativity into his weekly letters to H.H.

Twain entertained his patron with ripe misadventures, such as this one about getting lost going to the bathroom in the middle of the night in Rouen. (An indoor toilet in France in the 1890s meant they were staying at a fine hotel; people still carried candles, but Twain, wearing a loose flannel nightshirt, was apparently in a hurry.)

He described the Hotel d'Angleterre as a series of floors with four bedrooms on either side of a central winding staircase.

Would you think a person could get lost in such a place? I assure [you] it is possible for a person of talent. We are on the second floor from the ground. There's a W.C. [*i.e., water closet/toilet*] on the floor *above* us and one on the floor *below* us. Halls pitch dark. I groped my wall and found the upper W.C. Starting to return, I went *up*stairs instead of down, and went to what I supposed was my room, but I could not make out the number in the dark and was afraid to enter it. Then I remembered that I—no, my mind lost confidence and began to wander. I was no longer sure as to what floor I was on, and the minute I realized *that*, the rest of my mind went. One cannot stand still in a dark hall at 2 in the morning, lost, and be content. One must move, and go on moving, even at the risk of getting worse lost. I groped up and down a couple of those flights, over and over again, cursing to myself. And every time I thought I heard somebody coming, I shrank together like one of those toy balloons when it collapses. You see, I was between two fires; I could not grope to the top floor and start fresh and count my way down to my own, for it was all occupied by young ladies, and a dangerous place to get caught in, clothed as I was clothed, and not in my right mind. I could not grope down to the ground floor and count *up*, for there was a ball down there. A ball, and young ladies likely to be starting up to bed around this time. And so they did. I saw the glow of their distant candle. I felt the chill of their distant cackle. I did not know whether I was on a W.C. floor or not, but I had to take a risk. I groped to the door that ought to be it—right where you turn down the stairs; and it *was* it. I entered it grateful, and stood in its dark shelter with a beating heart and thought how happy I should be to live there always . . . and go out no more among life's troubles and dangers. Several of the young ladies applied for admission, but I was not receiving. Thursdays being my day. I meant to freeze-out the ball, if it took a week. And I did. When the drone and burr of its music had ceased for twenty minutes and the house was solidly dead and dark, I groped down to the ground floor, then turned and counted my way up home all right.

Twain entered his bedroom; he and Livy often slept in separate rooms due to his twenty-cigar-a-day snoring. He launched into a vintage tirade of cursing when all of a sudden a chilly voice came out of the darkness.

"When you are done with your prayers, I would like to ask where you have been all night." It was Mrs. Clemens waiting in the dark, waiting for a reposeful atmosphere and tranquilizing speech; for Susy's tossings and semi-deliriums had fagged her out and she had come to my room to rest her nerves a bit.

After his misadventure and scolding, Twain couldn't sleep that night of October 6 and wound up reading till dawn. He told Rogers that this marked the latest in a string of sleepless nights due to anxiety over the typesetter machine. Later that morning, mail from America reached the hotel, after a detour from Paris to Etretat to Rouen.

H.H. had sent a *Chicago Herald,* with pages printed by the Paige device.

"The Herald has just arrived, and that column is healing for sore eyes. It affects me like Columbus sighting land."

Susy's fever took two weeks to break, and the French physician recommended two more weeks' rest. An October 2 letter from Rogers included testimonials from a publisher, a manufacturer, and an engineer to the bright start of the Paige typesetter in the test.

On October 28, 1894, Twain wrote: "It seems to me that things couldn't well be going better at Chicago than they are. There's no other machine that can set type 8 hours with only 17 minutes' stoppage through cussedness. By and by our machines will be perfect; then they won't stop at all."

However, a few days later, just as they reached Hotel Brighton in Paris on November 2, a gloomy report arrived summarizing the first sixteen days of the test. Apparently, the machine was very fast but increasingly prone to errors and stoppages. (Twain did not know that the *Herald* did not allow any on-site repairs but required they be done at the company workshop two miles away; the logic was that the machine must pass a test without engineers and repairmen standing by to tweak it.)

Twain defended the Paige, claiming its speed, as much as fifteen times faster than a hand-setting compositor, more than compensated for the mistakes. He pointed out that the mistakes of an eight-hour shift could be fixed in half an hour, still leaving them far in the lead. He also blamed the two men running the machine for human error. "When the machine is in proper working order, it *cannot make a mistake.*"

While Twain worried, Livy found a place for "house-keeping"—the quirky studio-home of a wealthy artist named Pomroy, who was leaving for six months. He would rent his "large, rambling, quaint, charmingly furnished" four-bedroom house near the right bank of the Seine for $200 a month.

The artist's studio (40 by 30 feet with a 40-foot-high ceiling) would serve as drawing room/living room/dining room; it was flanked by a pair of massive fireplaces, even had a musicians' gallery at one end.

During periods of stress, Twain seemed very susceptible to illnesses. He developed a deep cough—the doctor "painted" his back and chest four times with iodine. Still coughing, he felt an excruciating pain in his left ankle. He suspected rheumatism; it turned out to be gout, and it hit his right ankle as well. The pain seemed to radiate out and fill every crevice of the room; the doctor administered repeated injections of pain-killers.

From his sickbed, he wrote passionate letters defending the Paige machine, especially against the Mergenthaler Linotypes, also in action at the *Herald*.

He was outraged that the Mergenthaler organization continued to make speed claims that didn't include error counts. "With a *concealed* machine, which couldn't bear daylight, and by gaudy advertising and large but poor-quality lying, those [Mergenthaler] people have splen-didly marketed their bastard."

Twain, in pain, was marooned in his bed, with both feet propped on pillows for the first fourteen days in the new house. H.H., meanwhile, cut his letter writing to a trickle. Wrote Twain: "I am putting in these dull hours of pain and cussedness with interesting anxieties and wonder-ments regarding the result of [the test]."

The ankle pain subsided enough that Twain could limp around in thick-padded slippers on Thanksgiving. He wrote a letter to H.H., deeply regretting that they had not tested the machine more thoroughly before going to the *Herald*.

> That would have been *fore*sight, whereas hindsight is my spe-cialty. I ought to have remembered that they used to test a mere sewing-machine a couple of months before they allowed it to go to a customer.
>
> I guess [engineer Charles] Davis ought to have "driven a stake" for he knew something about untried machines. Land, I wish now that the machine had spent those two months in the shop! Then we would give an exhibition just for speed. . . . The showing would leave the Mergenthaler not a leg to stand on.

Livy celebrated her forty-ninth birthday on November 27, Twain his fifty-ninth on November 30. He wrote that perhaps it was better that he wasn't in America because he would try to sway H.H. Rogers, no matter what common sense dictated. Twain's doctor forbade him from leaving the house, except on days of immaculate weather, and he had ventured outside only twice in a month.

His mood so soured that he refused to write any articles or *Joan* lest his "present spirit" infect his output. He craved distraction. "I need to be at work now especially, to keep my mind absorbed while I wait for the verdict concerning the machine," he wrote on December 7. "I'll be glad to get that. You'll cable it, won't you?"

Mrs. Clemens wouldn't allow him, sick as he was, to go to America, so he added a conspiratorial line near the end saying that H.H. must order him by "cable" to come when he needed him.

Hopes were dimming. "I note that you are not strongly expecting a favorable opinion from the *Herald*," he wrote on December 9. Twain then pitched H.H. about concealing any announcement about the results in order to buy Mergenthaler stock, which he expected to "boom" with Paige gone from competition.

Twain could no longer tolerate sitting around waiting, so he resumed writing *Joan*. He read out loud nightly to his daughters and wife about the peasant girl who heard voices and inspired armies. Joan was now imprisoned and her attendant visited.

> The sight of Joan gave me a shock. Why, she was but a shadow! It was difficult for me to realize that this frail little creature with the sad face and drooping form was the same Joan of Arc that I had so often seen, all fire and enthusiasm, charging through a hail of death and the lightning and thunder of the guns at the head of her battalions. It wrung my heart to see her looking like this.

Finally, a typewritten letter arrived from H.H. Rogers at noon on Friday December 21. He announced that he was withdrawing his backing of the Paige typesetter, in effect, dismantling the company. Rogers, with typical logic and directness, outlined point by point the machine's shortcomings, from repeated breakdowns to excessive manufacturing expenses. Twain wrote back:

> I *seemed* to be entirely expecting your letter and also prepared and resigned; but Lord it shows how little we know ourselves and how easily we can deceive ourselves. It hit me like a thunderclap. It knocked every rag of sense out of my head, and I went flying here and there and yonder, not knowing what I was doing and only one clearly-defined thought standing up visible and substantial out of the crazy storm-drift—that my dream of ten years was in desper-

ate peril, and out of the 60,000 or 70,000 projects for its rescue that came flocking through my skull, not one would hold still long enough for me to examine it and size it up. Have you ever been like that? Not so much so, I reckon.

Twain zeroed in on one thought only: that he must rush to America to witness the Paige dream die . . . or try by some miracle to resurrect it.

Still limping from the after-effects of gout, he race-hobbled to a travel office and asked if he could take the 9 p.m. train for London and Southampton and board the next transatlantic steamer . . . but the clerk told him a better plan would be to take the 6:52 p.m. Le Havre train and take the boat leaving tomorrow for New York.

Twain was standing "about two miles from home, no packing done, and with just barely head enough left on my shoulders to protect me from being used as a convenience by the dogs."

Then he realized it would be fruitless to rush to America if H.H. was not willing to delay action one month. So he sent a telegram and decided to wait for a response . . . and then he would decide whether to take the next steamer.

"By bedtime, Mrs. Clemens had reasoned me into a fairly rational and contented state of mind; but of course it didn't last long." The author became sleepless, stayed up the rest of night smoking, limping, and pondering. He finally dozed off at dawn and slept till noon, when he resumed writing to H.H.

He tried to rebut the main reasons the machine had failed: stoppages due to type breakage and repeated jamming and the excessive cost to manufacture a machine of such massive weight.

The Paige used thousands of matchstick-sized pieces of type with 108 different precise, tiny nicks on them to facilitate redistribution back to the correct channels for reuse. Dirt and caked ink were fouling the nicks/ indentations, jamming the machine, sometimes breaking the lead type. Twain now suggested the far-fetched solution of casting the type in a more durable metal, brass. He admitted the process was not yet scientifically feasible, but he reported that Paige had told him of a cold-brass stamp breakthrough.

He also proposed dropping 49 of the 108 keyboard characters, and just going with 26 upper- and 26 lowercase characters and 7 symbols. He said that would reduce size, weight and cost. (The machine didn't need 26 undersized small caps or the symbol π, for instance.)

He told H.H. *not* to tell Paige any of these fine ideas because they still controlled the fate of the machine and could make revisions or some deal with Mergenthaler. *"Don't* say I'm wild. For really I'm sane again this morning." The pages of the letter reveal how rattled Twain was because they are crammed with cross-outs, scrawls, inserts, even parentheses within parentheses.

He calmed down enough to promise to proceed with writing *Joan,* while H.H. pondered. "Meantime, I want Harry [*H.H.'s sixteen-year-old son*] to save some of the next soup for his Uncle Sammy, who would do as much for him." Twain was clearly addled, because he switched from his usual closing of "Sincerely Yours" or "Yours Sincerely" to "With love and kisses, SL Clemens."

For his part, H.H. was worried that his clear-eyed business decision would end their friendship, and he wrote a very warm, sincere letter (now lost), conveying feelings from his "old and hard" heart. Twain replied in the same spirit: "I am 59 years old; yet I never had a friend before who put out a hand and tried to pull me ashore when he found me in deep waters."

H.H. must have made some joke about completing the building of a 17,700-square-foot stable in Fairhaven—designed for nineteen horses and six cows but fine enough for humans—which would be located not far from his new eighty-five-room mansion. Twain took the mention as a hint.

I take that as a feeler—but it won't do. Now that I am in adversity I am prouder than ever. I intend to occupy Harry's room.

The Paige Compositor Company was indeed dissolved into a shell corporation, called Regius Manufacturing. H.H., years later, summed it up:

Certainly it was a marvelous invention. It was the nearest approach to a human being in the wonderful things it could do of any machine I have ever known. But that was just the trouble; it was too much of a human being and not enough of a machine. It had all the complications of the human mechanism, all the liability of getting out of repair, and it could not be replaced with the ease and immediateness of the human being. It was too costly; too difficult of construction; too hard to set up.

The Mergenthaler Linotype did win, and captured the world's typesetting market for nearly a century. Whitelaw Reid of the *Tribune* became fabulously wealthy from his investment.

————

Livy and Twain, with the realization crowding in, began making plans for their no-typesetter-windfall/heavy-debts-to-pay future. "Nothing daunts Mrs. Clemens or makes the world look black to her—which is the reason I haven't drowned myself." Twain would mention suicide several times, but implied that Mrs. Clemens forebade it.

They decided that the family would return to the United States in May when their lease ran out in Paris. They would live the summer for free at Livy's sister's place in Elmira.

Livy calculated that their empty Hartford house cost them $200 a month. They resolved to search for a tenant right away. ("We can never live in it again; though it would break the family's hearts if they could believe it.") Twain noted that he was paying their Hartford lawyer $40 a month; he asked Franklin Whitmore to take $20. He had already cut his brother Orion down from $100 to $50 a month. He wrote H.H. in late January:

> Meantime the thing for me to do is to begin to teach myself to
> endure a way of life which I was familiar with during the first half
> of my life but whose sordidness and hatefulness and humiliation
> long ago faded out of my memory and feeling.

Twain's diva lament about living in humble circumstances seems out of character and almost un-American. Was he posturing for his wealthy friend? Did Twain really consider poverty so hateful? As far back as 1867, he had written:

> No man can say aught against honest poverty. The books laud it;
> the instructors of the people praise it; all men glorify it and say
> it hath its reward here and will have it hereafter. Honest poverty
> is a gem that even a King might feel proud to call his own, but I
> wish to sell out. I have sported that kind of jewelry long enough. I

want some variety. I wish to become rich, so that I can instruct the people and glorify honest poverty a little, like those good, kind-hearted, fat, benevolent people do.

Mark Twain did not have extravagant tastes in clothes, meals, cigars; he did prefer luxurious hotels, a fine showy home, and first-class travel on ships and trains. Overall, he seemed to like the feeling of being wealthy more than many of the trappings. He wrote a maxim: "Man will do many things to get himself loved; he will do all things to get himself envied."

Twain's so-called "poverty" was relative. He figured out that Livy could still expect $4,000 a year from her Langdon inheritance (admittedly a comedown from the first twenty years of marriage, when it sometimes hit above $10,000 a year). He could count on receiving $3,500 annually from his backlist with American and British publishers. And he expected *Joan of Arc* royalties to help. (He wrote the "burned at the stake" final scene on January 29 and Susy wept when he read it to them.)

That $7,500 a year would probably put them in the top 5% of American incomes in the 1890s. He wanted them to have $12,000 a year for living expenses.

However, all of those revenue streams would not generate enough income to pay off about $60,000 ($1.8 million in today's dollars) in Webster publishing debts anytime soon. The debt hung heavy.

On February 2, 1895, Twain and his wife celebrated their twenty-fifth (silver) wedding anniversary. "I gave Mrs. Clemens a brand new five-franc piece [worth $1] & she will frame it," he wrote Rogers. "Nobody else put up anything, all the family but me being poor."

The author explained that he had come up with a drastic but potentially wonderful plan to pay off their debts and to escape the "phantoms" and "heavy nervous strain." He advised Rogers to "take a breath and stand by for a surge."

Twain would go *around the world* performing, mounting the platform, doing at least 100 nights, becoming "the only Yank" ever to show up to speak in Australia, India, South Africa. He thought he might clear $15,000 or more; his mere presence would help advertise a new complete works; he might get a travel book out of it. He wanted his family to join him, and H.H. and H.H.'s daughter and son Harry to come too. "Don't disappoint us," he wrote. "This is our last chance to go around the world; if we don't do it now we never shall."

CHAPTER 5

An Odd Homecoming

The family quickly ran into trouble over who would go on the trip. Twain toyed with the idea of taking the whole female troop, but that could double the expenses. (In that era, entertainers paid their own hotel and travel bills.) They decided to board the youngest and most troubled, Jean, along with one of the other daughters in Elmira with Livy's sister, Sue, and then possibly with a family in Hartford. So which daughter would come? Clara or Susy?

The very week that Twain decided to make the trek, the French steamer *La Gascogne* was lost at sea. A horrific winter snowstorm with "cyclonic blasts" ripped the Atlantic Ocean, with winds lathering up mountainous waves and the zero temperatures congealing New York Harbor with blocks of ice. *La Gascogne* failed to arrive on Sunday, February 3, and then days passed; other ships arrived with "iced shrouds, marble-coated bridges." Fears mounted.

The Clemens family spent that first week *not* daydreaming of exotic travel, but harried by relentless French news reports of likely death and drowning for hundreds of passengers. Then, finally, *La Gascogne* limped into port ten days late. It turned out that about one thousand miles from France, the steamer had broken a piston, and, after repairs, had battened down the hatches and rode out the storm like a 6,800-ton "cork."

Susy, as eldest, had first choice, but she leaned toward not going; Twain would cite to relatives her fear of the ocean voyages. Katy, the loyal family maid, said Susy's opera teacher had prescribed a year of farm living, exercise and fresh air to expand her lung capacity.

But twenty-two-year-old Susy's decision possibly had nothing to do with either reason. She was in love, and wanted to see her inamorata.

Six months earlier, Susy had learned that Louise Brownell, a fellow student from Susy's brief attendance at all-girls Bryn Mawr, was heading back from Europe (where the Clemenses were) to America and wouldn't even have a chance to say good-bye.

Fontainebleu, [France] Sunday [July 29, 1894]

Louise, *my darling,*

I would not, could not dream this would happen and that I should lose you now, *now* at the moment of having you again, after all these years of waiting. IT IS IMPOSSIBLE. I CANNOT BELIEVE IT. IT CANNOT BE TRUE. *Oh No,* dear dear Louise, my *darling* it is too dreadful! I cannot *cannot* bear it! . . . oh I have *lost* you and can do nothing. I am so miserably helpless. I love you so. I wish you were here to comfort me. I think I wrote you that we cannot now afford to live in Hartford & are likely to stay over here [in Europe] until we can. Do you realize what that may mean? another separation like this last,—another interminable unsatisfied longing to see you. This being apart *breaks* my heart. But you will not go. It is a *nightmare*. It isn't true. . . . I love you so much, so infinitely, and you are so near & I cannot *cannot* reach you.

Susy had met Louise, a pale-skinned brunette, at Bryn Mawr College in 1890–1891. For the next half decade, lovelorn Susy would be seeking to reunite with Louise. (More than a century later, it is hard to know whether their passions tipped over into the physical as well as emotional; Susy wrote about wanting to "kiss you *hard* on that little place that tastes so good just on the right side of your nose." She wrote about wanting to "throw my arms around you and kiss you over and over again.")

Now Susy, if she stayed in America in 1895, would almost certainly see Louise, who planned to study at Barnard in New York. Susy decided not to go. (She would regret the choice when marooned with Aunt Sue in Elmira and delight in it when lingering with Louise in Manhattan.)

Livy mentioned the possibility of not taking either daughter and not even taking a servant, to save money. Clara volunteered. She later recalled:

> It was decided that I was to be taken along as a sort of maid, secretary-nurse, being somewhat less unhealthy and unpractical than my sisters, though not very much so; even if all my shortcomings had not been discovered before my ticket was bought for Australia, they were discovered as soon as we were under way.

Twain returned to the States for a quick one-month trip in late February; he would come back to Europe to ferry the clan over in May. His agenda included forcing the lackadaisical lawyer Bainbridge Colby to make a payment to the creditors *before* Livy arrived. He also wanted to work with H.H. to strike a solid deal for publishing his complete works.

As soon at the SS *New York* docked and Twain set foot ashore, he was greeted by something deeply unpleasant: a public shaming over how he had handled his bankruptcy.

———

Twain had written a piece for *North American Review* harshly critiquing a French author, Paul Bourget, who had vaunted French culture and innovation over American. Another French author, Léon Paul Blouet, came to Bourget's defense in the March issue of the same popular magazine and, in the process, savaged Twain. (Their feud would result in a challenge to a duel.)

First, Blouet defended France.

> There is more artistic feeling and refinement in a street of French workingmen than in many avenues inhabited by American millionaires. [France] can teach [America], not perhaps how to work, but how to rest, how to live, how to be happy. She can teach her that the aim of life is not money-making, but that money-making is only a means to obtain an end.

Then Blouet attacked the American author.

> In France . . . a man who had settled his fortune on his wife to avoid meeting his creditors would be refused admission into any

decent society. Many a Frenchman has blown his brains out rather than declare himself a bankrupt. Now would Mark Twain reply to this: "An American is not such a fool; when a creditor stands in his way he closes his doors and reopens them the following day. When he has been a bankrupt three times he can retire from business"? Oh, but I hate saying such things as these.

(Word had seeped out that Twain had paid off Livy as Webster's biggest creditor, but it still was not widely known that he had done so *before* the bankruptcy.)

Obviously, Blouet didn't *hate* saying such things. Blouet wrote and performed under the bizarre stage name of "Max O'Rell." He had written his first book about England, *John Bull and His Island,* when he was teaching French there; it was an international bestseller; his stock in trade was to half-praise, half-raze the locals in a snide tone, while not-so-subtly elevating France. His book *A Frenchman in America* claimed that American employees, from waiters to shop clerks, bullied their customers in the United States. "The Americans are lions governed by bull-dogs and asses . . . tyranny from above is bad; tyranny from below is worse."

Twain, who had been collecting anti-French one-liners, would add a few more in his notebooks:

There is but one love which a Frenchman places above his love for his country, & that is his love for another man's wife.

There is a moral sense, & many nations have it. Also there is an Immoral Sense. The French have it.

The population of the world is now 1,500,000,000 & consists of the human race & the French.

Twain finalized little business-wise during this trip. He had some preliminary talks at H.H. Rogers's impressive home on 57th Street with book and magazine publishers about editions and articles. *Cosmopolitan* offered him $10,000 for twelve articles from his trip; he would later parlay that into $12,000 from *Century,* but he hesitated. He tried unsuccessfully to goad dapper twenty-five-year-old Bainbridge Colby into finishing his investigation into Webster's debts and assets after nearly a year.

With misgivings, the author decided to brave a visit to Hartford on Wednesday, March 20, just before Livy's dear childhood friend, Alice Day Hooker, and her husband and children were moving in. The visit would spark something of an epiphany for Twain.

Livy, darling when I arrived in town I did not want to go near the house & I didn't want to go anywhere or see anybody. I said to myself, "If I may be spared it I will never live in Hartford again."

But as soon as I entered this front door, I was seized with a furious desire to have us all in this house again & right away & never go outside the grounds any more forever—certainly never again to Europe.

How ugly, tasteless, repulsive are all the domestic interiors I have ever seen in Europe compared with the perfect taste of this ground floor, with its delicious dream of harmonious color, & its all-pervading spirit of peace & serenity & deep contentment. You did it all, & it speaks of you & praises you eloquently & unceasingly. It is the loveliest home that ever was. I had no faintest idea of what it was like. I *supposed* I had.

Twain had visited when all the furniture was covered under protective sheets and the carpets rolled up.

And so when I stepped in at the front door & was suddenly confronted by all its richness & beauty minus wraps & concealments, it almost took my breath away. Katy had every rug & picture and ornament & chair exactly where they had always belonged. The place was bewitchingly bright & splendid & homelike & natural, & it seemed as if I had burst awake out of a hellish dream, & had never been away, & that you would come drifting down out of those dainty upper regions with the little children tagging after you.

That steep staircase was wrapped in wallpaper designs hand-stenciled by Louis Tiffany's company (son of the jewelry store founder) to resemble mother of pearl. A theme of Victorian exoticism pervaded; a window stood over the fireplace to reveal snow falling above the flames while the smoke wafted upward in channels veering right and left. Twain had a billiards table in his third-floor office, not far from a small balcony, which allowed him, when presented with the calling cards of annoying visitors, to tell the butler—truthfully—he was "not in."

But the house was far more than decor and colored bricks. This was the *home* where Twain had played with the girls and filled bath soap bubbles with cigar smoke; where he had named the collies "I know," "You know," and "Don't Know"; where Clara had secretly kept squirrels as pets in an upstairs room (gnawing the wainscoting), where the coachmen had told the daughters that the cows would one day be horses fit for riding. The family had hosted weekly discussion groups and billiard parties for their clever Nook Farm neighbors; Susy had written and performed a play. Susy's fifteenth birthday was a candlelit supper for her friends, with flowers, Japanese name cards, strawberries, cakes and ice cream. In memory, 351 Farmington Avenue turned into Camelot.

Twain welcomed the Days to their first dinner in the house that night. As planned, the gardener, John, sent in some roses with a card from Livy, which deeply "touched" Alice.

Twain recorded all this in a letter to Livy, and he added a long, passionate postscript.

> Hartford is resounding with a thundering roar of welcome for you
> & the children—for I have spread it around that you & the chil-
> dren are coming to America. Words cannot describe how worship-
> fully and enthusiastically you are loved in this town; & the wash
> of the wave reaches even to me, because I belong to you; it would
> wash to your dog if you had a dog.
>   . . . I have made up my mind to one thing: if we go around the
> world we will move into our house when we get back; if we don't
> go around the world we will move in when the Days' time is up.
> I can't describe to you how poor & empty & offensive France is,
> compared to America—in my eyes. The minute I strike America I
> seem to wake out of an odious dream.

Paying off the debts and returning to the Hartford home now became the twin goals.

Twain sailed on the SS *Paris* on March 27 and detoured to London to be feted as an international celebrity at a gathering at the home of his friend, writer-explorer Henry M. Stanley (of "Dr. Livingston, I presume" fame). He queried Stanley on world lecturing, since Stanley, with his tales of Africa, ranked near the top of paid speakers. Twain learned that Stanley split the profits fifty-fifty with his Australian lecture agent, R. S. Smythe, and that Stanley had to pay his own expenses, food, lodging and travel. Forty attended the Twain dinner, including cabinet members, poets, playwrights, generals, professors and, as Twain put it with astonishment, "a number of people equipped with rank *and* brains."

Twain reached France and brought the family back on the *New York* on May 18 to the famous harbor with more than one hundred active piers, the busiest commercial port in America.

Livy still refused to go to Hartford, but she agreed to remain a few days in New York City. Twain had wanted to stay at the Waldorf, the recently built luxury hotel on Fifth Avenue at 33rd Street. Twelve glamorous floors of German Renaissance design with loggias and balconies, 500 guest rooms, fine restaurants, tea salons and bars, and a magnificent internal courtyard adaptable for winter or summer (all later torn down to make way for the Empire State Building).

Livy's brother, who often came to New York for medical treatment or business, happened to be staying there. Twain wrote H.H.:

> We were to have stopped at the Waldorf a few days as Charley Langdon's guests, but Mrs. Clemens's head is too level for that. People would think that we were splurging there on our own footing and it wouldn't look modest for bankrupts. Charley may take the children there if he will see to it that their names do not get into print, but the head of the family and I will stop at the Everett.

Humor helped dull the sting in that phrase "head of the family," but Twain was rapidly being forced to adapt to ceding financial control to his wife. Her money always filled family coffers, but Twain and her brother Charley had made almost all the decisions. Those days were gone. When he had visited Hartford, Twain had started to handle a small financial matter. He wrote his lawyer, Whitmore.

> At first I thought I would drop a note to Mr. Day and tell him to pay the rent to you; but next it occurred to me that I am warned

every day to venture no orders concerning Mrs. Clemens's properties and affairs.

And Livy would not tolerate her husband scrounging any money off H.H., even if it was H.H.'s pleasure to help a friend in need. The day that Twain returned from New York, she wrote to H.H. to please pay himself $270 out of her money to cover her husband's borrowing.

Livy's financial standards were often more chivalry than modern finance. She, with her husband's consent, decided that all investors in the Paige, lured personally by her husband's patter, must be reimbursed. Livy expected her husband to pay Bram Stoker ($100), Henry Irving ($500), and, above all, John Brusnahan ($850), a workingman, the head compositor at the *Herald*, who along with his wife, Mary, had invested their life savings.

By this point, Livy controlled the family home, her Langdon family inheritance, and (via the asset transfer) all Twain's books and syndication and stage rights as well. All that remained to Twain—besides $80,000 in Webster debt in his name—were magazine and newspaper articles. He worried that legally he would have to hire himself out to Livy to be able to lecture.

He was becoming the King Lear of his own writing empire.

With shame so clearly in her mind, Livy wanted some payment made immediately to the Webster creditors. Colby finally finished his paperwork, and just as they arrived in New York, he paid out $15,941, which equaled 20% of $79,705 owed to 101 creditors. This money came from the liquidation of Webster's assets, and the selling of books and printing plates and even office furniture. He paid sums to magazines where Webster ads ran, such as *Publishers Weekly* and *Dial*, to craftsmen such as Gill Engraving and Thomas Russell & Sons (bookbinders), to authors, such as $730 to General Custer's widow, Elizabeth, all the way up to $5,876 to Mount Morris Bank.

Twain's debt was now one-fifth paid; he had four-fifths and $63,764 to go.

H.H. Rogers was not pleased that these payments were made without any overall assignment concession plan in place. He advised delay to inspire some desperation. Through Colby, Twain had offered to give the creditors the remaining Webster assets (which hopefully would tally up to a third of the debts) in exchange for a quitclaim. He would also sweeten the deal by giving his "moral" promise to try to pay them all in full. The creditors rejected this offer. So Colby sent out this 20% payment, with no strings attached. Clearly, Livy was outvoting H.H.

———

Their new abode, the Everett House, overlooking Union Square, ranked as a tired but solid choice, favored by writers and actors. Livy clearly hoped to avoid their Hartford friends and neighbors but some tracked them down to offer their sympathies. (Twain still privately bristled that no one from Connecticut had stepped up in his time of need.)

A Hartford neighbor, George Warner, called, but only Twain and Susy came down to the hotel parlor. (They had already shipped off Clara and Jean.) George wrote to his wife:

> Mr. C[lemens] looks younger and thinner. Susy is thin, seems easily flushed and speaks huskily. I don't like it. She says a year at the farm will be good for her. Mr. and Mrs C and Clara go to Australia in July, Gone a year. Mr. C won't go to H[artford] Cant bear it. speaks of poverty etc Dont mention any of this.

A "Don't mention" usually starts the rumor mill.

Livy, Susy and "Youth" stayed only two more days in New York City after George Warner's visit. Twain left H.H. the task of trying to nail down a deal with Harper for publishing a complete works uniform edition. Twain himself began feeling out Major Pond for a quick U.S. tour before taking the ship from the West Coast to Australia. Twain had contacted Stanley's lecture agent, R. S. Smythe, and struck a deal.

The trio went to Penn Station and boarded the train to Elmira. Twain began filling his notebooks with possible selections for his performances. Pond offered to set up a trip for one-third of the profits; Twain countered with one-quarter and Pond accepted. The author was especially optimistic about San Francisco, and he hoped to do two consecutive nights in many places to allow Livy to rest. He wanted to charge $1 for general admission, $1.50 for reserved seats, and keep it intimate by never playing in theaters holding more than 1,500 people. Also, he wanted at least nine nights of practice before captive audiences such as at the Elmira Reformatory and Blackwell Island's House of Refuge.

Around June 1, Mark Twain was suddenly informed that several creditors were heading to the New York State Supreme Court to seek judgments against him. The Barrow family, led by upstate politician George Barrow, received a ruling in its favor on June 4 for $16,842 ($15,000 loan plus interest), and so did Mount Morris Bank for $10,098 (apparently Webster's debts *not* cosigned by Charley Langdon) and Thomas Russell & Sons for $5,046. The court in one swoop had ordered that Twain must pay $31,986, an enormous sum.

As long as Twain remained in New York State, he ran the risk of a sheriff showing up at his door demanding payment. With no debtor's prison in America, he couldn't be locked up, but the sheriff could seize any conceivable asset, such as the proceeds of a lecture or even jewelry. This new stress, a scant two weeks after rearriving in the United States, upended Twain and Livy.

Twain fell sick. Gout returned to plague him in his right ankle, and he developed a malignant boil "as big as a turkey's egg" on his left thigh. Boils/skin eruptions threatened in other places as well, even on his writing hand. His sufferings were starting to seem biblical, at least to him.

CHAPTER 6

Not Enough Time to Curse

Twain—the Missouri native—wrote some of his best books about the Mississippi while parked in upstate New York in Elmira. For twenty years, until their self-exile to Europe, the Clemens family spent summers at Quarry Farm on the elevated outskirts of Elmira overlooking the pastures and vales of the Finger Lakes region.

His in-laws, the Cranes—back when husband Theodore still lived—had built for their famous relative an octagonal carved-wood study shaped a bit like a riverboat pilot house, perched alone atop the mountain, away from the house noise, a haven of serenity with little cat doors and mighty views over the dairy lands below. Twain wrote *Tom* and *Huck*, also *Life on the Mississippi,* there as the breezes slipped through the eight windows and he puffed away on his endless cigars.

Now, he was stranded in a nightshirt in a stuffy bedroom in the main house (amid the clatter of daughters, dogs and servants), unable to pull on a pair of trousers over the nasty boil on his leg. At least he thought it was a boil, but the local family doctor, Theron Wales, diagnosed it as a "carbuncle," a diagnostic first cousin—a congealed clump of infected contagious boils.

Dr. Wales applied a slice of raw salt pork for several days. He then lanced it, but it hardly drained at all. Twain later claimed the most painful part of the treatment was not the needle or the bandaging but the relentless inane conversation. Twain rated Dr. Wales as "tedious, witless . . . a stayer [who] loved to hear himself talk" and often stayed for two hours.

Twain looked back and decided a cat could have stared at the wound as "effectively" and that the ex-slave cook, Rachel, could have administered the ham at no charge and changed the gauze.

The lancing failed, but in mid-June, the carbuncle erupted and "sloughed out a big hunk of decayed protoplasm like a Baltimore oyster . . . & left a corresponding raw cavity in my leg," he wrote his lecture agent. (A writer's precision can be a mixed blessing.) Twain expected that it "will heal fast, now." He was wrong.

From his sickbed, Twain tried to prepare his speeches, negotiate with his lecture agent, consult with his bankruptcy lawyer, and strike a deal for writing about his trip.

Twain was exchanging letters with his lecture agent, Major James B. Pond, a top figure in the industry, who handled stars such as Stanley and cartoonist Thomas Nast, as well as a handful of musical acts.

As soon as Twain beckoned, Pond—a fifty-seven-year-old with a long, thin, gray Uncle Sam beard—shunted off the rest of his seventy-five clients to underlings and personally took charge of Twain. He even decided that he and his twenty-six-year-old second wife, Martha, would accompany Twain for the whole route.

At first, plans called for a September departure, but the New York State court judgments prompted Twain to decide to leave as soon as he was physically fit and performance ready. He and Major Pond tentatively set July 7 for opening night in either Cleveland or Duluth. They settled on a northern U.S. tour, with Great Lakes steamer travel wherever possible instead of trains.

Then Pond fell sick with the flu. "We are determining nothing, accomplishing nothing," Twain confided to H.H., "& the devil is on deck and having everything his own way."

Twain wanted to do a dry run in Fairhaven, Massachusetts, as a present to benefactor H.H., but the carbuncle was foiling that; the author couldn't even come down to New York to discuss book or magazine deals.

That would leave bedridden Twain less than a month to finish preparing six or seven stories that would last about ninety minutes. (He had been noodling around with choices, but he had expected Elmira prep would be key.) Timing the talk was hard without an audience, as was memorizing it all, and he thrived on watching the audience to gauge delivering the perfect pauses for his punch lines. (Simple example: "Always obey your parents [P-A-U-S-E] when they are present.") He would also eventually need material for a second and third night in the same city, so that meant a gargantuan 180 more minutes to memorize. And he was supposed to be practicing being funny while in bed with an open wound on his thigh. Twain was running so far behind that he told Pond to schedule just one night in each city.

Twain had a tumultuous relationship with the profession of public speaking; he had sworn off paid public speaking several times. He was so nervous about his first lecture in San Francisco, he gave friends laugh cues, like a baseball third-base coach giving signals, in case the material fell flat. His first New York lecture at Cooper Union in 1867 had drawn so few ticket buyers that his promoter, Frank Fuller, had had to paper the house with teachers. He hit his stride with practice and later notched a successful run in prestigious New England.

Then he married an heiress, had a bestseller and quit with a flourish. He wrote the Redpath Agency.

> I guess I am out of the field permanently. Have got a lovely wife; a lovely house, bewitchingly furnished; a lovely carriage, and a coachman whose style and dignity are simply awe-inspiring— nothing less—and I am making more money than necessary—by considerable, and therefore why crucify myself nightly on the platform?

Over the next twenty-five years of marriage, he only unretired and dipped back into lecture tours four times, including a run in England and a tandem trip with New Orleans writer George W. Cable. Misgivings never left Twain. He confessed to his platform mate: "Oh, Cable, I am demeaning myself to be a mere buffoon. It is ghastly. I can't endure it any longer."

Livy always regretted his absences. This world tour—by far the most extensive—would be his first with family members.

Twain called his performances "readings" even though he didn't read and never held a book in his hand. He considered that author's head-down approach deadly; he pondered the strange alchemy required to transform the written word to spoken entertainment. And he found much of it simply inexplicable, beyond any formula of editing.

For speaking, he simplified the language, tightened the scenes, slowly built to punch lines or "nubs." He occasionally adopted voices to portray characters such as Huck or the slave Jim; for straight humor he often stood there as a rube who had no idea that he was saying anything funny. Deadpan humor is dangerous; he never laughed, and he loathed performers who chuckled or guffawed at their own material to highlight funny bits. "All of which is very depressing and makes one want to renounce joking and lead a better life."

So now he mined his own books for five- to fifteen-minute anecdotes, many of which he had been telling at private social gatherings or dinner parties over the years; he wasn't above "borrowing" a christening story from Bram Stoker. For his opening night in Cleveland, he intended to lean on several tried-and-true gems such as "Stealing My First Watermelon," "The Jumping Frog of Calaveras County," and "Grandfather's Old Ram." But Twain wanted a theme to string the half dozen stories together, so as to avoid jagged non sequitur leaps to new topics, and he came up with "Morals."

———

The American lyceum or lecture movement, which had started with Emerson and Thoreau, and heavy doses of piety and self-improvement, gained even more popularity after the Civil War with Henry Ward Beecher delivering his "Ministry of Wealth" and John Gough mimicking a drunkard's downfall.

Twain decided that he would spoof the ministers, such as William Booth, General of the Salvation Army, then spreading the gospel in Australia. Twain would preach that men and women *must* commit each and every sin imaginable, at least 450 different ones, to prevent themselves from ever perpetrating that particular sin again. The sinners would learn from their mistakes and never repeat them. He would stand there with that serious face and tell the audience he was two-thirds of the way to salvation, that he was an inspiration to them all. He figured he could tell a story to illustrate a sin such as stealing, lying or gambling. The "Morals" premise was packed with promise, but Twain, marooned in bed, stultified by Dr. Wales, engulfed in noise, hounded by debts, could not make it funny. (He would edit and buff the "Morals" intro for his entire trip until he at least mined a maxim of it: "To be good is noble; to teach others to be good is nobler—and no trouble.")

He and Major Pond argued over the route; Twain moaned that Pond wanted to skip San Francisco because apparently too many citizens flee in the summer. He would even slip into Canada twice.

Major Pond pushed for printing 30,000 four-page advertising pamphlets, an expense that would cut into their shared profits. Twain reluctantly agreed but stood firm on the theme.

> The chief feature when speaking of me should be that he (M.T.)
> is on his way to Australia & thence around the globe on a reading
> & talking tour to last twelve months—You get the idea? Traveling
> around the world is nothing—everybody does it. But what I am
> traveling for is unusual—everybody doesn't do that.

Twain was right: in that era of steamer (15 miles per hour) and rail (25 miles per hour), performers very rarely circled the globe, and an American author had never done it. Sure, a Conan Doyle or a Stanley or a Dickens might come to America, an American preacher might go to Australia, but globe circling was rare. P. T. Barnum—no novice in the promotion field—had sent Tom Thumb and his entourage around the world (1869–1872), and General Ulysses S. Grant had circumnavigated the globe in a kind of postpresidential triumphal parade (1877–1879). Albert Spalding world-chartered an American baseball team to demonstrate the strange new game (1888). Nellie Bly raced around in 1889 in seventy-two days, but she wasn't performing.

Pond ignored Twain's request about stressing world travel, but he compensated by buttering up the star: "Mark Twain is to-day the most popular writer in the English language." And: "Sentences and phrases that seem at first only made for the heartiest laughter, yield, at closer view, a sanity and wisdom that is good for the soul."

Twain wasn't only going to mount the platform, he also intended to cash in by writing either a series of articles or a book about the trip. Negotiating from Elmira, he agreed to do a dozen articles for a princely $1,000 each for *Century*. Then his old publishing house, under Frank Bliss, which was publishing *Pudd'nhead Wilson,* offered Twain a $10,000 advance for a travel book.

The bedridden, angst-ridden author began to realize that crafting a dozen magazine articles mid-trip would be much harder than sloppily amassing piles of notes, grabbing other travelers' accounts, and then writing a travel book in his post-trip leisure. He might even enjoy that process. He wanted to get out of the *Century* deal. H.H. Rogers was in Chicago on business, and Mrs. Clemens was adamant that her husband had "committed" to the magazine. He had agreed to sign a contract. Making matters worse, he now noticed a clause that made him absolutely furious.

> The Century people actually proposed that I *sign a contract to be funny* in those 12 articles. That was pure insanity. Why, it makes me shudder every time I think of those articles. I don't think I could ever write one of them without being under the solemnizing blight of that disgusting recollection.

Twain's fear of clown-dom continued. *Century* was a highbrow magazine that wanted Twain *only* for humor. H.H. Rogers—with his neat mechanical logic—advised a simple remedy: tell *Century* that he could not deliver as required. Twain informed Frank H. Scott:

> To be virile & fresh, the articles would have to be written as three-fourths of the Innocents Abroad was written—*intransitu* [*i.e., while traveling*]. To do that & at the same time run the lecture business and the social business would make a botch of all three. For an old man to write a young book under exhausting pressure of other work and in trying climates—well, it could not be done.
>
> And so, to save the making a bad mistake for both of us, let us stop now in time and give it all up. In the beginning I was charmed with the unhampered, uncharted $10,000 offer, which was made me last March but if the sum were doubled it could not tempt me, now that I have done my belated thinking.

Century would enact some revenge on Twain by requesting a bicycle humor piece from Twain and then rejecting it the following month. Twain's unpublished cycling piece included: "Try as you may, you don't get down [from a bicycle] as you would from a horse, you get down as you would from a house afire. You make a spectacle of yourself every time." Editor Robert Johnson called the piece "flat" and expected Twain's ire.

The carbuncle wound refused to close, even though Dr. Wales kept visiting daily and estimating just another week. Livy still chose not to go to Hartford, even though she wanted to protect their precious keepsakes from "careless servants or . . . unloving hands" while the Days or other renters occupied the house. Livy echoed her husband when she wrote their Hartford lawyer that she had "great hope" that the family would move back into their Hartford home in a year, in September 1896. This glimmered as the reward for paying off the debts.

Twain, now often on the parlor couch, kept practicing and kept stumbling over long passages. "I have found it exceedingly difficult to memorize readings & curse a carbuncle all at the same time," he wrote his friend Frank Fuller, who had organized his first lecture, "& I have done only one division of the job really well."

Twain had wanted nine dry runs for his speech before heading out to Cleveland, and he still hoped to travel to Fairhaven to speak and to explore Rogers's just-completed eighty-five-room mansion overlooking Buzzards Bay. At the time Rogers was literally deluged with money, as Standard Oil before its breakup in 1906 paid out astounding dividends of about $550 million ($16½ billion today), mainly to a handful of men including John D. Rockefeller, William Rockefeller, H. M. Flagler, John Archbold, and H.H. Rogers.

On June 26, a stranger knocked on the front door of the Quarry Farm house. He requested Mr. Samuel L. Clemens. The stranger stepped inside and handed the ailing writer a subpoena ordering him to appear in Supreme Court of New York in courthouse chambers in Manhattan on July 5, in ten days. Justice Patterson had granted the subpoena to lawyer William R. Wilder, representing bookbinder Thomas Russell & Sons, over an unsatisfied judgment for $5,046. The writ ordered Twain to come to be examined in supplementary proceedings and also to bring with him all his financial records about his personal assets, his transfer of assets, and Webster's profit and loss.

Livy was absolutely distraught. Twain immediately added a postscript to a letter he was writing to H.H. Rogers and asked whether he must "obey" the court order, adding that the doctor thought he would indeed be able to travel by then. (The mail—in that era of more efficient service—was picked up at that particular midday hour and would be delivered to Rogers in Manhattan the following day.) The subpoena with its block caps and gothic script stated, "The People of the State of New York . . . Command You" and it threatened a "contempt-of-court" conviction, damages to the plaintiff and a large fine.

Twain wanted to contact his lawyer, Bainbridge Colby, but the young man had just married Nathalie Sedgwick four days earlier and was off on his honeymoon. A respected local Elmira lawyer, John B. Stanchfield, claimed the New York State Supreme Court had no jurisdiction in this civil matter.

> How exasperating it is! The Devil and Colby would necessarily choose this time for junketing when I am tied by the hind leg and can't go and 'tend to my matters myself. . . . This carbuncle is not going to allow me to stand on my feet for two or three weeks yet. It is slower than chilled molasses. I'll go to Cleveland on a stretcher, sure.

Livy, "greatly distressed," overcame her shyness to write directly to H.H. Rogers, without first consulting her husband. She informed H.H. she held a mortgage for $30,000 (almost $1 million today) that *might* be paid to her in July.

> I know that Mr. Clemens and my brother will feel that it ought not to be used in that way—but if it could make us at ease on the Webster matters, during our trip, I should feel that it could not be better employed. My brother would not approve of this plan I know because he has felt very sorry to have my income so cramped as it has been by the machine and Webster & Co. . . . Would it trouble you to send me just a line telling me whether you think it would be a good plan?

It turned out that H.H. Rogers would hate the idea of rushing to pay any creditors before negotiating a tough quitclaim settlement and a vague promise to pay more. Once again, Twain would find himself pulled in opposite directions by two powerful advisers.

Livy echoed her husband and said that the Clemens family still hoped to come to pay a visit to Fairhaven.

Twain, for the next post, wrote more to H.H. as well. He regarded it as a "bad advertisement" for his round-the-world tour if newspapers portrayed him as sneaking away from the courts and fleeing the country. "If Colby had told me of this danger, I wouldn't have remained in [New York] State." The writer, acting on advice from the local lawyer, suggested sending a doctor's note and getting a brief postponement. And in the meantime, they should call a rush meeting of the creditors, including Thomas Russell, and sweeten the current offer of all Webster assets by adding 10% additional cash from Twain. "Mrs. C. is dead-set against having me keel-hauled and fire-assayed in that court for the benefit of the newspapers, though I myself do not much dread it."

Twain dashed off another postscript. "Look here, don't you think you'd better let somebody else run the Standard Oil a week or two till you've finished up these matters of mine? Why *I* can keep you busy, you don't need any outside industries."

William Wilder, the lawyer for Thomas Russell, had offered to settle out of court for 75% of the amount owed, but Twain and his lawyers turned it down. They had gained a brief medical adjournment to July 8. Livy was set to accompany him to Manhattan on Saturday, July 6, but the family feared for her health, she was so agitated. They convinced her to allow a professional male nurse to join him instead; he would have a private compartment on the train and a hotel room waiting.

Then a "telephone message from town" alerted Twain that the court date was further postponed till Thursday, July 11. H.H. had arranged it because by then the mogul would be back in Manhattan and could meet with Twain. "It is mighty good and lovely of you to be doing all this work and taking all this trouble for me, but I can tell you *one* thing—God shall reward you for it," Twain wrote on July 8. "I am going to look after that detail *personally*."

The performer was due in Cleveland on July 15. His performance anxiety seemed temporarily to trump his legal and financial anxiety. He wrote H.H.:

> I shan't be able to stand on a platform before we start west. I shan't get a single chance to practice my reading; but will have to appear in Cleveland without that essential preparation. Nothing in this world can save it from being a shabby poor disgusting performance. I've got to *stand*; I can't *sit* and talk to a house—and how in the nation am I going to do it? Land of Goshen, it's *this night week!* Pray for me.

CHAPTER 7

Twain Grilled, Livy Burnt

The stately carriage of H.H. Rogers rolled to a stop in front of the County Courthouse at City Hall Park in Lower Manhattan on the toasty morning of Thursday, July 11, 1895. A liveried coachman sprang down and opened the door.

Nearby newsboys hawked some of the city's seventeen dailies, including Joseph Pulitzer's leviathan *New York World* and Charles Dana's *New York Sun*. The scruffy youngsters sang out about the exploits of the city's brash new police commissioner, Teddy Roosevelt. As a yellow cable car moved down the center of Broadway, passengers hopped on and off. Not too far away, the Seventh Regiment Armory—one of a dozen throughout the city—protected the wealthier citizens against uprisings by the vast immigrant poor.

A male nurse in white descended from the carriage and helped Mark Twain out. H.H. Rogers followed. Both men realigned their top hats. Though they were similar in appearance, Rogers appeared far more dapper with his ramrod-straight posture, perfectly tailored suit, and lightly waxed mustache; Twain's clothes looked rumpled, his shoes unshined; his plush mustache bore signs of a half century of smoking. He had spent the previous forty-five days on his back and looked feeble.

They mounted the marble steps. Twain's lawyers, from the prestigious firm of Stern & Rushmore, quickly convinced Judge M. L. Stover to allow Twain's "examination" to be held in private, since the writer's health "would not permit . . . a public ordeal."

The clerk handed Twain a "ragged" Bible, and the judge swore the fiction writer to be truthful. The group, including lawyers for both sides, headed south; despite his carbuncle, Twain, along with H.H. and the nurse, decided to walk the half mile to Stern & Rushmore's offices at 40 Wall Street.

Newspapers reported that business executives turned and pointed to "the shambling figure surmounted by the shock of iron gray hair." In an age when most newspapers could not reproduce photographs, Twain was already a recognizable celebrity.

The session, held in an inner conference room, was closed to the public and press; it lasted from 11:45 a.m. to 6 p.m. with no break for lunch. (Twain ordered a glass of milk from a nearby restaurant.)

Based on later comments, it's clear that with no judge or referee present, both legal teams bickered and even descended to name-calling; Twain, for his part, tried hard to take H.H. Rogers's advice to remain calm and vague. William R. Wilder, the aggressive lawyer for Thomas Russell & Sons, later admitted to a straightforward agenda: find out under oath if Mark Twain had any "concealed assets," since it seemed inconceivable that one of the nation's wealthiest authors was dead broke. Ironically, a victory for proud Twain that day would amount to proving himself penniless.

Wilder's second mission was to probe the transfer of the author's assets to his wife. When did it occur? How much annual income did the book copyrights yield?

Wilder quickly elicited that the transfer had occurred *before* the Webster bankruptcy assignment. Twain justified it simply by stating that his wife had loaned the company $70,000 from her inheritance and that he wanted "to protect her from loss."

Wilder would tell a reporter: "I do not allege that this was done to defraud his creditors but I want to know exactly why it was done." Wilder was using lawyer-speak in the press to raise the threat that he might *later* accuse Twain of fraud. The lawyer, with the small office at 45 Cedar Street, always seemed one step ahead of Twain's high-priced solicitors.

Upon leaving the interrogation, Twain was uncharacteristically quiet. He told reporters that he had spoken enough for one day, although he did mention that on August 18 he would be departing from Vancouver for a round-the-world speaking tour.

The next day's newspaper headlines and coverage fulfilled Livy's worst nightmares. MARK TWAIN AS DEBTOR announced the *New York Sun;* MARK TWAIN IS RUINED blared the influential *Boston Globe* and added a quote from Twain's lawyer, Colby: "Mr. Clemens is a ruined man financially and . . . he has been very much depressed."

The *New York Herald* played the worst trick; it paired Twain's testimony side by side on page five with that of an accused murderess who had slit the throat of her foot-dragging bootblack fiancé from ear to ear. MARIA BARBERI ON THE STAND ran next to MARK TWAIN ON THE RACK. Then below: "Lawyers Pleads the Exasperation of Insulted Womanhood" alongside "Questioned in Relation to His Transfer of All His Copyrights to His Wife."

Seamstress Maria testified in Italian, which was translated.

> "I begged him to marry me," she said. "He said I must wait. He
> said he was furnishing our apartment. I told him furniture was not
> so necessary as my honor. I waited three days. Then he took me
> to No. 424 East Thirteenth Street, and said our apartment was
> ready. I went with him to an empty room. He abused me again."
> [*"Abused" was Victorian code for "raped."*]

The *Herald,* known for sass, would reword one of Twain's Pudd'nhead maxims: "October. This is one of the peculiarly dangerous months to speculate in stocks in. The others are July, January, September, April, November, May, March, June, December, August and February." The newspaper would replace "to speculate in stocks" with "for an author to go into business."

Even Twain's own lawyers didn't exactly help. Charles E. Rushmore explained the Webster failure to the *New York Sun:* "It was found when the crash came that the firm was loaded down with a lot of riff-raff, biographies and memoirs of people in whom the public had absolutely no interest."

After a brief second day of testimony, in which Twain showed up in a jaunty blue ship captain's hat supplied by Rogers, the lawyers left the building and announced they would have no comment. Also, the stenographer's 40,000 words would not be released.

Then lawyer William Wilder double-crossed them. He reached out to the press.

> Russell & Sons want to find out whether this [asset] transfer may
> be set aside. Mr. Wilder said yesterday that he had no doubts as

to the author's honesty but like many literary men, he is a very poor businessman. . . . He is unable to give with any exactness the receipts from his various books, and as Mr. Wilder expressed it, he is in business a big, overgrown boy.

Wilder also revealed that Twain's backlist generated only about $1,500 a year and that most of his royalties for the past decade had been "swallowed up" by Webster and plowed back into the company. He told the world that Twain would have been a wealthy man if he hadn't invested in the Paige typesetter and Webster publishing. The lawyer waved Twain's dirty laundry like a flag. Wilder's final off-the-cuff insult came in sharing that at the end of the session Twain had offered to sign any legal documents without reading them. Wilder hoped the courts would reverse the transfer and put a lien on Twain's copyrights.

National coverage, regurgitating snippets from other papers, was perhaps more brutal: MARK TWAIN PENNILESS (*San Francisco Call* front page); MARK TWAIN UP BEFORE A COURT: "Lawyers Suspect He Is Not as Poor as He Looks" (*Wichita Daily Eagle* front page). And the follow-up op-eds were harsh: "It is suspected that Mark Twain has money but that it is all in his wife's name. It is said, however, that he is utterly miserable. He may be forced into actually becoming humorous again in order to pay his debts" (*Wichita Daily Eagle*); "Mark Twain's failure was his own fault and yet he plans to lecture the world about it" (*San Francisco Call*).

Publishers Weekly chimed in, gloating about the inability of authors to self-publish. "[Mark Twain] was supposed to have every qualification of a good business man as well as of a clever author," stated the trade magazine. "And yet, at the examination of supplementary proceedings . . . his ignorance of, or indifference to even ordinary business details, proved astonishing."

The *Herald* paired him with the murderess again, plunking MARK TWAIN'S MONEY TANGLES next to MARIA TELLS OF KILLING CATALDO. (Judge Goff would sentence Maria to die in the electric chair, but a clemency drive, including a signature from Mark Twain, would gain her a new trial and an acquittal.)

Wilder had already landed subpoenas to examine H.H. Rogers (who had signed the transfer) and Bainbridge Colby (handling the assignment); now he convinced Judge Stover to add Mrs. Clemens to the witness list. The judge signed a wide-ranging subpoena, ordering her to his New York courtroom in one week, and also required that she bring all documents pertaining to the transfer of her husband's assets, to all loans she made to Webster, and to all income from Webster, as well as her bank books dating back to 1885. Wilder wanted *more* dirty laundry.

The night of Friday, July 12, a distracted Twain took the ferry from Harlem to Randall's Island to try out his stage act for the first time. On board with him—besides the nurse—was Rogers's six-foot-tall assistant, twenty-eight-year-old Katherine Harrison, the highest-paid salaried female executive in America, earning $10,000 a year. Precise and fiercely loyal, she knew all of Standard's secrets and guarded the clubby inner sanctum. In her spectacles and dainty hat, she towered over Twain.

Randall's Island, tucked between Manhattan and the Bronx, housed the Idiot Asylum, a potter's field, and also Twain's destination, the House of Refuge, for 700 juvenile delinquents. He bombed.

Twain didn't know it, but that afternoon there had been a riot when a guard noticed a knife in the pocket of a boy playing baseball. A dozen guards had wrestled with the boys, and eventually one guard swinging a baseball bat had succeeded in getting the knife from nineteen-year-old Tom Callahan.

Twain's talk—except for the part about stealing watermelons—had apparently whizzed over the heads of the restless boys. Twain called it a "comical defeat—delivering a grown folks' lecture to a sucking-bottle nursery." H.H. soon tried to shore up the faltering author. "It may have been a mistake to go up there to talk to a lot of hoodlums, nine-tenths of whom perhaps have never seen the inside of a book." He added that "Miss Harrison says anybody of sense would have appreciated and enjoyed it."

The following day, Twain, with his nurse, boarded the train north back toward Elmira. Once aboard, he happened to run into his lawyer Charles E. Rushmore. He asked him whether he thought Wilder could make trouble for Twain in Cleveland, maybe seize the box office money. Rushmore strongly doubted that Wilder would do that, but he couldn't be absolutely certain. "Mr. Rushmore thinks he knows Wilder," Twain would later write to H.H. "It is a superstition."

Twain reached Elmira, rode in a carriage up to Quarry Farm. He found Livy in an absolute state of "despair and misery" because of the newspaper coverage and the subpoena. She asked her husband if he could guarantee that Wilder would not harass them in Ohio, which would "float" another round of newspaper coverage. He admitted that he could not guarantee it.

She decided that she wanted to settle immediately with Thomas Russell & Sons—regardless of the cost—by drawing on Langdon family money. Twain failed to dissuade her. Since they were leaving for Cleveland the following night, he wrote immediately to H.H. "You will feel a good deal like blowing me up, I suspect,—*I've thrown up the Russell sponge.*" (Twain was using a boxing metaphor for surrender; in the 1890s, the phrase was not yet "throwing in the towel.")

The writer added, to lessen his shame: "[My wife] was ill over the situation and I at once administered the only medicine that could stop her from getting worse."

Twain informed H.H. that her brother, Charles Langdon, would supply the money. The author relayed his doubts that Wilder would now accept that 75% previously offered; he also doubted that anyone at Stern & Rushmore could knock down the price. He asked H.H. to pick someone to negotiate, unless that was one task too many. "It troubles me to put so many loads on your generous shoulders; and it troubles Mrs. Clemens, too," he wrote. "She thinks I ride you too hard."

Rogers received the letter the next day. With his strict business logic, he was clearly appalled by the decision to set the precedent of paying one creditor out of a hundred. He had also been informed by his son-in-law that Thomas Russell & Sons might have cheated by overcharging Twain for unused leather bindings, a fact to use for leverage. Nonetheless, H.H. within an hour sent a telegram to Olivia Clemens:

> I shall do everything to carry out your wishes even though it
> conflicts with my judgment. In order to make progress, I have
> talked with your brother on the telephone to-day and he is coming
> here. . . . Everybody is friendly.

H.H. clearly wanted to calm down both Mr. and Mrs. Clemens. "Don't worry about troubling me," he wrote Twain, adding: "Your [court] examination is like one of New York's nine days' wonders and will be forgotten within the prescribed time." (This cliché from the newspaper era preceded broadcast media's "fifteen minutes of fame.")

With the decision made to cave in to Russell, Twain could now return to worrying about his platform debut. He was squeezing in one last dry run at the Reformatory in Elmira. He would play to a captive audience in what was considered the nation's most progressive penal institution. Instead of the prevailing practice of fixed prison terms and hard labor, all prisoners in Elmira served "indeterminate" sentences of up to five years and could earn privileges and early "parole" release through good behavior, such as sitting still and laughing at Mark Twain's jokes. On the evening of July 14, inside the castle-like turreted walls, he fared better than at Randall's Island.

Afterwards, Twain quickly returned to his sister-in-law's house. As he awaited a carriage to carry him to the night train for Cleveland, he scribbled a brief note to his older sister, Pamela, in Fredonia, New York. "I can't make any more financial mistakes," he wrote. "I've nothing left to make them with."

Before signing off "In haste, Sam," he updated her on family news. Livy and Clara had already gone to the station, and Susy and Jean were remaining at the farm, with plans that they should all join up in London in a year.

When he reached the station, he saw a long line of satchels and trunks arrayed on the platform; the distant headlamp of the westbound train pierced the darkness. Family emotions heightened as the rumble approached. This parting was proving especially hard for Livy, already a wreck over the Webster matters. While her husband traveled often away from the family, she had *never* been parted from Jean, who was about to turn fifteen, and she had been separated only for about eight months from twenty-three-year-old Susy, during her stint at Bryn Mawr half a decade earlier.

Porters loaded the luggage. "The maid certainly has more to do than is possible," Clara had written in the predeparture days. Papa, Mama, and Clara settled themselves in a reserved private sleeping room. They looked out the window and saw Aunt Sue, Susy, Jean and the longtime family maid, Katy Leary, all waving good-bye under the new electric lights of the station. Tears flowed.

Major Pond and his young wife met the Clemenses aboard the train. Pond recorded in his journal that "Mark" looked "badly fatigued" and he feared that the family "baggage might be attached" in Cleveland. "My heart aches for both of them." Pond handed over $200 to Twain, as the author had asked to be paid in advance to avoid any unpleasantness by a sheriff at the box office.

In the morning, they reached hot, damp ninety-degree Cleveland, then the nation's eighth-largest city, a thriving Great Lakes port, the original home base of Rockefeller's oil-refining empire. They took a carriage to the prestigious Stillman House, and Twain went straight to bed. At 3 p.m., Pond woke him to do newspaper interviews. The talent agent charged reporters the price of admission to the show.

That night, more than 2,800 people filled the Music Hall. Twain, always nervous beforehand, seethed in the wings of the sweltering auditorium as the minutes ticked forward long past his scheduled 8 p.m. start time. Twain had several pet peeves about performing: start on time (no stragglers), do only ninety minutes, receive no introduction and tolerate no musical acts.

No one had told him that a couple of attractive young newlyweds, Fiora Drescher and Dewey Haywood, would open the night's show by performing chamber music—he on the flute and she, a glamorous brunette, on a 100-year-old violin—and that the wedding party of 250 would clap them to several encores. No one had told him to expect a forty-five-minute delay.

Also, no one had told him that since this Monday night performance served as a benefit for underpaid, overworked newsboys, 500 of them, ages six to sixteen, would be seated in bleachers on the stage behind him.

When the newlyweds finally finished, he hobbled out alone. He later explained his reasons for avoiding local amateur emcees who overpraised him in "a jumble of vulgar compliments and dreary effort to be funny." Twain had even tried planting an introducer in the audience. A big hulking man would reluctantly come up and stand there, dumbfounded, then say:

I don't know anything about this man. At least I know only two things; one is, he hasn't been in the penitentiary, and the other is [*after a pause, and almost sadly*], I don't know why.

Finally, Twain just discarded introductions altogether. That debut night in Cleveland, he reached the middle of the stage, and the perspiring, fan-waggling, handkerchief-mopping audience greeted him with enthusiastic applause, as did the newsboys behind him.

He launched right into it.

I was solicited to go round the world, on a lecture tour, by a man in Australia. I asked him what they wanted to be lectured on. He wrote back that those people were very coarse and serious and that they would like something solid, something in the way of education, something gigantic, and he proposed that I prepare about three or four lectures at any rate, on just morals. . . . I should like to teach morals to those people. I do not like to have them taught to me. . . .

His opening was still a slow starter, made even slower by his habit of speaking v-e-r-y s-l-o-w-l-y, never smiling. The newsboys behind him began to squirm and make faces, especially with no grown-ups assigned to chaperone them. Twain had their attention when he talked about stealing watermelons, but it was fleeting. "Why, with their scufflings and horse-play and noise, it was just a menagerie . . . they flowed past my back in clattering shoals, some leaving the house, others returning for more skylarking."

At one point, a dog got loose; the terrier nearly barked him off the stage. Twain did his best, but he was clearly flustered and accidentally switched the program order and performed a long tale about Jim Baker's blue jays.

Twain judged this night a "dead failure" and described the perspiring audience as paying "a dollar apiece to go to hell in this fashion." He especially resented the boys' behavior, which does seem a tad ironic from the author of *Huckleberry Finn*. He also hated running overtime, and toward the end, he abruptly surrendered.

I shan't attempt to go on with the rest of that program, but I will just close with that which is at the bottom. I have been in bed stretched on my back forty-five days and I am only five days out of that bed and I am, perhaps, not strong enough to stand here and talk. I will just close. It is unbusinesslike to jump at conclusions on too slight evidence and I will close with the case of christening a baby in a Scotch Irish family.

A little clergyman came and when he found that there was a great host of people assembled there, he would attempt to exploit his peculiar vanity. He could not resist that temptation. When he took the baby from the father's hands and hefted it, he said: "My friends, he is very little; very little; well, he is a very little fellow, but what of that? I see in your faces disparagement of him because he is little; disparagement for no cause but that he is little. You should reflect that it is from the little things that the great things spring. What is smaller than a grain of [. . .] sand? and yet it is from grains of [. . .] sand that this earth is formed. Very little is he. Take the little drop of water and out of little drops of water the great ocean is made. And very little is he and yet he may become like Napoleon, or like Caesar, or like both of them in one. He may conquer empires, he may turn all the world to looking at him. He may be like Hannibal, or like Alexander, or both in one, and become master of the universe. But what is his name? ***Mary Ann, is it?***

As Twain began to move toward the wings, the audience rewarded him with warm applause and newspaper reviews were kind, but he was deeply disappointed in his performance. Both husband and wife were still anxious. No sheriff had bothered them, but the lawsuit was not yet settled, and Livy was still officially scheduled to appear in a New York city courtroom in three days.

———

The North American portion of Twain's world tour would encompass twenty-two cities in thirty-eight days. Since the carbuncle had stolen his practice time, he would treat it as a dry run for the global jaunt. For his quarter of the profits, Major Pond would handle travel plans, bookings, press interviews, money collection, and receive the brunt of Twain's complaints.

All in all, Twain found Pond a "pleasant" companion, but the hyperbole-addicted agent had a few habits that irked Twain. "Pond never deals in small adjectives—'colossal' is a tame word for him." And Twain found the exaggerations a bit dull and predictable:

"Pond is not an interesting liar, it is the only fault he has. If his parents had taken the least little pains with his training, it could have been so different. He is destitute of the sense of proportion, & he has no imagination. These are fatal defects in a liar."

Tuesday morning the temperature hit 90 by 7:30 a.m. Twain was eager to leave Cleveland.

They took a carriage to the harbor; the Clemens party boarded the SS *Northland,* a luxurious steamship, to travel 450 miles over two days via two Great Lakes, Erie and Huron, to Twain's next stop, Sault Ste. Marie in northern Michigan.

On the monthlong trip, Major Pond carried a Kodak box camera and took dozens of informal shots of Twain and his family. Looking through the photos, one quickly discovers that women such as Livy and Clara, when traveling in that Victorian era, wore clothes that covered them from the leather shoe tips peeking out under their floor-length dresses up to the veils attached to their hats, an outfit that concealed them as effectively as a Muslim burka.

One of the first images Pond captured shows Livy—in heavy cape, hat and veil on the deck of the *Northland*—"urging" Twain, who is seated smoking a pipe, "to wear his overcoat," as Pond penciled in on the back. (Elsewhere in Pond's notes for the day, he recorded the temperature upon boarding at 98 degrees.)

After the stress of recent days, Twain tried to shed his worries and bask in the Great Lakes voyage. He would call the trip "sunny, balmy, perfectly delicious." He observed "spacious decks for promenading, just as luxurious & comfortable as a great ocean liner." And he was agog at the size of the ship, which he estimated at 350 feet. "I have seen no boat in Europe that wasn't a garbage scow by comparison." He learned that a machine churned out five tons of ice daily, while 2,700 electric lights aboard illuminated nightly diversions.

Fellow passengers gradually realized they were traveling with a celebrity. One elderly lady approached and thanked him for writing so favorably about cats. (He did adore the cats and often wore one draped around his neck; daughter Clara always tried to carry a kitten when she needed to interrupt him during writing hours.)

A couple from Washington offered to recite scenes from their favorite book, *Roughing It,* Twain's misadventure travelogue of old Nevada. A young man asked if Twain had ever seen a shaving stone and handed him a flat sandstone disc that he claimed could scrape off stubble. Twain smiled and slipped it into his pocket.

"That is just what I want," Pond overheard him telling the man. "The Madam will have no cause to complain of my never being ready in time for church because it takes so long to shave. I will just put this into my vest pocket on Sunday. Then when I get to church, I'll pull the thing out and enjoy a quiet shave in my pew during the long prayer."

The ship steamed past Detroit to the St. Clair River and on to Lake Huron. Twain especially enjoyed the narrow river passage at sunset, with banks full of summer cottages, many on stilts, with festive families and boating parties "all waving flags & handkerchiefs"; some revelers would fire off a cannon salute and the boat would reply "with a coarse toot of the hoarse whistle." The former Mississippi River pilot delighted in describing the "sinking sun, throwing a crinkled broad carpet of gold on the water—well, it is the perfection of voyaging."

The July 18 lecture at Sault Ste. Marie passed in a blur of minor improvements. The local newspaper claimed that one woman laughed so hard she had to be carried out of the Grand Opera House.

Boarding another ship the following day, Twain and his small entourage arrived around 4:30 p.m. on July 19 at one of the Midwest's premier resorts, the Grand Hotel of Mackinac Island. The wealthy of the heartland congregated at this large white, domed, neoclassical hotel perched on an island oasis cooled by refreshing lake breezes imported down from Canada. At meals, a twelve-piece orchestra played; fine chefs prepared French cuisine; guests wore formal evening clothes.

Pond was handling check-in when he discovered a telegram was waiting for Twain. H.H. Rogers informed Twain that the Russell lawsuit had been "silenced," but that Russell's lawyer Wilder had succeeded in extracting the full $5,048 amount, as well as an ample legal fee for himself. Twain quickly wrote Rogers that the settlement brought "solid relief" and "peace of mind," especially to Livy, and now enabled him to turn his "full attention" to his speeches.

But, perched in his hotel room, he couldn't leave the topic without some parting shots at his inept lawyers. "It is incredible, the worry and anger that that Russell business has cost me since the day my idiot lawyers allowed me to be dragged to New York by a court that had no more authority over me than the Mikado of Japan."

He was especially outraged that his lawyers had charged him $700 (approximately $21,000 in today's cash) for losing the case.

They never made a prophecy that came through—and they are fuller of prophecies than old Isaiah, they never made a move that wasn't silly; they were mere children in Wilder's hands; he played with them, told them lie after lie, and made them believe every *one* of them. That pitiful Rushmore had no more dignity than to repeatedly insult Wilder—acted like a child. And as for B.D.W.W.T.C.O.Y. Colby (Bainbridge Don't-Worry-We'll-Take-Care-Of-You Colby), he is a mere nine days' miscarriage, just a pulpy foetus. I reckon he wants that $700 to buy a sugar-teat with. [*"Sugar-teat" was a breast-shaped, sugar-filled linen sack that could be dampened and given to a baby as a pacifier.*]

Twain would later classify the twenty-four-year-old lawyer as in the running for "head idiot of this century." (Woodrow Wilson would appoint Bainbridge Colby to be secretary of state in 1920.)

CHAPTER 8

America

DRY RUN FOR THE WORLD

L ivy had some choice advice for her husband: Make it less funny. Give the audience a chance to catch its breath.

Never a champion of his vaudeville tendencies, she now wanted him to show off his narrative talents. Lesser men could tell that christening joke; she suggested that he insert at least one long, moving emotional story into his program, maybe Huck Finn and runaway slave Jim on the raft floating down the Mississippi. He could build to the key scene when the poor undereducated white boy, the hooligan son of the town drunk, agonizes over whether to do what everyone in Hannibal tells him is the right thing to do, that is, to hand over his best friend, Jim, to the slave catchers. Huck, in that moment, must decide whether to ignore his heart and obey the community "conscience" and the laws of the slave state of Missouri. It is immensely powerful in the midst of a novel, but would it work as a twenty-minute monologue?

Twain was skeptical, but he took her advice in Minneapolis, the sixth stop of the tour, and that Huck-and-Jim story would prove far and away the most popular of his round-the-world repertoire, singled out by critics and audiences from North America to New Zealand to India.

But before he could deliver in Minneapolis, he had to weather the fifth stop, Duluth, which had played out like a comedy of errors. The gargantuan steamship SS *Northwest* had hit a traffic jam of 600 boats waiting at the locks connecting the unequal water levels of Lake Huron and Lake Superior, and that delay had caused 1,250 paying customers to wait an hour in 100-degree heat in the unventilated First Methodist Church. Major Pond had shouted at the dock to the panicked church organizer:

"Don't worry, we'll have 'em convulsed in ten minutes." When Susy later heard about Pond's slick promise, she wondered how "poor little modest mama" was able "to put up with such splurge."

After some mix-ups in baggage transfers and unbooked sleeping cars, the Clemens entourage arrived, exhausted, in Minneapolis on the morning of Tuesday, July 23. Pond checked them into the city's finest, the eight-story West Hotel, so luxurious that it charged $5 a night per person, while other excellent places in town charged $2. (It's a tad ironic that Twain, trying to escape bankruptcy, almost always stayed in each city's best hotel; he seemed determined never to lower his heiress wife's standard of living.)

Minneapolis in 1895 was a fast-expanding commercial metropolis of 200,000 "including many Scandinavians," parked on the Mississippi River, harnessing "the power of 120,000 horses" at St. Anthony Falls to run flour and textile mills. Pillsbury produced more fine-grade flour than any other mill in the world, with quality equal to the "best Hungarian fancy brands," according to the Baedeker guide. Lumber mills north of the city band-sawed 400 million board feet of pine and hardwood logs a year. Prosperity attracted investment from East Coast enterprises, such as New York Life Insurance, whose building featured a famous French-inspired double-spiral staircase.

Major Pond had also booked Twain to have lunch with the mayor and other prominent citizens at the Commercial Club. A newspaper reporter claimed he overheard at least fifty people inform the author that *Innocents Abroad* was the first book they had ever read. In every city, celebrities attracted invitations. The author endured the glad-handing, but he admitted in his notebooks that he often found small talk very small, and preferred an audience of one thousand strangers to an audience of one stranger.

Twain was fagged out after the night train and chitchat, and his thigh was hurting. He begged off for an afternoon nap. Major Pond woke him to talk to six reporters. He refused to get out of bed, so the reporters interviewed him there, still under the covers.

He liked self-promotion but hated interviews; he even crafted a comedy segment—that he performed about a dozen times—on how to baffle interviewers with mounds of contradictory answers. He would cite three birthplaces; he would claim he was a twin and that he wasn't certain whether he or his brother had drowned. He'd say a birthmark might prove it, but he wasn't sure which twin had the birthmark. "There it is on my hand," he would say, confessing that he must have been the twin that drowned.

Being a former newspaperman, he expected to be misquoted. He also hated giving away material for free and loathed how reporters summarized and bollixed his stories. He would attend a banquet, make some remarks, and then read his quotes in the next day's paper. "You do not recognize the corpse, you wonder is this really that gay and handsome creature of the evening before."

But when those six reporters entered Room 204 of West Hotel, Twain charmed them. He explained about the carbuncle forcing him to stay in bed; he discussed some of his favorite living authors (William Dean Howells and Rudyard Kipling); he told a cute family story about how his then nine-year-old daughter Jean had once tried to jump into an adult conversation. "I know who wrote *Tom Sawyer*," Jean chimed in. All the dinner guests stared at the little girl. "Mrs. Harriet Beecher Stowe did!"

And the author waved the American flag, saying he was ending his four years of living in Europe. "I am going to settle down in my Hartford home and enjoy life in a quiet way."

As always, Twain addressed the reporters, as he spoke to friends, in a s-l-o-w manner with his mesmerizing voice with a hint of a twang, similar to his stage performance.

> His talk—I encountered him several times in London and New York—was delightfully whimsical and individual. The only drawback was that his natural drawl—freely punctuated, moreover, by his perpetual cigar being constantly put into and taken out of his mouth—made his utterance terribly slow. While waiting in a faithful and always justified hope that the point would come, you were reduced to admiring his magnificent head, leonine, with a snow-white mane.

So wrote Anthony Hope (1863–1933), English author of the huge 1894 bestseller *The Prisoner of Zenda*.

At the agreed cut-off time, Major Pond burst into the room. A scribe was just asking Twain if he had ever visited the city, and he replied that he had, eleven years earlier. Pond chirped: "Why, I was in Minneapolis when there were no saloons here."

Twain drawled: "Well, you didn't stay long." The newspapermen "laughed at the major's expense."

Twain rested and continued to memorize the new material.

Around 7:30 p.m., he and Pond took the short walk to the Metropolitan Opera House along sidewalks paved with thick cedar slabs. The ornate opera house was packed from the orchestra seats to the top gallery, with captains of industry and children, college students and mill workers. Twain attracted a diverse crowd. The *Minneapolis Times,* in its scene setter, estimated that no living American had made more people laugh than Mark Twain, especially in the wake of "the untimely death of Artemus Ward."

As he had put in his first flyer: "The trouble begins at eight." At the stroke of the hour, he strode out in the "swallow-tail [jacket] and immaculate shirt-bosom of fin-de-siecle society." One reviewer marveled at his transformation from the rough miner and suntanned riverboat pilot of the 1860s. The *Times* entitled its piece "Twice Told Tales" because for the most part Twain was telling his greatest hits.

Twain waited for the applause to die down, then said simply: "Ladies and gentlemen, with your permission, I will dispense with an introduction." More applause greeted him. (He was casting off that rambling "Morals" speech.)

He stood there, bushy brows, mustache and thick wavy hair—a caricaturist's delight—with the merest, faintest rumor of a hint of mischief in the eyes. He spoke slowly, not loudly, but his rich voice carried in an intimate way. He never smiled, seemed startled that anyone would laugh. Many claimed that hearing him topped reading him, a high bar indeed. (No recordings exist of Twain's performance or even of his voice; he feared he'd miss out on a payday if someone started making copies on Edison wax cylinders and selling them.)

He launched right into his first story. (The *Minneapolis Times* noted pauses and laughter.)

A man ought to know himself early—the earlier the better. He ought to find out . . . how far he can go and how much bravery there is in him and when to stop—not overstrain. I had the good fortune to learn the limit of my personal courage when I was only thirteen. My father at that time was a magistrate in Hannibal, Missouri.

Twain explained that his father was also the town coroner and that he kept a little bird-coop-sized office with a sofa.

Often when I was on my way to school I would notice that [the sky] was threatening; that it was not good weather for school (*laughter*) and very likely to get wet and I better go—fishing (*laughter*), so I went fishing. It was wrong—yes, it was wrong. That is why I did it. Forbidden fruit was just as satisfactory to me as it was to Adam. If he had been there he would have gone a-fishing.

I always had more confidence in my own judgment than I did in anybody else's. And now when I returned from those unorthodox excursions it was not safe for me to go home, for I would be confronted with all sorts of ignorant prejudice. (*laughter*)

And so I used to spend the night in that little office and let the atmosphere clear it (*laughter*).

Twain recounted that one day in Hannibal, while he was off fishing, a street fight had broken out. A man had been stabbed in the chest with a Bowie knife and killed, and his corpse—stripped to the waist—had been dragged to his father's office for an inquest the following morning.

Well, I arrived about midnight (*laughter*) and I didn't know anything about that (*laughter*), and I slipped in the back way and groped around until I found that [sofa], and laid down on it, and I was just dropping off into that sweetest of all slumbers, which is procured by honest endeavor. (*laughter*) When my eyes became a little more accustomed to the gloom it seemed to me that I could make out the vague, dim outline of a shapeless mass stretched there on the floor, and it made me uncomfortable. My first thought was to go and feel of it—and then I thought I wouldn't. (*laughter*) Well, my attention was carried away from my sleep. I was just beyond that thing.

Twain decided to wait till the moonlight through the window revealed the object.

But it got to be so dreary and so uncanny and sort of ghastly—waiting on that creeping moonlight, and that mystery grew and grew and grew in size and importance all the time and it got so that it didn't seem to me that I could endure it. And then I had an idea. I would turn over with my face to the wall and count a thousand (*laughter*) and give the moonlight a chance (*laughter*).

He made it as high as forty-five, drifted off a few times, whirled a few times, and then the next time, he saw a "pallid hand" in a square of moonlight.

I sat right up and began to stare at that dead hand and began to try—to say to myself "Be quiet, be calm, don't lose your nerve" (*laughter*). So I did the best I could and watched that moonlight creep, creep, creep up that white, dead arm, and it was the miserable, miserable . . . —I never was so embarrassed in my life (*laughter*). It crept, crept, crept until it exposed the whole arm and the white shoulder and a projecting lock of hair—it got so unendurable that I thought I must begin to do somethin' some time or other, some how or other.—I closed my eyes, put my hands on my eyes and held them as long as I could stand it, and then opened them. And then I got just one glimpse, just one glimpse and there was that drawn white face, white as wax in the moonlight, and staring glassy eyes, the mangled body. . . . Just that one swift glimpse and then, well, I went away from there (*laughter*).

   I did not go in what you might call a hurry—I just went (*laughter*) that is all. I went out the window (*laughter*). Took the [curtain] sash with me (*renewed laughter*). I didn't need the sash but it was handier to take it than it was to leave it (*laughter*) so I took it.

Ten minutes in and Twain was off to a very good start. He now made no pretense of using "Morals" to bind the stories together. He simply said, with absolutely no basis for saying it: "Now that brings me by a natural and easy transition to Simon Wheeler." He then told "Jumping Frog," which he had whittled down to thirteen minutes, and then "Grandfather's Old Ram," drawn from *Roughing It*. The brilliant punch line is that there is no punch line; the meandering storyteller veers off again and again. "My grandfather was stooping down in the level meadow, with his hands on his knees, hunting for a dime that he had lost in the grass and that ram was back yonder in the meadow when he sees him in that attitude he took him for a target . . . and came bearing down at twenty miles an hour." The story hinged on the teller always getting sidetracked and *never* revealing whatever happened to the old man and the ram. By the end, he had some audience members gasping for air.

Now Twain followed Livy's advice. Even though his comedy was flourishing, he sought the downbeat and told Tom and Huck. He needed an adept introduction to place listeners who hadn't read the book smack in the middle of the drama.

> And that brings me by the same process which I am following right along, regular sequence morally, and to an incident which made a great deal of stir at the time when I was a boy down there in [Hannibal], a sort of thing which you cannot very well understand now; that was the loyalty of everybody, rich and poor, down there in the South to the **institution of slavery,** and I remember Huck Finn, a boy who I knew very well, a common drunkard's son, absolutely without education but with plenty of liberty, more liberty than we had, didn't have to go to school or Sunday school, or change his clothes during the life of the clothes, and we preferred to associate with him because we envied him. Even Huck Finn recognized and subscribed to the common feeling of that community; that it was a shame, that it was a humiliation, that it was a dishonor, for any man when a negro was escaping from slavery—it was his duty to go and give up that negro. It shows what you can do with a conscience. You can train it in any direction you want to. I have written about that in a story where Huck Finn runs away from his brutal father and at the same time the slave Jim runs away from his mistress [*i.e., owner*], because he finds she is going to sell him down the river, and they meet by accident on a wooded island and they catch a piece of raft that is adrift and they travel on that at night, hiding in the daytime and they float down the Mississippi.

Now Twain needed to act out the scenes on the raft. He had marked up his own copy of Huck Finn, crossing out words, adding underlines for emphasis, and colloquial bridges. He even marked when to "blubber" or "bellow."

So, he described how Huck and Jim were approaching the "free" town of Cairo, Ohio, but Huck's conscience was troubling him.

That was where it *pinched*. Conscience says to me, "What had poor Miss Watson done to you that you could see her nigger go off right under your eyes and never say one single *word*? What did that poor old woman do to *you* that you could treat her so *mean*? Why, she tried to learn you your book, she tried to learn you your *manners*, she tried to learn you to be a *Christian*. She tried to be good to you every way she knowed how. *That's* what she done." I got to feeling so mean and treacherous, and miserable I most wished I was *dead*.

Then Twain described how Jim made Huck feel even worse because he told him that when he was free, that if he couldn't buy his children, he'd get an abolitionist to go steal them.

It most *froze* me to hear such talk. It was *awful* to hear it. He wouldn't ever *dared* to talk such talk in his *life* before. Here was this nigger, which *I had as good as helped to run away*, coming right out flat-*footed* and saying he would *steal* his children—The children didn't belong to him at all. (Laughter.) The children belonged to a man I didn't even *know*; a man that hadn't ever done me no *harm*.

Huck is torn and goes off in a canoe, maybe to tell on Jim, but as he's paddling away, he hears the runaway slave yell:

"*Dah* you goes, dar you goes, de *ole true Huck;* de on'y white genl-man dat ever kep' his promise to ole *Jim*." Oh, when he said that, it kind o' broke me all up.

Then Huck runs into a boat full of slave catchers. And one asks him:

"What's *that* yonder?"
"A piece of a *raft*," I says.
"Do you belong on it?"
"*Yes*, sir."
"Any *men* on it?"
"Only *one*, sir."
"Well, there's five *niggers* run off to-night up yonder, above the head of the *bend*. Is your man *white* or *black*?"

I tried to say he was black but the words wouldn't come. They hung fire and I seemed to hear that voice. I did not hear it at all, but it seemed just as natural as anything in the world, that voice a-saying "You true Huck. you only fren' left Jim now."

There was my conscience tugging after me all the time. It kept saying that anybody that does wrong, goes to the bad place [*i.e., Hell*]. It made me shiver and then I says "I don't care anything about it. I will go to the bad place. I will take my chances. I ain't going to give Jim up. And then I says, "The man on the raft is white."

And then he says, "It took you a good while to make up your mind what his color is. I reckon we'll go and see what his color is."

Twain has been acting out the voices: the boy, the slave, the men. The Minneapolis auditorium was dead silent, waiting. He slips back into Huck's voice.

Well, I was up a stump, I got to lie . . . Just in ordinary circumstances truth is all right but when you get in a close place you can't depend on it at all. So I had an idea and I says: "It's pap and he is sick, and so is Mary Jane and the baby and pap will be powerful thankful for you will help me tow the raft ashore. I have told everybody before and they have just gone away and left us," and he says, "That's mighty mean!" And the other says, "Mighty bad, too."

"What is the matter with your father?" "He is all right; it ain't catching."

"Set her back, John. Keep away, boy, keep to leeward. Confound I just expect the wind has blowed it to us. Your pap's got the smallpox and you know it precious well. Why didn't you come out and say so? Do you want to spread it all over? Good-bye, boy. You put twenty miles between us just as quick as you can. You will find a town down the river—tell them the family have got the chills and fever. Everybody got that down there. Don't you tell them, they have the small-pox. Good-bye, boy."

"Good-bye, sir," says I. "I won't let no runaway niggers get by me if I can help it."

The audience applauded, and over time as Twain realized the power of the story he expanded it and acted out Huck blubbering, begging the men to come help his sick family, all to make the lie more convincing.

And he would also work on sharing the moral while trying not to sound preachy. He would refine the introduction to include this pithy phrase: "In a crucial moral emergency a sound heart is a safer guide than an ill-trained conscience." Reread that line. Somehow, this concept seems to go to the essence of all Mark Twain's writings and beliefs. Forget the conventional wisdom, the current laws or religious teachings, try to follow the "sound heart" of a boy or youngster.

The message resonated. Audiences in Timaru, New Zealand, and Rawalpindi, India, applauded long and loud, and in the mill town of Minneapolis, Minnesota. "I am getting into good platform condition at last," he wrote to H.H. the next morning. "It went well, went to *suit* me here last night."

Twain told a few more stories, even gave a brief encore anecdote; then he bowed, soaked up the applause, and remained standing there center-stage for a long time as the house emptied. It was as though, at least in that triumphant moment, the financial woes and horrible stress of relearning his craft were finally melting away.

Major Pond wrote in his diary:

It was about as big a night as Mark ever had, to my knowledge. He had a new entertainment blending pathos with humor, with unusual continuity. This was at Mrs. Clemens' suggestion . . . the show is a triumph.

Twain now began filling his notebooks with speech ideas and travel observations. His leg healed. As he fine-tuned his delivery over the next few cities, he began to receive louder, longer ovations and even more effusive daily tributes in the newspapers. Editorials were sympathetic. He might have dreaded the platform, but he didn't dread the praise. As he once wrote to his youngest daughter: "I can stand considerable petting. Born so, Jean."

CHAPTER 9

Traveling with a Volcano

Major Pond would now lead this entourage through 2,500 miles of rail travel across the Dakotas, Northern Rockies, and Big Sky Country. Livy, who had lived in Europe for the past four years, would write to a wealthy friend, almost shocked: "It is impossible to believe what a great country it is until you travel across it—or at least it was for me."

Twain would perform in fifteen cities over three weeks; Clara and Livy would often go sightseeing while he would closet himself in the best hotel rooms to memorize his speeches. In transit, he would gush about the scenery he saw out the railcar window, such as the sprawling undulating wheat fields of the Red River Valley of North Dakota homesteaded by Scandinavians recruited by American railroad companies. "There is the peace of the ocean about it, & a deep contentment, a heaven-wide sense of ampleness, spaciousness, where pettinesses & all small thoughts & tempers must be out of place."

Travel brings out the best in *some* people.

Twain wrote those words just as he arrived in Crookston, Minnesota, a small town with unpaved streets, watered twice a day to keep the dust down. He performed, then the entourage had to catch the 4 a.m. train to reach Great Falls, Montana, in time for the next show even though Twain had asked Pond to avoid these middle-of-night transfers to protect Livy's health.

At 3:45 a.m., they alighted from two carriages and climbed the wooden steps in the dark, lit only by lantern to the train station. The hack drivers carried trunk after trunk and stacked them on the deserted lumber-plank platform. In the dim light, Major Pond noticed a handwritten sign: "Pacific Mail one hour and twenty minutes late."

Mount Saint Clemens erupted. He didn't use garden-variety curse words because Livy was present, but he unleashed his usual creative lava flow. The night was chilly, and since the waiting room was "dreary" and unheated, the group paced the platform to keep warm.

Twain kept the monologue going, berating Pond for not sending someone to check the train's arrival before waking them all up. "I have contracted with Mr. Pond to travel and to give entertainments and not to stand shivering around depots at this inhuman hour waiting for delayed trains that never were known to arrive."

He kept hammering Pond until finally Livy asked him if he was not being "a little unreasonable." Twain adamantly denied the charge of unreasonableness and sat down on a baggage cart and demanded that Pond honor his contract and get him "traveling."

Major Pond, the nation's leading talent agent for speakers, obliged and "wheeled" Twain around the station and platform at the break of dawn. Clara borrowed Pond's camera.

With the newly risen sun behind her, long-shadowed Clara captured the scene: the hulking Pond, straw boater on head, hands gripping the wheelbarrow-like cart, Livy in the background shading her eyes from the glinting sun (or perhaps from looking directly at her husband) and Twain, behaving like pouting royalty, perched on the cart, his bushy gray hair mushroom-clouding out from under his ubiquitous captain's cap. And off to the side, almost as interesting as the human drama, stands the group's bulky Victorian-era baggage, with at least seven massive steamer trunks visible, just a part of Pond's count of sixteen pieces of luggage.

The train lumbered into the Crookston station. The upcoming trip to Great Falls, Montana, (about 800 miles) would mark their longest single rail ride, taking more than twenty-four hours, a sunrise-to-sunrise trip at speeds exceeding thirty miles per hour across the level prairies. Ulysses S. Grant had driven the final spike ushering in transcontinental rail travel only a quarter century earlier, and this particular train line—Great Northern—had been completed just two years prior. Long-distance train travel was still relatively new—a miracle of speed and convenience. Baedeker's 1899 guidebook pointed out the contrasts between American and European rail travel. Europe had small train compartments for eight persons, accessed from the platform; the United States had long sixty-seat open carriage cars, with doors at each end. "A single crying infant or spoiled child annoys 60-70 persons," noted the influential guide, adding that any chance for sleep was spoiled by the constant sales pitch of newsboys roving the aisles, hawking "books, papers, fruit, lollipops and cigars." It did concede, however, that the opportunity to stroll the train, eat in a dining car and "the amusement of watching one's fellow-passengers" helped pass a long journey.

Pond secured five berths, which meant the entourage had some privacy. Twain watched the wheat give way to waving plains of tall buffalo grass; then in the morning, they started climbing into the mountains past the Upper Missouri River. He experienced a bit of déjà vu upon seeing "the crystal-clear atmosphere & deceptive distances." He opened the window and rediscovered "splendidly bracing & life-giving air."

Twain did not intend to include the United States in his upcoming world travel book. So the highlights of this trip begin to blur into a series of vivid vignettes, captured in the notebooks of either Twain or Pond.

Once they reached Great Falls, the hotel host and town founder, Paris Gibson, organized a little carriage trip for the entourage to visit Rainbow Falls (49 feet) and Giant Springs, a geyser of peacock-blue water that had amazed Lewis and Clark, and amazed Twain. He marveled that the blue aqua kept its color a half mile down into the muddy Missouri.

A young cowboy apparently noticed Clara (or maybe the celebrity Twain) and decided to do some "showing off." The man in the leather chaps tried to jump a barbed-wire fence. The horse's legs got tangled in the wire and badly cut, and the cowboy was flung forward. "The horse fell on him but unfortunately didn't kill him," noted Twain drily in his journal, extending all sympathy to the animal.

That same day, Twain felt strong enough to take a long walk with Major Pond out to the Norwegian shantytown on the outskirts of the town. Twain coaxed a pretty little girl into letting him "buy" two of her kittens; the whole exchange was, no doubt, a dodge to hand some money (but not charity) to an impoverished immigrant family—four generations of women—living in tarpaper shacks.

He performed in Great Falls; the theater collected $220. Pond had negotiated for them to keep 70%, or $154; Twain paid Pond 25% and kept a total of $115.50. He had to fork over a staggering $5 a person to the Gibson brothers' Park Hotel. So, the debtor-author had made at best $100 visiting Great Falls; it would be a long trek to clear close to $60,000.

In that summer of 1895, forty-four states belonged to the Union, and the Twain entourage was passing through four of the most recent additions: North Dakota, Montana, Idaho and Washington.

Montana meant cattle grazing and mining. (Baedeker reported that free-range grazing was giving way to having a single cowboy tend to a herd of 1,500 to 2,000 and haul in the strays.) The mining was world famous, including arguably some of the richest strikes ever found: gold at Drumlummon and silver at Granite Mountain, but especially copper in Butte to feed the new, seemingly endless demand for the electrical and telephone wires cobwebbing American cities and buildings.

The Twain party boarded the train for the 150-mile ascent to Butte (5,485-foot elevation), which at that time produced 250 million pounds of copper a year. Wheezing miners whistled hello as they descended, amid the noxious fumes of refineries. "[Butte] is a fearful place in which to live. . . . It is a flowerless, grassless, godless town." Refining the ore produces vapors that destroy vegetation, pollutes streams; it also creates the "stink pits" and slag heaps polka-dotting the town. The mining moguls had mansions but no lawns. The subterranean job, however, paid well: $100 a month, and the challenge was to leave before the place killed you. A deadly explosion in January had killed seventy-five, injured more than a hundred.

Butte, with its wealth, mixed high and low culture: 300 saloons and dozens of brothels shared the neighborhood with French dancing academies and opera houses and now, one night of Mark Twain. The author, who had read elitist Eastern newspaper accounts of drunken rowdies, was impressed by the caliber of the crowd, which he said was "compact, intellectual & dressed in perfect taste . . . [a] London-Parisian-N.Y. audience out in the mines."

Mark Twain had been fascinated by get-rich mining ever since he had tried prospecting and claim buying in Nevada back in the 1860s. Twain here recorded in his notebook: "The Hearst estate & Morris (?) Daly have the bulk of the stock of the Anaconda copper mines & smelting works, the greatest in the world." (Anaconda was both a mine in Butte and also a city, a short downhill train ride from Butte, which hosted the world's largest copper smelter.)

Throughout Twain's round-the-world trip, he would occasionally send letters—half business, half pleasure—or telegrams to H.H. Rogers back in New York.

By sheer coincidence, Twain now happened to be at the future site of one of H.H. Rogers's most notorious and most lucrative business deals. Less than four years later, H.H. and his partners would reap a $36 million profit (about $1 billion in early twenty-first-century dollars) without risking a single penny. At its simplest, Rogers and colleagues would agree to buy the vast copper mines of Marcus Daly and a few others for $39 million, giving them a check on National City Bank that could be cashed after a specified date. H.H. had two close friends at the bank, board member William Rockefeller of Standard Oil and bank president James Stillman, two men whose children happened to have married, further cementing ties. The collateral for what was, in effect, a $39 million bank loan to buy the copper mines was the signed contract to buy the self-same copper mines.

H.H. then created a $75 million stock company, Amalgamated Copper of New Jersey, harnessing his own Standard Oil business prestige to sell shares to a public agog about the potential of copper. The partners used the proceeds to pay off the $39 million loan to the bank, and H.H. and his pals divvied $36 million in profit.

By H.H.'s deal-making standards, Twain was out hustling for table scraps.

Twain played Anaconda (even more polluted than Butte). He then headlined in the state capital, Helena, which was once named "Crab Town" but after the gold strike voted to pay tribute to Helen of Troy, hoping, no doubt, to attract some dance hall girls who bore a faint resemblance. The city itself was quite beautiful, haloed by majestic mountains receding from view at greater heights, with the eastern edge of the Rockies lost in the clouds. A vast gold mine, Last Chance Gulch, split the city, which, with fifty millionaires, easily had more plutocrats per capita than New York City. Twain performed Saturday night, cleared about $140.

The lecture business in the 1890s respected the Lord's Day and took Sundays off. Of course, the Clemenses were staying at the best hotel in Helena. One Dr. Cole took Mr. and Mrs. Clemens for a three-mile carriage ride at dusk out to Broadwater, the famed mineral springs swimming pool, fed by 160-degree hot springs in the shallows but cooled by gushes of cold water in the deep end. "Parties of 50 hire the tank for a whole afternoon & have fun," wrote Twain.

Pond had charted this northern U.S. course—in that unair-conditioned era—to avoid deserted cities, to stay by water, and to climb up into the mountains. "The heat gave way to a delicious balmy breeze that invigorated everybody," wrote Pond of that Sunday, August 4, in Helena. "How delightful these summer evenings in the Rocky Mountains."

Montana's first U.S. senator, W. F. Sanders, for a bit of nostalgia, decided to accompany Pond and Twain on the 115-mile, five-hour trip through the Rockies to Missoula. A decade earlier, before the completion of the Northern Pacific, Sanders had joined Pond and his client Reverend Henry Ward Beecher on that same 115-mile trip between the then unconnected eastern and western rail ends; it had taken them four days to go by stagecoach.

The travelers entered the Rockies at the Continental Divide. The tracks headed toward the Columbia River under "savage and somber" crags with the snowcapped pyramid of Mount Powell in the distance; they passed Hell Gate Canyon and reached the Big Blackfoot River. Missoula was a budding railroad junction in a rich fertile valley, the former hunting grounds of the Blackfeet and the Flatheads. A carriage from Hotel Florence picked them up. Twain and Pond sat up top with the driver to catch the breezes.

Twain lectured that night ($75 net) and the next day decided to squeeze in a visit to Fort Missoula. For Twain, traveling with his wife and his lecture agent certainly made it harder to have any misadventures—his usual fodder for his stories—but in Missoula, Montana, he succeeded in having one, despite everyone's precautions.

Colonel Andrew Burt invited the Clemens party to an early lunch at Fort Missoula. Two U.S. Army wagon ambulances, each drawn by four mules, arrived at the hotel to carry them four miles to the fort. The women accepted the ride, but Twain decided he would walk. This fort was quite unusual in that all seven "companies" of the U.S. Army Twenty-Fifth Infantry stationed there were "colored," commanded by a handful of white officers. (The troops, though stationed there to save the settlers from Indians, wound up mostly protecting the railroad and mining companies from striking workers.) In 1895, four of the U.S. Army's twenty-five regiments were "colored," dubbed "buffalo soldiers" by the Indians, and received equal pay but served in segregated units and couldn't attain the highest ranks.

Twain set out on the four-mile hike to get some exercise now that his boil was healed. Major Pond stayed back an hour so as to coordinate baggage and railroad connections; then he hopped aboard the other mule-drawn ambulance, sat up front with the driver and reminisced about his Civil War days, as they made a leisurely trek along the dusty road. When they were about halfway there, far off to the left they noticed a man stumbling and rushing across an open field. Pond recognized the blue captain's cap, also the bushy mane visible "through the clear mountain" air.

Twain had taken the wrong fork, had walked six miles the wrong way, and was doubling back. "He was exhausted"—and Pond found him in a once-in-a-lifetime state of being too disgusted to complain. "[Twain] sat quietly inside the ambulance until we drove up to headquarters." The author, in his travel books—*Innocents Abroad, Roughing It, A Tramp Abroad*—mined the "lost traveler" motif for humor. While he exaggerated some personal traits for gags, he genuinely possessed this flaw, an open secret among his friends. Just a month earlier, he had sent an invitation from Elmira to H.H. Rogers: "Now you are to come up here. . . . I could explain to you which railroad to take and just how to come, but you would not have any confidence in it." And when he was planning to go from Elmira to Rogers's home in Fairhaven, Massachusetts, his branch-line switching plans hit so many snags that he wrote Rogers he wished he could just hang a baggage tag around his neck and be shipped there.

The moment Twain wearily alighted from the back of the ambulance into a cluster of white officers and their wives, a "colored" sergeant approached him and asked if he was "Mark Twain." The author nodded. "I have orders to arrest you and take you to the guardhouse." With his morning turning out so sourly already, Twain didn't even muster a retort and silently began trudging the hundred yards to the distant army jail.

When Pond saw the joke falling flat, he explained Twain's mood to Colonel Burt, and they climbed into a wagon and rushed to free the prisoner. Twain declined the offer of a ride back and muttered something about preferring "freedom." But he must have felt bad for the sergeant because he praised the man for showing "discipline" in following orders. Colonel Burt apologized for the practical joke.

The seven companies aligned in drill formation; the thirty-piece marching band—"one of the finest" in the country—performed an elaborate program on the dusty parade grounds. Pond and Twain—who also inspected the barracks, with soldiers at attention at the foot of each bed—were deeply impressed.

Splendid big negro soldiers; obedient, don't desert, don't get
drunk; proud of their vocation, finest & pleasant soldiers—& Pond
says great in battle. Some of these have been in the service 10 &
15 years & my escort 24 years. They all have the look & bearing of
gentlemen. The earliest ones were not educated & could not perform clerical duties; but the later ones can; been in public schools.
As a rule the army can't sing the Star Spangled Banner, but Burt
ordered these to be taught & *they* can sing it. The band all colored
but leader. Made beautiful music.

During the flag ceremony, a "Negro officer" reminded the author to
remove his hat, and during another ceremony to toss his cigar. Twain
noted that the Senate had appointed a black man to the rank of chaplain,
a commissioned officer to be saluted by all. "They take pride in it. *I* think
the negro has found his vocation at last," he wrote in his notebook.

Back on the train, Twain headed 200 miles that afternoon and evening
from Missoula, briefly through Idaho to Spokane, Washington, the family enjoying another magnificent taste of Big Sky country.

Lovely & oft majestic scenery. Along the skirt of the Flathead Res-
ervation noticed again the velvety softness of the barren mountains
& their rounded smoothness—as free of break as an apple—also
the exceeding delicacy of the shades of faint color . . .

Clark's Fork of the Columbia—green water & lovely. Never saw
a green stream in America before. Followed this perfectly lovely
stream all afternoon.

Vast towering castellated cliffs, with fronts with infinite shelves,
& a streak of yellowglass on each shelf, luminous with the slant
rays of the sun—the tint, old gold, old gold burnished, old gold
glowing. Perfectly beautiful. And new to me.

He had been invited to join a "special" private car of business executives handling the bankruptcy of the Northern Pacific Railroad, but the
invitation did not extend to his family so he instead chose to ride up front
with the engineer. He stuck that bushy mane out the window as they
roared through canyons and crossed steel bridges.

The entourage arrived that night in Spokane, the biggest city in eastern Washington, a beautifully situated railroad hub looking out on the

rushing snow-melt Spokane River. Islands of primordial stone divided the river into three streams, which reunited in the majestic Spokane Falls. It was postcard-pretty, primed for commercial growth, but the city of 20,000—after ambitiously rebuilding from a major fire in 1889—had crashed during the Panic of 1893.

In the morning Twain and Pond wandered near the massive Spokane House; they noted the fine asphalt streets and extensive electric lighting, but they also saw "buildings ten stories high, with the nine top stories empty, and . . . many fine stores with great plate-glass fronts, marked 'To Rent.'"

In the afternoon, the whole party went for an open carriage ride; the driver took them to see many fine mansions—pointing out this one was now occupied by the "receiver" for the failed Spokane Bank; that one, by the receiver for the failed Great Falls Company, several of whose directors were now in state prison. Twain judged "receiver" a very good career path for the youth of the region.

During flush times, Spokane had spent a fortune to build a 2,000-seat Opera House, which the manager told Pond he had never more than one-quarter filled. Twain wouldn't top the record. (He banked about $140, with 400 or so people there.)

Traveling with his wife and daughter brought some surprises for Twain. Clara was beginning to attract attention other than from lonesome klutzy cowboys. Pond wrote:

> As we passed out of the dining room into the great parlor, she sat down to the Chickering grand piano and began playing a Chopin nocturne. It was in the gloaming.
>
> Stealthily guests came in from dinner and sat breathlessly in remote parts of the boundless room listening to a performance that would have done credit to any great pianist. Never have I witnessed a more beautiful sight than this sweet brunette unconsciously holding a large audience of charmed listeners. If it was not one of the supreme moments of her mother's life, who saw and heard her, then I have guessed wrong.

Clara was vivacious, mischievous, at times flirtatious; she was far more comfortable in her own skin than her sisters. Susy mooned about, plagued by self-doubt, and Jean raged; Clara played the piano and sang and collected admirers.

The troop left Spokane to zigzag over the Cascade Mountains to Seattle. Pond noted that sometimes they had to travel thirty serpentine miles to go seven as the crow flies. Twain again rode with the engineer. His later notes describe how the train used engines at both ends to apply brakes on steep downhills, and the engineer sometimes had to throw the gears into reverse to slow the train.

Ninety miles outside Seattle, they stopped for some good old-fashioned fun at Wellington. They rolled rocks down the side of a cliff and ate fresh-caught trout.

They now found themselves traveling through one of the world's greatest unexploited timber forests, with the hills of the Blue Mountains thickly bristling with towering pine. As they crossed the mountains they smelled smoke. They saw smoke. A prolonged drought had sparked forest fires. The dense smoke would plague their entire week in Washington and Oregon. Twain never once saw Mount Hood or Mount Rainier. Major Pond wrote of the "rumor" of beautiful scenery. Local dignitaries apologized for the clouded/opaque conditions, and Twain placated them with small jokes about being a "perpetual smoker" himself. Hard to know if the forest fires were to blame, but Twain soon developed a bad sore throat and hoarseness that would jeopardize his speaking tour.

At Seattle, they caught the *Flyer,* the so-called Greyhound of the Puget Sound, which billed itself as the world's fastest steamer, to head thirty miles south to Tacoma. Twain watched the porters take their luggage from the train's baggage car, fling it onto hand trucks and then hammer-throw it again onto the deck of the ship. Twain fantasized aloud to Pond about at least one steamer trunk being "filled with dynamite and that all the baggage-destroyers on earth were gathered about it, and I just far enough off to see them hurled into Kingdom Come!"

Their entourage expanded as they stepped off the *Flyer* in smoky Tacoma. Twain's thirty-four-year-old namesake nephew, Samuel Moffett, the only son of Twain's sister Pamela, caught up with his "Uncle Sam." Moffett, who bore a family resemblance with thick curly hair, was a seasoned newspaperman for William Randolph Hearst's *San Francisco Examiner* and would soon be shifted to the flagship *New York Journal.*

The Clemens clan was "delighted" to see their nephew/cousin, and young Sam dutifully rushed daily updates to his pregnant wife, Mary, at home with their toddler in Berkeley, providing a fresh perspective on the trip. He reported that his uncle had greeted him with a tirade on travel fatigues and one-night stands, that his forty-nine-year-old Aunt Livy didn't have a gray hair and seemed to be bearing up well after they had lost almost all their property. "Uncle Sam is still not satisfied with his lectures and is continually working them over." The nephew was pleased to be able to confirm for his wife America's worst-kept literary secret, that Mark Twain was indeed the author of *Joan of Arc*, serialized in *Harper's* magazine. Moffett stated to his wife that Aunt Livy and Clara "agree with us that it is the best thing he has ever done." (Sam Moffett was a *serious* writer; his first book had tackled the import tariff and his second, just out, was entitled *Suggestions on Government*.)

Over the next week, he would accompany the family and squire his aunt and cousin on streetcars, on harbor boats, on outings to a park, to a play by a lake, filling the gap left by Twain and Pond, both off working the platform in other cities. He would rave to his wife about cousin Clara's piano playing, relaying that she had studied with a pupil of Paderewski's teacher and that Major Pond wanted to represent her for as much as $500 a night, but his uncle and aunt had swiftly nixed the idea.

"Uncle Sam" left Tacoma on Friday, August 9, with Pond for a performance in Portland. On the train, the twosome encountered two men in the smoking car. They chatted; one had gone to Yale, the other's father had been an editor of the *Missouri Republican*. Twain offered each a cigar from his cigar case, which he mentioned—in his deadpan drawl—was made from "the skin of a young lady." The two young men rose to the bait and asked him to explain.

Twain launched into a story about wandering in Europe and meeting a charming French astronomer who was the wittiest speaker and debater of his generation. The scientist was so popular that one of his admirers had once asked him what she might do to show her appreciation for his brilliant books and lectures.

She was a beautiful woman, with the fairest complexion and the most beautiful shoulders and neck [he] ever saw. [He] said to her: "I think if I had your beautiful neck and shoulders and complexion I would be perfectly satisfied. I would aspire to nothing higher. . . ."

She replied: "Well, when I am through with them I will send them to you."

She died a few years later, and to [his] surprise [he] found that she had left directions that the skin of her neck and shoulders be sent to [him].

Twain said the astronomer then pointed to "a beautifully bound volume on his center table" and said to him, "This book is bound with that lady's skin."

Twain paused, held up his case. "The lady of whose skin *my* cigar case was made probably had the smallpox very bad."

Twain's case was alligator.

Pond didn't record whether Twain earned belly laughs or not. Then again, the gentlemen had a 150-mile trip, and it wasn't too shabby to share it with Mark Twain.

They reached the thriving city of Portland, with its wide, navigable Willamette River, full of passenger steamers and all sorts of cargo vessels. They had to rush to the Marquam Grand Theater. Portland would mark the biggest payday of his North American tour; the next stop, Olympia, would mark the smallest.

Twain was delighted to see the crowds.

Splendid house, full to the roof. Great compliment to have a lofty gallery packed with people at 25 c[ents], as intelligent & responsive as the others. Floor & dress circle full too, many standing & the sign up early "Standing Room Only."

Pond and Twain cleared $480, which left Twain's share at $360, a spectacular one-night payday in that era for a solo speaker.

In Olympia, only two other guests were staying at their hotel, not a good omen. The state capital empties out in the summer. The hotel had one employee acting as clerk, bartender, waiter, bellboy. Twain cleared $52.

They returned to Tacoma, and nephew Sam found his uncle "overflowing with cheerfulness" thanks to the reception in Portland.

They all headed to Seattle, where the captain of the USS *Mohican* warship invited them to a formal shipboard luncheon in the harbor; the officers, in swallow-tail coats with brass buttons and gold braids, were quite attentive, especially to Clara. It was something of a magical day. That evening Twain discovered another standing-room-only crowd, and even though his voice was giving way, somehow his hoarseness lent an intimacy to the performance. The show was a big success; waves of applause engulfed him. After an encore of the whistler-stammerer, Twain was honored at the Rainier Club.

He woke up the next morning to a sore throat and some very bad news. He learned that a major newspaper (not identified) had run an article accusing him of doing the round-the-world performance tour to line his own pocket, and it claimed that he had no intention of giving any of the money to his creditors.

He was in a foul mood, all around. "Such a fearful hoarseness I could scarcely talk," he wrote in his notebook. Livy worried it would turn into "bronchitis" or "lung fever." The schedule called for him to head that morning to a place called New Whatcom, Washington; he would be staying in the Fairhaven Hotel.

"He worried and fretted all day," wrote Pond. On the train traveling the ninety miles from Seattle to New Whatcom, Twain, by himself in the smoking car, scrawled out in pencil a long note in self-defense to his nephew Sam for publication in the *San Francisco Examiner*. He left clear instructions that if the item were telegraphed to other papers, it must be marked: "On condition that it shall not be abridged." Here he was, circling the globe to pay off debt, and instead of a halo, he was getting splashed in tar.

Never mind interviewing me. I've nothing to do; lend me your pencil and let me say it myself.

What am I lecturing around the world for? Your question is easily answered: It is for the benefit of the creditors of the wrecked firm of Charles L. Webster & Co. I furnished the capital for that concern. It made a fortune the first year, and wasted it in the second. After that it began to accumulate debts and kept this industry diligently up until the collapse came.

My wife and I tried our best to save it; we emptied money down that bottomless hole as long as we had a penny left, but the effort went for nothing. When the crash came, the firm owed my wife almost as much as it owed all the other creditors put together.

By the advice of friends, I turned over to her my copyrights, she releasing the firm and taking this perishable property in full settlement for her claim—property not worth more than half the sum owing to her. She wanted to turn her house in, too, and leave herself and the children shelterless: but she hadn't a friend who would listen to that for a moment. And I can say, with what is perhaps a pardonable pride and satisfaction, that there is not a single creditor who would be willing to let her do it. No, I am mistaken. I am forgetting one creditor, a printer. The ruined firm owed him about $5,000. He had made a neat little fortune out of Webster & Co., but that didn't signify; he wanted his money: he could not wait on my slow earnings, so he persecuted me with the law.

No; I must not say anything more about that creditor just now. I will wait till I get time and room. As I understand it. Your journal's usual issue contains only sixteen pages.

I earned a good deal of money last year. I have left it all in New York. This money, added to the assets of our defunct firm, will pay off one-half of the firm's debts. A month ago I supposed it would take me a dreary, long time to earn the other half, but my eyes have been opened by this lecture trip across the continent. I find I have twenty-five friends in America where I thought I had only one. Look at that house in Cleveland, in the dead middle of July, with the mercury trying to crawl out of the top of the thermometer. That multitude has repeated itself in every big town clear across to the Pacific. . . .

I shall be sixty years old in November. A month ago it grieved me to be under this load of debt at my time of life, but that feeling is all gone now. Such a burden is a benefaction, a prize in the lottery of life, when it lifts a curtain and shows you a continental spread of personal friends where you had supposed you had merely a good sprinkling of folks friendly to your books, but not particularly concerned about their author.

Consider we fill the galleries of the opera-house to hear a lecture! I think that that is a compliment, worth being in debt for. The other day in Montana a stranger sent me this word: "You can draw on me for $5 a day until you are out of debt."

When our firm broke, Poultney Bigelow mailed me his check for $1,000 and didn't want to take it back again. Douglas Taylor, printer, New York, said: "Draw on me for $1,000, and if you think you can't find a hundred men to do the like, make me a bet and you will see." One dollar bills came in letters from here and there and yonder, from strangers, and I had to send them back. . . .

And so, let me sound my horn; it doesn't do you any harm, and I like the music of it.

Properly, one-third of our dead firm's debts should be paid by my partner; but he has no resources. This is why I must pay them all. If I have time and health, I can do it, and I think the creditors have confidence in me. And my wife and children are not troubled. They never knew anything about scrimping before, but they have learned it now; they know all about it these last two years, and whatever murmuring is done I do,—not they.

My books? Several of them are in the hands of my pioneer publishers, the American Publishing Company of Hartford; all the others are in the hands of the Harpers. The Harpers will begin to issue them from new plates presently. The books will help pay the Webster debts. I turned them over to my wife to keep them from getting scattered, which would of course destroy their earning capacity: but she will touch none of the profit that can be spared to the creditor.

My trip means a year's lecturing all around the world, and thereafter a lecture trip all over the United States. . . .

Now that I reflect, perhaps it is a little immodest for me to talk about my paying my debts, when by my own confession I am blandly getting ready to unload them onto the whole English-speaking world. I didn't think of that. Well, no matter, so long as they get paid.

Lecturing is gymnastics, chest-expander, medicine, mind-healer, blues-destroyer, all in one. I am twice as well as I was when I started out: I have gained nine pounds in twenty-eight days, and expect to weigh 600 before January. I haven't had a blue day in all the twenty-eight. My wife and daughter are accumulating health and strength and flesh nearly as fast as I am. When we reach home a year hence I think we can exhibit as freaks.

It was an upbeat pose—praising all the creditors but one, stating his deadbeat partner owed a third, calling the debts a blessing because of the audience's love. And he certainly *tried* to lighten the tone with that joke at the end.

Despite the unburdening prose and defiant stance, he stewed all day at the Fairhaven Hotel. "He had only two swearing fits with but a short interval between them," wrote Pond. "They lasted from our arrival in town until he went to sleep after midnight."

He showed up on time for the lecture on the fourth floor of the Lighthouse Theater in New Whatcom, but the audience didn't—neither did his voice. He later wrote to H.H. that he barely succeeded in "pumping out my voice *at all*." He waited, started speaking around 9, but by 9:30 p.m. more stragglers were still trickling in. He stormed off the stage. "Look at that damned audience," he shouted at Pond. "You'll never play a trick like this on me again." Pond explained that the trolley from the neighboring city ran only on the half hour. Twain eventually "cooled" down and returned to the stage. He even wowed the crowd, which demanded an encore.

Exhausted, hoarse, played out after the show, Twain nonetheless accepted an offer to be driven through the dark streets to the Cascade Club. The host and a handful of members climbed the three flights ahead of Twain, lit the place with candles, and then offered him a cocktail. (He had no idea that the club was pretty much out of funds and without staff.) He asked for his standard drink: a *hot* Scotch. The club had no kitchen; a member had to roust a Greek who owned a nearby restaurant and convince him to light his stove to boil some water. Twain dismissed members' concerns that the drink wasn't hot enough by ordering another. He stayed till past midnight.

Major Pond copied Twain's penciled press statement in ink, and they mailed it off at 12:30 p.m. Thursday, August 15, to nephew Sam at the *San Francisco Examiner* to be held for his arrival.

Twain personally carried a copy that same day to Livy, who, along with Mrs. Pond and Clara, had taken the ferry north to Vancouver, British Columbia, Canada.

Twain—still hoarse—went into his usual isolation to prepare for his performance that Thursday night in Vancouver. He had considered canceling the show but he hoped a *British* audience would be sedate and quiet enough to hear him at a whisper. Further souring his mood, he learned that their ship to Australia had suffered some kind of accident near Vancouver and would be delayed a week.

While Twain groused and prepared, Livy read her husband's press statement and was appalled by numerous passages in it, especially the several references to herself. She disliked the "shelterless" comment as well as the concept that the family was "scrimping" when she knew they were staying at the best hotels in America.

Sometime on Friday, nephew Sam—either in Seattle or San Francisco—did a major edit and rewrite of "Uncle Sam's" piece. (It is likely Livy contacted or encouraged him because it appears unthinkable that he would mangle the words without the blessings of his aunt Livy.)

At this point in Twain's career, anyone other than Livy attempting to change *anything,* even a comma, took grave bodily risk. A recent maxim: "In the first place God made idiots. This was for practice. Then he made proof-readers." (When Twain later in life received notes from a degree-dripping British editor, he wrote back: "See 119. I cannot permit 'an' hospital. Unless that #$@%& n is removed, you must allow me to append a disclaimer in the form of a footnote. Please see that it is removed. One might as well say an horse or an whore.") He was fanatical about changing punctuation as well, and more than fanatical about the replacement of any words.

The following piece would go out *under Mark Twain's name,* and the famous writer would be so furious that he would demand his version be published as well.

This edited statement often seems more like Livy's statement, and the wording often seems the work of a budding Hearst editorial writer, Sam Moffett. It is worth picturing Twain, hoarse, feverish, exhausted, cooped up in bed, worried about the damaged ship, being handed a copy of the Saturday, August 17, 1895, edition of the *San Francisco Examiner* and reading the following:

Sam L. Clemens (Mark Twain), who is about leaving [*sic*] for Australia, in an interview concerning the purpose of his long trip said:

I am idle until lecture-time. Write, and I will dictate and sign. My run across the continent, covering the first 4,000 miles of this lecturing tour around the world, has revealed to me so many friends of whose existence I was unconscious before, and so much kindly and generous sympathy with me in my financial mishaps, that I feel that it will not be obtrusive self-assertion, but an act of simple justice to that loyal friendship, as well as to my own reputation, to make a public statement of the purpose which I have held from the beginning, and which is now in the process of execution. [*Could anything sound less like Twain than "obtrusive self-assertion"?*]

It has been reported that I sacrificed for the benefit of creditors the property of the publishing firm whose financial backer I was, and that I am now lecturing for my own benefit. This is an error. I intend the lectures as well as the property for the creditors.

The law recognizes no mortgage on a man's brain, and the merchant who has given up all he has may take advantage of the rules of insolvency and start again for himself. But I am not a business man, and honor is a harder master than the law. It cannot compromise for less than one hundred cents on the dollar, and its debts never outlaw. [*Can the word "outlaw" even be used that way?*]

I had a two-thirds interest in the publishing firm, whose capital I furnished, and if the firm had prospered I should have expected to collect two-thirds of the profits. As it is, I expect to pay all the debts. My partner has no resources, and I don't look for assistance from him. By far the largest single creditor of this firm is my wife, whose contributions in cash from her private means have nearly equaled the claims of all others combined. In satisfaction of this great claim she has taken nothing, except to avail herself of the opportunity of retaining control of the copyrights of my books, which, for many easily understood reasons of which financial ones are the least, we do not desire to see in the hands of strangers.

On the contrary, she has helped and intends to help me to satisfy the obligations due to the rest.

The present situation is that the wreckage of the firm, together with what money I can scrape together, with my wife's aid, will enable me to pay the other creditors about 50 per cent of their claims. It is my intention to ask them to accept that as a legal discharge and trust to my honor to pay the other 50 per cent as fast as I can earn it. From my reception thus far on my lecturing tour I am confident that if I live I can pay off the last debt within four years, after which, at the age of sixty-four, I can make a fresh and unencumbered start in life.

I do not enjoy the hard travel and broken rest inseparable from lecturing, and if it had not been for the imperious moral necessity of paying these debts, which I never contracted but which were accumulated on the faith of my name by those who had a presumptive right to use it, I should never have taken to the road at my time of life. I could have supported myself comfortably by writing, but writing is too slow for the demands that I have to meet; therefore I have begun to lecture my way around the world. I am going to Australia, India and South Africa, and next year I hope to make a tour of the great cities of the United States.

In my preliminary run through the smaller cities on the northern route I have found a reception the cordiality of which has touched my heart and made me feel how small a thing money is in comparison with friendship.

I meant, when I began, to give my creditors all the benefit of this, but I begin to feel that I am gaining something from it too, and that my dividends, if not available for banking purposes, may be even more satisfactory than theirs.—MARK TWAIN

The wording veered toward pompous, but the statement was pithier and less prickly than Twain's; it was certainly more heroic and it mercifully lacked Twain's lame joke at the end about exhibiting as circus freaks.

Twain did not see it that way. He demanded that his version run as well verbatim, and it did a week later in the *Examiner*. Three months later, Twain would write his nephew that he had originally found the young man's version "too grave" even though Aunt Livy had regarded it as "exactly right to a word." But he now agreed with her and regretted that his version ran too. Clara had already written to her cousin: "We all like so much the interview you wrote for papa."

Twain, in future chats with journalists, would often wind up repeating his nephew's dandy lines that "honor is a harder master than the law" and "it cannot compromise for less than one hundred cents on the dollar."

These press statements mark a counterattack. In modern lingo, the Clemens clan—Sam, Sam, and Livy—were practicing the art of spin control. A handful of newspapers were making Twain look bad, and he wanted to regain the narrative upper hand. And Twain, America's great writer of fiction, did just that—with his nephew's help. They created a new narrative, an inspiring story, which contained . . . almost as much fiction as fact.

Boiled down, these statements proclaim that Mark Twain's unnamed business partner had made many bad business decisions without consulting him and that the partner should, by right, be forced to repay one third of the debts but wouldn't, because he had no money. The statements also proclaim that even though "insolvency" laws could have protected him, Twain would nonetheless take the high road and pay his partner's share and pay all the creditors in full. Also, that only one creditor was behaving badly. Also, that only Twain's copyrights were transferred to Livy.

————————

The unnamed partner was, of course, young Fred Hall, who had, in fact, sent dozens upon dozens of letters to Twain asking advice on business and book deals. Hall did this even though their partnership contract clearly stated that Twain "shall not be called upon to provide any service, or to take any supervision of said business." The contract also clearly stated that as one-third partner, Fred Hall was responsible only for debts up to the amount he has received in profits. Fred Hall received a salary but not a penny in profits. At best, Twain didn't know his own contract. He had recently written H.H. Rogers: "I've signed a lot of contracts in my time; and at signing-time I probably knew what the contracts meant—but 6 months later everything had grown dim and I could be *certain* of only two things, to-wit: 1. I didn't *sign* any contract; 2. The contract means the opposite of what it *says*."

As for "insolvency laws," they could *not* protect Twain for the simple reason that at the time, there was no federal bankruptcy law. When H.H. Rogers advised Twain to kill off Webster & Company in 1894, they did so under the New York State Laws of Voluntary Assignment. Basically, Twain appointed a lawyer as "assignee," in this case, young "idiot" Bainbridge Colby. The Columbia-educated lawyer then authenticated the legitimate Webster debts, which he tallied at $79,705 to 101 creditors, and then totaled up the assets, which he would eventually discover to be $22,075 or 27.7% of the debts. The process then called for Colby, with Twain's blessing as sole debtor, to make offers to the creditors so they would vote to release Twain from the debt. This "voluntary assignment" system seeks to avoid lengthy lawsuits, streamline repayment and allow fresh starts with the approval of the creditors. (No judge or referee can impose a settlement.)

Twain first offered to stop the clock on the debts and continue to operate the firm to pay them off; this was rejected. He then offered the Webster assets as payment with the promise that he would "try" to pay in full (rejected), then Webster assets plus 10% (rejected), then Webster assets plus $10,000 (rejected), until finally, in August, to pay 50% of the debts (i.e., with Twain ponying up about $15,000 cash on top of the remaining Webster assets) in exchange for a quitclaim and a best-effort promise by Twain to pay the rest. Colby expected this offer to be accepted by the vast majority of the creditors, but he was from the firm that made "more prophecies than Isaiah." (And, yes, he'd be wrong again, and Twain would dub him "that paltering ass.")

Another mistaken point: that only one creditor caused problems; in fact, the two largest creditors (in addition to that "one," Thomas Russell) had sued Twain—Mount Morris Bank ($30,000 debt) and the Barrows family ($15,000 debt)—and had already won judgments against him.

Twain's portrait of fans and friends shoveling money his way isn't completely accurate either. Envelopes of cash—that must be returned—did not arrive by the wagon load. In fact, Twain was deeply disappointed by the stinginess of his Hartford friends during his crisis. The one single extraordinary shining light was H.H. Rogers (and Livy didn't allow Twain to accept cash from him); the lesser light of generosity was Livy's brother, Charley, who came through but very grudgingly.

What was absolutely accurate, however, was that Rogers's advice on the transfer to Livy had saved Twain's books from chaos and made future complete editions possible. But these two press statements failed to mention that the original transfer to Livy in 1894 had also included Twain's Paige typesetter stock that he had then expected to be worth several hundred thousand dollars.

From the very first, Twain and Rogers had tried to keep the debt settlement as small as possible, coupling it with a high-flown promise to repay; from the very first, Livy insisted on full payment as quickly as possible. One day, Twain would talk tough with H.H. and the next he would talk "honor" with Livy. Twain could embrace H.H.'s cunning (the early transfer) *and* Livy's chivalry (full repayment).

This captures the man; his genius could entertain both viewpoints and be torn between the two. He chafed, and his humor came out. "Prosperity is the best protector of principle." "When people do not respect us we are sharply offended; yet deep down in his private heart no man much respects himself."

Twain, moralist *and* novelist, decided to embrace the "honor" narrative: "It may seem strange," Twain's sister wrote to her son, "but I am prouder of your Uncle Sam's determination to pay off all the debts of the firm a hundred cents on the dollar than of his fame as a writer."

Twain's choice would resonate with millions of Americans suffering through hard financial times—especially when they thought the debts were not his fault and that he had no legal obligation to pay. Good story line.

CHAPTER 10

Separation

M ark Twain lay sick in bed in Vancouver, with Livy hovering fretfully and rumors mounting about their dreadful ship to Australia, which had crashed upon some rocks.

The author sent a telegram to H.H. to inform him that the ship's departure was delayed until Tuesday, August 20. The raspy raconteur, ever hopeful for another payday, asked Pond to squeeze in a performance in Victoria, about a seventy-five-mile boat ride away, where the ship had traveled for repairs.

It made sense, since the 3,300-ton mail steamer RMS *Warrimoo* would now leave from there. The Clemens family tried not to despair over the tidbits they were hearing; recent newspaper accounts revealed that the captain, R. E. Arundel, in his first command, had run the ship aground not far from Victoria in the tricky strait of Juan de Fuca. The *Victoria Daily Colonist* stated that Arundel, a former first mate substituting for the regular captain on holiday, had gingerly entered the strait at half-steam during dense fog exacerbated by forest-fire smoke. He had ordered frequent soundings, and had just received a report of 200 feet depth when the sailors heard crashing surf ahead, indicating possible breakers or rocks. The captain ordered the engines cut and full speed astern, but the ship still skidded up onto the sandy shelf of Sea Lion Reef. The crew pumped water ballast out of the bow, lassoed a nearby rock, and with the rising tide pulled free the ship. The passengers were cheering, just as the *Warrimoo* crashed up onto another, far craggier ledge with a crunching sound and began to tip precariously.

Lifeboats were lowered; a sailor was sent to the nearby lighthouse to telegraph Victoria for help. Maritime steam whistles and gunshots brought Indian fishing boats to stand by for rescue. But once again, the rising tide liberated the damaged ship, which crawled into Victoria for repairs and a hearing before the Canadian Marine & Fisheries Department. That panel would soon decide whether Captain Arundel was fit to command the return voyage; ironworkers would gauge the damage.

Livy, already on edge, feared her husband would make himself far sicker if he traveled to perform the following night in Victoria, and possibly grow too sick to head to Australia. When he stubbornly refused to listen to her, she sent for a doctor, who judged it "perilous" for Twain, warning that "he could easily develop pneumonia." The family also received word that the ship's damage was more extensive than first thought. After being unloaded, it rode much lower than expected, and eight feet of water was discovered in one of the double-hull compartments. At least thirty steel plates of the exterior hull had "crumpled," one twisted badly enough to leave a one-foot gap. Repairs would take longer, so Pond sent a telegram to move back the Victoria performance three days to Tuesday night.

Twain, stuck in bed, but smoking constantly, found time to write a letter to young Rudyard Kipling, with whom he had struck up a passionate friendship, with a handful of meetings and lots of mutual admiration. Kipling, at age twenty-four, just before he struck fame for his tales of India, had made a pilgrimage to Elmira, New York, to seek out his favorite American author. Twain had graciously welcomed the young unknown Brit, and the pair smoked cigars and Twain talked for hours, flitting to many subjects but especially the role of conscience. Twain was always obsessed with that topic; in his personal life, he vacillated between doing the right thing and doing the wrong thing (swearing, lying, drinking, gambling, envying, bad-mouthing) just as his fictional characters vacillated too, from Tom Sawyer convincing his friends to whitewash that fence, to Huck on the raft torn over defying conventional wisdom to protect a runaway slave, Jim.

Kipling, in a later article, recounted the gist of Twain's opinion. "Your conscience is a nuisance. A conscience is like a child. If you pet it and play with it and let it have everything it wants, it becomes spoiled and intrudes on all your amusements and most of your griefs." Twain bragged back in 1890 that he thought he had come close to killing off his conscience. Clearly, his recent debts—and Livy—had helped resurrect it.

On Sunday, Pond wanted to do a little advance publicity for Twain's lecture in Victoria, so he lined up four reporters. Feverish Twain agreed to talk to them, on the condition that he could remain in bed. A Kodak snapshot taken by Pond reveals four wide-eyed young men and scruffy night-shirted Twain holding court and holding his meerschaum pipe in hand. (The link between smoking and respiratory illnesses was either unproven or dismissed in Twain's view.)

To avoid the endlessly repeated obvious questions, Twain rambled on about many topics, even describing how he carried candles to hotels in case the management stinted on delivering electric light. He was trying to remain on his best behavior. (A few days earlier, he had confessed in his notebook that when a very young reporter had asked him what the subject would be of his upcoming book about his travels, he had been very tempted to answer: "Hydrophobia, seamanship & agriculture.")

The rest of the Clemens entourage scrambled to amuse themselves with Twain stuck in bed and the ship stuck in dry dock. The thick gray-cotton smoke out the window also entombed them; it burned the eyes and throat. A family friend, a visitor named Mrs. Chase who knew Major Pond and knew he occasionally lectured about squiring celebrities, suggested Pond give a talk in the parlor of the hotel. Clara and Livy seconded the notion and a room was reserved, chairs supplied, announcement made.

Once all preparation was complete, Twain suddenly and forcefully refused to allow it because he said Major Pond was *his* manager and working for *him*. "Everything had to be stopped," wrote Pond. "It threw a wet blanket on all of us."

Years later, Clara would write of her father: "He was a constant surprise in his varied moods, which dropped unheralded upon him, creating day or night for those about him by his twinkling eyes or clouded brows."

On Sunday, the newspapers delivered the verdict of Saturday's maritime hearing on whether the novice captain Arundel must lose his certificate. Since the family would be traveling 8,000 miles on the *Warrimoo*, the article held great interest. The panel praised the captain for caution, and for taking frequent soundings, and good seamanship in getting off the reef, but it criticized him for not taking into enough account the level of the tide or the currents. Their ultimate decision: the captain's certificate should not be revoked. The verdict hardly ranked as resounding praise. The Clemenses would be traveling with a novice in a recently wrecked steamer.

"The smoke is so dense all over this upper coast that you can't see a cathedral at 800 yards," Twain wrote to H.H. "It makes navigation risky even in daytime—and at night very difficult and dangerous."

While the women were packing the trunks on Monday, Twain couldn't stand being cooped up anymore and demanded that Pond go for a walk with him in a light drizzle in the still-smoky streets of Vancouver. Pond found Twain quite discouraged and almost too feeble to walk. "It does make my heart ache to see 'Mark' so downhearted after such continued success." Twain told Pond that the unfavorable accounts of the *Warrimoo* were triggering Mrs. Clemens's "dread of the long voyage."

That day, Twain dashed off a dense near-frantic letter to H.H. and a similar one to an Elmira lawyer, plotting a lawsuit to get the near-worthless Paige typesetter shares back for him and his wife. He was grasping at financial straws.

The following day, the entourage headed to the docks to catch the noon ferry to go seventy-five miles south to Victoria (coincidentally passing near where the *Warrimoo* crashed). Although the *Charmer* arrived a half hour late from Victoria, that still left just enough time for the eight-hour return trip to deliver Twain to his performance that night. The captain announced that the ship would need *four hours* to unload 180 tons of cargo.

The ladies boarded the ship while Twain remained on the wharf and buttonholed the captain, and erupted "in very loud and unpious language," as Pond put it, about the greed of a passenger ferry line doing this to passengers for a few rotten dollars of freight. "They were a lot of blankety-blank somethings and deserved the penitentiary."

The captain stood stolidly listening, saying not a word, but growing redder in the face. Twain was shouting so loud that the Clemens women roaming the ship heard the rant.

Twain boarded, and apparently had a conversation with his wife. The author sought out Major Pond and asked him to go apologize to the captain for Twain's "unmanly abuse" and ask him how he could make it up to him.

Pond, throughout the trip and more so toward the end, marveled at Livy's ability to defuse her explosive husband. Elsewhere Pond noted:

"What a noble woman she is! It is Mark Twain's wife who makes his works so great. She edits everything and brings purity, dignity, and sweetness to his writings. In 'Joan of Arc' I see Mrs. Clemens as much as Mark Twain."

The lecture agent sent a telegram advising Victoria of a postponement to the following night. The theater not only distributed handbills but called any patrons wealthy enough to have telephones, such as the governor general of Canada, Lord Aberdeen.

The *Charmer* plowed through the smoke and fog and arrived in quaint Victoria after midnight. At the town's best, Hotel Driad, the entourage encountered Japanese elevator boys, male Chinese chambermaids and English waiters. Twain rested the following day. "He doesn't seem to get strength," observed Pond. "He smokes constantly."

Twain was ready to start his performance on time at 8:30 p.m. but was told he must wait for the governor general. Fifteen minutes later, Lord and Lady Aberdeen appeared with their little son in a highland kilt, and musicians played "God Save the Queen." Twain, for once, was pleased by the delay. "I wish they would always be present, for it isn't permissible to begin till they come; and by that time the late-comers are all in."

Twain's voice commenced strong but faded. Nonetheless, the night went well; the crowd was polite but appreciative. At one point, he earned a huge prolonged laugh that he wasn't at all expecting. (He later learned that a kitten had walked across the stage behind him.)

An aide-de-camp conducted Twain afterwards to the royal box, and the author soaked up the praise. A Mr. Campbell, a local dignitary, was supposed to come round to the hotel to take Twain to a private club, but he didn't show up. Twain was clearly disappointed so Pond and Twain went for a walk. "He was tired and feeble, but did not want to go back to the hotel."

Final preparations for the ocean voyage filled the next day. Pond recorded:

"Mark" and I were out all day getting books, cigars, and tobacco. He bought *three thousand* Manilla cheroots, thinking that with four pounds of Durham smoking tobacco he could make the three thousand cheroots last four weeks. If perpetual smoking ever kills a man, I don't see how "Mark Twain" can expect to escape.

That's Pond's version for his published memoirs, but in a letter to Twain's nephew Sam Clemens, Pond wrote they bought 500 cheroots, which again proves Pond's addiction to hyperbole. Three thousand cheroots would have meant 100 per day.

It was getting time to say good-bye. Twain inscribed a copy of *Roughing It* with the words: "Here ends one of the smoothest and pleasantest trips across the continent that any group of five has ever made." One senses that Livy hovered in the room.

The final financial accounting for the North America tour could now be done. Twain had netted about $4,200 in speaking fees from twenty-four appearances, but he had to pay for hotel and travel, and now he was shelling out $1,800 to buy three first-class $600 tickets from Victoria, B.C., to London, England. No record exists of Twain sending any money back to H.H. Rogers. Hopefully, he'd start to show a profit in Australia.

(Within a month, Twain would be confiding to H.H.: "Pond is superannuated, hasn't any sand or any intelligence or judgment. I must make no contract with him to platform me through America next year if I can do better. Who *can* I get?")

The RMS *Warrimoo* arrived at the Victoria dock at 1 p.m. on Friday, August 23, and the Ponds accompanied the Clemenses on board the ship. First impressions were bleak. "She looked dingy," Pond wrote to Sam, "smelled oily & musty and I think Mrs. Clemens was very homesick & almost heart broken & Mark kept silent & seemed disappointed when Miss Clara indignantly inquired if that was the great line of steamers that run to Australia." The Ponds and Clemenses ate lunch together for the last time, then lounged on the deck until time for departure.

Pond wrote in his notebook: "Mrs. Clemens is disappointed . . . our hearts are almost broken for the poor woman. She tells me she is going to brave it through, for she must do it. It is for her children."

The separation of the Clemens family was now becoming more tangible and vivid. The creaky ship and the questionable captain would place an ocean between Livy and her two other daughters.

A letter from Susy reached the family around this time. It was addressed to her sister Clara, but would be read by all.

Dear little spider [*Susy's nickname for her dark-haired younger sister*],

I will try to get one little word to you before you sail so far away out of our reach. Oh, dear, dear, the thought makes me ill! We have had so many good times together and it seems all wrong that we should be separated in this way. . . . Your sailing away seems like another terrible parting and good bye almost worse than the first, for we shall be such an eternity without news of you. . . . I love you most terribly, you dear little black thing, and long to be with you again, for we *are* a nice family.

Susy went on to recall that Clara had said many extremely sweet and supportive things to her before leaving, and Susy confessed that those words helped her when she was "cast down" over disappointing the family. "But perhaps I shall have a chance to try again," she added. "In any case, you *know* I love you all and *could not* have *wanted* more to be a 'nice child.' The only difficulty is that our duty doesn't end with wanting."

Major Pond, trying to cheer everyone up, had the three Clemenses pose on the rail next to the sign: NOTICE: ALL STOWAWAYS WILL BE PROSECUTED AT HONOLULU, AND RETURNED TO THIS PORT. — BY ORDER.

Twain is seen contemplatively smoking a long-stemmed pipe, and Clara and Livy look as though Pond just yelled, "Smile." The Ponds walked down the *Warrimoo*'s gangplank, and three-fifths of the "nice family" Clemens headed out to sea.

CHAPTER 11

At Sea

Mark Twain loved long sea voyages, and, with the abandon of a Carnival Cruise tourist, threw himself into cards, shuffleboard, stargazing, porpoise watching, even dancing. He read; he wrote; he practiced his speeches; he regained his health.

But Twain was Twain, and his very human traits bubbled up to spice up his days and everyone else's.

"Father was like a little child in his capacity for getting angry over cards," recounted Clara. She remembered watching the tiny muscles twitch under his eyes and seeing him fling down his cards and spew some sanitized curse, since she and her mother were nearby. "By the humping jumping—, who can play with a hand like that? Look at those cards! Just look at them! Products of the devil and his ancestors." They were playing Hearts for a running stack of worthless red and blue chips but no matter.

Clara said her "mother would then begin cooing out suggestions in an undertone and Father would gather up his cards with a little laugh. . . . 'I don't care a rap about beating, but I can't stand the sight of such cards. They make me boil—only a saint on ice could keep cool.'"

Twain, who all his life showed a marvelous talent for demonizing his enemies, found two worthy adversaries on this voyage: a pint-sized pug-nosed Japanese dog and the captain.

Twain apparently forgave the commander for beaching the ship twice off Victoria, but he had no patience for the man's pious behavior or his virulent anti-smoking policies.

He did not smoke or chew tobacco or take snuff; he did not swear, or use slang or rude, or coarse, or indelicate language, or make puns, or tell anecdotes, or laugh intemperately, or raise his voice above the moderate pitch enjoined by the canons of good form.

He seemed the Anti-Twain.

The man's piety extended to forbidding smoking in the staterooms and salons, to ordering the electric lights turned off in the designated smoking room promptly at 11 p.m. The captain's cabin stood next door, and he informed the author that the smell of tobacco smoke made him ill. Twain scrutinized tightly sealed walls and a bulkhead separating the rooms, and also observed the constant whirl of ocean breezes on the upper deck there. "Still, to a delicate stomach even imaginary smoke can convey damage," wrote Twain tartly in his later travel book.

Twain, who smoked ten to twenty cigars a day, had long ago given up trying to quit smoking. He found he could not write without it, but the challenge of quitting anything fascinated him.

When I was a youth I used to take all kinds of pledges, and do my best to keep them, but I never could, because I didn't strike at the root of the habit—the desire; I generally broke down within the month. Once I tried limiting a habit. That worked tolerably well for a while. I pledged myself to smoke but one cigar a day. I kept the cigar waiting until bedtime, then I had a luxurious time with it. But desire persecuted me every day and all day long; so, within the week I found myself hunting for larger cigars than I had been used to smoke; then larger ones still, and still larger ones. Within the fortnight I was getting cigars made for me—on a yet larger pattern. They still grew and grew in size. Within the month my cigar had grown to such proportions that I could have used it as a crutch. It now seemed to me that a one-cigar limit was no real protection to a person, so I knocked my pledge on the head and resumed my liberty.

As for the pug dog, Twain was infuriated that it enjoyed far more freedom than he did. "Notice has been put up forbidding smoking in cabins and salons but the little dog is free to discharge his inexhaustible bowels all over the ship."

The author asked questions and discovered the "vile little snub-nosed Jap dog" belonged to the regular captain, who was on holiday. "Instead of being in the butcher's keep where he would be if he belonged to a passenger, he sleeps in the berth with the second officer, and deposits his filth all over the ship."

Twain was so infuriated that he wrote in his notebook he would protest by "publicly breaking every rule of the ship" until the dog, like all other pets, was forbidden access to public areas. (That petulant passage was later crossed out—presumably after a conversation with Livy.)

All was not civil war and rebellion. Twain spent many long meditative hours at the rail smoking and staring out to sea. He found the waves hypnotic and peaceful. He saw "flocks of flying fish, with the sun on them" looking like "a flight of silver fruit knives." He caught a lunar eclipse, not long after a sunset, that reminded him of a "saucer of strawberry ice." He saw a school of follow-the-leader dolphins swim by at night that in their spiraling antics resembled a thirty-foot sea serpent.

The RMS *Warrimoo* was scheduled—one week out of Victoria—for a brief mid-voyage stopover in Honolulu. Twain eagerly looked forward to returning to those exotic islands, the place of his first literary successes.

At age thirty in 1866—after an up-and-down career in various trades—he had finally gained some national recognition with his irreverent articles from his five-month stay in the Sandwich Islands for the *Sacramento Union* in California. (Captain Cook had named the volcanic isles, the future Hawaii, after his patron in the British admiralty—the Earl of Sandwich.)

Twain had returned from Hawaii in August 1866 and soon afterwards gave his first lecture series. His clever ad proclaimed "A SPLENDID ORCHESTRA is in town but has not been engaged; A DEN OF FEROCIOUS WILD BEASTS will be on exhibition in the next block. MAGNIFICENT FIREWORKS were in contemplation . . . but the idea has been abandoned." He capped it off with: "Doors open at 7 o'clock. The trouble begins at 8 o'clock."

Not only was it his first big soloist payday, but it gave him an instant reputation as one of the funnier men in the country, a Pacific Slope humorist. From nobody to almost somebody by telling cannibal jokes.

In other cities I usually illustrate cannibalism on the stage, but being a stranger here I don't feel at liberty to ask favors, but still, if anyone in the audience would lend me an infant, I will go on with the show.

Of course his stand-up amounted to far more than cheap jokes. He showed a casualness, an informality that stood out in that booming, melodramatic Victorian era. (The audience had no idea that this informality resulted from intense practice.) Also, his material was darker and more intelligent than mere jokes.

> When these islands were discovered the population was about 400,000, but the white man came and brought various complicated diseases, and education, and civilization, and all sorts of calamities, and consequently the population began to drop off with commendable activity. Forty years ago, they were reduced to 60,000, and the educational and civilizing facilities being increased, they dwindled down to 55,000, and it is proposed to send a few more missionaries and finish them.

The Hawaiian or Sandwich Islands were still independent in 1895 when Twain was set to arrive. Sanford Dole of the sugar cane/pineapple empire had staged a coup and overthrown the Hawaiian monarchy and created a republic that wouldn't be annexed by the United States until 1898—in the jingoistic wake of the Spanish-American War.

Twain was excited to return to palm tree paradise. He looked forward to filling the largest hall in Honolulu. During his last visit he had been an unknown reporter; he was returning thirty years later as literary royalty.

Unbeknownst to Twain at sea, the local papers were already beating the drum for his Saturday-night August 24 appearance at Independent Park Theater at one dollar a ticket. "He told the truth about us in the early days and he made fun of our weak points," cited one op-ed writer who forgave the humorist.

With no telegraph, telephone or satellites, the Hawaiians had no way of knowing that Twain was delayed due to courteous Captain Arundel's reefing of the vessel off British Columbia.

A week behind schedule, on August 30, the *Warrimoo* reached Honolulu Harbor. The sailors switched from dress blues to dress whites for the occasion. Livy captured the moment in a letter to Susy.

Honolulu lights were in sight and we were just looking for our pilot to take us into port, when a little boat with nine or ten people in [it] drew up alongside. Everyone supposed it was the [harbor] pilot. When someone from the little boat said, "We cannot board you—there is sickness on the island, we want to speak with the Captain." The Captain was found and then came out their news. There was cholera in Honolulu! There had been five deaths that day.

Twain was crushed. He soon learned that $500 worth of seats had already been sold. Almost equally bad, the *Warrimoo* had to unload 700 tons of freight, so Twain could see paradise but not return to it.

No Hawaiian newspapers were allowed aboard, but he eventually learned from conversations that the cholera had only just hit Honolulu and been declared a possible epidemic. As recently as four days earlier, on August 26, 1895, the front page of the respected *Pacific Commercial Advertiser* had ignored cholera and chronicled an exhibition baseball game between the Kamehamehas and the Unknowns.

The proximity was torture for him. "Oahu just as silky & velvety & lovely as ever," Twain wrote in his notebook. "If I might, I would go ashore & never leave." He devoted pages to trying to describe the sun setting over a range of "billowy" mountains bathed in such warm soft light that it made "you want to stroke them as you would a cat's back." He mentioned dark blue, luminous bronze, light green, snow-white surf. "Finally," he exulted, "the cloud-rack was flooded with fiery splendors & these were copied on the surface of the sea & it made one drunk with an ecstasy of delight."

Livy's letter recounts the immense inconveniences of the outbreak, with some passengers forced to continue to Australia and some set-to-board passengers stranded in Hawaii. Livy—who later complained to her sister about the ship's food—especially regretted that no fresh fruit or vegetables could be delivered.

When the harbor ships came to offload the *Warrimoo*, the shore sailors tossed a rope aboard to link the ships. No sailor would touch it, out of fear of disease. "Ain't there *any*body in charge of that ship?" someone shouted up. "Hasn't she *any* crew at all?" Finally Clara Clemens picked it up and looped it around a cleat, and other passengers helped her with other ropes. The captain of one off-load vessel, a very fat man, struggled aboard; Clara took his photo and her father bravely shook his hand. The encounter made the papers, and Clara was described as a "Kodak fiend."

That night, a wealthy Canadian who drank far too much and whom Twain judged the ship's most interesting conversationalist, threatened to go ashore, carouse in the native quarter, and then come back aboard. For some reason, he hounded Livy with his plans. "I was rather afraid of him," she wrote.

With the ship anchored and unmoving, the tropics proved so swelteringly hot and humid that night that even the prim women could no longer sleep below deck. "We ladies put on wrappers," wrote Livy, "and took our pillows and lay down on the benches in the ladies salon. I found the seats too intolerably hard, so about quarter past three I went to my state room. Clara stayed with another lady in the salon until morning."

Clara might have had another motive for moving; she had found her cabin overrun by cockroaches. She later wrote her cousin Sam that she started imagining bugs everywhere, even had "brain-fever" nightmares of their antennae shooting bullets. "There was no article of furniture so large that I couldn't make a cockroach out of it, & their familiarity went beyond all bounds!"

As Twain's cherished Hawaii faded in the distance, he finally seemed ready to focus on preparing his speeches for Australia, two weeks away. He still had not mastered the new material he would need to perform several nights in the same city. He wanted three completely different ninety-minute acts so that local audience members could return without hearing repeats.

Around this time, he started having a very unpleasant nightmare that he was walking out on stage in Australia and was not wearing any pants.

For his second night, he wanted an emotional piece to play the same role as Huck and Jim on the raft. He tried "Aunty Cord," which he had written for the *Atlantic* about a slave woman being reunited with her long-lost, sold-away son during the Civil War. He returns in one of the "colored" regiments. Twain practiced telling it in slave dialect, playing the part of an elderly black female cook. It started with Twain asking: "Aunt Rachel, you are always laughing; haven't you ever had any trouble at *all*?" It was slow and melodramatic with no humor.

Twain also worked on writing a very silly poem using strange Australian animal names: emu, dodo and dingo, oh my. And he kept tinkering with the introductions to his already successful bits instead of rehearsing the new material. He took another crack at Morals. This time he would use doctors.

Fifty years from now the doctors will be inoculating for every *conceivable* disease . . . they will take the healthy baby out of the cradle & punch it & slash it & scarify it & load it up with the whole of the 1,644 diseases . . . and that child will be a spectacle to look at. But no matter; it will be sick a couple of weeks, & after that, though it live to be a hundred, it can never be sick again. The chances are that that child will never die at *all*. In that great day there won't be any *doctors* any more—nothing but just *inocula-tors*—& here & there a perishing undertaker. Now then *I* propose to inoculate for *sin*.

Twain planned on explaining that each sin committed brought a person one step closer to perfection. "The more crimes you commit, the richer you become,—*morally.*"

He took frequent breaks from memorizing to go play shuffleboard. He and Clara entered several tournaments, often playing before crowds of onlookers. The ship's roll made the sliding-disc game more challenging.

Father beat daughter to gain the finals of one tournament. Finally, with time running out on the voyage, the champions of two prior tournaments met for the big prize: Twain versus a Mr. Thomas. In his later travel book, *Following the Equator,* the author described the raucous crowd-pleasing start to the contest, when Mr. Thomas succeeded in landing four discs in the ten-point rectangle and Twain failed to knock any of them out.

I think it unlikely that that inning has ever had its parallel in the history of horse-billiards. To place the four disks side by side in the 10 was an extraordinary feat; indeed, it was a kind of miracle. To miss them was another miracle. It will take a century to produce another man who can place the four disks in the 10; and longer than that to find a man who can't knock them out. I was ashamed of my performance at the time, but now that I reflect upon it I see that it was rather fine and difficult.

Mr. Thomas kept his luck, and won the game, and later the championship.

High drama indeed, but Twain in his notebook and in a letter to H.H. stated that *he* won the final tournament. Just as with Twain's debts, apparently, the best dramatic story line wins. About a decade later, the author would tell his biographer: "I used to remember what happened and what didn't happen. Now I can remember only what didn't happen."

The ship continued to head southwest toward Australia and would soon cross the International Date Line. The captain announced that they would skip Monday, September 9. "While we were crossing the 180th meridian it was Sunday in the stern of the ship where my family were and Tuesday in the bow where I was," Twain later wrote. "They were there eating the half of a fresh apple on the 8th, and I was at the same time eating the other half of it on the 10th—and I could notice how stale it was, already."

The *Warrimoo* touched briefly at the British colony of Fiji on September 10 to restock. Clara, who had toured Europe, had never seen Pacific Islanders up close. "Was it possible that these savage-looking people were not imaginary characters in a musical comedy?" she later wrote. "Such heads of hair, like bushy halos around their heads! and such unconscious grace! A policeman with his monstrous club delighted Father. He wanted to buy the richly carved weapon. This greatly amused the strapping native." The island's governor showed Twain many artifacts, including one identified as a "cannibal fork."

Livy gauged her husband's mood in a letter to her sister.

> Mr. Clemens . . . is pretty cheerful—in fact he appears entirely
> cheerful—but underneath he has a steady unceasing feeling that
> he is never going to be able to pay his debts. I do not feel so, I am
> sure that if his life & health are spared to him that it will not be
> long until he is out of debt. Won't that be one joyful day.

Australia loomed less than a week away as the steamer plowed a solid 200 miles a day, heading to a remote outpost of the gargantuan British Empire, which covered one-fifth of the habitable globe, with footholds in the Caribbean, the Pacific, Asia, Africa, even South America, Hong

Kong and Gibraltar. As Tom explained to Huck in Twain's recent novella, *Tom Sawyer Abroad* (1894):

> Why, look at England. It's the most important country in the world; and yet you could put it in China's vest-pocket; and not only that, but you'd have the dickens's own time to find it again the next time you wanted it. And look at Russia. It spreads all around and every-where, and yet ain't no more important in this world than Rhode Island is, and hasn't got half as much in it that's worth saving.

That was the world in the 1890s: England, with its swaggering econ-omy and Royal Navy, was the colossus. The sun indeed never set on Queen Victoria's proud British Empire, which was good for Twain, since it meant more English-speaking customers for him.

CHAPTER 12

Greetings, Mate

Late on Sunday, September 15, 1895, the ship ducked between the "Heads," the craggy outer entrance to Sydney Harbor, and anchored in sheltered Watsons Bay for the night. Sacks of letters were tossed down to a Royal Mail boat; a newspaperman, who had bribed his way aboard, yelled up questions to Twain without much success. About the only thing the man heard clearly was Twain's last suggestion: "Don't forget my soulful eyes."

At dawn, Captain Arundel guided the *Warrimoo* through the famed five-mile "labyrinth of bays and channels" of the spectacular harbor. Spits of land seemed improbably perched far out into the sea; red cliff faces opened into secluded inlets; the charming old quarter of the city hovered above the landing spot, Circular Quay. Twain had already been warned that he would be called to "testify" to the greatness of the harbor; other travelers suggested tucking a note of high praise into one's hat before arriving. Young Captain Arundel, overeager, came in with too much speed and, despite ordering engines reversed, jolted the dock.

A newspaperman from the *Sydney Evening News* boarded immediately, searched the ship and found Twain eating breakfast alone. He peppered him with predictable questions about traveling and lecturing. "Do you think it is rather early to give your impressions of this country?" he asked at 7 a.m. "Well, yes," Twain replied. "The country has only been visible to me since half past six this morning."

The one unexpected question: Would Twain fight a duel with the French humorist Max O'Rell, who had insulted him? Twain instantly lost his temper and started to launch into a tirade about a second-rate writer seeking publicity just as Livy came by. She suggested it was time for her husband to pack.

The famous American's arrival ranked as big news in a place located many thousand steamer miles from Europe that in that era rarely attracted A-list entertainment. The main performers of that season were Russian pianist Mark Hambourg, English mesmerist T. A. Kennedy, Irish independence lecturer Michael Davitt, and several religious ministers, including the General of the Salvation Army, William Booth.

Australia was not yet a unified country; the immense island in 1895 consisted of five unfederated, often bickering British colonies (New South Wales, Victoria, South Australia, Western Australia, Queensland), which would be united into a Commonwealth in 1901. The landmass of 3 million square miles equaled that of the continental United States, but the United States had a population of 70 million, compared to only 3½ million people in Australia. Making the land Down Under seem even less inhabited, the vast majority of the Aussies lived in a handful of thriving seaports: Sydney, Melbourne, Adelaide, Brisbane. Elsewhere, sheep outnumbered people by twenty to one. Much of the "Australian Outback" was desert, and much of the so-called "Bush" was not green.

Captain Cooke had "discovered" the eastern coast of the island in 1770, and in less than two decades, the British Crown had figured out a use for it: create the penal colony of New South Wales. By 1868, when the transport of British convicts ended, the Crown had shipped 162,000 male and female convicts there to work the region.

This whiff of criminal ancestry made Australia far less class conscious than England. "There is no long line of moneyed heirs," pronounced *Lloyd's Guidebook*. "There is no idle rich to put fictitious values upon property." England in those days sent out a titled governor and some titled admirals to strut the decks of the men-of-war, and these gentlemen and their ladies ran what passed for high society in a place that usually favored the workingman. Twain would find Australians more like Americans than Englishmen. "No shyness; get acquainted in five minutes," he wrote in his notebook.

Twain, Livy and Clara walked down the gangplank and headed via carriage the short distance to the city's finest hotel, the Australia, on Castlereagh Street. They passed through the luxurious establishment's colorful Italian marble entryway and caught sight of the grand staircase leading to the tea salons and dining rooms. The hotel, avoiding excessive modernity, offered an elegant, airy mahogany staircase, backed by stained-glass windows, to all ten floors of guest rooms for those guests who distrusted elevators.

The Clemens clan arrived during the height of the Sydney spring social season, with Race Week at the horse track, Randwick. Both city and hotel were packed.

Since Twain's lecture agent couldn't predict the exact arrival date of the damaged SS *Warrimoo*, he had scheduled Twain's opening night for Thursday, which happened to be four days away, and that meant that Twain, uncharacteristically, had some free time on land. The agent, R. S. Smythe, a genial, short, thick-set former arts critic, set up interviews with all the major newspapers. (Eventually, pundits would joke about whether any journalist had *not* interviewed him.) The man from the *Melbourne Argus* found Twain "undersized" and unimpressive physically. "Intellectually he is like many another humorist; he seems cast in a somewhat somber mold."

The reporter from the *Sydney Morning Herald* seemed disappointed that Twain was not jolly and joking. Twain told him a bit defensively that no one was "properly funny" who was not at times quite "serious." They discussed humor, and Twain trotted out some famous views on the subject: "Life has been defined as a 'tragedy for those who feel and a comedy for those who think.'" He maintained that humor must be anchored by something absolutely authentic or it would fall flat.

Don't you remember what [famous actor David] Garrick said to a friend, "You may fool the town in tragedy. But they won't stand any nonsense in comedy." Any pretender can cast up the whites of his eyes to the heavens and roll out his mock heroics, but the comedian must have the genuine ring in him. Otherwise he couldn't be a comedian.

To other reporters, Twain told his canned story about retreating during the Civil War; he told about meeting Rudyard Kipling. He admitted that he avoided reading the current bestsellers, such as *Trilby* (about a Svengali corrupting a pretty Irish art model), because he feared they might infect his writing style. He loved Lewis Carroll, Gilbert & Sullivan, and Kipling. He was souring on Dickens.

Lecture agent Smythe scheduled an 11 a.m. Monday photo session for

Twain at the leading studio, Falk's. Herbert Low, a young reporter who hovered by Twain at the hotel, was rewarded by being invited to walk along to the studio. He described Twain as wearing a shiny top hat "with a rakish curl about the brim," dull black clothes, a black necktie fastened in a bow, and dusty tan shoes that needed a shine.

Thanks to Race Week, the streets had a "rattle and bustle" and were filled with young men in ribboned straw boaters and women in elaborate flowered hats. A water tram sprinkled the roads to keep down the dust. Hansom horse cabs were cocooned in white canvas. Twain noticed the unmistakable smell and smoke of forest fires. The sun resembled a hazy electric light.

As they walked the streets, the pair saw Twain's bushy-browed face plastered on numerous billboards, touting: FIRST APPEARANCE IN AUSTRALIA OF THE GREATEST HUMORIST OF THE CENTURY. He was not just the funniest man alive; he would have to live up to being billed as the funniest man for the past hundred years.

And here he was, walking along a tad gloomily discussing politics and other "serious" subjects with the reporter. Twain professed to be no expert, but he said he supported Free Trade, then a big issue in Australia, as *each colony* charged its neighbor import duties. "My instinct teaches me that protection is wrong." He pointed out that Californians could have bought cheaper products shipped from Asia or Australia but were forced to buy overpriced East Coast goods.

They arrived at Falk's. The photographer, H. Walter Barnett, asked if Twain would send for his wife and his daughter as well. He did, and a messenger brought the two women in about ten minutes. The talented photographer would capture Twain striving for the classic faraway ("I'm having profound thoughts") look, favored by famous literary people. But, perhaps more memorably, in that era of long-held poses, he crafted a wonderfully composed image of Livy and Clara, the schoolmarmish mother with the faintest smile of pride gazing slightly upward at her beautiful dark-haired, dark-eyed, full-lipped daughter.

The women departed. Twain lingered downstairs to explore some of the framed photos in the gallery. One headshot caught his eye. The image almost seemed etched—it was so three-dimensional; at a glance it looked like some rock outcropping, creased by cracks, half hidden in foliage. The photo was of long-time Australian politician Sir Henry Parkes, fearless eyes, flared nostrils, a huge fleshy Cro-Magnon head topped by white hair as thick as Twain's, and a chest blanketed by tendrils of his white beard. (Cartoonists would portray them comparing hairstyles.) Parkes's image emanated power, passion, experience. Twain and Parkes would soon meet and develop an almost instant comradeship.

Twain had some more free time and invited the newspaperman to give him a walking tour. They visited ornate Town Hall, and Twain couldn't resist testing the acoustics of the large empty auditorium. He stayed in the balcony and sent the reporter to the stage to speak in a conversational voice. He heard him clearly. "The size of the building don't count," said Twain. "It's the construction that is everything."

And acoustics played a key role for Twain, who strove for an intimate tone in his performances . . . no fire and brimstone, just a friend over for a chat. His performances were called "At Homes." The expression came from the Victorian practice of announcing certain days that a family—in those pre-telephone days—would be "at home" to receive visitors.

Reporter Herbert Low took Twain to one of Sydney's most beautiful vantage points for seeing the harbor, "Mrs. Macquarie's Chair." On a tentacle of land, they sat in an exposed sandstone outcropping, carved long ago into an oversized bench to suit a governor's wife, and they gazed in the direction of what would one day be the Sydney Opera House.

After spending hours together, Low judged Twain's conversation to be "peculiar" and halting, much like his walking. "Sometimes you think he has finished what he intended to say, and then just as you are about to chip in with a remark, you find your mistake out." Twain also told anecdote after anecdote, swerving far from the question and only teasingly returning.

When they approached Cooper's Wharf, several "genteel cadgers" recognized Twain: "Glory of my life to have shaken hands with you," said one and then asked for a few shillings. After the fifth cadger approached, Twain shook the next man's hand and informed him that he was performing around the world to pay off his own debts. "Could you oblige me with half a crown [*2½ shillings*] till I get back to the States?"

When Twain returned to the hotel, he found dozens of invitations waiting and bountiful bouquets of flowers. That first night in Sydney, sheets of rain poured down, bringing relief from the drought but muddying the race track. With no social secretary, Livy and Clara sorted and answered invitations. They chose to accept for themselves the most prestigious: a governor's ball and a high tea with an admiral on a man-of-war. Twain chose the racetrack.

The Clemens family attended Metropolitan Day at Randwick track. The rain and heavy air led to topsy-turvy results that day, with favorites faring badly, especially "Quiver" in the featured race. "The surroundings are made pretty comfortable for people who want to lose their money," Twain told a reporter.

On Wednesday, he holed up at the hotel, practicing for his Thursday night debut. His wife and daughter attended a tea aboard the HMS *Orlando*, hosted by Admiral Cyprian Bridge, whose wife Twain had met months earlier in London. That night Twain could not resist accepting a tribute at the prestigious Athenaeum Club, with near 100 top-flight politicians and businessmen attending. Twain met the photograph in person, the leonine-maned Parkes, a wooly mammoth. Parkes hosted and amused Twain, no small task. The politician—born in England but wildly patriotic toward his new home—would play a key role in uniting the bickering colonies of Australia; he also survived several bankruptcies, and the eighty-year-old would soon marry his twenty-three-year-old housemaid after outliving two wives. Twain allowed Parkes to suggest the author's toast, and Twain dutifully delivered Parkes's slogan "Advance Australia."

As opening night approached, Twain knew that despite all the colorful posters and publicity, he could either fly or flop. Would Australians understand his straight-faced humor? One newspaper had accused Twain's lecture agent, R. S. Smythe, of delivering mostly foreign has-beens and second-raters, such as the recent much-hyped American preacher, T. Dewitt Talmage.

Two thousand people, a standing-room-only crowd, filled Protestant Hall, from the private boxes to the top gallery. Most arrived by 7:30 p.m. Then one minute after 8 p.m., a "picturesque little figure stole out from the draping of the Stars and Stripes at the corner of the platform . . . and a shout went up that rattled the windows in their sockets."

The crowd cheered and cheered for Twain, and waved handkerchiefs and hats. They cheered more and stomped and kept clapping and clapping. "Few remember anything more spontaneous, heartier or more prolonged," wrote the *Sydney Morning Herald*. The American author who had suffered through so many financial setbacks seemed genuinely overcome by the warmth of the reception. He stood there, looking almost disoriented. Critics said he resembled his portraits but seemed older and frailer. "He looks all his 60 years, and his shaggy iron-grey hair and bushy eye brows give a roughly stern look that lasts till he smiles."

One newspaper noted that the only conventional aspect of the entertainer was that he wore a formal black suit, "which can make a Duke look like a butler and the reverse." Twain, once the hall quieted, seemed to stumble his way into his revised "Morals" inoculation intro but then abruptly gave it up and launched into the story of the corpse in the moonlight.

Audience members who had enjoyed his books might have read written versions of all five stories he would tell. But, for Twain, the difference between the written and the spoken versions was like the difference between the lightning and the lightning bug. He carried pince-nez spectacles, but he had no intention of reading anything. He despised author readings as a "crime" that troubled the world. He adapted his stories. He let audiences teach him what worked. Reviewers in Australia and elsewhere struggled to try to capture his secrets. Was he silly or profound or both? They all mentioned the crawling, drawling delivery, the well-timed pauses, the lack of a smile, the twinkling eyes. Then most surrendered. "Nothing short of some ingenious combination of photography and the phonograph, similar to that which Mr. Edison has just constructed, could furnish even a slight reproduction of his appearance last night, and it would be a very faint reproduction indeed."

Twain mesmerized the crowd that opening night in Sydney. All five stories soared; Huck and Jim brought tears to many in the audience, but the piece that drew the most laughs was one of the bravest, most unlikely bits of performance comedy in his repertoire, "Grandfather's Old Ram." He warns the audience up front—tells them to their faces that he will never get to the point, and he never does. He veers from what almost seems a drunkard's rambling tale to flights of hallucinogenic fancy. He even does some minimalist physical comedy.

And next I should feel it my privilege as a teacher to make war upon the wandering mind, the unconcentrated mind, the mind that wastes its forces upon irrelevant details that are outside of its subject . . . the ill-conditioned mind that starts with a distinct intention but wanders at once away from it to discuss a name or a family, & what became of the members of that family, & helplessly drifts from topic to topic . . . and circumnavigates the whole great globe of human interests without ever getting back to the subject it started with, any more.

Ben Harris had that kind of a mind. He lived in Nevada in the early days. He had concealed in him somewhere the facts concerning a most remarkable adventure, which his grandfather once had with a ram. He made many & many an attempt to unload those facts, but always failed. Once he did manage to approach so nearly to the end, apparently, that the boys were filled with an eager hope; they believed that at last they were going to find out all about the grandfather's adventure.

[*Twain now shifted into a backwoods accent.*]

Well, as I wassayin', he bought that old ram from a feller up in Siskiyou County and fetched him home and turned him loose in the medder, and next morning he went down to have a look at him, accident'ly dropped a ten-cent piece in the grass and stooped down—so—[*Twain bends over*] and was a-fumblin' around in the grass to git it, and the ram he was a-standin' up the slope taking notice; but my grandfather wasn't taking notice, because he had his back to the ram and was int'rested about the dime. Well, there he was, as I was a-sayin', down at the foot of the slope a-bendin' over—so—[*Twain bends over*] fumblin' in the grass, and the ram was up there at the top of the slope, and [Billy] Smith—Smith was a-standin' there—no, not jest there, a little further away—[*Twain walks to the place*] fifteen foot perhaps—well, my grandfather was a stoopin' way down—so—[*Twain bends over*] and the ram was up there observing, you know and Smith . . . [*Twain pauses, lost in thought*] . . . the ram he bent his head down, so . . . [*Twain tilts his head forward, pauses*] Smith of Calaveras. . . . no, no it couldn't be Smith of Calaveras—I remember now that he—b'George it was Smith of Tulare County—course it was, I remember it now, perfectly plain.

Well, Smith he just stood there, and my grandfather . . . was a-bending down just so [*Twain bends over*], fumblin' in the grass, and when the old ram see him in that attitude he took it fur an **invitation**—and here he come down the slope thirty mile an hour and his eye is full of business. You see my grandfather's back being to him, and him stooping down like that, of course, he, why so! it warn't Smith of Tulare at all, it was **Smith of Sacramento**—my goodness, how did I ever come to get them Smiths mixed like that—why Smith of Tulare was jest a nobody, but Smith of Sacramento—why the Smiths of Sacramento come of the best southern blood of the United States; there warn't any blood south of the line better than the Sacramento Smiths. Why look here, one of them married a Whitaker! I reckon that gives you an idea of the kind of society the Sacramento Smiths could 'sociate around in; there ain't no better blood than that Whitaker blood; I reckon anybody'll tell you that.

Look at Maria Whitaker—there was a girl for you! Why yes, she was little but what of that? Look at the heart of her—had a heart like a bullock—just as good and sweet and lovely and generous as the day is long; if she had a thing and you wanted it, you could have it—have it and [be] welcome [to it].

She had a glass eye. She used to **loan her glass eye** to Miss Wilson to receive company in. [*Laughter. Twain is standing there dead serious in a black suit.*] And it didn't fit Miss Wilson. There was just two sizes difference between them. Miss Whitaker's eye was No. 5 and Miss Wilson she was No. 7, and the eye didn't fit. It wobbled. [*Laughter.*] It was so small that when she would wink, it would turn over. [*Laughter.*] . . . But it was a very nice eye. It was a blue eye, her own eye was black. [*Laughter.*] Yes it was blue on the front side and it was gilded on the hind side. [*Laughter.*]

When [she] winked that blue and gilt eye would whirl over, and the other one stand still, and as soon as she begun to get excited that hand-made eye would give a whirl and then go on a-whirlin' and a whirlin' faster and faster [*Laughter*], a-flashin' first blue and then yaller and then blue and then yaller. [*Applause.*]

[Miss Wilson] married a Hogadorn. I reckon that lets you understand what kind of blood she was—old Maryland Eastern Shore blood; not a better family in the United States than the Hogadorns.

Sally—that's Sally Hogadorn—she married a missionary, and they went off carrying the good news to the cannibals out in one of them way-off islands round the world in the middle of the ocean somewhere, and **they ate her**; ate him too, which was irregular;

it warn't the custom to eat the missionary, but **only** the family, and when they saw what they had done, they were dreadful sorry about it, and when the relations set down there to fetch away the things, they said so,—said so right out—said they was sorry, and 'pologized, and said it shouldn't happen again, said 'twas an accident.

Accident! now that's foolishness; there aint no such thing as an accident. There ain't nothing happens in the world but what's ordered just so by a wiser Power than us, and it's always fur a good purpose. . . . Whenever a thing happens that you think is an accident you make up your mind it ain't no accident at all—it's a special Providence [and God's Will].

You look at my Uncle Lem—what do you say to that? That's all I ask you—you just look at my Uncle Lem and talk to me about accidents! It was like this: one day my Uncle Lem and his dog was down town, and he was a-leanin' up against a scaffolding—sick or drunk, or somethin'—and there was an Irishman with a [load] of bricks up the ladder along about the third story, and [the Irishman's] foot slipped and down he come, bricks and all, and hit a stranger fair and square and knocked the everlasting aspirations out of him; [Uncle Lem] was ready for the coroner in two minutes. Now then people said it was an accident.

Accident! there warn't no accident about it; 'twas a special *Providence* [and God's Will], and had a mysterious noble intention back of it. The idea was to save that Irishman. If that stranger hadn't been there, that Irishman would have been killed. The people said "special Providence—sho! the dog was there—why didn't the Irishman fall on the dog? Why warn't the dog appinted?" Fer a mighty good reason—the dog would 'a' seen him a-coming.

Twain sometimes had to wait a long time for that joke to sink in. It's a tribute to nineteenth-century theology and faith that the joke worked at all. But it did. (Livy and Clara loved hearing him tell that joke.) Twain was toying with the concept of free will and God's master plan, about how the faithful will accept that all deaths and disasters are part of God's master plan, even if we mere mortals don't understand. Now, here he was saying—earnestly, solemnly—that humans believe that other humans may often be "appointed" to play some unpleasant role in God's master plan—maybe dying in war or being dismembered by machinery—but that a dog couldn't be appointed . . . 'cause the dog would have "seen" him coming. "The absurdity of the situation always worked its way into the audience's mind," Twain later said, "but it had to have time."

For most of the world tour, Livy and Clara attended performances any night that Twain was doing "Grandfather's Old Ram" just to see how long it would take the audience to get the joke; they thought they could gauge a community's collective intelligence based on the wait.

He later explained the joke like some Comp Lit professor: "[The] dog [is] an instrument too indifferent to pious restraint and too alert in looking out for his own personal interests to be safely depended upon . . . even when the command comes from on high." Or as he put it, when doing his riff:

You can't depend on no dog to carry out a Special Providence. You couldn't hit a dog with an Irishman—lemme see, what was that dog's name . . . [*musing*] . . . oh yes, Jasper, and a mighty good dog too.

He warnt no common dog, he warnt no mongrel, he was a composite. A composite dog is a dog that's made up of all the valuable qualities that's in the dog breed—kind of a syndicate; and a mongrel is made up of the riffraff that's left over. That Jasper was one of the most wonderful dogs you ever see. Uncle Lem got him of the Wheelers. I reckon you've heard of the Wheelers; ain't no better blood south of the line than the Wheelers.

Well, one day, Wheeler was a-meditating and dreaming around in the carpet factory and the machinery made a snatch at him and first you know he was a-meandering all over that factory from the garret to the cellar, and everywhere, at such another gait as— why, you couldn't even see him; you could only hear him whiz when he went by. Well, you know a person can't go through an experience like that and arrive back home the way he was when he went.

No, Wheeler got wove up into thirty-nine yards of best three-ply carpeting. The widow was sorry, she was uncommon sorry, and loved and done the best she could for him in the circumstances, which was unusual. She took the whole piece—thirty-nine yards, and she wanted to give him proper and honorable

burial, but she couldn't bear to roll him up; she took and spread
him out full length, and said she wouldn't have it any other way.
She wanted to buy a tunnel for him but there wasn't any tunnel
for sale, so she boxed him in a beautiful box and stood it on a hill
on a pedestal twenty-one foot high, and so it was a monument
and grave together, and economical—sixty foot high—you could
see it from everywhere—and she painted on it "To the loving
memory of thirty-nine yards best three-ply carpeting containing
the mortal remainders of Millington G. Wheeler go thou and do
likewise."

After the laughter died down, Twain concluded: "No man ever found
out whether the grandfather found the dime or not, or whether he got—
interrupted . . . No, the unconcentrated mind always leaves the listener
smothered in a fog of doubts & uncertainties & its only function seems
to be to raise hopes which it cannot satisfy."

As one Sydney reviewer explained: "The evils of a wandering mind
were illustrated in a story that wound an interminable length along in
continuous laughter, and the most unexpected anecdotes were made to
point to the most unexpected conclusions."

Twain closed his performance with "Terrors of the German Language." He had studied German on and off since his trip to Europe seventeen years earlier. Livy was fluent, and while Twain could read the
gothic script, conversation often eluded him. "If [the] Viennese ladies
and gentlemen [who] called . . . were unable to speak anything but German, great misunderstandings took place as to what the topic of conversation really was," recalled Clara later. "[Father] thought the subject was
noted politicians, and the Viennese knew it was pigs."

Twain subscribed to low-key sign-offs as much as no-fuss introductions.

And he chats quietly for an hour and a half, and then dismisses
the audience with a sort of apology for keeping them so long. And
everyone regrets that the end has come. It may at once be said
Mark is not a lecturer—he never claimed to be. But he is the best
exponent and illustrator of his own creations, and some of them
live more vividly than ever they did before for many of those who

helped to welcome the master of American humor last night. (*Sydney Evening News*)

The "large audience cheered again and again." He bathed in it for long minutes. The reviews the next day were almost universally positive. And the payday was monumental. He earned about $400 ($12,000 in current dollars) for ninety minutes' work at Protestant Hall, which came in at double his nightly average in America and exceeded his biggest American haul, in Portland. Twain was finally reaping a big single-night reward: he had two more sold-out appearances scheduled for Sydney.

Newspapers all over the vast colonies immediately picked up the rave reviews. He had four performances pegged for Melbourne and four for Adelaide. All signs pointed to similar paydays. Australia might actually put a dent in his debts.

The only friction slowing Australia's budding love affair with the international celebrity came from some comments he had made during his nervous first few days in the country. These were now getting wide reprint play.

He had shared his opinion in favor of free trade between nations instead of protectionism, riling one set of newspapers against him; Twain also mentioned that socialist Henry George's captivating idea of redistributing all land would probably lead to "bloodshed," riling another set of newspapers against him.

He also candidly assessed popular fellow American author Bret Harte as a fraud and heartless, infuriating almost every literary critic in the country. Though largely forgotten today, Harte's "Luck of the Roaring Camp" and "Heathen Chinee" had put him atop any nineteenth-century list of American authors, making him one of the only Americans whose international fame rivaled Twain's. Harte's living in London further endeared him to British audiences. The two writers had once been close friends in California; Harte had even edited some of *Innocents Abroad*. They had collaborated on a play, *Ah, Sin!*, but the rupture came when Harte borrowed money from Twain and others, and dared to criticize Livy after staying with the Clemenses in Hartford.

Twain, who had once credited Harte with elevating him in the late 1860s from an "awkward utterer of coarse grotesquenesses," now proclaimed: "I detest him because I think his work is shoddy."

And then there was Max O'Rell. The Frenchman with the Irish stage name had toured Australia the previous year with the same lecture agent as Twain. The reviewers, who had found many of R. S. Smythe's clients has-beens, admitted that O'Rell was entertaining.

O'Rell/Leon P. Blouet had written those brutally cutting words about Twain's bankruptcy in *North American Review*. He had also once challenged Twain to a duel. The news had died down in America, but Australian newspapers now resurrected it for a laugh, envisioning a pair of fifty-plus-year-old comedians squaring off with boomerangs at twenty paces.

The duel sprang not from Twain's debts but from a printed joust Twain had with a famous French writer. Paul Bourget, needling Americans about their country's short history, had written: "I suppose life can never get entirely dull to an American, because whenever he can't strike up any other way to put in his time, he can always get away with a few years trying to find out who his grandfather was."

Twain counterattacked: "I reckon a Frenchman's got his little standby for a dull time too, because when all other interests fail, he can turn in and see if he can't find out who his father was."

Max O'Rell claimed he found Twain's jibe a "vile insult" to the wives and mothers of France. He did indeed challenge Twain to a duel, even allowing the Missourian the choice of weapons.

Of course, it was a stupid publicity stunt, but Twain couldn't let it go when Australian newspapermen asked him if he would fight.

I can disgrace myself nearer home, if I felt so inclined, than by going out to have a row with a Frenchman. (*Sydney Morning Herald*)

It was infamously offensive and impertinent in a person of Max O'Rell's literary standing (which is a cypher in America and England, I don't know what it is here), to introduce himself into a matter which did not concern him. . . . I have a family, and some self-respect acquired by great labor and pains, and I cannot afford to sacrifice them in fighting a duel. I never saw the day I would risk a life so precious as mine on the dueling field. (*Sydney Evening News*)

Twain supplied some more venom, then saw his wife coming: "Perhaps, I have said enough about Max O'Rell. I hope one day to meet him in—" Before Twain could finish the sentence, Livy clapped her hand on his mouth and smothered the last word.

Strangely enough, from his second week onward while in Australia, Twain, one of the most outspoken men of the age, muzzled himself—with his wife's help. Soon after, when asked his opinion of the British Empire, he begged off, calling it a "large subject for an infant to talk about." And he soon started giving vague answers about Bret Harte. Livy entered the room that Saturday just as he was finishing one such ambiguous answer about Harte. "I hope it was nothing critical; that was a great mistake you made," she said. "I think it would be better if your wife saw your interviews in print before they were published."

There's no record of Twain talking back. The interviewer then politely asked if Twain objected to the basic concept of an interview. The author replied that he didn't, unless the interviewer tried to ambush him into revealing flaws. "Every man has in his character weak places which he is ashamed of . . ." said Twain. "Fortunate men are like the moon, they never exhibit any but their best side."

His sold-out second night featured "Aunty Cord," the ex-slave cook, instead of Huck and Jim. On his third night, he tried out his "Australian Poem," which would prove to be his most popular piece Down Under. He delivered three unique shows. A fourth night was added; it too sold out all 2,000 seats.

Twain was quickly forgiven his offhand interview comments. The author—for better or worse—learned a profound lesson: he was traveling the globe to sell tickets for his performances. He could save his opinions on colonialism, imperialism, class warfare, British arrogance, decimation of native peoples, and sundry other outrages for his private notebook and his travel book, to appear a year or two later.

In person, during interviews, especially with Livy and his daughter at his side, he toned down the rhetoric. Mark Twain, at age fifty-nine, reluctant circumnavigator, was being hailed in this British colony with a near-royal welcome.

Twain luxuriated in bed on Wednesday morning, September 25, while Livy and Clara packed for Melbourne. Livy sent off a bundle of rave Australian reviews to H.H. Rogers in New York, and Twain wrote a letter to him. "We have had a darling time here for a week—and really I am almost in love with the platform again."

CHAPTER 13

Cashing in on the Platypus

A round 5 p.m. the Clemens family trio and Robert Smythe, the agent with the nickname "much-traveled," boarded the overnight train for the seventeen-hour trip west to Melbourne, Australia's largest city, in the neighboring colony of Victoria. Twain would now spend the next month entertaining in the South—in Melbourne, Adelaide, and a handful of prosperous country towns.

From out the train window, the author saw the famed Blue Mountains at sunset. Twain hoped to get a good night's sleep to the rhythm of the rails. He had been warned, but was nonetheless irritated to be woken up at 5 a.m. and put out into "the biting cold of a high altitude" at Albury to change trains "by lantern light." He was told the colonies of New South Wales (Sydney) and Victoria (Melbourne) could not agree on the width/ gauge of their railroad tracks (4′8″ versus 5′3″). In addition, Victoria charged import taxes on all "useful or ornamental" goods intended to remain inside its borders. He exited one train, passed through a customs house where the family's luggage was rifled, as though they were crossing a hostile border, and boarded another train.

"I believe in early rising . . ." Twain said sleepily and slowly to a reporter at Albury ". . . for everyone else." That's as far as he would let himself criticize. When details about the lack of Australian federal rail standards were explained to him, he begged off: "I haven't a bit of political knowledge in my stock that is worth knowing."

(The topic of disharmony among the Australian colonies actually did interest him. In his notebook, he soon jotted down that he was told that one politician here had suggested that New South Wales be officially renamed "Convictoria" to capture its heritage as a penal colony.)

At Spencer Street station in Melbourne, the American consul, Australian officials, numerous newspapermen and a crowd of about 200 people greeted Twain. They convoyed him to the fashionable, expensive Menzies Hotel, a national landmark that aimed to evoke the charm of a European grand hotel. Suites featured walnut wainscoting and French bedsteads. The author pled exhaustion and retired with his pipe and a book.

Civic leaders had wanted to show off their city, which they unhesitatingly referred to as "Marvelous Melbourne" and classed as the preeminent city in Australasia, with its neoclassical bank buildings on Collins Street and stately wide avenues. The population of Melbourne stood at a half million; in other words, one out of every seven of the continent's residents lived here. The numbers had skyrocketed from 23,000 at its founding in 1851, when the colony of Victoria was chipped off from the territory of New South Wales, just in time for the gold rush. Far and away the smallest Australian colony, detractors dubbed it the "cabbage patch," but it was certainly one wealthy cabbage patch. With safe harbor on Port Phillip Bay, Melbourne served as entry point for miners, as well as bank of choice for mining moguls.

Melbourne matched and exceeded Sydney in welcoming Twain. Five sold-out performances at the Bijou instead of four. "People were packed like sandwiches [sic] into the boxes," reported the *Melbourne Argus*, "the gallery was brimming over, there were two perspiring rows of spectators in the orchestra, and a side glance at the wings showed a background of eager faces."

Twain happened to arrive at the tail end of the annual Assembly week for the Church of England, basically Fleet Week for the clergy. The Bishop of Melbourne, in his opening salvo days earlier at the Anglican Cathedral, had mocked the Catholics.

The Pope invites us to reunion with the church of which he is the head, but on what terms? . . . The Pope's proposal as to terms of reconciliation has the merit of perfect simplicity. Differences of doctrine or of ritual are not to be discussed; no council, no conference, not even a committee meeting is to be summoned, in order to ascertain what concessions can be made on either side. The one condition of reconciliation is absolute surrender on our part to the church as represented by the Pope.

Australia, land of immigrants, was chockablock with various rival Christian sects. Into this tinderbox of warring faiths Mark Twain hobbled unknowingly. His audience that first night in Melbourne was full of visiting religious luminaries. He created a brief cease-fire.

That gentleman in the higher stage-box, who laughed till his face was scarlet and banged the end of his walking-stick on the floor, was an archdeacon, and close to him was a rural dean, backed by a number of the minor clergy, all cackling like schoolboys. Beneath them sat an aged senator leaning over the rail of the dress circle, and swaying to and fro in most painful enjoyment. Down below a bookmaker led the laughter with an unceasing metallic roll. He was always in time for the good points, for he never stopped. The clergy was the most notable element in the assemblage. The Church of England Assembly had evidently adjourned to the theatre in a body, and the Catholic priests had come to take the first steps towards that union of which so much is heard. There were several Presbyterians laughing really hard. . . . One burly Wesleyan exploded at regular intervals in the gallery—in fact, white cravats and black coats were dotted all over the building. It is suspected that there were even some particular Baptists present, but on such a point one must speak with reserve. Everybody in Melbourne who could get into the building seemed to be there, and there never was an audience that seemed more convinced that it had got the worth of its money. For two hours there was a continuous roar of laughter, with the exception of a seven minutes interval, and one or two places where the humorous and the pathetic met, and people did not quite know whether to laugh or cry. (*Melbourne Argus*)

Twain stood on the verge of a week of big paydays, but his carbuncle started to flare up. He was following the advice of Dr. Wales of Elmira, but he could tell the carbuncle was worsening. Besides the pain, he didn't relish the thought of it oozing through his dress pants on stage. He seemed headed for more cancellations. Someone recommended a popular local surgeon.

Dr. Thomas Fitzgerald devised a treatment that dulled the pain (hypodermic opium) and slowed the infection to gain Twain five days of shows, and then he would operate. The author wrote in his notebook that the doctor took the problem "at a bad stage" and "made brisk work with it."

Besides the carbuncle, another issue threatened his tour through the British Empire: a now-forgotten political wrangle between the United States and Great Britain.

England was then engaged in a border dispute with Venezuela over that country's boundary with the British colony of Guyana. Rumors of gold strikes exacerbated the situation. Great Britain hinted at the use of force to assert its claims; President Grover Cleveland demanded the dispute go to arbitration and cited the Monroe Doctrine about European powers not asserting any new territorial claims in "our" Western Hemisphere. Twain, for his part, wanted no part of the tussle.

On Saturday night after the show, he went to an eighty-five-person dinner in his honor thrown at the Cathedral Hotel by the Yorick Club, an association of leading literary and government men.

After acknowledging his princely welcome was "thoroughly deserved," he veered to politics and kinship.

Let one of us be far away from his country, be it Australia, or England, or America, or Canada and let him see either the **English flag or the American flag,** and I defy him not to be stirred by it. [*Cheers.*] Oh yes blood is thicker than water, and we are all related. If we do jaw and bawl at each other now and again, that is no matter at all. [*Laughter.*]

We do belong together, and we are parts of a great whole, the greatest whole that this world has ever seen, a whole that, some day, will spread over this world, and, I hope, annihilate and abolish all other communities. [*Loud cheers and laughter.*] It will be the survival of the fittest. The English is the greatest race that ever was, [or] will prove itself so before it gets done and I would like to be there to see it. [*Laughter.*]

This rhetoric—though at times tongue in cheek—seems strange in the wake of Twain's bitterly anti-imperialist tone in his later writings and in his travel book on this journey. But Mark Twain was selling tickets.

At the Yorick gathering, Twain strayed quickly from politics and talked longingly about his younger days on the Mississippi and about the delusions of trying to relive the past.

You don't suppose that I should enjoy being a pilot on a Mississippi steamboat *now,* and be scared to death every time it came a fog. Fogs and dark nights had a charm for me. I didn't own any stock in that steamboat. And that is one of the very advantages of youth. You don't own any stock in anything. You have a good time, and all the grief and trouble is with the other fellows.

One could almost hear his regret about owning Paige typesetter stock. Twain spoke for a very long time. (Perhaps he still had some opium in his system.) He told an uncharacteristically meandering tale about Mississippi piloting that never got to the point . . . until finally he blamed his carbuncle and thanked the crowd. He stayed drinking and talking till 2 a.m.

On his third night in Melbourne, he rolled out the Australian poem again. Twain was always a great judge of whether *spoken* material worked or didn't. He had an uncanny ear for audience reaction, and his notebooks marvel at subtle shifts from town to town or night to night.

However, it didn't take a genius to know that the poem on Australian animals was a huge hit, but it does require some subtlety on the part of the modern American reader to perceive its charm after more than a century.

This segment of his act—more than most—demands imagining Twain's slow delivery, his American twang pronouncing primeval Australian words, the nineteenth-century culture that venerated rhyming poetry. He is puncturing the Victorian-era pretense that any mouthful of polysyllables recited in a stately voice merited respect.

Twain was a terrible poet and it served him well. Also, in an unprecedented literary move, he decided he would immortalize the duck-billed platypus.

He informed the audience that he felt inspired to write a poem, once every thirty years.

I felt that sort of feeling the night I landed here. The time was up. The inspiration was ripe. If I am going to write a book about this trip round the world, why a book of such a character ought to have some poetry in it. I felt that.

When I landed from that steamer at Sydney, why of course I looked around for a subject. First I thought there of Sydney Harbour, but then I thought—maybe—somebody had attended to it.

[*The line drew a big laugh in this rival colony of Victoria.*]

I was too late for that. Nine poets had died on that subject already.

Then I thought of the fauna of Australia—the remarkable examples that exist here and don't exist anywhere else in the world. They have been written about and written about in prose, but they ought to be written in poetry. I thought that would be a very good scheme. I made a list of them. . . . I have got emu, kangaroo, jackass, or laughing jackass, and the bell bird. And the lyre. I have been told that the lyre is a bird but I do not believe it. I have met plenty without feathers.

I've got the great auk and the she-oak, and the ornithorhynchus [*Latin name for platypus*]. I think that is a daisy of a name. If I had a child I would christen it Ornithorynchus. . . .

And I also have a list of the extinct ones—the wonderful extinct ones like the dodo, the boomerang, and the great moa and the larrikin [*actually, Australian slang for a thug or hooligan; newspapers said the "larrikin" line played well in the cheap seats in the upper balcony*].

I can say now that the most difficult thing in the world to do is to write poetry when you don't know how. You see it is the rhymes that make the trouble. For if you get the sense right, why then there is no word that will rhyme with it. If your rhymes rhyme, then there is no sense in it. I will begin.

Land of the ornithorhynchus,

Of course, no one in the audience expected their homeland to be described as "land of the ornithorhynchus," that is, land of the duck-billed clawed-foot, beaver-tailed, egg-laying amphibious platypus; literally neither fish nor fowl.

He waited for the laughter to die down.

Land of the ornithorhynchus,
Land of the kangaroo,

And there you are. You see I am right against, a dead wall. You can
see there is nothing in the world that will rhyme with ornithorhynchus. Kangaroo? nothing rhymes with kangaroo.

[*Then Twain seemed to get an inspiration.*]

Land of the ornithorhynchus,
Land of the kangaroo
Old ties of heredity link us . . .

[*But he was still stumped by "kangaroo."*]

Of course, you can slyly let it off without rhyme, but it would fail.
I gave that up. I'll let it out by contract. I thought I would offer
a prize for it—chromos [*chromolithographs, i.e., photos/illustra-
tions*], or something like that. I started another way:

Land of the fur-tailed rabbit,
Land of the boomerang.

[*On some nights, he changed it to "Land of the fruitful rabbit." Australia's wild rabbit population had reached plague proportions of several
hundred million by 1895.*]

There it is the same thing. You can't find a rhyme for rabbit and
another rhyme for boomerang. Boomerang don't rhyme with
anything but boomerang. I saw the difficulty. You must start on a
simple basis.

Come forth from thy oozy couch,
Oh ornithorhynchus dear,
And greet with a cordial cheer
The stranger that longs to hear
From thy own, own lips the "tail" of thy origin all unknown,

Thy misplaced bone where flesh should be, and flesh where should
be bone.

Twain probably doled out those lines above one by one with some
commentary; then he eventually stumbled his way to reciting several
more ridiculous stanzas before ultimately surrendering.

You see I have got that animal wrong. He has got a beaver-
trowelled tail, but it is on the other end of him. I cannot help that.
The animal is not made right, and he must be made to fit. The creature has no teeth, but I cannot help that. I have got to rhyme, and
the animal has got to have teeth. . . . That animal must do his share
in this poem. . . . I cannot arrange the poetry and the animal too.

The banter more than the poem sent the audience into hysterics. As
one newspaper put it, "[We] could get no more of the poem, for the
audience would not stop laughing." No Australian paper succeeded in
capturing his patter regarding the later stanzas.

An Australian naturalist later gave Twain a stuffed platypus, an *Ornithorhynchus paradoxus,* and Mrs. Clemens called it his favorite present from the entire trip. The author sometimes conspicuously carried it
under his arm aboard ferryboats.

Performing in Australia was going astoundingly well, financially. On
Friday, October 3, Twain sent £437 home to H.H. Rogers through T. A.
Dibbs, Commercial Banking, of Sydney. That represented profit—
beyond theater and agent fees, and travel expenses. Two days later he
would receive another £252 from Smythe. At an 1895 exchange rate of
five American dollars to one British pound, that meant he had achieved
$3,445 profit. At least it marked a start to paying off the $60,000 debt,
unlike the American box office receipts, which had apparently gone to
travel expenses and the expensive steamship tickets.

Livy would later praise Australia as a very lucrative destination, but
she wished the place had another handful of conveniently located, large
cities.

When R. S. Smythe hastily added that fifth show for Friday night,
somehow an "idiotic" advertising mix-up occurred, stating that Twain
would perform the lineup of two *different* shows. Some came expecting

the second night's repertoire; others the third. Twain decided the only honorable thing to do would be to perform it all. Despite his carbuncle flaring, he raced through ten items in one and three quarter hours that would normally have taken at least two and a half. This might mark the only performance of the trip—maybe of his life—in which Twain talked fast. "Got through this prodigious bill," wrote Twain in his notebook. "It was a sweater."

The following day, Dr. Fitzgerald "froze" and then "lanced this damned carbuncle." The doctor accompanied it with another opium injection. Twain soon after made some notes that perhaps seem a bit opium loopy.

It is the loftiest of all human vocations—medicine & surgery.
Relief from physical pain, physical distress. Next comes the pulpit,
which solaces mental distress, soothes the sorrows of the soul.
These two are the great professions, the noble professions. The
gap between them & the rest is wide—an abyss.

Given Twain's repeated disappointment with doctors and his skeptical views on organized religion, he seemed to be in an exceptionally generous mood. Twain was indeed deeply grateful to Dr. Fitzgerald, especially because the surgeon explained to him and Livy how to treat future carbuncles and saved Twain from repeating the months-long misery.

Livy and Clara answered the mail and found time to attend teas in their honor as well as going to Marvelous Melbourne's Mayor's Ball at Town Hall, illuminated by hundreds of colored electric bulbs. Livy paid several calls and in the process, picked up a bit of "Strine"—that is, Australian pronunciations. She shared them with her sister. The butler had told her: "The Lidy will be down in a minute. Would you like to read the piper till she comes? It is on the tible with the kike."

Twain, meanwhile, was stuck yet again in bed, staring at the walls, reading, and smoking. He took the opportunity to fill his notebook with some musings on Australia, topics that could come in handy for his travel book.

Twain reminded himself to find a "good authority" who stated that some convicts became wealthy and rose to social prominence. He hoped that the felons left descendants who were not ashamed of their forefathers' criminal past.

One is not required to be proud of his ancestor's crime, but only proud that he rose above it & attained to honor & respect in *spite* of it. It is different from dukedoms reared upon the frailty of an ancestress. In that case, one's pride is strictly confined to the woman's sin itself, that being the only merit in the matter.

Unlike his wife, Mark Twain was profoundly unimpressed by noble titles.

He often made it a habit *not* to give royalty their due. A few years later, when the quirky, prestigious Savage Club of London made Twain an honorary member, he was informed that in the club's forty-year existence, they had conveyed that honor to only four men: "Stanley of Africa, Nansen of the North Pole, the Prince of Wales, & you."

He was asked: "Now what do you think of that?" And he replied: "Well, it must make the Prince feel pretty fine."

Several times during this trip, reporters sought his opinion on the recent news that American heiress Consuelo Vanderbilt would be marrying Charles Spencer Churchill, ninth Duke of Marlborough, in November, in exchange for a tidy payoff, rumored as high as $10 million.

Twain found the trend appalling. "These wretched American women, who buy titles (and noble tramps) with their money—mongrel breeders," Twain called them back in 1889 in his notebook. "[They] should have a bench show of their children." (A "bench show" is a dog show competition, usually for small dogs.)

Twain always exhibited an irreverent American casualness around royalty, which often set Livy a-flutter as she tried to teach him the rules of etiquette for when to bow, when to shake hands, when to speak.

Twain's bedside musings also drifted to Australia's passion for horse racing. He noted that the upcoming Melbourne Cup on November 5 would rank as the top social event of the year. "The ladies make it a grand display of dressing. Their 'cup gowns' call for their thought & invention & lots of their money."

By contrast, he also was amazed at the piousness of the Australian colonies, packed with churches of various denominations and willing to sacrifice their pleasures on Sunday, their only day off. He noted that newspapers were forbidden to publish Sunday editions and that streetcars didn't run before noon on Sunday. Most colonies forbade entertainments on Sundays, such as a Twain performance or the circus or plays; many communities ordered saloons closed. He jotted down that he thought the pulpit feared the competition.

Now Twain tried to create a crisp maxim to capture Australia. "When the people get to be as good as this, no amount of horse-racing can damn them." He later remodeled it: "The two Australian passions are horse-racing & keeping the Sabbath."

Twain was also surprised to learn that Australians used the word *native* to mean a "white person born in Australia," while they use *aboriginal* or *blackfellow* to characterize the tribal people living there. Twain had not seen a single dark-skinned aboriginal during his three-week stay. (Estimates vary but the aboriginal population had dropped to less than 100,000 by 1895.)

On Friday, October 11, Twain and company boarded the 4:20 p.m. train for the seventeen-hour journey west from Melbourne to Adelaide, the "White City" capital of South Australia, ringed by mountains. Twain observed that this colony would be more appropriately named "Middle Australia," since it extended 2,000 miles from southern to northern coast. (The "Northern Territory" would be created in 1911.)

The American consul, C. A. Murphy, prepared a special welcome to give them the best possible view when entering the city; the family left the train at Aldgate and rode the last twelve miles in the consul's open carriage.

> It was an excursion of an hour or two, and the charm of it could not be overstated, I think. The road wound around gaps and gorges, and offered all varieties of scenery and prospect— mountains, crags, country homes, gardens, forests—color, color, color everywhere, and the air fine and fresh, the skies blue, and not a shred of cloud to mar the downpour of the brilliant sunshine. And finally the mountain gateway opened, and the immense plain lay spread out below and stretching away into dim distances on every hand, soft and delicate and dainty and beautiful. On its near edge reposed the city.

Twain stayed at the city's best, the South Australian Club Hotel, which had just completed an ambitious two-year renovation. Swinging stained-glass doors under a cast-iron archway led into a spacious flower-strewn lobby. Electric lighting had been installed throughout, with hot and cold running water and elegant tiled bathrooms and new discreet servant staircases.

Outside, old-fashioned horse trams carried passengers up and down the grid of streets. The River Torrens split the city, with residential buildings to the north and commercial to the south.

On opening night, the inhabitants of Adelaide crushed into the Theatre Royale, with an overflow crowd of forty seated in chairs in a semicircle on the back of the stage.

"When the curtain rose upon him . . . the whole audience greeted him with waving handkerchiefs, hand-claps, stomping and lusty cheers." Twain—described as that "grey-haired remarkable man whose books are read and sayings quoted wherever the English language is spoken"—bowed several times. He delivered his standard first night. Like so many others, the reviewer at the *South Australian Register* singled out that irresistible line about "weather too rainy for school and just rainy enough to go fishing."

The scribe concluded, somewhat astonished: "No other man could compel the attention of a restless Adelaide audience for two hours" with such a slow delivery.

Twain sold out three performances, causing agent Smythe to add a fourth.

Overall, attendance Down Under was so brisk that agent Smythe decided to board a boat from Adelaide back to Melbourne to line up three more shows in that "Marvelous" region. (He handed guide/chaperone duties to his dapper thirty-year-old son, Carlyle.)

––––––––

Twain finished up in Adelaide and began a nine-day, seven-performance tour of five country towns—Horsham, Stawell, Ballarat, Bendigo, Maryborough—all commercial hubs. And he now felt well enough and comfortable enough with his performance to sightsee. Twain was eager to get outside and learn firsthand about Australia's two key industries: mining and sheep.

The family took the 4:30 p.m. train Wednesday, October 16, to Horsham, population 3,000, the smallest town he would visit.

Smythe—who didn't like to waste his own time or his clients'—had initially sniggered at inconvenient picayune Horsham. When contacted, he didn't want to book it; he then demanded a guarantee of £35 ($175; $5,250 today). A local branch of the Mechanics Institute (a British workingman's adult education society) tapped shoulders, queried merchants and found enough people willing to commit to tickets. The Clemens family arrived at 3 a.m. on October 17 and was greeted by the smiling secretary of the Mechanics Institute and his friend, who together promised to give the family a tour later during daylight hours.

That afternoon, they took the Clemenses in an open wagon out eight miles along a dirt road to the local agricultural college. The school taught forty city-born students, who worked in the fields one day and in the classroom the next.

> We saw the sophomore class in sheep-shearing shear a dozen sheep. They did it by hand, not with the machine. The sheep was seized and flung down on his side and held there; and the students took off his coat with great celerity and adroitness.

Twain noted that when the students accidentally cut the sheep, they would apply some tar on the end of a stick to help the wounds heal and keep off the flies. He also observed that the sheared fleece when patted flat looked as big as a bedspread. "The coat of wool was unbelievably thick," wrote Twain. "Before the shearing the sheep looked like the fat woman in the circus; after it, he looked like a bench."

Twain learned about many components of the industry, from lamb to slaughter. Each sheep might require up to five acres to graze, and the immense unpopulated lands supplied that. Itinerant sheep shearers, almost like American cowboys, traveled on horseback to far-distant ranches to collect £1 ($5) per hundred sheep sheared. They bunked under the stars, heated coffee in a billycan, and blew their wages at the nearest public house (saloon). He had also toured a refrigeration plant in Sydney where he learned that this New South Wales company could freeze for transport 1,000 sheep carcasses a day; he would later go to the hectic auctions at the wool market in Melbourne. "Bidders like barking dogs—Babel-racket-gesticulation-nobody calm but the President. Everybody yelps, yaps, barks, at once, & the Pres[iden]t decides which barked first—no appeal."

That night at Horsham, the overflowing working-class crowd at

Mechanics Hall who had scraped together a guarantee to bring the great foreign humorist to their little town exploded with laughter from the first moment of Twain's sheepish amble onto the stage.

"I think papa never talked to a more enthusiastic audience than that night," Livy wrote back to daughter Susy in Elmira. "They were entirely uproarious, taking a point almost before he had reached it."

Smythe told her that many had trekked great distances to attend, with one man traveling seventy-five miles and heading back the same night. The house was so "jolly" that she and Clara found themselves laughing at the unsophisticated audience's extreme fits of joy. "A young fellow who sat next to me (he brought Clara a lovely bunch of roses next day) began to pound his sides as if troubled with stitches in them and turning to me said, 'Well, if it is all as funny as this I shall die.'"

After the show, a dozen people came to the hotel, had a few drinks with Twain, and chatted for a half hour or so. Some of them then left to ride their horses home sixteen miles by lantern light in the dark, which would take a couple hours.

"And so it goes, it is constant unceasing adulation of papa," summed up Livy for her two daughters in Elmira. "They know his work so well out here, in fact they seem to know most of it by heart."

In the next stop, Stawell, Clara had an unlikely misadventure. She took a walk by herself in the countryside and noticed a sheep lying on its side, in pain, almost certainly dying. She decided she would do the merciful thing and put it out of its misery.

Clara belonged to the Society for the Prevention of Cruelty to Animals, and she had once forced a Parisian cab driver to stop using his whip; the horse then moved so slowly that her father had jumped out two blocks from the destination, shouting: "I wouldn't go to Hell at such a pace."

She returned to Horsham to find a drugstore to buy some ether. On her way back to the sheep, she encountered a man on horseback who happened to be the owner of the herd. He offered to help. They approached the sheep; he examined it and started laughing. He said the sheep, with a very full wool fleece at that time of year, had merely fallen over and was incapable of standing. "[The owner] gracefully raised the animal to its feet, and it toddled off, contented with the world."

The most unlikely part of that story is that beautiful twenty-one-year-old Clara was allowed to wander off alone in rural Australia. Mr. and

Mrs. Clemens were notoriously protective parents. Clara included the story thirty-five years later in her memoir, probably upholding a Clemens family tradition about facts and punch lines.

The family next traveled by train through rolling greenery to a place that seemed almost out of Twain's youth: a mining mecca called Ballarat where the first big gold strike in Australia occurred back in August 25, 1851.

Ballarat, then a cathedral city of 40,000 inhabitants, was famed for gold nuggets, including one that weighed 160 pounds. Twain marveled over the instant fortunes, but he also saw on arrival many graybeards who clearly hadn't struck it rich, not "young and gay" anymore but "patriarchal and grave."

Twain knew firsthand of the elusiveness of mining wealth, of the fevered delusional hopes and also of the straining hard work. Samuel Clemens, age twenty-five and adrift in 1861, had followed his brother to Nevada, where Orion was secretary to the territorial governor. Carson City shriveled to a tumbleweed town after the legislature closed its session. Nearby Gold Hill was prospering, and feverish accounts dubbed Humboldt County the next bonanza for miners.

"By and by I was smitten with the silver fever," he wrote in his mock travel memoir, *Roughing It*.

> "Prospecting parties" were leaving for the mountains every day, and discovering and taking possession of rich silver-bearing lodes and ledges of quartz. . . . Go where you would, you heard nothing else, from morning till far into the night. Tom So-and-So had sold out of the "Amanda Smith" for $40,000—hadn't a cent when he "took up" the ledge six months ago. John Jones had sold half his interest in the "Bald Eagle and Mary Ann" for $65,000, gold coin, and gone to the States for his family. [*Nevada was then a territory.*]
>
> I would have been more or less than human if I had not gone mad like the rest. Cart-loads of solid silver bricks, as large as pigs of lead, were arriving from the mills every day, and such sights as that gave substance to the wild talk about me. I succumbed and grew as frenzied as the craziest.

So, Sam Clemens, who didn't adopt the name "Mark Twain" until 1863, and three companions headed out in December 1861 to trek 175 miles in a creaky wagon with two creakier horses toting a ton of mining supplies.

> I confess, without shame, that I expected to find masses of silver
> lying all about the ground. I expected to see it glittering in the sun
> on the mountain summits. . . . My fancy was already busy with
> plans for spending this money.

They filed claim for a patch of solid rock and dubbed it "Monarch of the Mountains." They blasted it with dynamite but progressed only twelve feet downward in a week when Clemens quit for the first time. He rejoined when they decided to try to dig a tunnel inward; he resigned again when they took another week to clear three feet and had 900 more feet to go. He decided it was wiser to buy and sell other people's mining deeds. He later claimed that he had accidentally let his claim lapse on one of the biggest strikes in Nevada, but no one was buying that, either.

Twain could talk the miner's talk in Ballarat, but unfortunately he couldn't get out and walk the miner's walk. He was invited several times to tour the mines but was stuck in bed because yet another carbuncle was flaring, his third. During yet another bed interview in which he was asked his opinion of regions such as Ballarat which he had not seen, he turned to his increasingly useful non-answer.

> No, I've been down on the blankets pretty well ever since I
> arrived, and have done little else—outside lecturing—but study
> wallpapers. Every kind of wallpaper you possess in Australia has
> come under my purview, and if I fail as a lecturer, I shall write a
> book on Australian wallpapers, for I don't intend to be swindled
> out of everything by a carbuncle.

In Ballarat, the first batch of letters for them from America caught up with the travelers. Livy received five letters, and the dates on them—two months prior in August—reinforced for her the "heartbreakingly long" distance separating her from her daughters.

The Clemenses had expected Robert Smythe to rejoin them here, but he did not. His son Carlyle, who explained his father's absence, would have to run the show.

R. S. Smythe had boarded the RMS *Cuzco* in Adelaide and arrived in

Melbourne harbor three days later. A quarantine doctor/health official had boarded at 5 p.m. and by 6 p.m. had diagnosed one crew member with smallpox. Almost all the Melbourne passengers, at least 160, disembarked for the quarantine station, but Smythe, being the veteran traveler, decided to gamble that the sailor actually had chicken pox and that doctors in Sydney, the next stop, would free the ship. He gambled and lost. The one case of smallpox turned to a half dozen by the time the *Cuzco* reached Sydney, and the "much-traveled" Smythe was looking at two weeks of quarantine, far away from his famous client.

Young Carlyle added a detail that Twain much appreciated. One passenger had indeed succeeded in leaving the *Cuzco* in Melbourne: a bride set to wed in two days. Luckily for her, she had already been vaccinated. "They will fumigate her & her trousseau to-day [&] set her ashore," he wrote in his notebook.

Having Carlyle instead of his father turned out just fine for Twain. Carlyle was born in the Himalayas when his agent father was taking around his wife, a popular and pregnant Melbourne soprano. Carlyle was handsome, literate, intelligent, and, best of all, he agreed to play pool with Twain at all hours, whenever possible. The son would remain with them for almost a year, taking them on to India and South Africa and even accompanying them to England. Clara would later judge him "a most attractive companion" in a letter to Major Pond's young wife and note: "Everything runs smoothly & he takes any amount of trouble to make us comfortable."

Twain and young Carlyle would form a bond, and the agent-in-training, a former writer himself, clearly understood Twain. He called him a "sedate savant who has been seduced from the paths of high seriousness by a fatal sense of the ridiculous."

They boarded for Bendigo, but Twain's trip to the next mining town, just seventy-five miles away, was marred by delayed railroad connections and took nine hours, including three hours waiting at Castlemaine.

Upon arrival, however, he was impressed that Bendigo—turning out 200,000 ounces of gold a year—seemed to be thriving even more than famed Ballarat, boasting 144 square miles of mining operations, five parks, seven auditoriums, nineteen churches, an electric trolley, electric street lights. Population: 27,500.

But, apparently, the prosperity of the mines, as expressed in beautiful civic monuments and buildings, didn't trickle down to the miners. Twain encountered his first half-full house, and local residents complained about high ticket prices even though Smythe was charging 20% less than in the major cities.

He might not have been helped by a column, called "Twain's Poverty," on page 2 of the *Bendigo Advertiser*.

If Mr. Clemens had been content with his profits as one of the most successful authors of the world, he might have been comparatively speaking, a rich man. But he dabbled in publishing, and seems, like a much greater man—the immortal Sir Walter [Scott]—to be paying the penalty for it in his declining years.

Sir Walter Scott (1771–1832), author of *Ivanhoe* and other historical novels, owned the publishing house Ballantyne, which failed during a financial crisis in 1825; Scott refused to declare bankruptcy, placed his home and income in trust for his creditors, and spent the last seven years of his life grinding out books to repay his debts. (Twain believed the man literally wrote himself to death.) Scott refused any charity, including from the king of England. His novels continued to sell posthumously, and soon after his death, his debts were paid.

Op-ed writers and journalists in both the British Empire and America would increasingly—and somewhat inaccurately—draw parallels between the two embattled authors, Sir Walter and Mr. Samuel L. Clemens.

A half-full house was not good. Carlyle Smythe, with his father in quarantine, lowered the ticket prices another 25% for the second night at Bendigo and came within a few chairs of selling out the Royal Princess Theatre.

Twain finished the country town circuit with a stop in Maryborough and headed back by rail to Melbourne to squeeze in three more performances before his next major excursion, to New Zealand. The tight schedule led the nearly sixty-year-old author with a brewing carbuncle to spend a very hectic Saturday, October 26, 1895, a day that reveals his will and energy.

He and the entourage rose in the dark to board the 5 a.m. train from Maryborough to Melbourne. He battled a conductor who wanted to throw them off the train for having the wrong tickets. Their tickets, bought in Sydney, covered 1,500 miles or so of track but did not include

12 miles of a branch railroad. The conductor informed them he could not sell tickets, which could be purchased only in stations.

> The RR is the only unAmerican [*later crossed out*] & thoroughly
> European thing here. That is, they build fine stations (the one at
> Maryborough with its dumb clock . . .) & then have all the idiotic
> European RR system in perfection: slow trains, no drinking water,
> no sanitary arrangements . . . the jackass system.

Carlyle Smythe interceded and somehow fixed the ticket problem. They arrived in Melbourne, after nine hours, in time for Twain to rush by carriage to Athenaeum Hall to give a "farewell" 3 p.m. matinee. Large crowds, large ovations, good payday. Soon afterward, he and his classical music–loving wife and daughter attended a piano recital by a well-known Russian-British piano prodigy, sixteen-year-old Mark Hambourg, a favorite of Paderewski. When Twain entered Town Hall, loud cheers erupted, which he acknowledged with a bow. Hambourg played works of Liszt, Chopin, Schubert and others, but Twain ducked out at intermission.

He hobbled a few blocks away to the Cathedral Hotel on Swanston Street, where the Australian Institute of Journalists was honoring him with a "Smoke Night" dinner. One of the hosts gave him a basket of flowers from his own garden to deliver to Mrs. Clemens and Clara. This gave Twain a theme.

> We have come a long distance, which at first it was my purpose
> to traverse alone. But I always have many purposes which fail, for
> reasons which those who are married among you will understand.
> I am technically "boss" of the family which I am carrying along—
> (laughter)—but I am grateful to know that it is only technically—
> that the real authority rests on the other side of the house.
>   It is placed there by a beneficent Providence, who foresaw
> before I was born, or if he did not, he has found out since, that I
> am not in any way qualified to travel alone. And so, it has been my
> good fortune to be furnished with a wife who is always capable,
> both by brain and by heart, to make up all shortcomings, which
> exist in me. She has brought me through for twenty-five years
> successfully.

Twain's travel incompetence was a running joke in the family, but so was his inability to handle mundane tasks. "He has the mind of an author exactly," wrote Susy at age thirteen in her biography of him. "Some of the simplest things he can't understand."

The Australian Institute voted him an honorary member. He concluded his long day of train travel, lecture, music recital, dinner by staying past midnight, drinking and chatting.

Many of the journalists came away with the impression that Twain would rather chum around with fellow newspapermen and eat street food such as "hot saveloys" [*i.e., frankfurters*] at the curb than dine on silver plates.

Twain certainly had that common-man side, but his highbrow family often didn't share those tastes. The Twain clan spent the following day and night at the newly built mansion of one of the "squatters" (i.e., sheep ranchers), John Wagner, in Malvern, east of Melbourne. Livy, with her jeweler's eye, assessed the furnishings and layout in a letter to her sister.

> He is a very wealthy man with this superb house looking on a most
> beautiful view. We had a very large bedroom, with six windows in
> it, three of them leading onto a very extensive porch. Our bedroom
> was almost thirty feet square—perhaps a little more. Out of it was
> a dressing room with a bed in it. So when we took our afternoon
> naps, Mr. Clemens took the dressing room and I the big room.

Twain returned the hospitality by doing a favor. He wrote a letter of recommendation to Henry Harper, his publisher, for Wagner's son. He mentioned he was "snatching a visit" at the "palatial" home of John H. Wagner, a Canadian who had spent forty years in Australia with his American wife from Stonington, Connecticut. He said their son was pitching an illustrated article on Samoa to *Century* magazine. "He seems determined to earn his own living, in literature, but if *I* lived in this palace & had a father equipped with 100,000 sheep & 500,000 acre of pasture land, damned if *I* would."

(Wagner's article, "Lotus-Land of the Pacific," would eventually run in *Harper's* in September 1897.)

Mr. Wagner personally drove the family back to Melbourne in his carriage on Monday. That afternoon, Twain performed in nearby Geelong, and was rewarded with his worst reviews of the trip. Apparently, his "Terrors of the German Language" offended some Teutonic types in the audience. (Geelong had a large, venerable Germantown.) The critics contended that Twain's "alleged complexities of gender in the German language . . . [were] based upon an entirely erroneous hypothesis." Twain spun out his entire tale from the fact that the German noun for *fishwife* was not feminine. He had explained earlier in *A Tramp Abroad* about male and female nouns: "In German, a young lady has no sex, while a turnip has. Think what overwrought reverence that shows for the turnip, and what callous disrespect for the girl." The piqued critics added they didn't find his Australian poem amusing either.

Twain squeezed in yet one more payday via an appearance in nearby Prahran, then headed with his family and Carlyle Smythe to catch a boat to New Zealand on October 31. New friends in Melbourne begged the Clemens clan to stay five more days and wait for the Melbourne Cup—the big horse race, the sprawling party—which was falling on Guy Fawkes Night, making it a double celebration with plenty of fireworks. But they passed. "Too bad," wrote Twain with genuine regret in his notebook. Livy: "We dislike extra much coming away from Melbourne." Clara in a letter called it an "eternal life of goodbyes."

They were heading off to yet another remote part of the vast British Empire. Despite the unamused Germans, Twain was thriving. What had started for him as a desperate lunge for money was starting to seem magically transformed into a victory lap for the "humorist of the century."

CHAPTER 14

Maoriland

T wain, who had gotten lost strolling out to Fort Missoula, glanced at a map and expected to reach New Zealand—quickly.

All people think that New Zealand is close to Australia or Asia, or somewhere, and that you cross to it on a bridge. But that is not so. It is not close to anything, but lies by itself, out in the water. It is nearest to Australia, but still not near. The gap between is very wide. It will be a surprise to the reader, as it was to me, to learn that the distance from Australia to New Zealand is really twelve or thirteen hundred miles, and that there is no bridge.

Twain would be taking a four-day voyage across the Tasman Sea; once there, he would perform twenty times over five weeks. The island colony lay so far off the beaten track, so close to nowhere, that it didn't lure many top-notch performers. That year's bright lights included General William Booth, saving souls for the Salvation Army, violin-playing Reverend Haweis, several drama troops, and Irish Home Rule advocate (i.e., freedom fighter) Michael Davitt, who just happened to be sailing on the SS *Mararoa* with Twain.

The pair struck up a brief friendship, and Davitt would follow a similar speaking route to Twain's. Davitt, forty-nine years old, tall, lean, thinning hair, one-armed from a childhood work accident, had proved himself a charismatic speaker on the need to break up the gargantuan estates owned in Ireland by a few dozen absentee aristocrat landlords. He had served seven years in an English prison for what he deemed a trumped-up charge of running weapons to Ireland and had recently been elected to Parliament but was prevented from serving because of his convict status. He was now lecturing around the Empire to tell everyone of the daily injustices inflicted upon the Irish and also to pay his legal bills to continue his fight for reinstatement. (He would become a member of Parliament.) Davitt found Twain warm and accessible, and garrulous with a crowd.

> No celebrity can be more readily approached than Mark Twain. . . . The kindliest of smiles and of laughing good-natured grey eyes, make you immediately welcome. You are made to feel at once that you are in presence of a man whom fame or fortune could not deprive of his natural disposition to make you laugh away the worries and troubles of the moment. He was, needless to say, a favourite with everybody on board.

Davitt recounted that Twain told several stories in the ship's smoke-room. He relayed a tale about a customs-house prank.

Twain had crossed the Atlantic from Liverpool, with a handful of American friends. The "boys," as he styled them, had slipped dozens of expensive cigars into Twain's suitcases, figuring it would look like Twain was smuggling and that he'd have to pay import duty on them.

> The [boys] all crowded round [me] when the Customs officer came along. They counted upon [me] being compelled to pay up for the cargo. They stood round when the critical moment arrived, and were ready to explode with laughter at my expense.
> This is how it ended;—
> The Customs officer: "Your name, please?"
> "Mr. Clemens."
> "Are you Mark Twain?"
> "Yes."
> "Then pass on."
> So, I was neither asked to pay nor to lie, and I had all the cigars to myself, for you may be sure I did not deliver any of them to those who tried to play that little game upon me.

The *Mararoa* was slated to make a midway stop in Hobart, Tasmania. On November 2, Saturday morning, just before dawn, the ship curled around the notorious prison peninsula of Port Arthur and reached gorgeous Hobart Harbor. The rising sun soon illuminated the towering rocky peak of Mount Wellington hovering above the sloping, lush greenery and numerous little inlets. Twain, who had read the history of the harsh penal colony, found the beauty incongruous, almost jarring.

Twain remained tight-lipped in public during this trip on controversial anti-British topics but he would later write of the decimation of the indigenous peoples. "And it was in this paradise that the yellow-liveried convicts were landed, and the Corps-bandits [*i.e., guards*] quartered, and the wanton slaughter of the kangaroo-chasing black innocents [*i.e., Tasmanians*] consummated . . . in the brutish old time. It was all out of keeping with the place, a sort of bringing of heaven and hell together." Twain would write of the fast decline of the Tasmanians, who had numbered 10,000 or so when the British arrived. "The Natives were not used to clothes, and houses, and regular hours, and church, and school, and Sunday-school, and work, and the other misplaced persecutions of civilization, and they pined for their lost home and their wild free life." The last native Tasmanian, a woman, died in 1876.

At 7 a.m., a local young man named Dobson boarded the *Mararoa* to invite the Clemenses to breakfast. The Dobsons, one of the elite families of Hobart, were friends of the Days, who were then renting Twain's Hartford home.

The Dobsons eagerly greeted the Clemens family, served them a fine meal, and offered to take them anywhere for the remaining five hours before the *Mararoa* sailed. Livy and Clara chose beauty, a carriage ride to the hillside summer bungalows; Twain—who sometimes showed a near-ghoulish fascination for details of the suffering of slaves and prisoners—chose to seek a "glimpse of any convicts that might still remain."

Twain headed off in the carriage with the Dobsons, that is, Mr. Dobson, a barrister and former premier, and his brother, currently chief justice. They took Twain's request to see a living convict literally and drove him to the "Refuge for the Indigent" that housed more than 200 male and female ex-convicts, many quite old. With his sixtieth birthday less than a month away, he found the prospect of a wrinkly joyless long life more disturbing than inspiring. He considered the place *too* healthy.

The Dobsons also took Twain to meet Sir James Agnew, the wizened eighty-year-old former surgeon for the nearby convict station of Norfolk Island. Dr. Agnew confirmed that some prisoners indeed received the horrific punishment of 300 lashes—one man for the crime of stealing silver spoons. The doctor, who was required to attend, had "seen men's backs flogged to a bloody pulp; [had] seen a man receive 150 lashes without crying out—then receive 150 more."

Twain learned from Dr. Agnew that prisoners used to put a pebble or hunk of lead between their teeth so they would not cry out; and those who made it through silently were called "pebbles," a term of high praise from fellow convicts.

Someone had suggested that Twain read *For the Term of His Natural Life* by Marcus Clarke. Twain read it and handed it to Clara. (They would also see the stage version.) The historical novel—despite fanciful plot twists about bastard stepbrothers and inheritances—graphically depicts some of the cruelest aspects of the convict life: "transportation" sentences for trivial crimes, vicious guards, horrific floggings, cannibalism during a desperate escape.

Dr. Agnew, also an ex-premier, and ex-premier Dobson both claimed that Clarke exaggerated, chose a handful of extreme cases, and tried to palm them off as the rule. Twain filled his notebook with what he considered authenticated atrocities. "Three [convicts]—one killed another by lot—the third was witness. This to get themselves hanged." And he later wrote:

Convicts were "assigned" to Tom Dick & Harry to work [*that is, to various wealthy farmers and ranchers*]. Story of one who, for a fault, was made to walk 14 miles & get an official flogging, then walk back with his torn back; other assignees warned that if they washed his wounds or succored him in any way they would get the like.

These stories clearly reminded him of Southern slavery. Mrs. Dobson gave Twain a very rusted leg iron found in the bushes, probably tossed by some prisoner during an escape attempt.

When Twain reboarded the *Mararoa* just around 1 p.m., he chatted with Davitt as the ship sailed out of the winding harbor "past dreadful Port Arthur," which Twain described as "bush-covered hills & table lands—foodless—[a] peninsula joined by a low neck to the mainland—used to keep dogs & officers here to catch escaping convicts."

Seeing the actual peninsula, a kind of massive natural prison, made the writer feel that anyone sentenced to this place ought to have had the option of being hanged.

Davitt later wrote that Twain told him he deemed meeting the old scarred ex-convicts "one of the most interesting but saddening experiences of his life." Twain recounted to him how some high-ranking gentlemen had denied the accuracy of Marcus Clarke's book, but he told Davitt he believed the "fiendish cruelties" had indeed occurred. The Irish lecturer added that Twain "grew indignant at the thought of doctors having looked on and sanctioned the savage punishments which could leave such evidence of their force and ferocity after so many years."

The *Mararoa* steamed toward New Zealand. When Livy and Clara went to their stateroom, they were surprised to discover that the Dobsons and others had filled it with fresh-cut flowers,

A thousand miles across the choppy Tasman Sea remained. "Huge waves . . . come rolling up from the Lord knows where and lift the vessel like a cork on their crests," wrote Davitt in his book. Livy recorded a "great deal of creaking" in the ship's bones that night.

On November 5, the *Mararoa* reached Bluff, an unimpressive one-street town at the base of a 500-foot hill that needed to be climbed to catch the train to the main towns of the South Island. (The two main islands take up about 100,000 square miles, about the size of the state of Colorado.)

New Zealand in 1895 was a shocking place. *Women* could vote. (American women wouldn't win the vote until 1920; French women till 1944; Saudi Arabian women until 2015.) New Zealand, followed by Australia, stands first in the modern world.

The social customs of the place immediately set travelers a bit off kilter. Although it was a British colony, no titled aristocrats tormented their inferiors; in fact, almost no upper class existed at all. Vast waves of more or less prosperous middle-class ranchers and merchants thrived, even worked in the fields side by side with laborers who were protected by a slew of labor laws that limited workdays and boosted wages. Michael Davitt, who crusaded for Irish land reform, found New Zealand a fine relocation destination for the workingmen of England, Ireland and Europe.

Lush green open spaces still dominated; many regions resembled Switzerland. The population of 750,000 in all of New Zealand was less than the combined tally of Melbourne and Sydney.

The place evoked a rough-around-the-edges irreverence, a feisty, independent streak. Twain would encounter more hecklers here than anywhere else.

The violin-playing lecturer Reverend Haweis, who had visited six months earlier, found many New Zealand colonists more interested in practical skills such as wool-shearing techniques than in highbrow culture. One traveling European drama troupe complained that it couldn't survive there without a "whistling woman, prize comic or acrobat." The reverend himself found audiences preferred performers playing "bones and banjo" to his classical repertoire; crowds were more provincial and less polite than in Europe.

New Zealand, unlike parts of Australia, hadn't started as a penal colony; it had followed the more traditional pattern of befriending the dark-skinned locals and then battling them. The Maori proved worthy adversaries during a quarter century of fierce conflict; the victorious whites would eventually borrow place-names from the conquered and enshrine their artifacts in museums. The living, breathing Maori of 1895, however, were mostly being squeezed onto ever-shrinking properties to the north.

Twain and his family and Michael Davitt rode up the hill from Bluff and boarded the train toward Invercargill and Dunedin. Davitt immediately recalled the green lushness of County Cork, Ireland, in the rolling hills of this part of South Island; only the far-off mountains were taller than their Irish counterparts; he saw similar-to-home blackbirds and hedgerows of hawthorns and of furze bushes. Twain and Davitt would perform a few days apart in many New Zealand towns over the next month.

The train passed a handful of "neat comfortable" towns; they then crossed a river of gold, the Clutha. Gold flecks came down from the Ragged Range mountains and then were dredged out of the river sand bottom, using barges on cables. The next stretch toward Dunedin, as viewed by Twain out the window, featured "vast level green expanses snowed over with sheep" with color schemes varying from vivid green to paler shades.

Dunedin, at 50,000 people, was one of New Zealand's largest cities; the Scottish had settled there and erected a statue to poet Robert Burns, which Twain found oddly tucked between a church and a taproom.

Twain's first night in Dunedin happened to coincide with several religious gatherings: the Presbyterian and Anglican synods. A local reporter noticed many churchmen in attendance, as well as professors, bankers, doctors, lawyers and a hefty portion of youngsters. The venue, the auditorium at City Hall, overflowed. Twain enjoyed being told how far some audience members had traveled. One woman came from 200 miles away (on an "express" train traveling 20 miles per hour), setting a new record for distance.

At 8 p.m. on the dot, Wednesday, November 6, some people in the cheap seats in the back began rudely rapping walking sticks on the floor.

A minute later, Twain in a formal black suit stepped out, his Bohemian shock of gray unruly hair eye-catching as ever. The crowd erupted, delivering "an exceedingly hearty and long-sustained salvo of applause—the most cordial welcome, in short, which has ever been extended to a lecturer in Dunedin," according to the *Otago Daily Times*.

Twain chose not to entertain the churchmen with his moral crusade of striving to commit all sins, but rather did a variation on his standard opening night. He began with "Corpse in the Moonlight" but opted to shake it up a bit with "Mexican Plug Horse" for his second number. On his ride into town he had seen the vast sheep runs and sheep shearers galloping around on horseback.

He told the story of how he—a former printer's apprentice, a riverboat pilot—had bought his *first* horse and learned a life lesson about trust in the process.

> Everybody rode horseback there. They were most magnificent riders. I thought so at least. And I was just burning with impatience to learn more. I was determined to have a horse to ride, and just as the thought was rankling in my mind an auctioneer came along on a beast crying him for sale, going at $22, $22, horse, saddle, and bridle.
>
> I could hardly resist. There was a man standing there. I was not acquainted with him. [*pause*] He turned out to be the auctioneer's brother. [*long laughter*]

You have to hear Twain's slow drawl, see the blank, dumbfounded look on his face. The audience "roared," according to the *Otago Times*. "There was apparently only one serious person in the building, and that was the entertainer himself, who told his stories in a matter-of-fact way as if utterly unconscious of their drollery."

[The man] observed to me, "It's a sin to let a good horse go so cheap." I said I had half a notion to buy it. He said: "I know that horse—know him perfectly well. You are a stranger, and you may think that he is an **American** horse. He's nothing of the kind; he's a **genuine Mexican plug**; that's what he is." Well, I didn't know what a "genuine Mexican plug" was, but there was something about that man's way of saying it that I made up my mind to have that horse if it took every cent I had, and I said: "Has he any other advantages?"

Well, he just hooked his forefinger into the breast pocket of my army shirt, led me off to one side, and in a low tone that no one else could hear, said: "He can outbuck any horse in this part of the country. Yes," he repeated, "he can outbuck any horse in America."

The auctioneer was crying him at $24, $24, going at $24. I said, $27—"and sold." I took the "genuine Mexican plug," paid for him, put him in the livery stable, had him fed, then I let him rest until after dinner, when I brought him out into the plaza, where some of the citizens held him by the head while others held him down by the tail, and I got on him. As soon as they had let go, he put all his feet together in a bunch. He let his back sag down and then he arched it suddenly and shot me 180 yards into the air. I wasn't used to such things, and I came down and lit in the saddle, then he sent me up again and this time I came down astride his neck, but I managed to slide backward until I got into the saddle again. He then raised himself almost straight up on his hind legs and walked around awhile, like a member of Congress, then he came down and went up the other way, and just walked about on his hands as a schoolboy would, and all the time kept kicking at the sky. While he was in this position I heard a man say to another, "But don't he buck!" [*pause*]

So that was **"bucking."**

[*The audience "roared" again, according to the newspaper account.*]

I was very glad to know it. Not that I was particularly enjoying it, but I was somewhat interested in it and naturally wanted to know what the name of it was. While this performance was going on, a sympathizing crowd had gathered around, and one of them remarked to me: "Stranger, you have been taken in. That's a genuine Mexican plug," and another one says: "Think of it! You might have bought an American horse, used to all kinds of work, for very little more money." Well I didn't want to talk. I didn't have anything to say. I was so jolted up, so internally, externally, and eternally mixed up, gone all to pieces. I put one hand on my forehead, the other on my stomach; and if I had been the owner of 16 hands I could have found a place for every one of them.

Well, that horse gave me such a buck-jump at last that it sent me out of the saddle up and up—and up so high I came across birds I never saw before. I kept on going and just missed the top of a steeple. But when I got back, the horse———[*PAUSE*]———was gone.

Daughter Clara faithfully attended most of the lectures on the trip and observed closely, and she is the one who wrote down the exact words of the closing and the delivery.

Father knew the full value of a pause and had the courage to make a long one when required for a big effect. And his inimitable drawling speech, which he often lost in private life, greatly increased the humorous effect on the stage. People in the house, including men, got hysterical. Cries that resembled cries of pain could often be heard.

She said her father always claimed to detest mounting the platform to deliver paid lectures, but even he wasn't immune to a theater full of people laughing and cheering. "I believe that [he] was often elated by it himself," she later wrote, and on some nights when a big audience was roaring, she thought his cheeks and eyes "glowed with color that resembled tinted sparks."

The first pair of nights in Dunedin sold out, so a third was added. Twain, who rarely found time to explore, caught a break. On this, just his fourth day in New Zealand, he and his family were invited to the home of one of the colony's leading collectors of Maori artifacts. Dr. Thomas Hocken was a respected doctor, the Dunedin coroner for twenty-two years, only five feet tall, with a dapper goatee and an infectious enthusiasm for amassing all things Maori, from canoe-prow carvings to meticulous color drawings of tattooed chiefs. (His collection would wind up in a university museum.)

Twain pored over illustrations and also photographs and artifacts, such as four-fingered figurines and greenstone Maori war clubs shaped like Ping-Pong paddles. Dr. Hocken showed Twain his translation of a rare diary and explained his theory about the origins of the Maori. He believed their long straight black hair revealed they arrived centuries earlier by boats from Polynesian islands.

Twain later wrote of the "frescoed" bodies and faces:

The tattooing in these portraits ought to suggest the savage, of course, but it does not. The designs are so flowing and graceful and beautiful that they are a most satisfactory decoration. It takes but fifteen minutes to get reconciled to the tattooing, and but fifteen more to perceive that it is just the thing. After that, the undecorated European face is unpleasant and ignoble.

And he also was impressed by the carvings, which inspired more cannibal conjectures. "The totem-posts were there, ancestor above ancestor, with tongues protruded and hands clasped comfortably over bellies containing other people's ancestors—grotesque and ugly devils, every one, but lovingly carved."

Adding that extra night in Dunedin, however, jumbled his schedule. Now, Twain would have to perform next in Timaru, 125 miles away, on Saturday, then double back fifty miles along the same track to Oamaru for Monday—all mostly at ten to fifteen miles per hour. To avoid the nuisance, Livy and Clara headed on directly to Christchurch, New Zealand's largest city.

Twain found "beautiful hill & ocean scenery" on the way to Oamaru, where he changed trains. There, he discovered he missed American rudeness. He encountered a "peremptory big frowsy blonde waitress" that made him miss "our home-made article." He then crossed the amazingly fertile Canterbury Plains, "splendid sheep ranches & billowy piles of snowy alps lying under the horizon . . . everywhere a spring freshness & vividness under this luxuriant early summer vegetation."

His notebook depicts Timaru as a bustling little town of 20,000, with breweries and flour mills, set amid rolling hills that created "folds of land," "green and trim," with nearby Mount Cook, showing off "its crested helmet of perpetual snow."

The author noted "a beautiful bathing beach" near town "appreciated by crowds of children but not by adults much—not many bathing houses or machines." (Victorian grown-ups, especially women, still changed in "bathing machines," i.e., small sheds on wheels that were rolled out into the surf. The women, once in their bathing dresses, could discreetly dunk in the water, holding a rope attached to the shed; many men still wore what resembles modern neck-to-knee long johns.)

Twain performed there on November 9, the national holiday of the Prince of Wales's birthday, to a packed (and possibly intoxicated) house. He would be heckled, and more than a few people exited the theater, grumbling their disappointment.

The reporter for the *Timaru Herald* stated somewhat vaguely that Twain's "monologue" became a "dialogue" and that the audience contributed "repetitions" and "interjections."

One critic attending that night tried to capture the audience reaction for the local literary monthly, *Triad*. C. N. Baeyertz was ashamed of the boorish behavior of his fellow countrymen, whom he accused of craving nothing but vulgar dumb jokes, dirty double entendres and buffoonish blackface. By way of apology, Baeyertz wrote: "[Twain] could certainly supply any one of his detractors with sufficient brains to double his intellect and not be greatly inconvenienced by the loss."

Agent Carlyle Smythe admitted—long after the financially successful tour—that the humorist considered platform speaking "undignified work" and resented audiences that "insist merely that he shall crack jokes to them for an hour or so."

The critic Baeyertz queried some of the crowd leaving that night: one man thought the humorist collected money under false pretenses and was more suited to serve as "second cook" on a sheep ranch; another said he had already heard the story about the grandfather's ram. Another found Twain's English baffling.

Twain spent a family-less Sunday in the town. He stayed in bed, reading George Augustus Sala's *Under the Sun,* which he found "brilliant & breezy." Not surprisingly, after the heckling, his thoughts turned a bit dark.

It is the strangest thing that the world is not full of books that scoff at the pitiful world, & the useless universe & the vile & contempt-ible human race—books that laugh at the whole paltry scheme & deride it. Curious for millions of men die every year with these feelings in their hearts. Why don't *I* write such a book? Because I have a family. There is no other reason. Was this those other people's reason?

With time alone, his mind veered to his debts, which gnawed at him.

The fact that man invented imprisonment for debt, proves that man is an idiot, & also that he is utterly vile & malignant. How can imprisonment pay a debt? Was the idea of it to pay the creditor in revenge?

————

Next stop: backtrack to Oamaru, an unusual place that would seem perfect for a travel memoir. Twain would exclude it. Here, his hecklers would be of the four-legged variety.

Oamaru's claim to fame was that, despite being a smallish coastal town, it had streets full of ornate, classical stone buildings. As Michael Davitt put it, "You think . . . you have dropped down upon a New Zealand Athens." The town had very few wooden or brick buildings.

All the houses are built of a handsome, cream-colored limestone which abounds in that section. The stone is so soft when first taken from the quarry that it can be cut with an ordinary saw and chisel. On exposure to the air it hardens, and enough lime is dissolved by the rain and crystallized between the blocks to fill up the crevices, the whole building becoming literally one piece.

Davitt described seeing "numbers of . . . buildings [that] look like Grecian temples, with colonnades, pillared porticoes and palatial designs—out of all character to a small place having about four or five thousand of a population."

Twain performed that night. A sign proclaimed NO DOGS ALLOWED IN THE DRESS CIRCLE, which meant dogs *were* allowed in all the other less expensive seats. Canines were then extremely popular pets throughout Australasia. One lecturer, Sherman Denton, a famed American naturalist and illustrator who did a stereopticon show in the 1880s, tried to forbid dogs at his shows. Some nights Denton resorted to kicks, and one night he missed the dog and kicked "an English dude, with excessively thin legs" and feared arrest or lawsuit. Denton devoted pages to his pique over pampered pets in these British colonies.

> The less property a man possesses, the more dogs he requires
> to guard it, and if he has five or six half-starved and poorly clad
> children there must of necessity be two or three great dogs to keep
> them company. On every railway train, running under the seats of
> the cars was a long box, into which dogs belonging to the passengers were forced, and conversation along the road was enlivened
> by their muffled yelps.

Denton was more harassed than Twain by dogfights during his talks. Denton's ultimate solution, however, sounds almost Twain-like: "In my exasperation I used to think that if all dogdom were heaped together, I should like to stand about half a mile off with the most destructive of modern Gatling guns, and turn the crank until the last of the race expired with a howl."

Twain, on the other hand, was uncharacteristically terse. "Plenty dogs attend my lectures. They have had a fight only once—at Oamaru." Unfortunately, no more details are forthcoming. He did jot down the "dress circle" sign.

On Tuesday before leaving, Twain took a four-mile carriage ride with a longtime fan, a Mr. Miles, who had written Twain a letter a half decade earlier about a strange and amusing public incident in New Zealand. The legislature had been considering importing and introducing a species of wild goat/antelope called a "chamois." When argument broke out over the exact nature of the animal, one legislator handed another, named Kerr, a book on the subject to read aloud. Mr. Kerr read:

> The lauded chamois is not a wild goat; . . . it is not a horned animal; . . . it is not shy; . . . it does not avoid human society; and . . . there is no peril in hunting it. The chamois is a black or brown creature no bigger than a mustard seed; you do not have to go after it, it comes after you; it arrives in vast herds and skips and scampers all over your body, inside your clothes.

The legislature dissolved in laughter. A representative from a neighboring district had handed Mr. Kerr a copy of Twain's *A Tramp Abroad,* in which the author had confused the goatlike chamois with a flea.

Twain headed 160 miles by train to reunite with his family in Christchurch, and was slated for at least a dozen more New Zealand appearances. He boarded an express train that raced 20½ miles per hour, which he compared favorably in design to American models; this one had a long, narrow railed porch along one side of many cars that allowed for clear viewing of sea and countryside.

Christchurch, unlike predominantly Scotch Presbyterian Dunedin, had been founded to be an exclusively Anglican religious enclave, with streets named after English and Irish cathedral towns. Twain adjudged the orderly city and its environs a "Junior England," with weeping willows bordering a winding river called the Avon. The original Anglican-only plan nonetheless faltered in the face of New Zealanders' open democratic spirit. "Other sects crept in," as Michael Davitt observed.

The American humorist would perform three times here to large crowds. He did receive one of his rare bad reviews from a traveling Australian, writing for the *Queanbeyan Age,* who seemed dead set on being disappointed at seeing and hearing an author of such great written works as *Innocents Abroad*.

> There are very few halls that he could be properly heard in, as he speaks in a private sort of style, and if you are any distance away you want an ear like an elephant's flap to gather in enough of the yarn.

The reviewer thought Twain tried too hard to stand out with that mess of hair.

> Our own [*Sir Henry*] Parkes can knock him out at that in quantity, quality, and colour. From the distance Mark's head appears covered with a long combing mousey-coloured, grey, Southdown kind of deck-swab [*i.e., a ship's mop*]. . . . If he now gets traveling much in the back country with it, where the wily emu layeth up her eggs, he will have to fence it off or she'll seize it for a breeding spot.

The cranky critic claimed that stripped of the hair and funny American accent, little of note remained. About all the reviewer from New South Wales liked was Twain's unadorned entrance and his tart comment when people started drifting out "for a nip" *before* intermission: "Some of you would like fresher air than I can supply and I will wait."

In Christchurch, as on so many stops along his trip, one of the town's leading citizens shepherded the Clemens party. A photo survives of Twain in top hat with curls squished downward, seated in an elegant open carriage with a satisfied-looking Livy and their wealthy host, Mr. Joseph Kinsey.

The carriage ride took them to the lush Botanical Gardens and to the museum, full of more Maori artifacts and rare indigenous animals.

Twain was especially impressed by the "ten-foot-tall" skeleton of the giant moa, an extinct giraffe-like bird, a caricaturist's delight. For once, hyperbole-prone Twain might have been underselling. Reverend Haweis pegged the same skeleton at "fifteen feet tall."

Twain imagined the war kick of this flightless bird. "If a person had his back to the bird and did not see who . . . did it, he would think he had been kicked by a wind-mill."

The author noted these skeletons came from actual bones, not fossils, which meant a relatively recent demise. Reverend Haweis was told of a Maori expression, which might explain the bird's extinction: "As stupid as a Moa."

The Christchurch Savage Club of fifty first-tier citizens threw a last-night-in-town dinner for Twain at the Provincial Council Chamber. The gathering featured the usual gracious toasts to the queen and to the United States. Twain loved to find a local theme to spur a riff, and this time he tackled the New Zealand Prohibition movement, which had left several cities, such as Dunedin, entirely dry and others dry on Sundays. He had a joke ready to adapt.

> In our country several years ago there was a man who came into a prohibited town, and, unlike you savages here, they said to him, "You can't get a drink anywhere except at the drugstore." So he went to the druggist, who said, "You can't get a drink without a prescription from a physician." But the man said, "For pity's sake, it don't want a physician's prescription to see that I am exhausted." "Well," said the druggist, "if you were suffering from snake bite, now, it might be all right."
>
> "Well," the man said, "where's the snake?" So the druggist gave him the snake's address, and he went off. Soon after, however, he came back and said, "For goodness sakes, give me a drink. That snake is booked for six months ahead." (*laughter*)

Belly laugh or not, that joke traveled around the world in five months. The *Christchurch Press* reported it immediately, then other British papers picked it up, then a trade journal in London, *Wine & Spirit Gazette,* then America's *Bonfort's Wine and Spirit Circular* on March 25, 1896. It was a timely topic. Police Commissioner Teddy Roosevelt was then enforcing a Sunday saloon ban in New York City, while the Temperance movement was accelerating toward Carrie Nation touring with her bar-smashing hatchet.

His host, Mr. Kinsey, was a bona fide dues-paying "savage," and they enrolled Twain in the local club. The city of Christchurch embraced the Clemenses, who attended numerous teas and small gatherings. Livy counted thirty-eight gifts on parting, including photographs, flowers, chocolates and a stuffed platypus. In her later thank-you note to the Kinsey family, she revealed:

> Mr. Clemens does not allow "Ornithorhynchus dear" to leave his arms while we are moving from boat to train and train to boat. He says it is his most treasured possession. He does not think even his [Maori] wife beater [stick] surpasses it.

Kinsey—father and daughter—accompanied the Clemens family on the dark rainy night of Saturday, November 16, on the eight-mile train ride to the port of Lyttelton. A prior outbound ship had been canceled, and the Union Steamship Company crammed both passenger lists aboard the *Flora* for the journey to North Island.

"We went from our pleasant quiet chat in the railway carriage into a perfect pandemonium," Livy later wrote to Mr. Kinsey. Twain would write Mrs. Kinsey and call the vessel a "floating pigsty with 500 Christians crowded into accommodations more proper for 25 cattle." Foul weather and choppy seas intensified the misery.

The family's stateroom reservations were ignored. Livy and Clara were directed to share a tiny room with "two strange women." The floor was so crammed with luggage and mattresses that Clara found it impossible to walk without stepping on someone. In addition: "No towels to wipe with, no pillows to sleep on and no sheets to protect one from the grimy blankets." She encountered a dozen of the largest cockroaches she had ever seen, and by the middle of the night, she was begging her mother to be allowed to return to the United States.

Livy reported every corner and crevice of the entire ship was allotted for sleeping, and she made the upper-crust joke in her letter to Mr. Kinsey that we "comfort ourselves" that now we would make no new discoveries if we were ever "compelled to go steerage [class]."

Both Livy and Clara agreed that Papa and young Smythe had it worse. They were assigned to sleep in the large open salon, with women on one half, men on the other, separated by a curtain strung down the middle. Her father told her that as the ship rolled, a woman kept driving her elbow into his ribs through the curtain. Some slept on the floor; others in chairs or on tables. "Fat people were selected to sleep on the tables," claimed Clara, "in the belief that they would be less likely to roll off."

Twain described it as one of the worst nights of his life, one he could never live long enough to forget.

> I had a cattle-stall in the main stable. . . . The place was as dark as the soul of the Union [Steamship] Company, and smelt like a kennel. When the vessel got out into the heavy seas and began to pitch and wallow, the cavern prisoners became immediately seasick, and then the peculiar results that ensued laid all my previous experiences of the kind well away in the shade. And the wails, the groans, the cries, the shrieks, the strange ejaculations—it was wonderful.

Twain himself got seasick; he couldn't tolerate the vomit smell of the main dining room, and he spent the rest of the night with many others standing on the hurricane deck. He found the smell in the room assigned for breakfast "incomparable for efficiency" in making even more people seasick. (The British edition of his travel book would tone down his tirade about "murder," "monopoly," and a government official winking aboard a dangerous excess number of passengers.)

He had promised to treat his family to quality accommodations and felt dreadful about this slipup, even if he and Smythe could never have predicted the overbooking. At the first way port of Wellington, the party switched to the "perfect little bijou, clean & comfortable," the 240-ton *Mahinapua*, a "bridal-parlor" of a ship, to go to Auckland.

The route took them through French Pass, a narrow gateway of rock, with strong currents that caused the steamer to shoot forward "like a telegram." At the exit side, the eddies spun the boat and "picked her up and flung her around like nothing and landed her gently on the solid smooth bottom of sand—so gently indeed that we barely felt her touch it, barely felt her quiver when she came to a standstill." Twain stated that fishing poles were brought out, but "before we could bait the hooks, the boat was off and away again."

Clara revealed—a bit cattily—in her later memoir that her father was bluffing and had actually *slept* through the "only shipwreck" of his life. She reported that a storm had seesawed the ship so badly that everyone took refuge in bed and that when the ship first got stuck, the captain feared the worst. She personally observed passengers "dressed and undressed" rushing to the lifeboats. The captain quickly realized it was a sandy bottom with a rising tide. "[Father] was disgusted to have missed the excitement, for he always loved relief from monotony in almost any form."

The Clemenses arrived in deep-harbor Auckland at 6 p.m. on November 20, with majestic volcanic Mount Eden towering. Twain, who would perform there two nights, hoped to squeeze in a quick sightseeing visit to some of the world's most fascinating natural hot springs and baths in Rotorua. The vividly named springs attracted him: "Dragon's Mouth" spewing sulfur and steam and "Lightning Pool" with its strange underwater flashes. In another pool, Maori women cooked potatoes; nearby, they used a natural steam oven to bake bread.

But the ten-hour trip each way would require Twain to catch a 4 a.m. train back, and then he feared he'd be too tired to perform well. "Traveling and lecturing are like oil and water; they don't mix," Twain told an Auckland reporter. "There are many fine sights in New Zealand that I haven't seen." He did get a carriage ride up local Mount Eden: "rolling green fields, hot bursts of flowers . . . distant stately mountains."

He spoke in Auckland on November 21 and 22 and drew more than a thousand paying customers each night. Livy was quite pleased with the "large and very enthusiastic" audiences.

Then his health took another turn for the worse. Just as it seemed to Livy that he was growing more energetic, a new carbuncle threatened in a horrible place: his armpit. "Naturally that makes him feel very much discouraged," she wrote her sister. So far it was one single boil, and Livy was confident that Dr. Fitzgerald's methods would stop it.

Also, their milestone birthdays loomed within a week; Livy's fiftieth would be followed three days later by his sixtieth. Neither spouse seemed eager to celebrate the passage. And right in the midst of all that, unsettling letters would arrive from Susy back at home.

CHAPTER 15

Birthdays and Longing

Livy was scheduled to be in Gisborne, New Zealand, to celebrate her fiftieth birthday on November 27, as Twain was speaking there that night. Gisborne was a cute river town, just past Poverty Bay, not far from where Captain Cook first landed. The day before had been pleasant with a coastal trip out of Auckland and some serendipitous whale watching. "Nothing could be daintier than the puffs of vapor they spout up when seen against the pink glory of the sinking sun, or against the dark mass of an island reposing in the deep blue shadow of a storm cloud."

But they couldn't reach Gisborne because the weather turned, and very rough seas kicked up. The captain of the *Rotomahana* deemed it too dangerous to approach the dock. A little tugboat, the *Snark*, steamed out—plunging and rising in the storm, doing somersaults, as Twain put it—to ferry passengers ashore. In the choppy sea, a "primitive basketchair" was rigged to the yard arm of the larger *Rotomahana*, filled with a passenger or two, swung out into the sky and lowered at the right time onto the *Snark's* rolling deck, to be corralled by sailors in yellow slickers. Twenty-five travelers arrived this way and twenty-five departed, including four prisoners bound for jail and one blind woman. A "young fellow" from the *Rotomahana* was parked in the chair, as "a protection to the lady-comers." To save time, two women sat in his lap at once and he encircled each with an arm. (An illustration in Twain's later travel book portrayed the sailor as smiling broadly.) The Clemens family—no one reveals who made the decision—decided it was too risky or risqué, to go ashore that way.

Livy wound up spending her birthday on a tippy boat in the harbor. Twain tried to distract Mrs. Clemens from dwelling on reaching half a century. He pointed vaguely eastward to the nearby International Date Line—which happened to be located just a handful of miles offshore at 180 degrees longitude. Gisborne boasted of being the first town on planet Earth to receive the new day's first rays of sunlight. Twain made some calculations and crossed November 27, 1895. "I claimed that her birthday has either passed or is to come; that it is the 27th as the 27th exists in America, not here where we have flung out a day & closed up the vacancy." The man tried.

The fiftieth passage was not exactly bringing out chipper thoughts in her. She wrote to her sister:

> Oh, dear me! I wonder if we ever shall get our debts all paid, and live once more in our own house. To-day it seems to me as if we never should. However, much of the time I believe we shall; but it is a long way. Mr. Clemens continues to have large and *very* enthusiastic houses.

The Clemens clan exited Gisborne, skipped safely south along the coast to Napier, a flourishing small city with streets named after British poets, not noblemen. Twain called it a "little Boston." He gave one performance there, then canceled the second and collapsed into bed to spend his November 30 birthday and the next few days recuperating and pondering, and fighting off flies, canaries and carbuncles.

Turning 6-o didn't creep up on him; Twain seems to have been mulling aging at intervals along the trip. Two months earlier at the Yorick Club in Melbourne, in the boozy late hours, he had confessed:

> My friend on the right (Mr. Deakin) and I were talking just now about [growing old]. I said I thought that if I had created the human race—(laughter, and a voice, "You did some of them")—oh! I could have done it. (Laughter.) I was asked nothing about it, and I didn't suggest anything. (Laughter.) But I thought that if I had created the human race, and had discovered that they were a kind of a failure—(laughter)—and had drowned them out—(loud laughter)—well, I would recognise that that was a good thing. And then fortified by experience, I would start the thing on a differ-

ent plan. (Laughter.) I would have no more of that 969 years' [Old Testament] business. I wouldn't let people grow that old. I would cut them off at 30. Because a man's youth is the thing he loves to think about, and it is the thing that he regrets. It is the one part of his life that he most thoroughly enjoys. My friend on the right suggests that we should go as far as 40 years, as he doesn't want any of his 40 years rubbed out. Well, perhaps you really might go up to 40, because then you get a perspective upon youth, and that has its value. That has its charm. But, oh, dear me, I never would have created age. (Laughter.) Age has its own value—but that is to other people, not to those who have it. (Laughter.)

Livy and a local doctor were treating the boil with Dr. Fitzgerald's methods, which ultimately called for freezing, lancing and an opium hypodermic. Twain counted it a blessing that his bed rest happened to occur at Napier because the family had wonderful hotel rooms right on the ocean, with a porch looking seaward. He wrote of "the solemn deep boom of the swells breaking on the shore" making a "luxurious lullaby . . . full of contentment & peace, & persuasions to sleep."

His incipient bliss, however, was quickly interrupted by three cages of canaries outside his room. He compared their music to "scratching a nail on a window pane," and he wondered "what sort of disease enables a person to enjoy the canary." He encouraged the hotel staff to haul off the cages immediately.

On Saturday, the day of his birthday, his room was invaded by one of those "whizzing green Ballarat flies." He compared the insect's noise to a buzz saw and its speed to a lightning flash. "No peace while he is here . . . harder to endure than 100 mosquitos."

The American mail reached them and Twain received letters from, among others, his good friend Reverend Joe Twichell of Hartford—a missive a mere two months and five days old. He learned that *Harper's* had assigned Twichell to write a profile of Twain, which, not surprisingly, delighted both of them. Twain wrote back and showed off some fine writing to impress (or amuse) the New England minister. "Away down here fifty-five degrees south of the Equator this sea seems to murmur in an unfamiliar tongue—a foreign tongue—a tongue bred among the ice-fields of the Antarctic—a murmur with a note of melancholy in it proper to the vast unvisited solitudes it has come from."

And Twain marveled to his friend at how well both wife and daughter were handling the "nomadic life," surviving foul food, hard beds and bobbing little ships. He judged they were displaying a "heroic endurance that resembles contentment."

Twain also tried to give himself a humongous birthday present. He wrote to H.H. Rogers in New York and suggested that H.H.'s son-in-law, who had bought the Library of American Literature for $50,000, now be persuaded to buy five-year rights to Twain's next travel book for $40,000. The man with the boil in his armpit just happened to choose a dollar figure that would free him from debt in one swoop, and he pitched the offer through his millionaire pal H.H. instead of contracting W. E. Benjamin directly. (The self-gift would not succeed.)

The author also wrote to turn down an offer from Major Pond to lecture fifty nights in England. Twain replied he wanted to rest and write his travel book. Pond later suspected that Twain's phenomenal success in Australia had gone to his head, catapulting his compensation scale.

———

But the mail included more disturbing missives. Livy and Clara received letters from America, at least one each from an unhappy, bored, self-blaming Susy, and both would reply. Half a world apart, paired with a two-month lag in communication, makes for an agonizing way to mend a damaged relationship, or to try to comfort one another, or to smooth over regret.

Two and a half months earlier, on September 16, when Susy wrote the letter, Major Pond and his wife had just arrived to visit them at Aunt Sue's Quarry Farm in Elmira, New York. The couple came bearing trip photos and anecdotes from just traveling cross-country with the other three Clemenses. They all sat in the parlor: Uncle Charley Langdon, the struggling coal businessman; Sue Crane, their relentlessly upbeat aunt; troubled Susy; and strange Jean. They looked at the late summer photos from Montana, Washington and British Columbia. Susy saw her father perched in the Great Northern locomotive, saw her mother and sister next to a massive stuffed buffalo, and finally, the traveling Clemens trio standing by the "stowaway warning" sign on the SS *Warrimoo,* just before their August 23 departure out into the Pacific.

Susy, looking at photos and listening to the Ponds, felt an agonizing pang of regret, which she conveyed to Clara:

We have enjoyed [Major Pond and his wife] so immensely much. They do bring you near again. . . . These last [photos] are certainly the best of all the wonderful collection. Ah me, was I not a fool to stay here instead of going with you? How happy and adventurous and chic you do look in these pictures!

[Major Pond] enthuses and enthuses and gushes and gushes until he has no more breath or language at his command. But he has a full and discerning appreciation of you all and it is a joy to hear them both talk about you. *If* I ever can be with you again, I shall stick like a burr indeed! There will be no extricating and separating me from you again. We *are* such a congenial family. It seems to me no one ever understands us as we understand each other. We *do* belong together.

When I think of you and Mamma and Papa, your superior charms and attractions make me look upon other mortals with contempt and a *profound* indifference. Oh dear, you are so lovely and I am missing you so terribly!—how, how, why, *why* did I ever let you go? I do not dare to think but rarely of going to meet you in England, for the thought makes me kind of insane. To leave Elmira and all its bores to rejoin *you*, brilliant, experienced, adorable people, to whom I belong, and to rejoin you in Europe!!! Oh quel bonheur! *can* it ever come true?

Susy wrote that she was living in a "haze," a horrid daydream during "this strange long desolate year." The social scene in Elmira offered little to a twenty-three-year-old girl who had lived in Paris and Berlin. "It is a mistake to separate from the people we love and whom we belong to. I do not really love anybody but you dear three, and of course, nobody else loves me."

(It's interesting she doesn't include her fifteen-year-old sister Jean, who was already starting to show odd behavior. Pond took many photos in Elmira; in one, Jean is standing in the background on the *roof* of the first story of Aunt Sue's house.)

Just like her father, Susy would have binges of self-reproach. She had apologized to her sister for not being a "nice child." Part of her decision to remain—besides the aching hope too see Louise Brownell—seems to have hinged on her strained relationship with her mother. She knew that traveling and bickering would have been rough on them all. Jean—in her brusque way—pointed out that Susy was polite with affable Aunt Sue but often "rude' or "disagreeable" to Mamma. "I don't suppose I ought to write this, and don't show it to Mamma if it will offend her, and *on no account* to Papa. Mamma is a *great* woman and Aunt Sue is infinitely little. I would rather have a lifetime of Mamma's honest reproof than a month of Aunt Sue's false sweetness."

The "honest reproof" makes it sound like Livy found the need to scold her daughter often.

Among Pond's numerous photos from that fall day, one captures Susy sitting at the dining room table, staring wide-eyed, almost angry, frowning slightly, while her aunt looks over at her with a rueful smile.

Her letter to her mother has not survived, but based on Livy's reply, we can tell that Susy clearly wrote about trying to correct her health and behavior problems through "Mental Science"—some form of mind over matter.

Her mother's reply of December 2 congratulates her on embracing Mental Science and then tries hard to cheer up her daughter by shouldering some blame for their squabbles, and stressing the bright side.

> You dear sweet darling little child in your self-reproachings—
> you seem to entirely forget that we had many, many, many happy
> beautiful hours together, beautiful hours that I remember with
> such infinite pleasure. Do you remember oftener the times that I
> was impatient and disagreeable to you, or the times that we were
> happy together? I am sure you do not think very often of the fact
> that I often spoke in a way that a mother ought not to speak—
> I am sure you do not hold those things in your heart; neither do
> I. I think *much* MUCH oftener of your lovable, dear, sweet ways
> than I think of the times when you were not absolutely perfect. . . .
> So my darling child do not repine for the things that you did that
> were wrong. I feel when we come together again we shall feel alike
> that we never shall want to be separated.

In the rest of her very long letter, Livy captures the family vacation aspect of the trip, in a way that Twain's notebook and travel book do not. It is as though she wants to invite Susy onto the trip, back into their lives.

Palmerston North, New Zealand. December 2nd, 1895

Here we are in most beautiful summer weather! Cherries and
strawberries and pineapples. This morning it was very warm, not
hot, but a bright sunny warm morning when you could wear thin
clothing, and yet there was a little breeze that made it entirely
comfortable. Papa said it was the kind of day that made one happy
to be alive.

Our trip today was through a most beautiful country, fields and
woods and mountains and waterfalls. We saw one of the great
sheep runs. Mr. Smythe thought there were a thousand sheep. . . .
I should think there were fully that; you never saw anything like it
and I never did before. One of the gorges was most beautiful and
we could just stand out on a little balcony of the car and look up
and down the gorge. . . .

We cannot at all realize that it is nearly Xmas time and that we
have only warm weather, and shall have it warmer & warmer.

She shares a little epiphany with Susy about wealth and what truly
brings contentment. Olivia Langdon Clemens at times almost seemed
cursed with the burden of needing to demonstrate to her neighbors a
rich lifestyle, with servants and carriages and fine furniture; her husband often seems to share the burden, though he makes fun of himself
for it.

She wrote Susy: "Our experiences are most interesting, and in spite
of the fact that our lives are not now all luxury, we enjoy ourselves *very
much*."

Livy then haltingly, apologetically, informed her daughter that even
though they had "not loitered *one day* for sight-seeing" they would not
reach England by spring. Late summer or early fall was more likely. She
stressed it wasn't pleasure chasing that delayed them. "We are seeing
almost nothing of the wonders of this land that we ought to see." She
even worried whether "Papa" would have enough material for his book.

Their new plans after returning now called for spending the fall and
winter of 1896 in England. "Papa feels that he does not want to go back
to America until he is able to arrange the Webster matters." (If Twain
returned before full payment was made, he would be vulnerable to

humiliating legal action by the most aggressive creditors, such as Mount Morris Bank or the Barrow family.)

"I hope this [delay] will not be too much of a shock to you." And she closed her letter: "To you, my precious child, a hug & a kiss & unchangeable love, always, Mama."

———

Surprisingly to all involved, Livy and a local doctor cured Twain's armpit boil, which did not turn into an infected mass (i.e., a carbuncle). His mood improved; his jotted notes resume a playfulness.

They were staying at the somewhat odd Club Hotel in Palmerston North with tiny rooms and paper-thin walls. There, Twain encountered a "stunning Queen-of-Sheba style of barmaid [who] always answered the bell & then got up on her dignity & said lighting fires, brushing clothes, boots, &c. was the chambermaid's business. Would she please tell the chambermaid? (No answer. Exit.)"

Twain would shout after her: "Why do you *answer* the bell?" and receive no reply. (Hotels had pull strings hidden in the walls tied to numbered bells in the servants' area; it's extremely unlikely this New Zealand hotel had an electric bell system.)

And earlier, when the family had arrived to check in, Twain had noticed a sign informing guests that the landlord was NOT responsible for lost or stolen property. Twain requested his room key, wanting to lock the door especially after seeing a couple of drunks wandering around the lobby. The beefy, red-faced owner told him he couldn't find a key to Twain's room, and that he had forgotten to label the keys and he had a drawer full of them. An elderly woman humiliated Twain by offering to give up her room, which had a key and lock, saying that "*she* wasn't afraid to sleep without a key."

The landlord woke them up to deliver a key around midnight. The Clemens family, after that intrusion, tried to sleep in late but failed.

Early in the morning a baby began—pleasantly—didn't mind baby—then the piano . . . played by either the cat or a partially untrained artist—certainly the most extraordinary music—straight average of 3 right notes to 4 wrong ones, but played with eager zeal & gladness—old old tunes of 40 years ago . . . & considering it was the cat—for it *must* have been the cat—it was really a marvelous performance. It convinced me that a cat is more intelligent than people believe.

After a Monday night performance, they boarded the train to Wanganui. At their next hotel, Twain's life was threatened by a lunatic.

Clara and her father both left versions of the event, and they agree on almost no details. Twain wrote that a man burst into the parlor room of his hotel suite in Wanganui on December 4 and told him that Jesuits were going to "cook" him to death, by putting poison in his food, or maybe three men would execute him on the stage. The lunatic had seen the assassination signal—a square with a diagonal slash and numbers—on Twain's poster, and he claimed to have saved him the previous night by scaring off the assassins. The man also boasted that he had recently performed the same service for violin-playing Reverend Haweis by telling him where to stare to ward off death. He whispered that Twain's death plot was orchestrated by *Century* magazine, which was a Jesuit tool steeped in "carnage & murder."

Twain said that before departing the man told him that he "had saved so many lecturers in twenty years, they put him in the asylum."

Clara's version stars Clara. She was sitting alone, reading in the hotel lobby when a man with bloodshot eyes began hissing at her, and bouncing about as though his toes were on fire. He offered to save Mark Twain's life. "Tonight when Mark Twain lectures, three men—his enemies—are going to try to kill him, but you and I can save his life. I have a little bottle here, the contents of which Mark Twain must drink between periods."

Clara stood up, told the jittery man to wait there, and then rushed to her room; on her way, she yelled to a bellman that there was a lunatic in the lobby who needed to be thrown out.

Twain survived performing there two nights.

With their New Zealand stay winding down, up here on North Island, all three Clemens family members tried to soak up as much Maori culture as possible. The Maoris fascinated them. In the American West, they had seen almost no Indians; in Australia, they had seen no aborigine; in Tasmania, the natives had died out two decades before their arrival. But now, this North Island of New Zealand provided their first chance to closely observe an exotic culture, a culture without long pants or neck-to-ankle dresses, or lace-up shoes.

When they arrived in Wanganui, Twain wrote: "Plenty Maoris here.

Plenty horseback riding. Plenty comely girls in cool & pretty summer gowns." The Maori women wore bright-colored cloth wraps, and many of them sported geometric tattoos on their chins and lips that, from a distance, resembled goatees.

Twain visited a *pa* or long council house, with carved poles; then, on a different day, Clara and Livy explored one. An old man in a shawl offered to let the two Clemens women go inside. He muttered something in Maori, which they could not understand. The 200-foot-long *pa* housed meetings by day and accommodated sleepers on mats and ferns at night. The women admired the carvings but found the inside—lit by just two windows—dark and unappealing. "When we got back to the carriage we began to feel the result of being in a dirty place as we had evidently many insects about us," Livy later wrote. "Since we came back we have killed seven fleas, of course that does not begin to represent the number that we have seen."

Livy's curiosity about all things Maori was short-lived. "I have been very much interested in the Maoris since we came here, and have been anxious to see more of them, now I have had enough."

A few days later, Twain had the opportunity to dine with some of the nation's highest-ranking Maori, including a descendant of the war hero Hone Heke and one of the four Maori elected to the seventy-five-member House of Representatives.

The author learned that the word they use for white man or foreigner was *pakeha*, which was derived from the Maori word *pakepakeha* for magical creature or fairy. "When the white man came, they took him for a kind of fairy because of his complexion." (The etymology was accepted in Twain's time, but is now questioned.)

Before Twain left the Wanganui region, he found himself profoundly disgusted by a monument in the heart of Maoriland built by whites to celebrate the heroism of twenty Maori warriors who died fighting for whites. He deemed it a monument to traitors, disloyal to their own families and people, and thought it could be fixed only with "dynamite." He saved these thoughts for his travel memoir.

The Clemens party left New Zealand on Friday, December 13, at 3:15 p.m. on the *Mararoa* for the trip back to Sydney. Twain immediately began praying for bad weather. "Now let us have a storm & a heavy one," he wrote. "This is the damdest menagerie of mannerless children I have ever gone to sea with."

The four-day voyage gave Twain ample time to reflect on Australasia. One overriding trait he found deeply irritating: the colonial insecurity that craved constant compliments. He found himself having to dodge questions about which was the best city, best colony, best view, best audience, and he thought the queries clearly fell into the category of the "guilelessly idiotic sort, which only another idiot would answer."

They reached Sydney just after a "burster" storm with winds up to forty-five miles an hour had suddenly lowered the temperatures from 96 degrees to 67. The first night there, they attended a theater version of Marcus Clarke's *For the Term of His Natural Life*. Twain's notebook: "No play goes far [enough] to enable one to realize that old convict life— invented in hell & carried out by [Chris]tian devils."

That same day in America, December 17, President Grover Cleveland addressed Congress and spotlighted the Venezuela dispute, in which the British were threatening to intervene in South America, and he reaffirmed the Monroe Doctrine, forbidding any European power from meddling in territorial affairs in the Americas. He also suggested a congressional commission to settle the dispute. Many in the British Empire chose to interpret the speech as a veiled threat of war.

Twain, who was squeezing in five performances before leaving Sydney, immediately addressed the Venezuela issue at the end of his show at the School of Arts.

> He said he wished to express . . . the earnest hope, that "the little war cloud" which was lowering over England and the United States of America would quickly blow away under the influence of cooler and calmer counsels. (Loud cheers.) He trusted sincerely that the fruitful peace which had reigned between the nations for 80 years would not now or ever be broken (cheers) and that the two great peoples would resume the march shoulder to shoulder in the van of the world's civilisation. (Prolonged cheering.)

Many Australian editorialists, however, were not amused by President Cleveland's speech or placated by Twain. Here's a typical one from Grafton in New South Wales:

> By their insane howlings about the British claims regarding Venezuela, the Americans have earned the contempt of all the conti-

nental nations, and the sooner they come to their senses the better it will be for their reputation. That they will fight over the matter is extremely improbable, and certainly they will not intimidate John Bull [*i.e., England*] by their ridiculous blustering.

Twain knew that a belligerent attitude on his part would not bode well for ticket sales in India. He also happened to have strong pacifist leanings.

The Clemens family shipped their winter clothes in trunks to South Africa. They would not be needing any in India, or anywhere for the next few months. They spent their first summertime Christmas, in Melbourne. They returned to the palatial spread of John Wagner, and Twain played billiards for most of the next two days. Livy found time to forward even more architectural details to her sister—"very large, very wide and very long . . . irregular shaped porch with bays and pillars and unevennesses . . . most charming."

And she observed her husband having a delightful time. "He was born for just this kind of luxury, I think." Twain concluded his final performance in Melbourne "by bidding Australia good bye, and wishing every prosperity to this land, where for several months I have had a good time and have been so hospitably and kindly treated."

The Clemens family, with Carlyle Smythe in tow, sailed west to Adelaide. Mark Twain, who had earlier wired home £437 and then £200 to H.H. Rogers from Sydney, now sent another £850 from Adelaide. That tally of £1,487 (at five dollars to the British pound) equals $7,435 (about $223,000 today). The reluctant storyteller had done quite well in three months. Twain kept just £97 for expenses until he would start earning again in India.

They went to the Adelaide Zoo, where a laughing jackass bird finally laughed for them. On New Year's Eve they boarded the fine clean Peninsular & Oriental steamer *Oceana* to head from Adelaide to Ceylon (Sri Lanka) and on to India. They plowed out to sea for the two-week voyage, soon rounding Cape Leeuwin on the southwestern tip.

His parting comments on Australia, confided to his notebook, were hardly charitable.

One must say it very softly, but the truth is that the native Australian is as vain of his unpretty country as if it was the final masterpiece of God, achieved by Him from designs from that Australian. He is as sensitive about her as men are of their <~~womenkind~~> sacred things—can't bear to have critical things said about her. Thinks he is going to build a mighty nation here, & someday be an independent one—a republic—cut up his 60[,000] & 100,000-acre sheep runs into farms, maybe—irrigate the deserts, &c—Federation is *sound*; but better not hurry to cut loose from England.

Twain softened considerably for his next and final entry there off the coast. Maybe he remembered his conversations with Irish nationalist Michael Davitt: "Australasia is the modern heaven—it is bossed absolutely by the workingman."

And speaking of work, after six hard months on the road, circling the globe at twenty miles an hour, the creator of Tom and Huck was one-quarter of the way toward paying off his debts.

CHAPTER 16

To India

The luxurious steamer RMS *Oceana* beelined northwesterly across vast open seas toward the equator and Colombo, Ceylon. Each day it grew hotter as the yellow-disc sun beamed down from a cloudless sky. Twain, the former riverboat pilot, would deeply enjoy the first ten days of the two-week voyage—before he suddenly got sick.

The author watched guests play cricket under nets; he played progressive euchre at night on the top deck, with light cool breezes that didn't send the cards flying. He strayed from his usual nonfiction and read three novels in a week: Robert Louis Stevenson's *Prince Otto* ("an easy flowing tale"), Henry Kingsley's *Geoffry Hamlin* ("gushes . . . like a mother whose baby is showing off before company") and his favorite, *The Master* by Israel Zangwill ("characters real, incidents . . . natural").

He sprawled in lounge chairs and often stood at the rail. "The porpoise is the clown of the sea," he wrote in his notebook. "Evidently he does his wild antics for pure fun, there is no sordid profit in it." (Sometimes all roads led back to his forced tour.) He created another maxim: "Give & take—especially the latter."

As the ship approached the toasty equator, the crew stretched canvas awnings across the entire top deck to provide shade; they fixed up "punkahs," long cloth strips that dangled over the tables and were kept in motion by Indian servant boys pulling ropes.

He enjoyed watching the exotic-looking brown-skinned lascar crew go about their duties, wearing baggy white pants and a red sash belt, matched by a red scarf tied around a brimless straw hat. He even remained calm in the midst of a swarm of "ungoverned," "fractious noisy" children because he reminded himself that ungovernable youths often turned into "valuable" adults. He made a short list of Hannibal residents, but maybe he was also thinking of himself. He, however, did find the irony "irritating."

At mealtimes, the first-class passengers "dressed" up for formal dinners, with the men in black evening wear and the women in ball gowns.

> Beautiful dresses, low necks, vivid colors, with the broad shield of the other sex's shirt-bosom interspersed, officer in uniform at the head of each table, electric light, richly decorated dining saloon— why it looks like a swell banquet.

On January 9, the guests switched to summer whites, and Twain eagerly did so as well. He slept well, thanks to "long, slow, gentle rocking of the ship, soothing & lulling as a cradle's motion."

Then in the Doldrums surrounding the equator, the trade winds ceased and rainstorms hit hard—in "deluges." Twain's throat got sore and he began coughing. That didn't stop him from hiking from his stateroom to enjoy an occasional cigar. His diary entry:

> To the smoking room—an interminable trip through a dark tunnel to the second saloon—a lady showed me the way—up 2 flights, along canvas-roofed deck, a dart across the bridge, a spring through a ray of rain for the smoking-room door—made it without catching a drop—slipped on a grating & fell sprawling on the swimming deck.

He had vowed that morning to stop swearing. He broke his vow.

The damp heat at the equator made the air seem steamy and thick. Clara said her stateroom felt like "such an oven." Several women "could not endure the heat & came out & slept in the large hatchway well." Twain's cough was worsening. Carlyle Smythe also fell sick, as did "many passengers," according to Clara.

Twain's mood shifted sharply in a day. He went from enjoying an "infinitely comfortable & satisfying" time to being furious that he was sick. He informed H.H. Rogers in a letter that he had a "hell-fired cold" on his chest, which he downgraded to "all-fired cold," no doubt at Livy's suggestion. She had him gargling with watered-down Listerine to "doctor up his voice" so that he could perform in Ceylon. "But I don't care if it *never* gets audible again; I have been persecuted with carbuncles and colds until I am tired and disgusted and angry."

The big steamship reached Colombo two days later, on January 14. A couple of reporters rushed aboard to ask about that night's performance, but Carlyle Smythe nixed the appearance. Twain, who clearly didn't feel well, drifted away from the reporters and over to the ship's rail to watch the catamarans and the boys diving for coins tossed by passengers.

Carlyle Smythe took up the slack and informed the journalists that this was the longest speaking tour ever attempted and that Twain's audiences in Australia surpassed all the big names: Stanley, Forbes, O'Rell.

Twain told a reporter that he could watch the scene forever, but he quickly drifted away from the newspaperman. The author soon found himself surrounded by a horde of hustlers endeavoring to sell him a "tortoise shell shoe horn, a comb or a sapphire ring."

Carlyle Smythe was stuck trying to arrange for their trunks to be switched to the creaky SS *Rosetta* for the 975-mile voyage the next day to Bombay. Twain and his wife and daughter soon took a carriage to the city's finest, the Grand Oriental Hotel, but it was completely booked. He demanded the suite held in reserve for presidents but was told there was none. The family was shunted off to the nearby Bristol. He collapsed in bed there at 4 p.m., exhausted, and ate dinner in the room. In his delirium, he found it uncomfortable to undress in front of a Sinhalese *male* servant when the man had his back turned. All Twain saw was a petite person with beautiful long black hair gathered in a tortoiseshell comb, who was wearing a bright-colored floor-length gown.

Twain, though ill, was determined the next morning to go sightseeing. He asked a reporter and a major he had met to take him to see the sights, and they took him "with that wild beauty & life all about" to . . . the new post office. A Victorian building that could have been in London. This elicited "the incurable stupidity of man" in his notebook.

Twain bailed on that duo and instead joined his wife and daughter for an excursion. They climbed aboard rickshaws and were hauled to the crowded market at Cinnamon Square and along the seaside esplanade at Galle Face. Twain harbored mixed feelings toward human-drawn vehicles.

He makes good speed for half-an-hour, but it is hard work for him; he is too slight for it. After the half-hour there is no more pleasure for you; your attention is all on the man, just as it would be on a tired horse.

Clara added another reason that her father disliked rickshaws. He was afraid that he would fall out if the driver stopped suddenly, and he would plunge into the tired sweaty fellow.

When Twain later felt well enough, he recorded his initial impressions of the people and clothes he saw in Ceylon, that teardrop island at the triangular tip of India.

The most amazing varieties of nakedness & color—& all harmonious & fascinating. Ingredients: a shining black body nine tenths naked & one or [two] bright colored rags, & you have the perfection of dress—grace, comeliness, convenience, comfort, beauty.

He later buffed up his enthusiasm when writing his travel book:

What a dream [Ceylon] was of tropical splendors of bloom and blossom, and Oriental conflagrations of costume! The walking groups of men, women, boys, girls, babies—each individual was a flame, each group a house afire for color. And such stunning colors, such intensely vivid colors, such rich and exquisite minglings and fusings of rainbows and lightnings!

. . . Sometimes a woman's whole dress was but a scarf wound about her person and her head, sometimes a man's was but a turban and a careless rag or two—in both cases generous areas of polished dark skin showing—but always the arrangement compelled the homage of the eye and made the heart sing for gladness.

Twain's delight in sightseeing on that Thursday morning of January 15 was suddenly interrupted. A dozen Ceylonese young women, students at a nearby missionary school, walked by, wearing "prim," "pious" European clothes.

Those clothes—oh, they were unspeakably ugly! Ugly, barbarous, destitute of taste, destitute of grace, repulsive as a shroud. I looked at my womenfolk's clothes—just full-grown duplicates of the outrages disguising those poor little abused creatures—and was ashamed to be seen in the street with them. Then I looked at my own clothes, and was ashamed to be seen in the street with myself.

Twain adored the exotic, the unpredictable, the colorful. His brief blurry stay in Ceylon would whet his appetite for India. Livy called Colombo the "most fascinating, picturesque place" she had ever seen but noted that night that she had heard Bombay was "even more interesting."

They boarded the old tub *Rosetta,* a rusty step down from the *Oceana,* and Twain curled up in his cabin for the entire three-day journey. Livy thought her husband's room "intolerably hot," but he claimed not to "feel" the heat. Livy and Clara, escaping the sauna-like conditions, slept on mattresses on deck, enjoying two "glorious" breezy starry nights. They modestly scampered to their sweltering rooms at 6 a.m.

Livy marveled: "Winter! How ridiculous it seems to say winter when we are in this broiling heat."

The family reached Bombay on January 18, and so began Mark Twain's unlikely love affair with India.

CHAPTER 17

Bombay!

I t seems surprising, verging on incredible, that this petulant
performer, this grouchy, exhausted traveler, could fall in love with
any place at that point in his life. But the American author found
himself mesmerized by the eclectic, brazen color-charged chaos of India,
of ashes-splashed naked holy men, of cinnamon-tinted women twirled in
gaudy gauze, of cows ruling corners, of monkeys enshrined in temples, of
corpses devoured by vultures, of fakirs running freak shows, of jeweled
maharajahs aboard even more bejeweled elephants, of harems ported in
swaying palanquins, of the stately Taj Mahal and the holy river Ganges.

Twain's fascination with India was no literary pose; his uncharacteristically gushing observations spill off the pages of his private notebooks and
into letters and then onto the pages of his later travel book. He never
outgrew a sort of child's delight in encountering the exotic—the circus,
rafting pirates; he kept his keen pleasure at running smack into something never expected to turn up in Hannibal, Missouri.

Years later, he would call India "the *only* foreign land I ever daydream
about or deeply long to see again." That means India outranked England,
France, Italy, Germany, Austria, Sweden, Switzerland, Egypt, the Holy
Land, Australia, New Zealand, South Africa, to name some places that
the author visited.

"Father seemed like a young boy in his enthusiasm over everything
he saw," wrote Clara of their stay in India. "He kept reiterating: 'This
wonderland land, this marvelous land! There can be no other like it.'"

Twain's sojourn in India began badly. He felt truly ill with a bronchial cough. The American vice-consul Samuel Comfort had planned a big welcome at the dock, but the SS *Rosetta* arrived three hours early, spoiling it. (Comfort also happened to be Standard Oil's agent for the region, so he no doubt had H.H. Rogers's orders to cater to the famous guest.)

Over the previous few days, Twain's cough had worsened, taking most of his voice with it. The family boarded a carriage and rode to one of the city's best hotels, Watson's Esplanade, a four-story Moorish-Victorian palace with arabesque bay windows and curved, arched verandas, built in 1863 on the edge of University Gardens. The place featured exotic Taj Mahal–style decor with electric lights in the rooms till midnight.

Outside the carriage, he glimpsed the swarms of color, the brown skin. He shuffled into the lobby, coughing, on Saturday, January 18, 1896, and was immediately charmed.

> The lobbies and halls were full of turbaned, and fez'd and embroidered, cap'd, and barefooted, and cotton-clad dark natives, some of them rushing about, others at rest squatting, or sitting on the ground; some of them chattering with energy, others still and dreamy.

The unreliable hydraulic elevator was not working, so the "burly" German manager led the Clemens family to their rooms two flights up on the front of the building. Twain was amused to see a chain of about seventeen solemn servants—like porters on a big-game safari—carrying their luggage. The last few men had little to tote: one had a box of cigars, another carried an umbrella, but each later "waited patiently" until a family member found time to give him a coin.

The manager fussed to set up the family in their rooms. When a servant failed to fix the door that led to the balcony, the manager suddenly cuffed him across the face and scolded him loudly. Twain, in his feverish state, felt transported back to pre–Civil War America, to a time when his father used to cuff the "harmless slave boy," Lewis. The Indian servant meekly accepted his beating, saying nothing, just as Lewis had done. That was the way of the world in the antebellum South and also apparently in British India. In both cases, Twain felt "sorry for the victim and ashamed for the punisher." (When he felt better, he would fill several notebook pages on this incident.)

The servants unpacked some of the luggage and installed the patient in his bedroom. Dr. Sidney Smith, who came recommended by *Murray's Handbook,* paid a house call. The doctor prescribed bed rest and throat lozenges. He would return for three more house calls and order the patient kept indoors for Twain's first six days in India.

Twain promised to rest, but he felt frustrated and tantalized by the panorama that he could see from his window.

> There is a rank of noble great shade trees across the way from the hotel, and under them sit groups of picturesque natives of both sexes; and the juggler in his turban is there with his snakes and his magic; and all day long the cabs and the multitudinous varieties of costumes flock by. It does not seem as if one could ever get tired of watching this moving show, this shining and shifting spectacle.

That night, the hotel servant shut the curtains and shrouded the bed in mosquito netting, and Twain soon fell into a deep sleep. He was awoken abruptly in the dark, at first not sure if he was dreaming. He jotted in his notebook.

> The hotel noises begin about 5 in the morning. Hindoo servants yelling orders to each other from story to story. It is equal to a riot and insurrection for noise. And there are other noises—roofs falling in, windows smashing, persons being murdered, crows squawking, canaries screeching, fiendish bursts of laughter, explosions of dynamite. By 7 o'clock one has suffered all the different kinds of shock there are & can never more be disturbed by them.

Twain drifted back into a deep sleep around 7 a.m. He luxuriated in it. He needed rest to recuperate. Then the crows started. Hundreds of crows lived in the rows of trees across the street by the Gardens. They squawked and jabbered almost exactly for an hour, then stopped abruptly. Twain, in his feverish state, would become a bit obsessed with the birds, deciding since they lived in India, a land of reincarnation, that this bird or that bird had passed through various human lives, such as "a gambler, a low comedian . . . a fussy woman . . . a thief . . . a reformer, a lecturer . . . an infidel, and a wallower in sin for the mere love of it."

He found the crow remorseless. He expected its next incarnation to be as an author. Since Twain couldn't sleep that Sunday (and many following days), he lounged out on the balcony. In his delirious state, he was convinced the crows were gossiping about him.

> They would sit there, in the most unabashed way, and talk about my clothes, and my hair, and my complexion, and probable character and vocation and politics, and how I came to be in India, and what I had been doing, and how many days I had got for it, and how I had happened to go unhanged so long, and when would it probably come off, and might there be more of my sort where I came from, and when would they be hanged,—and so on, and so on, until I could no longer endure the embarrassment of it; then I would shoo them away, and they would circle around in the air a little while, laughing and deriding and mocking, and presently settle on the rail and do it all over again.

He survived Sunday. On Monday, the family hired a manservant to help him. *Murray's Handbook* advised: "A good travelling servant, a native who can speak English, is indispensable, but should on no account be engaged without a good personal character or the recommendation of a trustworthy agent."

The Clemens family scrutinized a pile of recommendations and selected "Pedro" because he was judged extremely competent and his English skills were spoken of "with warm admiration verging upon rapture."

Livy went downstairs and met Pedro. She hired him for a trial week. He was fiftyish, tall, slender, a tad stoop-shouldered, timid-eyed, wearing faded European clothes, born of a Portuguese Catholic father and a Goa mother, of Brahmin descent. (Twain found him religiously "well-equipped" if not capable in many other areas.)

Twain sized up the man's language skills: "Quaint & pleasant English, & a little hard to understand at first."

The recuperating author was excited to have a servant, or as he put it "something new to play with." He had read the guidebooks; he knew how important they were.

> You hire him as soon as you touch Indian soil; for no matter what your sex is, you cannot do without him. He is messenger, valet, chambermaid, table-waiter, lady's maid, courier—he is everything.

He carries a coarse linen clothes-bag and a quilt; he sleeps on the stone floor outside your chamber door, and gets his meals you do not know where nor when; you only know that he is not fed on the premises, either when you are in a hotel or when you are a guest in a private house. His wages are large—from an Indian point of view—and he feeds and clothes himself out of them.

Twain chatted up Pedro and learned he had been to Ceylon: "I been there—been shooting three gentlemen there. Also elephants. Also tiger." The author called it "bearer" English. "Where he gets his English is his own secret. There is nothing like it elsewhere in the earth; or even in paradise, perhaps, but the other place is probably full of it."

By Wednesday, cooped-up Twain realized that he could barely make sense of anything that deferential Pedro said. He tried to order him around with often bizarre results. A command to clean up the bathroom led Pedro to tidying the wardrobe.

That day, an invite arrived to dine on Thursday with the most powerful man in the region, the British governor, Lord Sandhurst, at Government House on Malabar Point, but Twain felt too ill. "Had to decline lest my cough jump on me again."

He did allow a handful of reporters to interview him in his room to build traffic for his upcoming Friday show. One of them observed him filling "a capacious briar-root pipe, which was kept busily engaged as he paced up and down the room, enveloped in a rich cloud of smoke." To repeat: he was suffering from a bronchial cough.

Twain told the reporters that his well-meaning family was torturing him. "My wife and daughter overwhelm me with the fascinations of Bombay and so make my imprisonment all the harder to put up with."

Livy, who had started a letter to her sister in Bombay harbor, still had not yet finished it. "Absolutely, the *most* fascinating place I have seen," she would write on Friday, "and for a week I have been trying to write you about it, but could not snatch a moment. Social life and sightseeing *all* the time—breakfasts, lunches, teas, dinners, balls."

One senses no one stayed and held Twain's hand, except his newly hired servant, Pedro, who didn't survive his trial period.

[Pedro] was a failure, poor old fellow. His age was against him. He was desperately slow and phenomenally forgetful. When he went three blocks on an errand he would be gone two hours, and then forget what it was he went for. . . . He couldn't wait satisfactorily at table—a prime defect, for if you haven't your own servant in an Indian hotel you are likely to have a slow time of it and go away hungry. We couldn't understand his English; he couldn't understand ours; and when we found that he couldn't understand his own, it seemed time for us to part. I had to discharge him; there was no help for it. But I did it as kindly as I could, and as gently. We must part, said I, but I hoped we should meet again in a better world. It was not true, but it was only a little thing to say, and saved his feelings and cost me nothing.

By Friday, performance day, Twain was ready to hire a new servant. He chose someone young, full of vitality, wearing the garb of the region. He gave him a very brief trial.

[He] flitted in, touched his forehead, and began to fly around here, there, and everywhere, on his velvet feet, and in five minutes he had everything in the room "ship-shape and Bristol fashion," as the sailors say, and was standing at the salute, waiting for orders. Dear me, what a rustler he was after the slumbrous way of [Pedro], poor old slug! All my heart, all my affection, all my admiration, went out spontaneously to this frisky little forked black thing, this compact and compressed incarnation of energy and force and promptness and celerity and confidence, this smart, smily, engaging, shiney-eyed little devil, feruled on his upper end by a gleaming fire-coal of a fez with a red-hot tassel dangling from it. I said, with deep satisfaction—
"You'll suit. What is your name?"
He reeled it mellowly off.
"Let me see if I can make a selection out of it—for business uses, I mean; we will keep the rest for Sundays. Give it to me in installments."
He did it. But there did not seem to be any short ones, except Mousa—which suggested mouse. It was out of character; it was too soft, too quiet, too conservative; it didn't fit his splendid style.

Nonetheless, they called him "Mauzie." Twain, fresh from a week in bed, showed up at the Novelty Theatre on Friday. The show was set for

5:30 p.m., which pleased the author as the early time would cater to restless housewives and to workingmen who preferred not to come home and then have to leave again. All 1,400 seats were sold. He walked out on stage, coming off ten days of sick leave. "His appearance was greeted with round after round of loud, prolonged and enthusiastic applause," reported the *Times of India*.

The author performed his dependable opening night: "Corpse," "Mexican Plug," "Old Ram," "Huck/Jim," and "Christening." The audience was three-quarters Caucasian British, but with a surprisingly large sprinkling of Parsee, Muslim, and Hindu ladies and gentlemen. Despite being hoarse, he was a huge success, according to the English-language papers. "The ninety minutes seemed a mere ten."

Twain would mount the platform twice more in Bombay in sold-out theaters.

The British newspapers would lionize him, but the various Indian-language papers would largely ignore him. Over the next weeks, almost no one would recognize him in the streets. Because of illness and long travel distances, he would perform only eighteen times in two months there. But India, for Twain, wasn't about a coronation of his comic skills or receiving a regal welcome.

India didn't discover Twain; Twain discovered India.

CHAPTER 18

Eyes Wide

Released from his cage, Twain needed to make a purchase before he could begin his touring. He bought a white birch bark–covered pith helmet, which matched his white don't-care-a-damn suit. Over the next three days, the author would cram in the most sightseeing, party-attending, club-hopping and hobnobbing of any similar stretch of his entire trip.

He climbed into the carriage of Vice-Consul Comfort along with wife, daughter and Smythe, and headed north through the crowded island section of Bombay. The Brits had corrupted the original Portuguese name of *Bom Bahia* (meaning "Good Bay"), and the name, unlike Greenland, didn't lie: a beautiful strip of land, tapering down to curved inlets with magnificent bays and harbors.

The family was invited to a reception at the home of a wealthy Jain merchant who was honoring a fellow Jain, Mansingji Saringhji, Thakore Sahib of Palitana, a region in Gujarat. On January 1, 1896, Queen Victoria had raised him to Knight Commander of the Most Exalted Order of the Star of India.

Twain adored the exotic-sounding titles of the rulers of these various Indian or Native States. "The barbaric gorgeousnesses, for instance; and the princely titles, the sumptuous titles,—how good they taste in the mouth!" later wrote Twain. "The Nizam of Hyderabad; the Maharajah of Travancore; the Nabob of Jubbelpore; the Begum of Bhopal; the Nawab of Mysore; the Ranee of Gulnare; the Ahkoond of Swat; the Rao of Rohilkund; the Gaikwar of Baroda."

In his notebook, Twain couldn't resist concocting a few more titles: "Slambang of Gutcheree, . . . the Hoopla of Hellasplit, the Breechclout of Buggheroo . . . his Highness the Juggernaut of Jacksonville . . . the Jamram of Ramjam."

The subcontinent of India was then composed of territory under direct British control, about two-thirds of the acreage, while the rest was filled with hundreds of mostly small, semi-autonomous Indian states, with heavy emphasis on *semi-*. Kingdoms such as Hyderabad and Kashmir paid hefty financial tribute to Queen Victoria, Empress of India, for defense (mostly from Britain); meanwhile, British political agents could depose any Indian ruler for misconduct. Twain learned:

> Every year the Empress distributes knighthoods and adds guns for public services [*such as building schools or hospitals*] done by native princes. The salute of a small prince is three or four guns; princes of greater consequence have salutes that run higher and higher, gun by gun,—oh, clear away up to eleven; possibly more, but I did not hear of any above eleven-gun princes. I was told that when a four-gun prince gets a gun added, he is pretty troublesome for a while, till the novelty wears off, for he likes the music, and keeps hunting up pretexts to get himself saluted. It may be that supremely grand folk, like the Nyzam of Hyderabad and the Gaikwar of Baroda, have more than eleven guns, but I don't know.

Actually, Twain erred a tad; the percussive scale ran up to 21 blasts for Indian royalty, 31 for the British viceroy, and 101 for Queen Victoria herself. The monarch's cannon-greeting scheme seems akin to a modern boss giving an employee a promotion and fancy new job title in lieu of a raise.

Before the congratulatory party began, a learned Jain took the Comforts and the Clemenses and Smythe to visit a Jain temple in Byculla. Their guide was named Gandhi. Several respected biographers have identified the man as the soon-to-be-famous Mahatma Mohandas Gandhi, but records indicate he was actually one Virchand Gandhi, who had visited the 1893 Chicago World's Fair.

They mounted white marble stairs polished so finely as to almost seem clear, walking between two massive stone elephants. Livy found it remarkable that they had to remove their shoes as they trod on the colored marble, set in geometric patterns with mystic symbols.

Twain saw a swastika (not yet borrowed by the Nazis) and asked about it. Gandhi explained it was the main symbol of Jain philosophy, representing the four levels of existence: demon, animal (including insects and plants), human, and heavenly. Jainism, espousing a fully vegan nonviolent life, ranks as one of the world's oldest surviving religions. Twain noticed portraits of holy men in a chapel. The man who had been to Chicago explained: "You have also your demi-gods like George Washington, Abraham Lincoln and others and while you place statues of such great men in parks and public places, we place them in temples and sanctuaries."

The earnest, respectful group climbed to the sanctuary on the roof and enjoyed a magnificent view of Bombay, of Hindu temples and Muslim minarets, of the sprawling forty-eight-acre Victoria Gardens, on land donated by an Iraqi Jewish merchant, David Sassoon.

The entourage was taken to the party, already half full of guests, with more arriving in carriages, almost no Europeans. Twain marveled at the variety of colors, especially in the turbans, which he learned varied according to a person's place of origin.

Twain glanced at a group of attractive young dancers, in "gorgeous" jeweled costumes, and then he did a double-take. "These children were professional nautch-dancers, and looked like girls, but they were boys," later wrote Twain. "They got up by ones and twos and fours, and danced and sang to an accompaniment of weird music." He found their bobbing and slithering movements to be "elaborate and graceful," but he was not a fan of the singing. It ranked for him down near a Richard Wagner opera. "Their voices were stringently raspy and unpleasant, and there was a good deal of monotony about the tune."

In the vast hall, not a single woman was present except Olivia and Clara Clemens. Not surprisingly, they were asked if they would like to tour the zenana, or women's quarters.

Livy recounted walking with a relative of the host and being shown the women's and children's costliest dresses and "treasures." With luxury everywhere, she was quite surprised, though, by the eating arrangements. "The dining room is really the kitchen and during meals they squat in front of little tables about six inches in height."

Huzzahs were heard echoing outside, heralding the arrival of the guest of honor, the "Star of India" recipient. Livy and Clara were escorted back to the party and even seated on the dais near the prince, but none of the Jain wives or mothers were allowed to attend.

Amid the crush, there entered a "large stately" man "festooned with ropes of gems," which Twain described in his notebook as "pearls & *green* rubies." (When Livy later corrected him for the book, he told her: "All right, I'll make it emeralds, but it loses force. . . . Green rubies is a fresh thing. And besides it was one of the Prince's own staff liars that told me.")

Twain was impressed by the grandeur of the ceremony, which included tributes and a poet reciting with booming voice. Twain compared the Indian prince's stern-faced and solemn stride across the stage to a Julius Caesar accepting tribute. Seeing the man, awash in emeralds, flanked by his jeweled son and surrounded by ornate armed Gujarati guards, Twain felt as though he was almost time traveling to some long-ago historical scene of royals, perhaps King Solomon receiving the Queen of Sheba.

He had written about Joan of Arc, about King Arthur, about princes and paupers. This pageantry suited him mighty fine.

The Thakor Sahib (his title) of Palitana expressed his thanks, with regal brevity, in English and two other languages. He lingered for a few moments afterwards, long enough to have a servant invite Twain and family to visit his Bombay mansion later in the week.

The next day, Sunday, Twain had lunch at the home of an even more powerful personage, Lord Sandhurst, thirty-nine-year-old governor of Bombay. The Lord and Lady lived at Government House, a brace of breezy bungalows on Malabar Hill, an elephant's tail of land jutting out to sea at the southern tip of Bombay, with magnificent views.

To Twain, the understated power of the mansion symbolized the British Raj "with the quiet elegancies and quiet colors and quiet tastes and quiet dignity that are the outcome of the modern cultivation." Clusters of large turbaned *chuprassies* in crimson robes guarded the grounds.

Throughout his trip, he would be hosted by very high-ranking British civil and military officials and wealthy businessmen. Ultimately, he would sharply criticize the British subjugation and humiliation of native cultures in Australia, Tasmania and South Africa, but he would decide the British brought great benefits—railroads, telegraph, schools, hospitals—to the warring petty-state chaos of India. He found it astounding and impressive that 150,000 white British-born citizens (half of them soldiers) could somehow devise a smooth orderly way to control 300 million brown-skinned natives across a subcontinent.

After a leisurely lunch, at around 4 p.m., Twain and his group rode through beautiful gardens to higher ground on scenic Malabar Hill to visit one of the most remarkable holy sites in Bombay: the Towers of Silence. Here, the Parsees dispose of their dead by exposing them to vultures.

Carlyle Smythe had sent a letter requesting permission to see inside and to photograph, but his request had been denied. The Parsees apparently feared ridicule and misunderstanding. They believe that corpses should not contaminate the sacred elements: not the Earth by burial, not Fire by cremation, not Water by sprinkling of ashes. So they expose their dead to be devoured by vultures in elaborate, brilliantly designed stone structures.

Twain and his party alighted from the carriages. They saw five white-washed cylindrical masonry towers; the largest was twenty-five feet high and about eighty-five feet across. Twain noted a row of vultures perched along the top of the walls. At first glance, he thought they were stone statuary, gargoyles, till a wing flapped and a bald head twitched.

The visitors were fortunate to see a funeral. A procession of 100 or so mourners—symbolically linked by a white rope and followed by a lone dog—accompanied the corpse up the hill to the vicinity of the towers. From there, two Parsee funeral workers, outcasts—even though they wore gloves and used large tongs to avoid touching the "unclean" dead body—carried the corpse up steps and into the large, squat tower. "When the iron gate was opened & the corpse carried in, Clara & Livy had a glimpse thro' the distant iron door, of the vultures flying down in." So Twain wrote in his notebook. He claimed in his later book that "nothing was left of it but a clean-picked skeleton when they flocked-out again a few minutes afterward."

A Parsee gentleman, Jewanjee Jamshedjee Modi, took the group to a separate building, which housed a scale model of a tower. He explained that inside the tower were concentric stone layers with shallow troughs for the corpses, with channels cut to allow bodily liquids to flow down through charcoal filters. Once the sun and winds further cleaned the bones, an attendant picked them up with tongs and tossed them into a well in the center. Rich and poor, wise and foolish, their dust comingles for eternity . . . no name plates, no family plots . . . just dust in a well on a Bombay hill.

A British travel writer found the place disturbing. "It seemed horrible to watch the great vultures perched near the buildings, some gorged with their meal of yesterday, others waiting eagerly for that of to-day."

But Twain, the contrarian, was impressed on both social and hygienic grounds. He liked the equality in death that didn't elevate the pharaoh's pyramid over the pauper's grave. He also commented in the visitors' book:

> One marvels to see here a perfect system for the protection of the living from contagion derivable from the dead—I mean one marvels to see this proof that modern science is behind the ancients in this important matter.

He made no jokes on the Towers of Silence in his travel book, and that section happened to be chosen to be excerpted in the *New York World* for prepublication publicity. (A Parsee in New York would find a few small mistakes, such as Twain claiming the body was carried naked in the procession instead of being stripped *inside* the tower.)

The 60,000 Parsees of Bombay formed an elite and very philanthropic community, praised by Twain as "energetic, enterprising, progressive"; they spread their wealth during their lifetimes, especially by building hospitals for humans and animals. They often acted as intermediaries between the Hindus and the British.

Several Parsee gentlemen, afterward, took the Twain party for a carriage ride amid the lush gardens and sea views of Malabar Hill. The view, as they coasted along at sunset, remained etched among the most memorable of Twain's yearlong odyssey.

> This is the drive around the sea-shore to Malabar Point, where Lord Sandhurst, the Governor of the Bombay Presidency, lives. Parsee palaces all along the first part of the drive; and past them all the world is driving; the private carriages of wealthy Englishmen and natives of rank are manned by a driver and three footmen in stunning oriental liveries—two of these turbaned statues standing up behind, as fine as monuments. Sometimes even the public carriages have this superabundant crew, slightly modified—one to

drive, one to sit by and see it done, and one to stand up behind and yell—yell when there is anybody in the way, and for practice when there isn't. It all helps to keep up the liveliness and augment the general sense of swiftness and energy and confusion and pow-wow.

In the region of Scandal Point—felicitous name—where there are handy rocks to sit on and a noble view of the sea on the one hand, and on the other the passing and repassing whirl and tumult of gay carriages, are great groups of comfortably-off Parsee women—perfect flower-beds of brilliant color, a fascinating spectacle.

Tramp, tramp, tramping along the road, in singles, couples, groups, and gangs, you have the working-man and the working-woman—but not clothed like ours. Usually the man is a nobly-built great athlete, with not a rag on but his loin-handkerchief; his color a deep dark brown, his skin satin, his rounded muscles knobbing it as if it had eggs under it. Usually the woman is a slender and shapely creature, as erect as a lightning-rod, and she has but one thing on—a bright-colored piece of stuff which is wound about her head and her body down nearly half-way to her knees, and which clings like her own skin. Her legs and feet are bare, and so are her arms, except for her fanciful bunches of loose silver rings on her ankles and on her arms. She has jewelry bunched on the side of her nose also, and showy clusterings on her toes. When she undresses for bed she takes off her jewelry, I suppose. If she took off anything more she would catch cold. As a rule she has a large shiney brass water jar of graceful shape on her head, and one of her naked arms curves up and the hand holds it there. She is so straight, so erect, and she steps with such style, and such easy grace and dignity; and her curved arm and her brazen jar are such a help to the picture—indeed, our working-women cannot begin [to compete] with her as a road-decoration.

It is all color, bewitching color, enchanting color—everywhere all around—all the way around the curving great opaline bay clear to Government House.

———

Twain woke up Monday morning knowing he had a performance that night, but he decided to break his rule about not sightseeing on show

Be good + you will be lonesome.

Mark Twain

The frontispiece of *Following the Equator*.

LEFT: Twain's formal onstage attire (seen here, aboard the USS *Mohican* in Seattle harbor).

BOTTOM: Twain expected this "mechanical miracle," the Paige typesetter, which weighed four tons and had 18,000 moving parts, to revolutionize the publishing industry. Instead, it bankrupted him.

TOP: Throughout their 1895–96 trip, the thoughts of the Clemens family often wandered back to their much-loved Farmington Avenue home in Hartford, Connecticut. They hadn't been able to afford to live there since 1891.

RIGHT: Livy urging her husband to put on an overcoat, on a Great Lakes steamer in July.

BOTTOM: Twain, who loved cats, holding a pair of kittens by a tarpaper shack in a Norwegian shantytown in Great Falls, Montana.

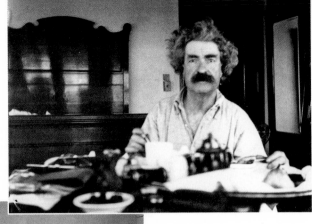

RIGHT: Twain at breakfast in his room in the near-empty hotel in Olympia, Washington.

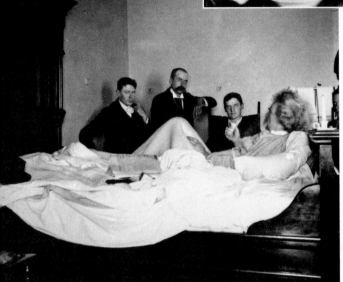

LEFT: Twain recuperating from bronchitis, doing interviews and smoking a pipe. Vancouver, British Columbia.

BOTTOM: An irritated Twain demanded his lecture agent "travel" him along the platform in Crookston, Minnesota, since the predawn train was more than an hour late. Mrs. Martha Pond, Major James Pond, Twain, Livy (left to right) *and* Clara's shadow.

TOP: On the rail of the SS *Warrimoo*, heading to Australia from Victoria, British Columbia, August 23, 1895. Twain, Clara, Livy (left to right).

BOTTOM: Sydney, Australia, 1890s. George Street.

THE USUAL SPIRIT.

TOP: The artwork of *Following the Equator* sometimes deftly combined anti-imperialism with nudity. Here, an Australian rancher is accused of serving a poisoned Christmas pudding to the aborigines.

RIGHT: Livy and Clara Clemens at Falk's studio in Sydney, September 16, 1895.

In New Zealand, Twain saw a similar skeleton of this extinct bird, a giant moa; he was quite impressed. (James Gault erected this one at Slovens Creek.)

TOP: Celebrity Twain was often hosted and pampered by wealthy families such as the Kinseys in Christchurch, New Zealand.

RIGHT: Twain with his lecture agent, Carlyle Smythe, who accompanied him through Australia, New Zealand, India, South Africa, and on to England. Smythe booked theaters, hotels, and transportation, and graciously handled all requests, including playing pool with his boss.

TOP: The Clemens family, though deep in debt, traveled in style, on the luxurious 468-foot SS *Oceana,* of the Peninsular & Oriental line, from Australia to India.

BOTTOM: The elegant lounge, dining room, and grand staircase.

TOP: Twain loved the unpredictability of sightseeing in India. Here is a holy fakir at work. Twain envied their income.

BOTTOM: Snake charmers set up on a street near Twain's hotel in Bombay.

TOP: Twain described the cows in Hindu India as "lordly" and said he always gave them right-of-way on the sidewalks.

BOTTOM: Twain was disturbed to witness people drinking Ganges water near the cremation ghats in Benares (Varanasi).

RIGHT: The Gaikwar of Baroda, one of the world's ten wealthiest men, hired Twain for a private performance in his palace for two hundred close friends.

LEFT: Twain rode an elephant like this jeweled one at Baroda. He rode alone and later admitted he couldn't stop worrying that the elephant might break away and start running through the crowded town.

BOTTOM: A loop on the Darjeeling railroad, with vast chasms below. Twain railroaded up and roller coastered down.

Twain enjoyed the dancing of the "nautch girls" who often performed at weddings, but he wasn't fond of their nose rings.

TOP: Twain described riding in "cab substitutes" or "open coffins, in which you sit and are then borne on men's shoulders." He even took one up a mountainside in Darjeeling.

RIGHT: The observant Twain noticed the phallic nature of this Calcutta monument to David Ochterlony.

BOTTOM: Zulu rickshaw drivers in Durban, southern Africa. Twain discovered uncomfortable parallels to the pre–Civil War South.

TOP: Cheerful Aunt Sue (Susan Langdon Crane) playing with Osman (a Saint Bernard) and Bim (Major Pond's son). Notice Twain's troubled fifteen-year-old daughter, Jean Clemens, on the roof.

BOTTOM: Susy, looking sad, marooned in Aunt Sue's dining room in Elmira, New York, while her parents traveled.

Twain with H.H. Rogers, American oil, steel, and copper tycoon,
on vacation in 1908.

days. He and Clara took a carriage to the Natural History Society. His private tour included seeing "boy's toes" found in the stomach of a panther, which confirms "the beast is a man-eater upon occasion." He saw hibernating cobras and vivid chameleons, but the animal that riveted his attention was the pet of the main official, H. M. Phipson, who had seen Twain twenty-two years earlier in London.

A two-year-old giant hornbill bird named "William" lived in a large cage behind Phipson's desk; it would grow to be more than four feet tall, could catch tennis balls thrown from thirty feet, and once swallowed a lit cigar with no ill effects. The bird with its large, distinctive orange, yellow, and white beak lived twenty-six years, and was referred to as the "office canary." Phipson, an original Society founder, told Twain that the bird "colors his vast bill every morning . . . [since] it rubs off." The humorist wrote that in his notebook but wised up enough not to put it in the book.

Twain performed Monday evening at 5:30 p.m., delivering a second-night lineup that included the Aussie Poem, which especially wowed the sold-out audience. Afterwards, he rode from the Novelty Theatre to the prestigious Bombay Club, where he was the guest of honor for dinner at the male-only enclave.

Meanwhile, Livy and Clara attended a ball at the equally prestigious Royal Yacht Club. The long veranda offered spectacular views of sailing ships and regattas, while club officials could climb a tall teak lookout tower to judge the races. The club also featured a fine billiards room, a massive dining room with an open timber roof, and a huge ballroom with shoulder-high wainscoting.

The Yacht Club had earlier sent a note offering Twain an "honorary membership" for a month for 16 rupees (about $4, which equals $120 in today's dollars), in effect waiving the hefty 200-rupee initiation fee ($50, or $1,500 today). Twain, however, found *any* fee for something called "honorary" just plain wrong. "A club should not pay a compliment wh[ich] it can't afford," he scratched in his notebook. "They ought to . . . call it a Temporary Membership, a word which carries no deception with it." Needless to say, he did not pay, and he apparently shared his pique with other gentlemen in Bombay.

Twain lingered a few minutes at the Royal Yacht Club, then the entire entourage, with Smythe, headed at 11:30 p.m. to a wedding ceremony at the home of a wealthy Hindu merchant. To reach the address, they drove through a usually crowded part of town, a vibrant market. But at this hour, they saw all the shops shuttered, an occasional oil lamp, and hundreds of people curled up near each other sleeping on the sidewalks and streets. The stillness reminded Twain of battlefield dead. The carriage could barely weave through the sleeping bodies; rats occasionally scampered out, startled by the horses' hooves.

They turned a corner and encountered a sudden glare of light. Row upon row of small candles in tumblers hung "thick as stars" along lattices up and down the street. They reached the gas-lit wedding house, with gaudy decorations and clusters of men everywhere. The only female present besides Livy and Clara was the bride herself, a "trim & comely little" twelve-year-old dressed in black velvet pants embroidered with silver. Around her neck dangled a thick sixteen-inch rope of "big diamonds" with a "superb" green emerald as the pendant. She politely greeted them, and they learned that her future husband, also twelve years old, had already gone to bed.

The Clemenses entered the large main room of the home. Soon after, two female nautch dancers arrived with musicians "who played upon instruments which made uncanny noise which made one's flesh creep," according to Twain. At one point, a man played snake-charmer music upon a flutelike pipe while the young women danced and wriggled, imitating snakes being coaxed out of hiding places. Twain, for his part, did not think that that "unlovely squawk" of music could charm anything, but a nearby Parsee gentleman assured him that snakes were indeed drawn to those sounds. He told Twain that he had recently attended a similar gathering and that a half dozen snakes showed up. The musicians stopped, and a snake wrangler captured the snakes to carry them elsewhere, because the devout hosts would not kill any creature.

As they prepared to leave at 2 a.m., Twain noticed a massive muscular fellow on the porch of the house, whom he discovered to be "a turbaned giant, with a name according to his size: "Rao Bahadur Baskirao Balinkanje Pitale, Vakeel to his Highness the Gaikwar of Baroda." Twain noted: "Without him the picture would not have been complete; and if his name had been merely Smith, he wouldn't have answered." This vakeel, or emissary, relayed his master's invitation to Twain to come perform at Baroda, 250 miles due north. The Gaikwar, who also rated the title of maharajah, would pay 1,000 rupees, about $250 ($7,500 today). (Twain would check his schedule with Smythe and then accept.)

Before leaving, the author asked again about the bridegroom. "As I understood it, he and the bride were to entertain company every night and nearly all night for a week or more, then get married, if alive. Both of the children were a little elderly, as brides and grooms go, in India—twelve; they ought to have been married a year or two sooner; still to a stranger twelve seems quite young enough."

Clara later wrote: "Father was touched by the helplessness of the tiny child whose grandmother was only thirty-eight years old." Twain's own last comment in his notebook ran in a different direction: "Within an hour it began to embarrass me to see people with clothes on."

He lectured Tuesday in Bombay, then Wednesday 100 miles away in Poona. He returned Thursday morning on the night train and squeezed in a handful of visits. First, he paid a call on that new Knight Commander, the Thakore Sahib of Palitana, in his Bombay palace. Twain enjoyed the earnest conversation of the sixty-year-old, but he found himself preferring the company of the two young heirs, the ten-year-old prince, who had been to the 1893 Chicago World's Fair, and the eight-year-old princess. Twain, who would later collect "angelfish" (young platonic female friends) à la Lewis Carroll, described her as

> a wee brown sprite, very pretty, very serious, very winning, delicately moulded, costumed like the daintiest butterfly, a dear little fairyland princess, gravely willing to be friendly with the strangers, but in the beginning preferring to hold her father's hand until she could take stock of them and determine how far they were to be trusted. She must have been eight years old; so in the natural (Indian) order of things she would be a bride in three or four years from now, and then this free contact with the sun and the air and the other belongings of out-door nature and comradeship with visiting male folk would end, and she would shut herself up in the zenana for life, like her mother, and by inherited habit of mind would be happy in that seclusion and not look upon it as an irksome restraint and a weary captivity.

The Clemens ladyfolk again departed to the zenana, while Twain tried to learn how to wind a turban, that is, how to deftly twist and turn forty-plus feet of thin tissue fabric around his famous mop of gray hair. He failed. He asked lots of questions on lots of topics. He found out that the silverware was locked up—to protect it from theft, from the touch of the lower caste and from the application of poison.

> I believe a salaried taster has to taste everything before the prince ventures it—an ancient and judicious custom in the East, and has thinned out the tasters a good deal, for of course it is the cook that puts the poison in. If I were an Indian prince I would not go to the expense of a taster, I would eat with the cook.

Their visit ended with garlands of yellow flowers draped around the necks of Mr. and Mrs. Clemens and Clara, and the gift of some breath-freshening, mood-stimulating betel nut to chew.

Twain also found time to squeeze in a visit with one of the most powerful and wealthiest men in the Muslim world, then eighteen-year-old Mohammed Aga Khan, the leader of the Ismaeli Shi'ite Muslims, a direct descendant of the Prophet and great-grandson of the Shah of Persia (Iran). Twain wrote in his notebook: "Sells indulgences; is worshipped; has a great following; they get the parings of his fingernails from his barber & set them in gold & wear them as . . . amulets."

Mohammed Aga Khan was indeed fabulously wealthy; his followers later gave him his weight in gold, then in diamonds (243 pounds in 1946), then in platinum; his horses won the English Derby five times. Pro-British, he would one day be president of the League of Nations. In his memoir, he recalled Twain as having "unassuming charm" that "captivated the serious-minded lad that I was." Twain was impressed that the young man had read *Huckleberry Finn*.

After all that chatting, Twain craved a cup of coffee before his night train to Baroda. He decided to have it at the Bombay Club, which had made him an honorary member. No members were present, but the servants let him in and served him a cup of coffee. He drank it; he asked for the check. They brought him another cup of coffee. He drank it; he again asked for the check. They brought him yet another cup of coffee. He drank it; he once again asked for the check.

> When I had drunk nine cups & could not hold any more, I turned out to see if I could find a waiter who could understand me. But every time I approached one, he dodged away. Then something

occurred to me which should have occurred to me before: that the waiters had quite naturally taken me for an unauthorized interloper, & that they didn't know what to do with me or how to get rid of me in the absence of their officers, & had conceived the idea of pacifying me with coffee until Providence should have pity & interfere. It was a delicate situation. It was embarrassing to stay, & it was embarrassing to try to go. On the whole, I thought I would try to go. On the stairs I came across that first waiter, & told him my trouble, & asked for my bill, & said I had tried my best to make the others understand. but he said—"Oh, they understood!"

That was a surprise.

"They understood? Then why didn't they bring the bill?"

"Oh, they had their orders—it was all right."

"What orders?"

"The [Club] President's. He told us to watch out for you, & remember your face, & said we must give you whatever you wanted & not let you pay anything, you being the guest of the club."

One can picture the Bombay Club president not wanting to be damned in the same paragraph as the Royal Yacht Club. Twain pursued the topic with the waiter and tried to discover if he had asked for the bill *forty-five* times whether he would have received *forty-five* cups of coffee. The Indian servant looked at him and said solemnly: "Why, then, sir, I am sure you wouldn't need any more coffee today." The author left deeply impressed that the servant never once cracked a smile; and he left convinced that they would have kept politely serving him coffee until it ran out of his ears.

Twain loved India.

CHAPTER 19

Rails, Riches and Elephants

On the evening of January 30, the Clemens family headed to the train station to go to Baroda, accompanied by Smythe, Mauzie and a new servant for the women. "We named him Barney for short; we couldn't use his real name, there wasn't time." Twain also later decided to change Mauzie's nickname to Satan.

The author, who had accepted the offer to play private jester for a crowned prince, would entertain 200 of the man's closest friends in the durbar hall of a three-century-old palace, whose white stucco exterior resembled wedding cake frosting. He would meet and socialize briefly with the thirty-two-year-old maharajah of Baroda, Sayajirao, who ruled (and owned) an area almost twice the size of Connecticut, with a population of 2½ million. The maharajah, whom *Time* would rank in 1910 as the world's sixth wealthiest man, had recently finished building a gargantuan new palace, almost four times larger than Buckingham Palace.

Twain was frequently drawn toward wealthy men, such as Andrew Carnegie or H.H. Rogers, but perhaps what appealed to him most in this case was that this prince had formerly been a pauper. The backstory seems right out of the pages of Kipling.

A popular maharajah had died back in 1870. His pregnant maharani had given birth to yet another girl, leaving the throne vacant; his brother, who had been imprisoned for conspiring to hire a British assassin to murder his sibling, had ascended to the throne. According to the British, he proved cruel, greedy, pleasure mad; he ordered up a pair of cannons cast in solid gold, each weighing 280 pounds, to outdo a silver pair commissioned by an ancestor. He created a "carpet" of pearls. He administered whimsical justice. When Great Britain complained about misrule, he tried to poison the British resident agent with arsenic. After four years, the Secretary of State for India, Lord Salisbury, ordered the lunatic shuffled off the throne and into house arrest in Madras.

Hence, the hunt for heirs in 1875. Dozens of distant cousins flocked to Baroda to seek the throne. Three penniless brothers walked 400 miles. According to Twain, Great Britain judged the eighteen-year-old too grown up to be pliable and thought the ten-year-old would be a minor for too long. The British chose the twelve-year-old middle son. According to lore, when he was asked why he had come to Baroda, he replied: "To be maharajah, of course." (Twain added a detail in his account, that the boy was "making mud pies" when he was summoned to court.)

After six years of seasoning by both Indian and British tutors, lessons in reading and writing Marathi, English and Gujarati, and training in cricket, cheetah-hunting and pig-sticking, he ascended the throne and had been ruling quite successfully for the past fifteen years. He was a passionate Anglophile who wore Savile Row suits and later bought Tennyson's home, but chafed under the bullying of local British rule in India.

The Clemens family reached the Bombay train station that night, and the American author yet again became hypnotized by the kaleidoscopic scene: brown skin, bright fabric, motion, noise.

> It was a very large station, yet when we arrived it seemed as if the whole world was present—half of it inside, the other half outside, and both halves, bearing mountainous head-loads of bedding and other freight, trying simultaneously to pass each other, in opposing floods, in one narrow door. These opposing floods were patient, gentle, long-suffering natives, with whites scattered among them at rare intervals; and wherever a white man's native servant appeared, that native seemed to have put aside his natural gentleness for the time and invested himself with the white man's privilege of making a way for himself by promptly shoving all intervening black things out of it. In these exhibitions of authority Satan was scandalous. He was probably a Thug in one of his former incarnations.

Neither Clara nor Livy were huge fans of aggressive behavior, although boarding a train in India, finding seats or sleeper berths, loading luggage—all of it required some aggression. "Such rows as went on between private servants or official porters carrying baggage would only seem excusable during an earthquake," later wrote Clara. "We were always relieved when we failed to discover our own Indian servant in one of these station brawls."

Her father, meanwhile, enjoyed the whole show and couldn't shift his eyes away from it. He noticed colorful family clusters from newborns to great-grandparents, all of them poor people but most women, covered in gaudy gold jewelry, especially nose rings, toe rings, wrist and ankle bands.

These silent crowds sat there with their humble bundles and baskets and small household gear about them, and patiently waited— for what? A train that was to start at some time or other during the day or night! They hadn't timed themselves well, but that was no matter—the thing had been so ordered from on high, therefore why worry?

Twain saw an unthinkable mass of humanity cram into some of the cheap third-class cars of another train; it seemed like a three-dimensional human jigsaw puzzle, trying to fit all of them inside that space. He learned about a problem he hadn't expected. Higher-caste Hindus didn't want to be defiled by touching lower-caste Hindus. So, each caste clustered together as others of unknown castes wriggled to find a vacant spot. Train travel at times became easier for the lower castes and a perilous obstacle course for the likes of the Brahmins.

Twain caught sight of Barney and Satan and found them commanding a line of porters to enter a railway car to deliver bedding and satchels, parasols and cigar boxes. Hand baggage was tossed into a netting; two leather-strapped shelf beds in the wall could be folded down over the permanent sofa beds below; blue-tinted windows that opened allowed light without glare; a little storage closet held a wash bowl. He found the space "light, airy, homelike," and Barney and Satan came back a bit later and made their beds with Twain's sheets and pillows. Twain and Smythe shared a room, as did Livy and Clara; Barney and Satan disappeared to parts unknown. The train left at 10 p.m. for the 255-mile ride north, set to arrive in Baroda at 7 a.m., jogging at a fine twenty-eight-mile-per-hour pace with stops.

During their descent the following morning, as they rubbed sleep out of their eyes, the moment seemed out of a fairy tale. The prince's massive turreted palace loomed a mile away; an elegant gilt carriage with a driver and three footmen, "drawn by picture-book horses with glossy, arched necks," came to pick them up.

They had a whole day free before Twain's 4:30 p.m. performance. After a delicious breakfast at the guest house, the prince's underlings took the Clemens party for a tour and some unannounced activities. They drove through a manicured park that grew progressively wilder and more unkempt. All of a sudden three large gray apes pranced across the road. Twain called it an "unpleasant" surprise, for he expected such creatures in a zoo, but "they look artificial and out of place in a wilderness."

The family arrived in the city portion of Baroda, an "intensely Indian" place of 115,000, not usually on most tourist itineraries. Twain loved seeing authentic Indian houses, "with rude pictures of elephants and princes and gods done in shouting colors." He was amazed by the frantic industry of workmen squatting at little booths "hammering, pounding, brazing, soldering, sewing, designing, cooking, measuring out grain, grinding it, repairing idols."

Their string of sightseeing carriages exited the city for a long lazy quiet ride through the lush countryside of fertile Gujarat; barefoot natives padded along in the still landscape. A string of "stately camels passed by . . . velvet-shod by nature and made no noise." The rare discordant sound came from the unexpected clink of iron from a chain gang, working the road.

They reached their destination: the elephant stables. The Gaikwar, being so wealthy, owned thirty elephants, with sixteen gaudy howdahs in gold, silver and ivory, even solid gold hoops for the elephants' ankles. The prince's mahout, or elephant trainer, beckoned the American humorist.

I took a ride; but it was by request—I did not ask for it, and didn't want it; but I took it, because otherwise they would have thought I was afraid, which I was. The elephant kneels down, by command— one end of him at a time—and you climb the ladder and get into the howdah, and then he gets up, one end at a time, just as a ship gets up over a wave; and after that, as he strides monstrously about, his motion is much like a ship's motion.

The mahout prodded the elephant with a metal pole and whispered into the beast's flapping ear. The mahout eventually judged Twain safely aboard, and he went elsewhere.

Twenty-one-year-old Clara witnessed her white-pith-helmeted *pater* up there in his howdah perch.

> Father seated on an elephant defies description. There was something particularly funny about the sight to me; and Father, suspecting what I was giggling about, said: "What are you laughing at, you sassmill?"
>
> "If you could see yourself, Father, you would laugh, too. The elephant looks so unreal with all his important trappings and you have a troubled air, as if you realized your hat didn't match the blue-and-red harness."

Twain confessed to his daughter he did feel a tad nervous since the mahout had walked far away from him. He asked her: "What could [I] do if the elephant decided to run?" And he later admitted that he was up there in the howdah imagining the damage a mad elephant could do barreling forward and crushing the narrow stalls in the town's marketplace.

Fortunately, he never needed to find out the "what if" answer. Clara also boarded an elephant, and so did the young jeweled son of the Gaikwar, who led the procession on the largest elephant of them all. "We were never free from the impression of living in a fantastic dream," she wrote.

With little time remaining before Twain's 4:30 p.m. performance, the group asked to see the prince's world-famous jewel collection, which included the gold cannons, the 125-karat Star of the South diamond, and that tapestry woven entirely of pearls and precious stones.

Unfortunately the guide thought they had said they wanted to see the gigantic new palace. So he took them to Lukshmi Vilas, the most expensive private building project in nineteenth-century India. Designed by a pair of British architects imitating aspects of Indo-Saracenic style (zenana, durbar, etc.), so massive as to create its own exotic skyline, the palace incorporated dozens of motifs, as though pulled from random pages of an architectural history book. Longer than 200 yards, taking a dozen years to construct, the place was either a dream of one-stop viewing of centuries of design (including a Venetian mosaic floor, Flemish stained-glass windows, Mughal-style panels, French chandeliers and Gothic arches), or a nightmare hodgepodge.

Twain brusquely called it "mixed modern American-European [that] has not a merit except costliness; it is wholly foreign to India, and impudent and out of place." He added: "The architect has escaped."

At 4:30 p.m., Twain appeared in the durbar, or large meeting hall, of the *old* palace, Nazarbagh, which had been built in 1721. With its Moorish colonnades, it fit into the landscape. The wealthy prince used the building to house his library and art collection.

Twain loved the room even if it did echo a bit. He performed before the most Indian audience of his trip, including a soon-to-be internationally famous yogi, Aurobindo, and was warmly received, especially by the sophisticated, well-read Gaikwar. He did "Corpse in the Moonlight," "Mexican Plug," "Mrs. McWilliams Afraid of Lightning," "Australian Poem," "German Language," "Christening" and "Interviewer." That marked a longer-than-usual performance.

Clara, who sometimes seemed to delight in puncturing Papa's successes, felt the need to note in her memoirs that the performance fell flat before a cluster of humorless wives in purdah. The maharani and her attendants sat high up in a balcony behind a screen—so as to listen but not be seen.

> Some of the little women understood English very well, but laughed so little that our impression was that their sense of humor was certainly not of the American variety, if they possessed any at all. A deadly affair for the poor humorist, who had not even the pleasure of scanning the faces of his mute audience.

After his performance, the maharajah sought out Twain for some conversation.

The author was surprised to learn that Sayajirao, though thirty-two, had already been to Europe five times. He spoke impeccable English. His closest confidant for years was his British tutor, F. A. H. Elliot. Twain kept silent on the topic, but Clara later reported that the maharajah complained to her father about the need for the British to leave India, that the two cultures were incompatible. In the twentieth century, Sayajirao would become famous/infamous for snubbing King George V in 1911, during the first visit to India by a king of England. The maharajah was supposed to wear his most exotic jeweled costume and be one of several hundred Indian princes to bow three times to King George V; instead he wore a plain white tunic and bowed once and turned his back on his majesty.

The Clemens family had some time to rest before catching the 10 p.m. train. Back in the guest house, Clara was changing her clothes in the bathroom. She stepped on something, a "hard-soft mound"; it moved; to her it looked like a narrow stream rippling along. She screamed very loudly.

Servants came running and rescued her from the snake. As a card-carrying SPCA member, she begged them not to hurt it, but they had no intention of killing it. They respectfully carried it away on a pile of clothes.

The fairy-tale carriage toted them a mile to the train station. Satan and Barney went ahead and secured train rooms again and the coveted lower sofa beds, but then they had to go tend to the luggage and some other errands. Livy and Clara arrived in time to witness a loud, pushy American woman—"growling and snarling and scolding," as Twain put it—order a squadron of Indian servants to snatch Clara's lower-berth sofa bed and hurl Clara's bedding up onto the upper shelf.

Twain and Smythe confirmed their lower berths, took a bounce on them, and then decided to take a walk. When they got back, Smythe's linens had been transported up to the hanging shelf. Twain had now spent four months with young Carlyle, and the whole family liked the handsome efficient young man very much. Did Twain fight for his new colleague?

> When we came back . . . an English cavalry officer was in bed on the sofa which [Smythe] had lately been occupying. It was mean to be glad about it, but it is the way we are made; I could not have been gladder if it had been my enemy that had suffered this misfortune. We all like to see people in trouble, if it doesn't cost us anything.

Twain added in his notebook: "Slept all the way to Bombay—10 p.m. to 7 a.m." So he evidently enjoyed the *schadenfreude* and then rolled over on his wide couch and drifted off to sleep to the gentle rhythm of the rails.

CHAPTER 20

Holy Cities

The family had a few hours to rest and pack at Watson's Esplanade Hotel before leaving the coastal area for six weeks of long-haul sightseeing and performing. The ambitious itinerary would zig them northeasterly across India, and then zag them up into the Himalayas and then to the very far north. They would eventually log more than 4,000 railroad miles, and everyone but that rock of health, Livy, would fall sick for a full week.

In their handful of hours in Bombay, Twain found time to pick a fight. He was furious when he learned that Dr. Sidney Smith had charged him two and a half times the local going rate, even for "well-to-do patients." Twain had received a bill for 100 rupees ($25, or $750 in today's dollars) for four brief house calls to the hotel. The debtor/author *might* have given Smith the benefit of the doubt if the doctor had prescribed something more than cough drops or if his office was farther than around the corner. Twain sent a check for 40 rupees ($10, or $300 today) and a seething note that "there seems to be a mistake somewhere" and that if Dr. Smith could find it and "rectify" it, he should feel free to write to him. Twain never heard from Dr. Smith.

At 10 p.m., the family and Carlyle Smythe boarded the train for the 866-mile, two-night-and-one-day cross-country trek to Allahabad, then hosting one of the world's largest religious festivals, the Megh Mela.

The trip got off to a rocky start. Twain tried pajamas.

He spelled it "pyjamas"—the newfangled clothing option featured baggy pants with a drawstring, and a button-up top. The Missourian had been wearing nightshirts all his life; housemaid Katy used to sew home-made flannel ones for him in Hartford.

He did not sleep well that night on the train for overheating, under-heating and other problems. "I missed the refreshing and luxurious sense, induced by the night-gown, of being undressed, emancipated, set free from restraints and trammels," he later wrote. "In place of that, I had the worried, confined, oppressed, suffocated sense of being abed with my clothes on."

Twain stared out the window at the desiccated landscape. A severe drought had been gripping central India for almost two years, damaging crops, inflicting famine and starvation. He saw expansive dry plains, the color of "brickyard" dust, with an occasional "spectral" tree leading to a village. "Should have had a week of rain at Xmas—hadn't a drop; every-thing is parched, the wheat crop cannot be saved; in some regions the people are already eating roots & leaves."

As always, he found the human scenery fascinating; again, he pon-dered apt descriptions of clothes and skin. "A loin-cloth . . . amounts to a bandage, and is a white accent on his black person, like the silver band around the middle of a pipe stem." The only other bit of clothing for the many "lanky" men he saw was an occasional "fluffy and voluminous white turban."

He found the villages in this region of Madhya Pradesh mostly depressing mud huts amid squalor. Twain, back in his nightshirt, slept much better that second night. He then briefly lost his servant.

[Satan] got out of the train to see if he could get up a misunder-standing with somebody, for it had been a weary, long journey and he wanted to freshen up. He found what he was after, but kept up his pow-wow a shade too long and got left.

This happened in the middle of the night at Manikpur, 60 miles from Allahabad, so Twain woke up to discover that he had no servant. Twain was actually very fond of Mauzie/Satan, even if the other family mem-bers were not.

He was an astonishing creature to fly around and do things. He didn't always do them quite right, but he did them, and did them suddenly. There was no time wasted. You would say: "Pack the trunks and bags, Satan."

"Wair good" (very good).

Then there would be a brief sound of thrashing and slashing and humming and buzzing, and a spectacle as of a whirlwind spinning gowns and jackets and coats and boots and things through the air, and then with bow and touch—

"Awready, master."

It was wonderful. It made one dizzy. He crumpled dresses a good deal, and he had no particular plan about the work—at first—except to put each article into the trunk it didn't belong in. But he soon reformed, in this matter. Not entirely; for, to the last, he would cram into the satchel sacred to literature [*Twain's work valise*] any odds and ends of rubbish that he couldn't find a handy place for elsewhere. When threatened with death for this, it did not trouble him; he only looked pleasant, saluted with soldierly grace, said "Wair good," and did it again next day.

He was always busy; kept the rooms tidied up, the boots polished, the clothes brushed, the wash-basin full of clean water, my dress clothes laid out and ready for the lecture-hall an hour ahead of time; and he dressed me from head to heel in spite of my determination to do it myself, according to my lifelong custom. . . .

Speaking of noise, he certainly was the noisiest little devil in India—and that is saying much, very much, indeed. I loved him for his noise, but the family detested him for it. They could not abide it; they could not get reconciled to it. It humiliated them. As a rule, when we got within six hundred yards of one of those big railway stations, a mighty racket of screaming and shrieking and shouting and storming would break upon us, and I would be happy to myself, and the family would say, with shame:

"There—that's Satan. Why do you keep him?"

And, sure enough, there in the whirling midst of fifteen hundred wondering people we would find that little scrap of a creature gesticulating like a spider with the colic, his black eyes snapping, his fez-tassel dancing, his jaws pouring out floods of billingsgate upon his gang of beseeching and astonished coolies.

I loved him; I couldn't help it; but the family—why, they could hardly speak of him with patience.

When Twain arrived at Allahabad, he sent a telegram to the station-master at Manikpur: "Kindly forward my detained servant by next train."

The family installed themselves at a hotel and rested up after their long train journey. Twain was scheduled to perform that evening at the Railway Theatre, and he hoped to squeeze in a trip to the Megh Mela fair the next morning. Twain noted the absence of servant Satan: "It seemed very peaceful without him."

The stationmaster did indeed "forward" Satan.

The physical site of Allahabad—at the junction of two holy rivers—was very sacred to the Hindus, but it had been conquered by the Muslims, who had ruled it for six centuries and renamed it after their Supreme Being. The Hindus preferred to call it Prayag. Twain split the difference and called it Godville, but he shuffled off responsibility for the blasphemy, claiming to have heard it from a babu, i.e., an Indian servant who mangles English.

Since Twain found himself in a religious place, he decided to revise his opening number to give it a more pious twist. The carriages rolled up to the Railway Theatre at 9 p.m.; it took three Hindu servants and a horse to deliver a white man three blocks or so. "Apparently the European [in India] never walks."

The theater filled; Twain strode out onstage. He started in on the "Corpse in the Moonlight" story about finding the weather too drizzly for school but perfect for going fishing, even though he knew it was wrong.

For the forbidden fruit had the same attractions for me that it had for Adam. Some unthinking people criticize Adam—find fault with him because he was weak & yielded. O, that is not fair, that is not right. He hadn't had *any* experience—we have had ages & ages of experience & tuition—we who criticize him—& yet . . . just see what *we* are [like] when there's any forbidden fruit around. I've been around a good deal, but I've never been in any place where that apple would be safe—except Allahabad. Why, it is the *prohibition* that *makes* many things precious. There is a charm about the forbidden that makes it unspeakably desirable. It was not that Adam ate the apple for the apple's sake, but *because* it was forbidden. It would have been better for us—O, infinitely better for us if the *serpent* had been forbidden. He would have eaten the serpent.

Twain did five more stories and, as usual, basked in the applause. He ate a postperformance meal with his family and picked up Satan at the train station at 11 p.m. Then hoping for some male companionship, he strolled by the North West Province Club, but the members had all retired. His notebook entry states that he wanted to leave "P.P.C. cards" there. That's a Victorian touch, probably lost on most modern readers. He couldn't pick up the phone and leave a message at the club, but he had wanted to tell them he was leaving the next day and give a forwarding address. "P.P.C." stands for *pour prendre congé*. Victorian callers stopped by homes on days when families were "at home" or "receiving" guests; if there was a mix-up, the visitors dropped off their "calling" cards or, if they were leaving town, their P.P.C. cards.

Twain woke up early to go gather Smythe and go sightseeing; as he rushed around the hotel veranda, he was saddened to see the Hindu servants sleeping curled up on the cold outdoor tiles; one servant, who had shined his master's yellow boots, now squatted barefoot by the door waiting. Twain wanted to shoo the man to some warmer place, or at least have him jump about to stay warm, but he couldn't remember the right foreign words. "It was a curious and impressive exhibition of meekness and patience, or fortitude or indifference, I did not know which," he wrote. "But it worried me, and it was spoiling my morning. In fact, it spoiled two hours of it quite thoroughly."

The early sightseeing did not go swimmingly. Their schedule called for a late-morning train to Benares, so they had a small time window. Though haste was required, they headed out of town "with a pair of dead horses and dead driver," as Twain put it, to the famous old fort near the festival, located at the intersection of the blue Jumna and muddy Ganges rivers, both near dry in the drought.

The British had retrofitted a sixteenth-century Muslim fort there to serve as an arsenal. It still had tall stone walls and a fillable moat. Twain found fascinating the history of all the religions jockeying for supremacy at that spot, with key moments of it recorded on a fifty-foot-tall stone monolith: Buddhist scripts from 240 BC, then Hindu victories in the second century AD, then seventeenth-century Muslim conquest. Now the British had re-erected the fallen Pillar of Asoka and built a church inside the fort.

From the walls of the fort, they could see the Megh Mela along the two-mile-long spit of land where the Jumna meets the Ganges. The vast multitude of Hindu pilgrims camped out in a temporary city of reed-and-wattle huts and fakir booths and preaching platforms . . . with attendance approaching 2 *million* people most years. On the especially holy twelfth-year celebration, attendance was said to reach 20 *million* people.

Twain recorded arriving on February 4, 1896, at "the fag-end & finish of the great January *mele* when . . . natives swarm to Allahabad to bathe in the sacred waters." He said sick pilgrims came to be healed or die, and many hundreds of thousands walked hundreds of miles to get there from all over India to be cleansed of sin. He marveled at the "faith" and "devotion" which were "beyond imagination . . . to our kind of people, the cold whites."

The heart of the pilgrimage lay in the bathing. The Hindu men had to groom themselves to be worthy of the holy plunge.

Priests, or *pragwallahs*, advertising with colored pennants along the shore, stood ready—for a donation—to shave the men from head to foot, and leave only the traditional "celestial tuft" at the back of the head. Most pilgrims had avoided barbers for months. "The sand is literally strewn with fine silky black hair, of which, at the close of the day, we saw piles five or six feet in height!" wrote British traveler Constance Gordon-Cumming in her travel book, which Twain had read. She noted that Hindu women also had the tips of their long hair cut by *golden* scissors.

Bathers emerged "purified" of their sin from the river. That represented the solemn part; the tent city on land marked one of the craziest carnivals imaginable, with priests, contortionists, self-mutilators, beggars, deformed cows, musicians, near-dead pilgrims. Twain hoped to see

a man who hasn't sat down for years, another who has held his hands above his head for years & never trims his nails or hair—both very long—& another who sits with his bare feet resting upon a lot of very sharp spikes—all for the glory of God. Human beings seem to be a poor invention. If they are the noblest work of God, where is the ignoblest?

Numerous Western travelers recorded what seemed to them a competitive freak show. W. S. Caine, who passed through near the same time, described observing "on a little platform . . . [a] horrible dwarf, who has the facility of twisting all his joints about under his skin, till his arms and legs look like bags of eels [and] a dusty ringletted fakir, who has been standing for fifteen years, who has gone to sleep in the midst of the Babel, leaning on a board slung from a tripod of bamboos."

The fair attracted thousands of fakirs and beggars. Twain saw gaunt naked "fakeers in plenty, with their bodies dusted over with ashes and their long hair caked together with cow-dung; for the cow is holy and so is the rest of it; so holy that the good Hindoo peasant frescoes the walls of his hut with this [dung], and also constructs ornamental figures out of it for the gracing of his dirt floor."

Some of the extraordinarily limber fakirs contorted themselves into uncanny yoga positions such as the both-ankles-behind-head naked walk-on-hands waddle. All of them expected a donation, even from the poorest pilgrim, who would toss anything from a grain of rice to a piece of fruit to a brass coin onto a dirty cloth. The fakir, per tradition, greeted the gift "with stony indifference." Twain envied their steady income.

In addition to the fakirs, thousands of beggars paraded their deformities and clustered around tourists. A six-legged cow was a gold mine. The withered-arm man was famous from many travel accounts: his raised arm culminated in a shrunken hand with very long corkscrewing fingernails and a large thumb permanently stuck between his second and third finger. His face was smeared with yellow saffron, and his hair matted with dung, which "gave him a wild and demonish appearance."

Twain's final comment on the fair revealed that the great writer for once felt himself stumped to capture something on paper: "*Costumes:* I give it up. The costumes—for variety—are clear & away beyond the flight of the craziest imagination."

Twain reluctantly returned by carriage from the fort, and unfortunately as he alighted, he saw the servant who had shined the yellow shoes *still* squatting by the doorway.

The Clemens family rushed to catch the train to go ninety-six miles to Benares. They observed more parched land of "unimaginable poverty and hardship"; they disembarked at 2:10 p.m. at Mogul Serai to wait for a branch railroad train to go the final *nine* miles west to Benares. The other train was running late; Twain hunkered down, expecting to be irritated and bored.

> We could have found a carriage and driven to the sacred city, but we should have lost the wait. In other countries a long wait at a station is a dull thing and tedious, but one has no right to have that feeling in India. You have the monster crowd of bejeweled natives, the stir, the bustle, the confusion, the shifting splendors of the costumes—dear me, the delight of it, the charm of it are beyond speech.

He saw a "backwoods" rajah come bustling in with an entourage of twenty or thirty "ragged soiled" men in strange scarlet turbans carrying "rusty old flintlock muskets & bayonets." He saw nose rings and red-stained betel-juice teeth. He saw four small closed padded palanquins that apparently contained four small Hindu women from the zenana, who could not have lain down.

The connecting train arrived and the natives swarmed aboard. "The two-hour wait was over too soon," he concluded.

Twain was now heading to India's holiest Hindu city, Benares/Varanasi/Kashi. He had read up a bit on Hinduism; he would later recount his findings. A twentieth-century Hindu scholar, Keshav Mutalik, called Twain's observations "platitudinous and superficial." That seems harsh: "superficial" maybe, but not "platitudinous." Cynically irreverent might be fairer, like covering the Catholics but focusing only on Ash Wednesday, papal castrati choirs, nuns' headgear and relic boxes with saints' body parts. Twain's disgust with *all* organized religions mounted year by year until his late-in-life rants against Christianity, especially its sought-after heaven that featured such dull entertainment as harps, choirs and prayers.

He explained that Hindus had their own "trinity" of Brahma, Shiva and Vishnu and that each of them had numerous wives with multiple names, and multiple children with numerous names. "It is not worth while to try to get any grip upon the cloud of minor gods," he advised, pegging the number of them at 2 million.

He avoided any of the more serious philosophical areas that might have led him to sound "platitudinous." For instance, he did not attempt to explain dharma (duty) samsara (reincarnation), karma (correct behavior), or moksha (enlightenment/liberation from the cycle of birth and death).

By reading Reverend Arthur Parker's *Hand Book of Benares* (1895 edition), he learned that Hindus consider Benares the origin of creation.

> It was merely an upright "lingam," at first, no larger than a stove-pipe, and stood in the midst of a shoreless ocean. This was the work of the God Vishnu. Later he spread the lingam out till its surface was ten miles across. Still it was not large enough for the business; therefore he presently built the globe around it. Benares is thus the center of the earth. This is considered an advantage.

Twain very quickly became fascinated with the concept of *lingam*. Scholars nowadays find numerous interpretations for the Hindu term, but in Twain's era the dominant definition was that of a phallus, a representation of a male organ, a penis.

The train reached Benares at 4:40 p.m.; the Clemens party stayed at a hotel on the outskirts of town. They woke up very early the following morning to go sightseeing. Twain refused to allow a repeat of the Allahabad rush.

The guidebook writer himself, the Reverend Arthur Parker of the London Missionary Society, took them around. (He might have conveyed a certain bias, since he considered Hinduism to be "ignorant folly.") As they walked to board boats for the classic tour along the Ganges to see the pilgrim bathers and the cremations, they got a sense of the ancient crumbling, mesmerizing holy town where Buddha once preached. Reverend Parker pointed out that one out of every eight of the 222,000 residents was a priest. "Religion, then, is the *business* of Benares, just as gold-production is the business of Johannesburg," interpreted Twain, who judged the place a kind of humongous department store, "theologically stocked."

Another thing became increasingly clear to Twain:

> Shiva's symbol—the "lingam" . . . is worshiped by everybody, apparently. It is the commonest object in Benares. It is on view everywhere, it is garlanded with flowers, offerings are made to it, it suffers no neglect. Commonly it is an upright stone, shaped like a thimble—sometimes like an elongated thimble. This priapus-

worship, then, is older than history. Mr. Parker says that the lingams in Benares "outnumber the inhabitants."

(One can almost hear Twain's cackle at slipping the word *elongated*
into his later travel book, past his editor and sometime censor, Livy.)

Twain and his entourage wandered the streets en route to the boats.
Twain would later call Benares "one of the most wonderful places" he
had ever seen. "Every thing is so strange, so utterly unlike the whole of
one's previous experience." And as a man in debt, he clearly envied the
priests opening up their umbrellas and selling services and items to pilgrims who joyfully handed over their life savings.

As they walked the streets, Twain indeed was amazed to see sacred
cows and Brahmani bulls with right-of-way everywhere, even into shops
and homes. He later discussed them with a reporter:

> "Very fine looking cattle too . . . peaceable enough. They certainly
> had a fine lordly way of going and taking what they liked."
>   "Did you ever have to make room for them?"
>   "Well, yes, I will make room for a bull any time."

The Clemens clan and Smythe and Satan boarded the canvas-covered
boats. Benares sits perched on a hillside bend of the Ganges. They saw
the river's curve blanketed with a crazy-quilt of ancient buildings, of
bathing ghats (stone stairs to platforms at river's edge) and verandas, and
porticos, and temples and maharajah mansions and holy wells and pencil-
thin minarets. Centuries mingled. Hindu pilgrims scurried up and down
narrow passageways. But with fifty bathing ghats, Twain mostly saw bathers, thousands clustering together in a human collage, immersing themselves in the holy river and gulping water from their cupped hands or
from brass *lotas* (i.e., pitchers). Twain was mesmerized.

> I think one would not get tired of the bathers, nor their costumes,
> nor of their ingenuities in getting out of them and into them again
> without exposing too much bronze, nor of their devotional gesticu-
> lations and absorbed bead-tellings.

The men in the water often unwound their turbans and let the long
strips of colored cloth float in the breeze; the wet women remained

wrapped in their saris, and the marvel, noticed by other male travelers beside Twain, was that after bathing the women could unwrap a wet sari and spin into a dry one with no loss of modesty.

Besides living Hindus purifying themselves in the water, dead or dying Hindus were brought to Benares for public cremation at river's edge. Twain stated they witnessed *nine* cremations that day. First they saw an older, well-muscled man, who was placed upon a flat pile of dry wood, his feet in the Ganges, doused with some flammable oil, while a nearby fakir screamed what seemed a funeral oration. Then a young man, presumably his son, walked round the corpse seven times and touched sacred fire to the head and feet.

Hindu male corpses were wrapped in a white sheet; women in red. Bearers carried bodies shrouded and covered in flowers on biers and set them down at the Ganges's edge.

For the funeral, only "holy fire" could be used, and priests negotiated a price; the "outcast" funeral workers also charged for wood and oil. Debtor Twain envied the priests' "monopoly" in the fire business. "There is hardly an hour in the day when the smoke and fumes of the burning dead are not ascending from this rude crematory," wrote one visitor.

The wealthiest, like the maharajahs, would pay for precious sandalwood; the corpses of the friendless poor were carried to the river in a winding sheet strapped to a pole, to be burned at government expense during off-peak hours. Twain meticulously observed the process:

Sometimes they hoisted the half of a skeleton into the air,
then slammed it down and beat it with the pole, breaking it
up so that it would burn better. They hoisted skulls up in the
same way and banged and battered them. The sight was hard to
bear; it would have been harder if the mourners had stayed to
witness it.

Hindus believe the soul of this dead person will now migrate to another form of life. This sacred cremation speeds the soul onward. Other travelers who passed by the cremation ghat at dawn claimed they saw the workers "carrying yesterday's ashes to the water's edge, washing them in sieves and pans like any placer-miner to recover the gold, silver, and jewels burned with the bodies."

Twain's party made several trips along the river, and he said he would have made more if he had time. He found himself worrying about the Hindu worshippers' health and hygiene. Men and women and children, smiling, bathing, were drinking Ganges water, which happened to be downstream from a toilet sewer and from the funeral ghat area. "When . . . I see a Hindu—the very man, perhaps, who fears defilement so much through [touching] the other man's *lota* [water pitcher]—when I see him going down to the muddy, filthy Ganges, and washing himself in and drinking out of water only fifteen yards away from where a dead body is lying—I can't help thinking he is at least sincere."

The Clemens party had time for two more stops: a mosque with a great view from the minaret and the monkey-infested temple of the dreadful goddess Kali. Dominating the skyline of the holy city—infuriating the Hindus—were two magnificent slender 142-foot minarets of the mosque of the Mughal conqueror Aurangzeb. The cylinders stood only 8½ feet wide at the base and 7½ feet at the summit. Twain called them "fairy like candles" and he trudged up the endless spiral staircase. (Hindus had closed the front entry to the mosque and made worshippers and tourists enter through the back.)

When he reached the top, with the extraordinary holy city unfurled below, he happened to notice a gray monkey scampering over the parapets of the mosque and over rooftops. The monkey leaped across ridiculously wide chasms. "He got me so nervous that I couldn't look at the view." Twain kept focusing on the monkey, and he found himself gasping out loud and mimicking the monkey's reaching and grabbing at each exploit of the furry daredevil. "He came within an ace of losing his life a dozen times, and I was so troubled about him that I would have shot him if I had had anything to do it with."

He gave up trying to look elsewhere, descended (advising future tourists to carry a rifle), and moved along to the Temple of Kali. She is the goddess of death; she wears skulls around her neck; her long bulging red tongue sticks out of her grotesque silver face; she is a nightmare and one of the last Hindu deities still honored with blood sacrifice—commuted from human victims to goat. Twain suggested switching to monkeys, who were notoriously aggressive.

The monkeys could be quite rude to the Hindu pilgrims, especially to the women. The hairy imps became such a nuisance that the pious local government once asked the British to intervene, but without shedding any simian blood. Her Majesty's army arrived, captured hundreds of monkeys, crated them and dropped them off far away in the jungle. (The monkey population revived quickly.)

Twain had time only to see a fraction of the holy sites in Benares; he had spent much of his visit on the river, but that didn't stop him from reading Parker's guidebook and devising a "logical" orderly step-by-step itinerary for the devout Hindu.

Here is the highlight version:

Go to **The Well of Fate** at Dandpan Temple . . . The sunlight falls into it from a square hole in the masonry above. You will approach it with awe, for your life is now at stake. You will bend over and look. [If you do not see your reflection,] you have not six months to live. There is no time to lose. . . . Get yourself carried to the. . . .

Well of Long Life. This is within the precincts of the moulder- ing and venerable Briddhkal Temple, which is one of the old- est in Benares. You pass in by a stone image of the monkey god, Hanuman, and there, among the ruined courtyards, you will find a shallow pool of stagnant sewage. It smells like the best limburger cheese, and is filthy with the washings of rotting lepers, but that is nothing, bathe in it; bathe in it gratefully and worshipfully, for this is the Fountain of Youth; these are the Waters of Long Life. Your gray hairs will disappear, and with them your wrinkles and your rheumatism, the burdens of care and the weariness of age, and you will come out young, fresh, elastic, and full of eagerness for the new race of life. Now will come flooding upon you the manifold desires that haunt the dear dreams of the morning of life. You will go whither you will find . . .

Fulfillment of Desire. To wit, to the Kameshwar Temple, sacred to Shiva as the Lord of Desires. Arrange for yours there. And if you like to look at idols among the pack and jam of temples, there you will find enough to stock a museum. You will begin to commit sins now with a fresh, new vivacity; therefore, it will be well to go frequently to a place where you can get . . .

Temporary Cleansing from Sin. To wit, to the Well of the Ear- ring. You must approach this with the profoundest reverence, for it is unutterably sacred. It is, indeed, the most sacred place in Benares, the very Holy of Holies, in the estimation of the people.

Twain noted that Reverend Parker seemed irritated that a thief, an adulterer, or a murderer could take one dunk and be cleansed of sin. Twain then advised:

Make Salvation Sure. There are several ways. To get drowned in the Ganges is one, but that is not pleasant. To die within the limits of Benares is another; but that is a risky one, because you might be out of town when your time came. The best one of all is the Pilgrimage Around the City. You must walk; also, you must go barefoot. The tramp is forty-four miles, for the road winds out into the country a piece, and you will be marching five or six days. But you will have plenty of company. You will move with throngs and hosts of happy pilgrims whose radiant costumes will make the spectacle beautiful and whose glad songs and holy paeans of triumph will banish your fatigues and cheer your spirit; and at intervals there will be temples where you may sleep and be refreshed with food. The pilgrimage completed, you have purchased salvation, and paid for it. But you may not get it unless you . . .

Get Your Redemption Recorded. You can get this done at the Sakhi Binayak Temple, and it is best to do it, for otherwise you might not be able to prove that you had made the pilgrimage in case the matter should some day come to be disputed. . . . You have nothing [left] to do but go and pray, and pay at the . . .

Well of the Knowledge of Salvation. It is close to the Golden Temple. . . . And there also you will see a very uncommon thing—an image of Shiva. You have seen his lingam fifty thousand times already, but this is Shiva himself, and said to be a good likeness. It has three eyes. He is the only god in the firm who has three. The sacred water is being ladled out to a mob of devout and eager pilgrims. With it comes to them the knowledge, clear, thrilling, absolute, that they are saved; and you can see by their faces that there is one happiness in this world which is supreme, and to which no other joy is comparable.

Irreverent? Yes. Platitudinous? No. As Twain once wrote in his notebook of the Christian afterlife: "Dying man couldn't make up his mind which place to go to—both have their advantages, 'heaven for climate, hell for company!'"

The Clemens family spent the night at their hotel on the outskirts of town. The following day Twain met God, or at least a living god.

The sixty-year-old living god's name was Sri 108 Swami Bhaskarananda Saraswati. He had 108 names, or else his name must be repeated 108 times when addressing him. Twain wasn't certain.

The Hindu god lived in a beautiful garden, donated by a wealthy worshipper. In a gazebo stood a marble statue of this Hindu who had achieved perfection. Twain described him as "tall," "slender," "emaciated," looking older than his years, but "much study and meditation and fasting and prayer, with the arid life he had led as hermit and beggar, could account for that."

Twain later told an interviewer: "It's just as though you had taken a very fine, learned, intellectual man, say, a member of the Indian Government, and unclothed him. There he is, . . . he hasn't a rag on his back. But he has perfect manners, a ready wit, and a turn for conversation through an interpreter."

Twain is the king of straight-faced humor, so it's often hard to tell when he's fooling, but it seems as though he took great joy in meeting a living god. He saw a Hindu pilgrim, who had traveled hundreds of miles, arrive and immediately prostrate himself before Saraswati and kiss the living god's feet. Moments later, the god shook Twain's hand. The swami, having achieved perfection through the various long stages of family life, study, begging, desert dwelling as a hermit and meditation, could not be defiled by contact with a person of lower caste or even a Presbyterian.

As soon as I had sobered down a little we got along very well together, and I found him a most pleasant and friendly deity. He had heard a deal about Chicago, and showed a quite remarkable interest in it, for a god. It all came of the World's Fair and the Congress of Religions. If India knows about nothing else American, she knows about those, and will keep them in mind [a]while.

He proposed an exchange of autographs, a delicate attention which made me believe in him, but I had been having my doubts before. He wrote his in his book, and I have a reverent regard for that book, though the words run from right to left, and so I can't read it. It was a mistake to print in that way. It contains his voluminous comments on the Hindoo holy writings, and if I could make them out I would try for perfection myself. I gave him a copy of *Huckleberry Finn*. I thought it might rest him up a little to mix it in along with his meditations on Brahma, for he looked tired, and I knew that if it didn't do him any good it wouldn't do him any harm.

This living god was something of a tourist attraction. Other Western travelers visited. Pretty twenty-five-year-old Delight Sweetser, who noticed Mark Twain's signature in the guest book, described meeting a wizened "toothless" old man with remarkable kindly eyes. He took her for a walk in the garden and plucked wine-red rose petals and gave them to her, along with his book and photograph.

Twain told an interviewer that *another* person's religion poses challenges for a stranger. "You can't revere his gods or his politics, and no one expects you to do that, but you could respect his belief in them if you tried hard enough; and you could respect him, too, if you tried hard enough."

Sometimes Twain tried hard; sometimes he didn't. He told an interviewer that instead of repeating the Swami's name 108 times, he stopped at 104. He also doubted that Saraswati had really heard of "Mark Twain" or read his books, since he didn't read English. "Gods lie sometimes, I expect."

But where Twain really earned the wrath of faithful Hindus was in his later riff on reincarnation, and the risks of dying on the wrong side of the Ganges.

The Hindoo has a childish and unreasoning aversion to being turned into an ass [*i.e., a donkey*]. It is hard to tell why. One could properly expect an ass to have an aversion to being turned into a Hindoo. One could understand that he could lose dignity by it; also self-respect, and nine-tenths of his intelligence. But the Hindoo changed into an ass wouldn't lose anything, unless you count his religion. And he would gain much—release from his slavery to two million gods and twenty million priests, fakeers, holy mendicants, and other sacred bacilli; he would escape the Hindoo hell; he would also escape the Hindoo heaven. These are advantages which the Hindoo ought to consider; then he would go over and die on the other side.

There's Twain in a nutshell, playful on *both* sides of the topic: awed and amused at the same time. Carlyle Smythe's line about him holds: "a sedate savant who has been seduced from the paths of high seriousness by a fatal sense of the ridiculous."

In his notebook, Twain claimed he had heard that although various Christian missionaries had achieved little success converting Hindus, they had scored some breakthroughs with . . . monkeys. "In 2 years, at a cost of $60,000, 4 [monkeys] converted & 11 hopefully interested."

CHAPTER 21

The Heart of the British Raj

They left "Lingamburg," as Twain styled it, and caught the 1:28 p.m. train for the 476-mile overnight journey to Calcutta, the capital of British India. The 17½-hour railroad journey took them from the chaos of pious Hindu "delirium" to the disciplined epicenter of British civil and military power. And they reached Calcutta on Friday, February 7, at a moment when the British Lion was preening and roaring, at the time of the annual Grand Military Tournament. The city was jammed with spit-shined, uniformed, chest-medaled officers and rifle-toting soldiers and their Indian servants, from all over the country. The very top brass were hosting dinners and attending the tournament.

With Twain's first lecture not till Monday, the family looked forward to a pleasant weekend of social calls and military displays, but the harried author somehow had caught a sudden chest cold with a cough.

The family, with help from Satan and Barney, checked into the recently built posh Continental Hotel and were quite pleased to discover a large stack of mail from America waiting for them, from the family in Elmira, of course, but also from mogul-friend H.H. Rogers and Major Pond, lecture agent.

Twain, who was stuck in the room recuperating yet again, opened the letter from Pond, and out spilled numerous Kodak photographs of Pond's visit, with his young wife and son, to the Elmira farm back in September. Mr. and Mrs. Clemens could see four-and-a-half-month-old black-and-white images of their two other daughters. It must have been a bittersweet pleasure for Mama and Papa to see the girls—half a world and a third of a year away.

Twain took up the rest of the correspondence reclining in a chaise longue. He wrote Susy a letter (answering hers—now lost), praising her for studying Mental Science, which could overcome ailments via positive thoughts, and wishing he could have used it to drive away his "exasperating colds and . . . carbuncles." Twain often read his letters aloud as he wrote them.

"Mama is busy with my pen, declining invitations. I caught cold last night coming from Benares and am shut up in the hotel room starving it out, and so instead of river parties and dinners and things, all three of us must decline and stay at home."

One can hear Twain's playful emphasis on "*all three of us* must decline." But apparently his preemptive strike failed. The pair abandoned him; he would have to make do with Smythe, but then Smythe set out to arrange some interviews and coordinate with the theater.

With his forced isolation, Twain had time to write a long business letter to H.H. Rogers, tackling the bankruptcy repayment and concocting plans for selling his travel book and creating a complete works.

He had just learned from Rogers—five months after the fact—that Bainbridge Colby expected the creditors to accept Twain's offer to deliver them 50% of the money owed in exchange for a quitclaim and the moral promise to repay the rest. He also learned that Colby expected the defunct company's assets to pay 38% of the debt. Some math simple enough for Twain revealed that the author would only need to supply 12%, or about $10,000, and he could easily amass that much money. That must have been a relief.

Unfortunately, Colby—the false prophet—was wrong as usual: the two largest creditors would reject the 50% offer, as would more than half of the others, and Webster's assets wouldn't bring close to 38%. Sometimes handling negotiations via letters with a two-month lag time can have a surprisingly positive effect.

The author learned that *Century* magazine was claiming the "moral right" to Twain's next travel book, since he had backed out of his agreement to supply them with $1,000 monthly travel articles. Twain dismissed that claim curtly; he pointed out that he had legitimately rejected their *written contract* offer, which had included that "insulting" requirement to be funny.

For the book, he leaned toward going back to Frank Bliss, the son of his nemesis Elisha, at American Publishing, and accepting Bliss's offer of a $10,000 advance. His main reason was that he desperately wanted to strike a complete works deal, and, as of now, Bliss held the copyrights to six of Twain's most important books, such as *Tom Sawyer*. To make matters worse, it looked as though U.S. copyright law would allow Bliss to renew the expiring twenty-eight-year copyrights on books such as *Innocents Abroad* (1869) and *Roughing It* (1871) and add another fourteen years. Twain, who would crusade on international copyright issues, called it an "everlasting shame," but for once he let common sense rule over righteous anger in a business decision.

He knew that his best hope for long-term financial survival lay in striking a deal with Bliss to allow his new publisher, Harper (*Joan of Arc*), to issue his fifteen-plus books in a so-called "uniform" edition. Twain couldn't keep traipsing all around the world, making people laugh at 75 cents a head. He would grind himself to a nub. He'd be a mosaic of carbuncles with an earthquake cough.

———

After twenty-four hours of starving himself, the American author felt well enough to go to an elite dinner on Saturday night at the lieutenant governor's magnificent mansion. He probably read this portion of his letter to H.H. aloud to Livy and Clara:

> That will be my first outing here, whereas the family have been gadding about and dissipating socially just the same as ever since they left home. It is wonderful the way they keep up, considering the tax that is put upon their strength.

They dined in an intimate assemblage of a dozen of the crème de la crème of British civil servants and officers—at Belvedere House, a colonnaded pale beauty of a building in the midst of thirty private acres, the former residence of the viceroy, now allotted to the lieutenant governor. Remodeled several times, the place somehow combined tasteful Italian Renaissance arched windows with hints of Indo-Saracen flair. The massive ballroom featured extensive electric lighting, something of a marvel for a country house. *Murray's Handbook* stated somewhat cryptically: "The electric light is worked from the neighbouring jail." Inmates on treadmills? Perhaps, since no river was nearby to generate power.

Over the next week, Twain would meet and be feted by some of the most powerful Brits in India: the viceroy himself (the fifty-six-year-old full-bearded Lord Elgin), and by the lieutenant governor of Bengal (fifty-three-year-old "Star of India" knight Sir Alexander Mackenzie), and the lieutenant general of the army (fifty-eight-year-old career military man Sir William Elles). He would eat, drink, rub elbows with these august gentlemen and their underlings, and that might have colored his impressions.

For a man who has gone down in history as an ardent anti-imperialist, Twain gave the British a pass on its snatching and governing of India. In interviews over this stretch, he quite praised the Raj. He told the reporter for the *Calcutta Englishman*: "When one considers [the] security and prosperity, one cannot help coming to the conclusion that the British Government is the best for India, whether the Hindus or Mohamedans like it or not." And he continued—unless he was misquoted—by asserting that the British race was physically and intellectually superior to the Indian race. "[The British race] is vigorous, prolific and enterprising. Above all, it is composed of merciful people—the best kind of people for colonising the globe."

The following day, Sunday, he took a carriage ride over to the "Black Hole of Calcutta," a guardroom in the old Fort William. A simple brass engraved placard marked the now vacant spot, then being excavated. Twain accepted the famous account as absolutely accurate that on June 20, 1756, the Muslim conqueror of Calcutta, Suraj-ud-Daulah, the "Nabob of Bengal," had "packed" 146 English prisoners into a room only eighteen feet square, and by morning 123 of them had died in the crush. This account (or propaganda) fueled British distrust and anger toward the brown-skinned races.

Sir William Elles, the highest-ranking military officer in India, who had also fought in the Crimean War and the jungles of Burma, invited Twain to join him on an inspection of the Calcutta garrison at 7:30 a.m. Monday, ten hours before his Calcutta debut. One suspects that Livy refused to allow her temperamental husband to turn down the invitation, even though it was rare for him to sightsee on a platform night.

Twain rose early, witnessed the rank and file of hundreds of immaculate sepoys and British soldiers displaying polished weapons and stern-faced obedience. The author, who often resented shaving or changing his shirt, left no notes of that morning. His show was already sold out, with a huge influx of high-ranking military attendees, in town for the tournament. Theater staff carried in extra rows of chairs. Rave reviews from Australia had been ricocheting around the Anglo-Indian newspapers.

He decided to tailor his act and slip in a piece on his own not-so-illustrious military career. In some tellings, he would "refine" the narrative to the point of having a young Colonel Ulysses S. Grant of the Union troops coming within a few miles of capturing a raw Confederate army recruit by the name of Samuel L. Clemens, of the Missouri company.

So, Twain opened with a bit about learning the limits of his own courage in "Corpse in the Moonlight" and then tried out his soldiering riff. Twain told this tale, straight-faced, to this battle-hardened audience, to these men with scars who had heard bullets whizzing by their heads.

(*Please honor—the pauses.*)

My courage has been tested as a soldier, for I was born for military glory.

I served—for two weeks at the beginning of the Civil War as an officer in the Infantry and then I—resigned.

I was a Sergeant—with the rank of—Captain and the authority of—Lieutenant General.

My merits were acknowledged by everybody, who said I had more—discretion than anybody else.

In two weeks, we—retreated—thirteen hundred miles, and I brought my people through—without a single casualty, while four-fifths of the pursuing force died—of fatigue.

I have been out this morning and have witnessed the Commander-in-Chief inspecting the Garrison. That is not in my line of business. I will better enjoy the Tournament which I am going to see tonight. If there is to be any—retreat, I could enjoy that and put on the old war spirit.

A veteran British soldier, Lance Corporal E. J. Creasey, reviewed the performance for the regimental monthly, *Bengal Tiger*. He noted that the audience listened intently, and he perceptively judged that the humor lay in Twain's delivery and accent. (Creasey felt the need to use CAPS to capture it.) "It WAS not SO much what he SAID as the funny way he SAID it."

Creasey's favorite was Huck and Jim on the raft, but he found the ending confusing. "At last, the [slave-hunters] leave [Huck], but he is quite at a loss whether to be proud or ashamed at what he has done." Perhaps the implied punch line of Huck embracing his heart over the laws of the land was a difficult one for a well-trained British soldier. (Then again, perhaps, it's difficult for lots of people.)

The show ended about 7 p.m. Twain ate a quick dinner and attended the Grand Military Tournament from 9 p.m. to midnight. "We have struck it fine here," Twain enthused to H.H. Rogers, "for the Indian Army is turning itself loose on a series of magnificent tournaments— regular mimic war."

The night began with a crisp marching drill of all the soldiers, brandishing arms, hauling cannon; and then the regimental bands played rousing martial and patriotic tunes, highlighted by the "musical ride of the 16th Lancers." The bag-piping, kilt-wearing Scottish "Pipers of the 1st Battalion Highland Light infantry" performed sword dances and earned enthusiastic applause.

But the highlight of each night's performance was the mock war, the storming of the wild Pathan hill fort by British soldiers, which delivered enough "battle, murder and sudden death to satisfy the most bloodthirsty baboo," according to the *Bengal Tiger*.

Brown-skinned sepoy troops—a generation and four decades removed from the Munity of 1857—played the wild Pathans, proud hill people who stubbornly resisted the British in regions that are today's "ungovernable tribal areas" near the Afghanistan-Pakistan border. There was mock gunfire, mock swordplay on and off horses, and mock bayonet battles. The *Bengal Tiger* reviewer noted that Tommy Atkins (i.e., a white British soldier) tended to "die" with much rigidity of limb—à la stage deaths of the era—while the wild Pathan used "gymnastic feats" to portray his last moments.

The military challenge in India for the British, with relatively few troops available and large distances to cover, was often to arrive at an ongoing battle in time to help.

Of course, the Pathan Hill Fort was at last taken by our gallant defenders, amidst the boom of distant artillery fire, the rattle of the musketry, soon to be followed by the roll of the drums and the hoarse cheering of the victorious troops, driving the enemy from fastness to fastness into the heart of their native mountains, from which we know they will return punctually in time for "The Combined Display of All Arms" in the next performance.

Lieutenant Creasey continues, with a bit of war-hardened humor:

Above the roar of battle . . . could be heard at frequent intervals the groans of the dying and the shrieks of the wounded, consisting chiefly of tender-hearted ladies [in the audience]. These felt deeply for the poor Pathans and evidently were of opinion that Maxims and Field guns did not give the hairy warriors a fair chance and might be discontinued with advantage.

Holding a military tourney, showcasing a British victory over wild Pathans might seem like good propaganda, but clearly the reporter for the *Bengal Tiger* felt a tad uneasy about having (loyal for now) native troops portray the enemy. He added on the front page: "We imagine the Sepoys who acted as the part of Umra Khan's men with so much spirit would have made those mountaineers look very silly either with knife, rifle or any other weapon."

Twain especially enjoyed his seat in the commander in chief's private box. "The mimic storming of a native fort . . . was as good as the reality for thrilling and accurate detail, and better than the reality for security and comfort."

The rest of his week in Calcutta was a whirlwind of high-ranking house calls. Tuesday featured "Government House," residence of the viceroy, to see the portrait gallery, then an hour at the Indian Museum viewing antiquities, followed by a call on the lieutenant governor of Bengal, conveniently at lunchtime, so they stayed, then a social call on Sir William Elles, commander in chief, finally a visit to the swank Bengal United Service club. He also found time to buy a silver mug to display at the Players Club in New York, in his niche as one of the club founders.

All that visiting required the hiring of several horse-drawn cabs.

Apparently no Calcutta *garrywallah* is acquainted with any street or place in the town. After infinite instructions they always go wrong. It took my cabman half an hour to find 3 Esplanade East after having it pointed out to him from the hotel front. I allowed him to pass it 4 times—he & the *syce* [*i.e., stable man*] jawing at each other all the time. I wanted to see how long the idiot would be in finding it.

Twain also jotted in his notebook a dark little tale he'd heard about a particular street in Calcutta. A British gentleman in his carriage had accidentally run over and killed an elderly Indian lady, and had paid the family ten rupees as compensation. "It was said for a time that little street was full of grandmothers waiting for the chance to earn 10 Rs when he should drive along."

The humorist on Wednesday again tailored his performance to the military. He added Huck's confusion over Tom Sawyer wanting them to join the Crusades and attack the Holy Land. Huck is unschooled but logical, while Tom is full of half-baked conventional knowledge. (Once Twain got rolling after the setup, he would assume the different voices, and there'd obviously be no need repeat the names "Tom" or "Huck.")

HUCK: What is a crusade?

TOM: A crusade is war; it is war to rescue the Holy Land from the heathen cannibals.

HUCK: Which Holy Land is it?

TOM: Why there is only one Holy Land. Do you think there is a million?

HUCK: Tom Sawyer, how did we come to let them get it?

TOM: We did not come to let them get hold of it. They always had it.

HUCK: If they always had it, it belongs to them.

TOM: Why, certainly.

HUCK: It seems to me that if I had a farm and it was my farm and it belonged to me and another fellow wanted it, would it be right for him to take it?

TOM: They own the land, just the mere land, and that's all they DO own; but it was our folks, our Jews and Christians, that made it holy, and so they haven't any business to be there defiling it. It's a shame, and we ought not to stand it a minute. We ought to march against them and take it away from them.

HUCK: Why, it does seem to me it's the most mixed-up thing I ever see! Now, if I had a farm and another person—

TOM: You don't understand it at all. You don't get the hang of it at all. It has nothing to do with farming. It is on a higher plane. It is religious.

HUCK: What, [it's] religious to go and take the land from the people who own it?"

TOM: Why, of course it is, it has always been considered so.

Another large crowd came that night and a big favorite was the Australian poem—one colony laughing at another. Twain added a new touch about how he regretted that he hadn't applied in time for the post of poet laureate of Great Britain. Queen Victoria back on January 1 had appointed Alfred Austin to replace the popular Lord Tennyson, who had served for forty-two years.

The next day Twain attended a meeting of the Supreme Legislative Council and sat next to a newspaper reporter; Twain was apparently a guest of the viceroy, Lord Elgin.

The official, below the queen, who ultimately governed India was the Secretary of State for India, but the man on the ground, reachable by relayed telegraph messages, was the viceroy. Lord Elgin, a somewhat dour Scot, presided over the Supreme Legislative Council, which was attended by native princes as well as British resident agents and local governors. The members sat at a long table, closer or farther away from Lord Elgin according to rank, according to how many gun salutes, and so forth. The most amusing moment for Twain was not the donkeys-traveling-on-railroad debate, but when an Indian prince, who had been sick, surprised everyone by showing up mid-session, and they all had to play musical chairs. "Several had to get up & move down a peg to give him his place."

Twain found himself, in Calcutta, this city on the Hoogli River, at the vibrant heart of the British Raj. And in this city, one monument stood out, towering above all others. He expected it would be dedicated to Major-General Robert Clive, who had notched so many victories to cement the East India Company's grip on the country, or to Warren Hastings, who had conquered Bengal. The "cloud-kissing" structure was a fluted column 157 feet tall that dominated the skyline. Twain inquired; it was for a fellow named "Ochterlony." No one in the neighborhood had heard of him. Someone thought he might have been a mayor.

The tall white rod captured Twain's imagination. In his notebook, he made it 165,000 feet tall; in his later travel book, he showed restraint.

It is a fluted candlestick 250 feet high. This lingam is the only large monument in Calcutta, I believe. It is a fine ornament, and will keep Ochterlony in mind. Wherever you are, in Calcutta, and for miles around, you can see it; and always when you see it you think of Ochterlony. And so there is not an hour in the day that you do not think of Ochterlony and wonder who he was.

Twain appears to be the only travel writer who ever referred to the monument as a lingam. One glance at a photo explains all.

The author rejoiced that the British did not believe in reincarnation, because he thought if Clive ever returned, the general might declare: "With three thousand I whipped sixty thousand and founded the Empire—and there is no monument; this other soldier must have whipped a billion with a dozen and saved the world."

Twain discovered little about Ochterlony except that the monument was built after his death: "He doesn't suspect that it is his monument. Heaven is sweet and peaceful to him. There is a sort of unfairness about it all."

David Ochterlony (1758–1825), it turns out, was born in Massachusetts, in British colonial Boston, and sent to India as an eighteen-year-old, and he climbed the ranks, fought under Hastings, made a fortune, and was famous for conquering Nepal. He also was infamous for adopting local customs and collecting beautiful young wives for his unofficial harem. Jealous whisperings had it: "Sir David Ochterlony took the evening air in Delhi followed by his thirteen wives, each on [her] own elephant."

When Twain was drafting his travel book a year later, he occasionally would jot down promising phrases or concepts in his notebook so he wouldn't forget them. The following sentence never made it into the book, but it serves as a fine exit line before the family's departure to the Himalayas: "The last thing we saw was Ochterlony's lingam, standing erect & fine, & then Calcutta was gone."

CHAPTER 22

Himalayan Joy Ride

The Clemens family boarded a train at 4:30 p.m. on Friday, February 14, 1895, to head 385 miles due north to spend a weekend at the mountainside resort of Darjeeling at the scenic edge of the Himalayas, near Tibet. The British Railway—thanks to contacts Twain had recently made at the highest levels—extended V.I.P. courtesy to him. The author paid half-fare rates, but the railroad bumped him up to traveling in the Chief of Traffic's elegant private railcar, which had a separate servant's car attached. Livy, who often had an appraiser's eye for luxury, mentioned "easy chairs, sofas, a good-sized table, &c" and a pair of servants who delivered them high tea with bread, butter, and cake. "The servants remained standing behind our tables until we had finished our tea," she later wrote to daughter Jean.

Twain and entourage—along with hundreds of Indian passengers— exited the train four hours later to cross the Ganges on a night ferry. They found several top railway officials waiting at the ferry boat stop to host a "sumptuous" lamp-lit dinner for them as the boat slowly headed to a railroad connection terminal thirteen miles away.

At the station, they found a private sleeping car waiting. Twain's notebook: "Sound sleep, all night. Up early, refreshed. Put on double shirt of flannel—bright & frosty." They were heading, in the middle of winter, up to Darjeeling (mean temperature 55 degrees), which was one of the most popular summertime "hill station" excursions for the British elite. (The lieutenant governor of Bengal had his summer capital there: "The Shrubbery.")

They descended at Siliguri to board the Darjeeling Himalayan Railway. (Sometimes referred to as the "Darjeeling Himalayan Express," the term "Express" is used loosely.) As recently as fifteen years earlier, the only way up to Darjeeling was "bullock cart," or *dak gharry,* bouncing for four days on the steep, crumbly switchbacks of the Hill Cart Road. But once British businessmen terraced more than a hundred lucrative tea plantations up near Darjeeling, a group of private investors found enough financial incentive to try to build a railroad to climb 7,000 feet through rocky rugged terrain. At its completion, with more than 500 bridges of various lengths, it was considered one of the engineering marvels of the world. "All day long the train winds in and out along the valleys," wrote one travel writer, "skirting dizzy precipices on the edge of mighty gorges, opening up vista after vista of the grand wooded mountains that form the foothills of the giant Himalayas."

Several travel writers called it the "grandest railway journey in the world."

The steepness in places required four horizontal loops and four reverse-direction zigzags, many of these at the edge of straight cliff drops of more than a thousand feet. One travel writer compared the line of train cars to "a snake winding up in the clouds."

The first locomotive, custom built in Manchester, England, pulled freight and a string of short passenger cars—holding only six exposed, anchored chairs and a canvas awning. One guidebook warned of showers of soot and ash from the snorting engine. "Ascended the mountain— all curves," wrote Twain in his notebook, ". . . it takes 7 or 8 h[ours] to climb the 40 m[iles] to Darjeeling." The official railroad rules called for a seven-mile-per-hour speed limit going up, but "on special occasions sixteen miles per hour has been easily attained." (Going down, almost *any* speed could be achieved—but not safely.)

A rainstorm, at a place called the "Mad Torrent," had once wiped out 500 feet of track, and disaster threatened repeatedly during the region's 125 inches of annual rainfall.

The train—sometimes called a "toy train" because of the narrow gauge and odd cars—attracted an equally unusual clientele. The rail station at Siliguri represented a kind of crossroads of human continents, as it seemed to fall on the border between Oriental/Mongolian Asia and Hindu India. Mingling in the station were dagger-toting, high-cheekboned men of Bhutan, Tibet and Nepal, alongside lanky Bengal Indians, alongside khaki-jacketed British tea planters and a sprinkle of Kodak-carrying Swedish tourists.

The Clemenses boarded the train, which didn't begin the steep ascent right away; first it traversed farmland and then entered a thick jungle, plowing a shadowed corridor through swaying giant fifty-foot bamboo canes. The family squinted for a glimpse of animals mentioned in a popular handbook: wild elephants, rhinoceroses, tigers, leopards, buffaloes, wild cattle, deer, as well as hogs, wolves, wild dogs, monkeys. They didn't see any, although Twain would later remark about meeting "a man who conversed with a man who knows the man who saw a tiger come out of the jungle yesterday & eat a friend of his who had just put on his breechclout and was starting to pay calls."

The family found the journey up mesmerizing:

The [rail]road is infinitely and charmingly crooked. It goes winding in and out under lofty cliffs that are smothered in vines and foliage, and around the edges of bottomless chasms. . . . By and by we were well up in the region of the clouds and from that breezy height we looked down and afar over a wonderful picture—the Plains of India . . . shimmering with heat, mottled with cloud shadows.

At 6,000 feet, Twain said they actually entered the clouds. And that was (and is) the risk of going to Darjeeling for a brief visit. Just as in the Alps at Zermatt, clouds sometimes block the view of the snow-capped mountaintops.

The train ascended to Ghoom (elevation 7,000 feet) then descended a rapid thousand feet to Darjeeling. Porters waited with poles to lift palanquins, or "open coffins," as Twain called them, to carry the arriving tourists uphill to the hotel, the Woodlands. Clara in her memoir noted that fog and clouds shrouded the peaks on arrival. And Twain said tourists warned him about people waiting three weeks for a clear sighting of the world's tallest mountains in the Himalayas, which would then seem almost overhead in the crystal-clear air but were actually forty miles away.

After the spectacular trip up, they had time for dinner and a bit of a look-see before Twain's performance that night.

Darjeeling (population 155,000) was a bustling hill town, with nearby tea plantations producing 8 million pounds of top-grade tea a year. The thriving local economy and gorgeous location had led the British elite to spend sizable sums to renovate and spiff up the place.

One traveler said he arrived "prepared for grand emotions" at seeing the awe-inspiring mountains but instead discovered he was in an English resort town, with posters hawking English amenities: Colman's mustard, Pears Soap, Beecham's Pills (laxative). He saw privileged English schoolchildren either on horseback or walking, always followed by a submissive Hindu servant . . . with tennis courts available and English-style bungalows and creeping roses . . . and an English stone clock tower . . . and assembly rooms for dances, Protestant chapels, and everywhere soldiers in red coats, living as gentlemen—fit men with pomaded hair. At the boardinghouse, he found politeness, piano, and Gilbert & Sullivan or patriotic songs. "Of all the races living abroad, the English adapt themselves the least to foreign cultures," groused André Chevrillon. "They defy assimilation of any sort and re-create home while abroad."

Twain had no problem with Colman's mustard, or with much of anything else about Darjeeling. (He wasn't too fond of Frenchmen, especially in the wake of the Dreyfus verdict, when the Gallic nation "lost its head entirely, also such odds & ends of dignity as were left in stock.") The American author gave his speech that night at 9:30 p.m. at Town Hall. He weaved in a few new jokes for the 200 or so British planters and soldiers in attendance. When an Indian servant handed him a glass of water, he sputtered at its coldness. He told the audience that water in the rest of India was usually lukewarm and it had given him fevers; he hoped this cold mountain water wouldn't give him a cold.

He noticed the fog outside and admitted he wasn't optimistic about seeing the snow-capped peaks. "You surely can't expect everything for the price of a *single* railway fare." He also said that he had been warned in Calcutta by nine different people to add a layer of clothing, so he was now standing there in *nine* suits of clothing.

Giddy from the altitude or not, he then slipped into his Grade A opening-night speech, and he brought the house down, as always: "Corpse in the Moonlight," "Mexican Plug," "Australian Poem," "Huck and Jim" and "Terrors of the German Language." The greatest hits played well, and the audience laughed very enthusiastically. However, pathos won out with the local reviewer, who called Huck and Jim "the finest effort of Mark Twain's imagination."

After the show, some wealthy plantation owners invited Twain to their gents-only private "Planters Club." The newspaper reported he had a "peg" (i.e., a shot of whiskey) and drew such a crowd that nobody could wield a cue stick in the billiard room. He told stories and smoked "American Eagle" cigars, which he noted were made in Hamburg, Germany.

The following day, Sunday, with fog still blocking the view, Twain went for a leisurely tour of the bazaar, or weekly market. "Throngs of Hill people and tea-coolies" arrived to shop and meet friends, with plenty of "chaffering, howling, shouting, singing."

Twain pointed out in his notebook that four other countries lay within a half day's ride: Bhutan, British Sikkim, Tibet and Nepal. He called it a "strange and striking pageant."

Twain encountered Asiatic peoples new to him. The local Lepcha had squat, muscular bodies and Mongolian facial features with sallow complexion, broad flat face, flat nose, oblique eyes, thick black hair, pigtail, scant facial hair. One helpful guidebook author noted that if visitors found themselves briefly confused as to the gender of the Lepcha encountered: women wore *two* pigtails, the men only *one*.

Gaudy barbaric jewelry abounded on the women, and the men of Nepal strutted impressively with long broad-bladed knives, *kukeries,* at their belts. "Every man carries a knife that would disembowel an elephant," wrote a tourist, who also observed a large consumption of intoxicants at the bazaar. Locals drank *murwa* (spiced millet beer served in a bamboo pipe), but the law forbade selling it to British soldiers. Twenty barbers worked outdoors; Bhutanese women sold "great crocks full of snow-white curds, the favorite dainty of the place, which they serve out to their customers in square vessels ingeniously twisted out of plantain leaves."

The Clemens family plans—due to prior appearance commitments—called for leaving Monday morning. Some of the guests at the Woodlands decided to mount a predawn excursion to Observatory Hill for a better view of the lofty range and the second-highest peak, Mount Kinchinjunga, hopefully lit up in a cloud-free sunrise. (Mount Everest required an even longer trek to a viewing spot on Tiger Hill.)

Clara and a gentleman from the hotel rode horses; Carlyle Smythe walked briskly and Livy traveled in a rickshaw, pulled by two men and pushed by a third. Her husband refused to go at 5:30 a.m. by *any* mode of transportation. Livy recalled leaving him in his nightshirt and robe at the window.

"I stayed at home for a private view for it was very cold," later wrote Twain, "and I was not acquainted with the horses anyway. I got a pipe and a few blankets and sat for two hours at the window, and saw the sun drive away the veiling gray and touch up the snow-peaks one after another with pale pink splashes and delicate washes of gold." He claimed a sighting.

As for the excursion party, they experienced one of those majestic ethereal travel moments. The sun lit up several of the sixteen snow-clad peaks; they also saw what tourists raved about: the mighty granite crag of Mount Kinchinjunga rising dramatically above the snow line. "We did not regret the effort or the early hour, for never again did we behold such a dazzling expanse of bluish white snow," wrote Clara much later. "We were awed and humbled by the sight."

Travelers, even that irritated Frenchman, Chevrillon, strained to find words to capture the view. He called it *"le plus grand panorama du monde"* ("the greatest panoramic view in the world . . . to the south, the plains of India, to the north the Himalayan peaks").

The Clemens clan all reconnoitered for breakfast at the hotel by the coal fire. Clara suspected her father was bluffing about his clear view, but a newspaper reporter confirmed the feasibility of seeing Kinchinjunga that Monday morning from town. They soon headed to the station. Twain told some of his new pals from the Planters Club that he was pleased the sunny weather had saved him from lying.

At 10:30 a.m., they took the locomotive-pulled train up to Ghoom. From there they would go cartwheeling down on their private free-falling roller coaster. Wrote Twain:

We . . . then changed to a little canvas-canopied hand-car for the 35-mile descent. It was the size of a sleigh, it had six seats and was so low that it seemed to rest on the ground. It had no engine or other propelling power, and needed none to help it fly down those steep inclines. It only needed a strong brake, to modify its flight, and it had that.

The British Railway, which was giving Twain V.I.P. treatment for that whole excursion, could not risk maiming or killing a celebrity. "Mr. Barnard, chief engineer of the mountain-division of the road, was to take personal charge of our car, and he had been down the mountain in it many a time."

The railway also sent a police inspector named Mr. Pugh ahead in a handcar, with two local men: "Everything looked safe. Indeed, there was but one questionable detail left: the regular train was to follow us as soon as we should start, and it might run over us. Privately, I thought it would."

Twain described seeing the tracks drop sharply in front of them; he claimed the first moment felt like that first instant of pushing off on a toboggan slide—"a mixed ecstasy of deadly fright and unimaginable joy." The weather was cold, in the 40s, and Twain and Livy and Clara and Smythe sat bundled up in their anchored outdoor seats. Anyone who has ever ridden in a go-cart knows that the closer one is to the ground, the faster the speed seems. (It's hard to picture Olivia Clemens in her Victorian dress in that chair.)

The family watched the tester car whiz down through curves and straightaways, along cliffs. The first half of the trip, while plenty steep and dangerous, did not yet feature any of the loops or zigzags, which would began at about twenty miles down.

At one point, Mr. Barnard noticed a wild Tibetan dance play being performed near the tracks and hit the hand brake, which, as Twain enthused, could stop the car "on a slope as steep as a house roof."

They alighted, and heard "barbaric" music and saw entertainers in bright costumes "spin around with immense swiftness and vigor and violence, chanting the while, and soon the whole troupe would be spinning and chanting and raising the dust."

Apparently, it was a famous historical play. Twain said an old Chinese man kindly whispered explanations to him in "pidgin English" as the drama unfolded. He later complained: "The play was obscure enough without the explanation." His notebook contains a bizarre diagram, which might or might not reveal something about the play.

The locomotive local train passed them. They reboarded the handcars. They soon chose another stop: the hillside cottage of one of the railroad executives, where they ate lunch on a fine veranda with a spectacular view. The local train also stopped for lunch, and now they were back in the lead. They stopped to pick wildflowers. It passed them.

Now came the terrifying reverse-direction zigzags—the design something like a giant crooked Z slashed in the steepest hillside. Intermixed with these were four horizontal loops. At about 3,000 feet up, they hit their first loop as the handcar barreled down toward a tight-radius curve at the edge of a cliff, offering a kind of infinity-pool view because one couldn't see down over the edge.

The even crazier third loop resembled a misshapen corkscrew, as the track did one horizontal loop and then curled in upon itself and went down under a fifty-foot-tall trestle tunnel carved out of the rock.

Twain said they decided to get out and stand on the trestle, and wait and watch the passenger train slither through. "[We] saw the locomotive disappear under our bridge, then in a few moments appear again, chasing its own tail; and we saw it gain on it, overtake it, draw ahead past the rear cars, and run a race with that end of the train. It was like a snake swallowing itself."

As they descended toward Calcutta, the heat returned. "We started in rugs and furs and stripped as we came down, as the weather gradually changed from eternal snow to perpetual hellfire," Twain later wrote.

They reached Siliguri and were greeted by a high-ranking railroad official, who offered them an ornate dinner in a private dining car aboard their overnight train. Livy wrote to Jean about the evening: "There was a rare fish that reminded me of a Connecticut river shad, rare birds, meats, two puddings, ices, champagnes, wines, fruits, nuts, candies &c. Pleasant talk and a much larger amount of eating done by all the party."

The railway president met them in Calcutta, and he had a servant carrying a gift of ten tins of double-wrapped tea, including "two of their finest and most costly teas."

All three family members had a wonderful time in the mountains, but especially on the handcar down. Twain summed it up for H.H. Rogers: "We never enjoyed ourselves so much in all our lives."

CHAPTER 23

Mutiny on the Ganges

Twain and Smythe left Livy and Clara in Calcutta and departed that same evening on an overnight train to Muzaffarpur, a small town about 370 miles to the northwest. A wealthy British indigo planter was hosting them, and providing a private supper at a local club to follow his "At Home" show. (Due to illness and long rail journeys, Twain would perform only eight more times over his last six weeks in India.)

In a flood of memorable places visited around the world, this one was forgettable. Twain scribbled some notes about the price of indigo dye.

Clara and Livy would remain an extra day in Calcutta before meeting up with Papa for a brief sightseeing jaunt in Benares on the way to Twain's next performance.

The following morning, Tuesday, February 18, with her father speeding far away on a train and her mother spending her time packing and repacking, Clara innocently asked if it would be okay to go out sightseeing with a servant to visit a temple. Her mother agreed.

Clara later admitted that she had failed to inform Mama that she would be going to a Hindu temple of death and destruction to watch animal sacrifices.

The twenty-one-year-old Clara and the quiet servant Barney took a horse cab to the Kalighat Temple, dedicated to the goddess of mayhem, Kali, the crazed one with the obscenely long tongue, corpse earrings, skull necklace, and midriff wrapped in a string of severed human hands. Kali, Shiva's angry wife, demanded blood from her worshippers.

Clara would write up the incident immediately afterwards in a letter to

Major Pond's twenty-six-year-old wife, Martha, her frequent pal on that U.S. trip.

> I went out this morning with the servant—to a Temple to see a goat sacrificed & I assure you going into that place was like going into the lowest parts of New York (I should think). One of their musical bands was playing, crowds of natives were yelling their prayers out, many were throwing flowers & fruit to the idol & all were ready to fight for a few coppers. A young black priest offered to lead me through the crowd & the creatures in their demand for money hit the priest two or three times because he didn't encourage me to give them any & several attacked my servant with such violence that he had to scatter coppers.
>
> . . . I was naturally timid, so we hurried along as quickly as possible to the sacrificing block where all ready twelve goats had been butchered. The pools of brilliant blood were sickening & the stench enough to knock one down. As we stood there a man brought up a bleating lamb by the legs but I couldn't wait any longer; much as I adore horrors, I fled from this one, it was a little too much.

Clara confirmed that if the family had known the exact nature of the spectacle, she "could never have gone alone with a servant."

After his Muzaffarpur outing, Twain, along with Smythe, departed at 1 a.m. to catch two trains to meet up with Livy and Clara at 7 a.m. so they could all spend another twenty-four hours together in Benares. Clara excitedly wrote to her aunt Pamela about seeing the spectacle of hundreds of Hindus bathing in, drinking in, praying in the holy river, more "absorbed and serious" than any Christian, and wearing "dazzling yellows and greens" that no gallery goer would believe on any painted canvas in America.

———

The next six days of Twain's trip could be dubbed the "Mutiny of 1857 Tour." The family would be visiting Lucknow and Cawnpore, the sites of two infamous battles, usually referred to by British guidebooks as the Siege of Lucknow and the Massacre at Cawnpore.

British tourists still descended in droves on the landmarks of war, but for some, after almost forty years, the thrill had passed. Wrote American Eliza Scidmore:

> One has rather too much of the Mutiny in India. It is decidedly overdone; it may be well to keep the great incident alive in native memory, along with the justly terrible reprisals, but the tourist gets sated with England's woes and foes of '57, and recalls other wars and sieges since, and trusts that the next generation is not to be harrowed with the sieges of Ladysmith and Mafeking, Tientsin and Peking.

Twain, who had a soft spot for derring-do, felt differently. He would devote numerous pages in his later travel book to the heroic British acts; he swelled with pride at the courage and sacrifice:

> The military history of England is old and great, but I think it must be granted that the crushing of the Mutiny is the greatest chapter in it. The British were caught asleep and unprepared. They were a few thousands, swallowed up in an ocean of hostile populations. It would take months to inform England and get help, but they did not falter or stop to count the odds, but with English resolution and English devotion they took up their task, and went stubbornly on with it, through good fortune and bad, and fought the most unpromising fight that one may read of in fiction or out of it, and won it thoroughly.

Indian historian Keshav Mutalik, who celebrated Twain's writing and was thrilled that Twain loved India, was absolutely baffled by Twain's blindness to the oppressions and humiliations of British rule.

The English East India Company—arguably, the world's most successful *private* company—controlled India for more than a century until 1858 and had already weathered a handful of mutinies by the darkskinned sepoy troops. In 1764, the British had famously struck down a mutiny, tied twenty-four ringleaders to the mouths of cannons, and blew them up, scattering their chances for reincarnation.

Over that hundred years, the vast wealth of the subcontinent showered down upon a handful of lordly British stockholders. The Crown profited by taxing the company and often borrowing huge sums from it.

The company controlled India by directly conquering the land and also through alliances with native states. To speed up the swallowing of all of India, Lord Dalhousie of the company created a convenient policy, the Doctrine of Lapse, stipulating that if an Indian state lacked a legitimate male heir or was mismanaged, the company would take over that province and its treasury of gold and silver and all its lands. "Lapse" was in the eye of the beholder (i.e., the eye of Lord Dalhousie, governor general). The company confiscated thirty kingdoms, including in 1854 a very wealthy proud one, Oudh (which included Lucknow and bordered Cawnpore), and this inflamed the locals. Even *Murray's* quite pro-British guidebook conceded that this appeared "like a policy of unjust and high-handed aggression."

Another spark to the "Indian Mutiny" was that the British army supplied its Muslim and Hindu troops with new Enfield rifles with cartridges, "unfortunately greased with hog or cow fat," that had to be bitten during the loading process. It was a masterstroke of insensitivity to both religions.

The Clemens family arrived in Lucknow late Friday, February 21, 1896, after a sweltering train ride through flat dusty plains of central India. On Saturday, Twain went sightseeing with a young officer named Stirling. They toured the famed "Residency"—a cluster of ornate buildings that had been a kind of hilltop palace for a prior company resident agent—in which 1,700 British, including many women and children, had survived a months-long siege by tens of thousands of attacking mutineers.

Starting in the heat of summer, from July 1, 1857, onward, the enemy tried to tunnel its way in; it stormed the walls; it placed snipers in the Shah Najaf mosque and in the clock tower of Chattar Munzil palace. The British defenders made frequent sorties to spike guns and blow up buildings and tunnels.

Owing to the fire of the enemy, the windows had to be barricaded, and even the men were shot in their beds. One great torment was the flies, which swarmed in incredible numbers. The ground was black with them. The besieged could not sleep; they could scarcely eat on account of them.

Just prior to the siege, the commander, Sir Henry Lawrence, had wisely built a perimeter wall around the Residency and had shipped in enormous amounts of food and supplies. Lawrence died July 4, 1857, and is buried there.

Twain performed Saturday night in Lucknow and drew his usual ovation. The following morning, an Indian orderly on a "picturesquely dressed" camel delivered an invitation to go on a tour of the exact route of Colin Campbell's famed rescue march to save the British besieged at Lucknow. Twain's guides, Major & Mrs. Aylmer (Sixteenth Lancers) and Captain & Mrs. Dallas, offered to carry him and his family in the "regimental drag," a large official coach, drawn by four horses.

A siege is a deadly waiting game. The first relief forces, led by a pair of generals, James Outram and Henry Havelock, reached the Residency by September 25, but their troops were so depleted fighting their way in that they too became stranded. Then two months later, Sir Colin Campbell—a legendary Scottish general with triumphs around the Empire who had been lured out of semi-retirement in England at age sixty-four—headed to Lucknow.

> The last eight or ten miles of Sir Colin Campbell's march was through seas of blood. The weapon mainly used was the bayo-net, the fighting was desperate. The way was mile-stoned with detached strong buildings of stone, fortified, and heavily garri-soned, and these had to be taken by assault. Neither side asked for quarter, and neither gave it.

(Battle writing might rank as Twain's least effective genre, and his latest, *Joan of Arc,* was crammed with it.) Campbell arrived on November 17 and was able to deliver the women and children to safety five days later. Approximately 1,000 of the 1,700 British had survived the siege.

The author took time to walk through the cemetery. He tried to re-create the battles on site based on battle plans, but he complained he was born with east and west reversed in his brain. He was feted that Sunday night at the United Service Club at the "elegant" century-old Chattar Munzil, otherwise known as the Umbrella Palace for its magnificent dome. Twain gave another of his American-Anglo unity speeches at the Club:

> I feel all thro' to my marrow, that the names England, America, India, Canada, Australasia, are but geographical expressions, that

they but indicate the several homesteads of one great family—
the great English speaking family . . . a tradition milestoned with
immemorial names: who are the Black Prince, Henry V, Elizabeth,
Shakespeare, Milton, Cromwell, Clive, Nelson, Wellington, Washington, Lincoln, Franklin, Lee, Grant, ... kinsmen of English
blood. . . . And, please God, no drop of that rich blood shall ever
again be spilt in fratricidal war.

That night, when they returned to the hotel, Twain found his favorite hyperactive Hindu servant, Satan/Mauzie, stumbling around drunk.
The author tried to cover for him with Mrs. Clemens by claiming Satan
was ill.

I said it was a fever, and got the family's compassion, and solicitude
aroused; so they gave him a teaspoonful of liquid quinine and it set
his vitals on fire. He made several grimaces which gave me a better
idea of the Lisbon earthquake than any I have ever got of it from
paintings and descriptions. His drunk was still portentously solid
next morning, but I could have pulled him through with the family
if he would only have taken another spoonful of that remedy; but
no, although he was stupefied, his memory still had flickerings of
life; so he smiled a divinely dull smile and said, fumblingly saluting:

"Scoose me, mem Saheb, scoose me, Missy Saheb; Satan not
prefer it, please."

Then some instinct revealed to them that he was drunk. They
gave him prompt notice that next time this happened he must go.
He got out a maudlin and most gentle "Wair good," and saluted
indefinitely.

Twain knew that Satan was at risk. The famous writer had schooled
himself to drink no more than one or two hot scotches a day in front of
Livy.

They took a train forty miles southwest to Cawnpore and were hosted
by Lieutenant Colonel P. Baddeley. This fortified city, strategically
located on the Grand Trunk Road and the Ganges, with an immense
arsenal, was the site of what some Union Jack–waving British historians

would call "the blackest crime in human history," that is, the massacre by knife and cleaver of women and children prisoners.

The native sepoy troops in Cawnpore mutinied in 1857 under the command of Nana Sahib, a local, adopted thirty-two-year-old Hindu prince, whose massive annual revenues had been stopped by Lord Dalhousie at his father's death in 1851.

With Cawnpore at risk, Sir Hugh Wheeler, the sixty-seven-year-old British general married to a Hindu wife, somewhat bizarrely decided to leave the arsenal/fort and place the thousand or so British (more women and children than soldiers) in a newly built encampment with four-foot-high walls in an exposed plain nearby. "The worst rider on the worst horse could have jumped over [and in,]" stated *Murray's*.

After an absolutely wretched twenty days of being bombarded with British munitions from the recently evacuated British fort and with food running out, General Wheeler agreed to surrender. "If they surrendered at least there was a chance for safety," wrote F. W. Pennefather. "The vilest wretches in the world have sometimes reverenced the sanctity of an oath."

A deal was struck on June 26, 1857, that the 300 women and children could float on boats to Allahabad, and 150 British soldiers could carry their weapons and sixty rounds each of ammunition. Nana Sahib would supply boats; they would depart the following day. But only one boat would make it downstream. All but four persons would be killed.

Who fired first? There was no doubt in the minds of the British. (Four survivors told the tale.) They heard a bugle sound, and Nana Sahib ordered his troops to open fire. Indian historians state that the Indian boatmen jumped overboard, and the British, fearing betrayal, fired at them first.

The mutineers killed all the British men except for those on the escaped boat; they dragged the surviving 125 women and children back to the Bibighar, a mansion once owned by a British resident's Indian mistress. On July 7, when Nana Sahib heard the advance guns of Havelock approaching Cawnpore, he (or possibly another rebel leader) ordered the women and children murdered. Sepoys with rifles fired through the windows but apparently had no heart for the task. Butchers in aprons were hired and did the slaughter with cleavers and long knives. The bodies were tossed down a deep well. Some Indian historians said it was payback for similar executions of non-combatants recently committed by British troops near Allahabad.

Twain wrote: "The soldiers had made a march of eighteen days, almost without rest, to save the women and children, and now they were too late—all were dead and the assassin had flown."

The British soldiers discovered blood ankle deep in some rooms of the Bibighar and the well overflowing with corpses, each of which was lifted out and buried. The troops also found liquor while looting the town.

Twain makes no mention of the savage retribution the British soldiers took upon most any dark-skinned man in the vicinity. The troops rounded up local Hindus and Muslims, whether involved in the battle or not, and forced them to lick up the blood in the Bibighar, then hanged them, sometimes inside a pig's carcass, or tied them to cannons and exploded them. Some British historians claim those tales exaggerated—except for the licking and hanging.

In the immediate aftermath, British newspapers also amplified the atrocities with Victorian code words, reporting that the women were "violated" (i.e., raped) and their bodies "mutilated" (i.e., breasts hacked off). Indian historians claim 9,000 dark-skinned local men were randomly chosen and hanged.

Twain approached the horrific well. There he saw a somewhat incongruous large white marble statue of the Angel of the Resurrection by sculptor Carlo Marochetti, depicting a female with wings folded across her breast in sad resignation, which cost £30,000 ($4½ million today), paid for by the Indian residents of Lucknow:

Sacred to the perpetual memory of a great company of Christian people, chiefly women and children, who near this spot were cruelly murdered by the followers of Nana Dhunda Pant, of Bithur, and cast, the dying with the dead, into the well below, on xvth day of July MDCCCVII.

The battle cry "Remember Cawnpore" fired up British troops for generations. The atrocities of the mutiny led the Crown to take over India from the East India Company the following year and to double the Caucasian British troop count in India. One of the four British soldiers to survive Cawnpore wrote a memoir that concluded:

The [Indian people] have acknowledged the sceptre of Queen Victoria, and have become constituents of the great British Commonwealth. Under the sanctions of unrestricted commerce, the vast natural resources of the land will multiply beyond all conception; hideous superstitions will give place to pure faith; righteous laws will rectify tyrannic abuses; science will clear the jungle and irrigate the desert. There is room enough here for all adventurous heroism and indefatigable perseverance that ever made the name of England great.

A French traveler in Twain's time put it slightly differently: "The English see the Hindu only as a 'boy' who is good to carry his bags and shine his shoes; just as they see in the countryside an agriculture or industrial business opportunity."

And Mohammed Aga Khan, descendant of the Prophet, leader of the Ismaelis and an Anglophile, found the atmosphere poisoned between the races in India by the mid-1890s.

The color bar[rier] had to be kept rigid and absolute, or some mysterious process of contamination would set in, and their faith in their own superiority and in their right—their moral, intellectual and biological right—to rule others would be sapped.

The next speaking stop was only forty-five miles away, but travel was often not easy in those days. The Twain entourage had to board a train at 3 a.m. to reach Agra and the Taj Mahal, a Persian-Muslim masterpiece built for a favorite harem wife who died during her fourteenth pregnancy. It's a tad ironic that predominantly Hindu India's most famous building is a Muslim mausoleum with lines of the Qur'an on some walls, a shrine to Mumtaz Mahal, the dead wife of one of India's Moghol conquerors, Shah Jehan. His name in Persian means "Ruler of the World"; a devout Muslim, he was rather intolerant of Hindus.

Twain and his family saw the marvel by day—also by night, from close, from afar. Twain even stated in his notebook that he saw the Taj at midnight during an eclipse of a full moon.

At that moment, to our surprise, an eclipse began & in an hour was total—an attention not before offered to a stranger since the

Taj was built. Attempts were made to furnish an eclipse for the
P[rince] of W[ales] in 1876, & in recent years to 2 other princes
of that house, but without success. However, Col. Loch, political
agent, has much more influence than any of his predecessors have
had.

It appears that Twain was just trying out that gag because the eclipse
never made it into his travel book, just a viewing by straight "moonlight."

The author was clearly feeling the pressure of writing about the sub-
lime Taj. Guidebook writers have emptied dictionaries combing for new
adjectives to capture the exquisite beauty and harmony of this 1647 tomb
for a shah's soul mate.

He built for her the most splendid mausoleum that the world has
known and he dedicated it "To the Memory of an Undying Love."
And truly everything that is lovely in love seems to have found
form and shape in that wondrous structure.
— DELIGHT SWEETSER

What jewels can equal its lustrous brilliancy as it rises against the
clear, cloudless sky?
— F. W. PENNEFATHER

It is a dream that floats, something airborne, weightless, such is
the perfect equilibrium of its lines, and so delicate and pale are the
shadows that play about the pure and translucent stone.
— ANDRÉ CHEVRILLON

Twain decided not to enter the joust of superlatives. He weighed in
instead on anticipation, on Niagara Falls, on ice storms, and on almost
anything but his own personal opinion of the Taj.

He complained that his brain was overloaded with *other* people's versions of the Taj, which clouded his vision.

You cannot keep your enthusiasms down, you cannot keep your
emotions within bounds when that soaring bubble of marble
breaks upon your view. But these are not your enthusiasms and
emotions—they are the accumulated emotions and enthusiasms

of a thousand fervid writers, who have been slowly and steadily
storing them up in your heart day by day and year by year all your
life; and now they burst out in a flood and overwhelm you; and
you could not be a whit happier if they were your very own. By
and by you sober down, and then you perceive that you have been
drunk on the smell of somebody else's cork. For ever and ever the
memory of my distant first glimpse of the Taj will compensate me
for creeping around the globe to have that great privilege.

He reminisced about how he had first arrived at Niagara Falls expecting the Atlantic Ocean to be pouring over the Himalayas, and it took him
fifteen visits before he could see the falls for himself. He spent pages
doing a truly exquisite description of the morning after a New England
ice storm that has coated trees in a thin frozen veneer.

A gust of wind sets every branch and twig to swaying, and in an
instant turns the whole white tree into a spouting and spraying
explosion of flashing gems of every conceivable color; and there it
stands and sways this way and that, flash! flash! flash! a dancing and
glancing world of rubies, emeralds, diamonds, sapphires, the most
radiant spectacle, the most blinding spectacle, the divinest, the
most exquisite, the most intoxicating vision of fire and color and
intolerable and unimaginable splendor that ever any eye has rested
upon in this world, or will ever rest upon outside of the gates of
heaven.

And he slyly concluded: "The Taj is man's ice storm." And that was
as close as he came to revealing his own impressions of the magnificent
building.

At Agra, the most powerful man in the region hosted the Clemens
family. They were guests of Lieutenant Colonel William Loch, the political agent, now in charge of three territories. A rajah had been deposed
nine months earlier, which Livy stated had added greatly to the workload
of this "lovely interesting man."

Livy luxuriated in the regal reception. She immediately relayed details
of her accommodations in this "most beautiful bungalow" to her sister.
Her bedroom, a massive airy windowed cube, measured thirty feet in

each direction, including the ceiling, and looked out onto a large pillared veranda. She had a large dressing room and bathroom as well. Her husband had a similarly large setup, as did her daughter. As did several other houseguests.

None of the rooms had doors, just curtains that caught the breeze. But none of them fretted over the lack of locks; Livy could see outside her window a near-constant parade of white-turbaned natives patrolling. She found the place "delightful—good food, nice interesting, homelike people, great comfort and great independence."

Four waiters and a boy served the meals, which she judged among the best they had eaten in India. Servants seemed to be everywhere. "As you go along a hall or enter a room in these eastern houses they will rise up from the floor where they are squatting anywhere from two to six or eight servants, sometimes they remind one of monkeys."

Her husband had taken a different tone about the servility in his notebook: "The cringing salaam of the native (hand held to forehead, & bow) which the white man does not pay attention to. Piteous."

While the lieutenant colonel's guests slept in feather beds, the servants slept outside their rooms on the veranda. Livy told her sister that one must be careful not to trip over a "servant rolled up like a cocoon" when leaving early in the morning. She did point out that the Clemens family chose to pay their servants almost double the going rate of twenty rupees a month, which equaled $5, and that whole families lived on $1 a month.

When Twain heard about the lieutenant colonel's increased workload, he volunteered to help. "I offered to depose a Rajah or two for him—or drown them—this for novelty." One senses a certain impatience on Twain's part with the master race.

The Clemens family returned late that night from the Taj and found that Satan/Mauzie wasn't sleeping in his appointed place either under a tree or on the veranda but had passed out in the entranceway of Lieutenant Colonel Loch's mansion. He was apparently drunk again. "[He] was sleeping like a log on the marble steps of the great portico, with his head on the bare flags[tones]."

Twain was heartbroken because he knew, with Livy staring down at Satan and also staring over at the august British officer, there would be no reprieve for Satan this time. The day was February 29, 1896.

So he had to go. When I told him, he said patiently, "Wair good," and made his parting salute, and went out from us to return no more forever. Dear me! I would rather have lost a hundred angels than that one poor lovely devil. What style he used to put on, in a swell hotel or in a private house—snow-white muslin from his chin to his bare feet, a crimson sash embroidered with gold thread around his waist, and on his head a great sea-green turban like to the turban of the Grand Turk.

With help from the lieutenant colonel, the Clemenses were able to find a replacement very quickly:

His successor was a Mohammedan, Sahadat Mohammed Khan; very dark, very tall, very grave. He went always in flowing masses of white, from the top of his big turban down to his bare feet. His voice was low. He glided about in a noiseless way, and looked like a ghost. He was competent and satisfactory. But where he was, it seemed always Sunday. It was not so in Satan's time.

In Twain's boyish universe, nothing could be worse than eternal Sunday. Did karma quickly come into play here for discarding Satan/Mauzie? Everyone would fall sick at the next stop, the elephant-venerating, pink city of Jeypore.

CHAPTER 24

Feverish in the Pink City

Twain tried to ignore an intermittent numbness and pricking sensation in his left arm; he had a harder time trying to ignore stomach issues as well as exhaustion. The British doctor in Jeypore "immediately ordered [him] to throw up Delhi & other engagements & rest a week or 10 days."

Clara also fell sick on arrival, and so did Carlyle Smythe. (Livy, as always, remained fine.) The two younger travelers ran a fever.

It was a strange place to fall ill. It was a strange place. Period. Sick or healthy, Jeypore could seem like something out of a feverish delusional dream. The main boulevard, wide as a football field and two miles long, was flanked by buildings—private homes, palaces, temples, stores, warehouses—all painted *shades of pink,* all "the soft rich tint of strawberry ice-cream," as Twain put it. "One cannot look down the far stretch of the chief street and persuade himself that these are real houses . . . the impression that it is an unreality, a picture, a scene in a theater, is the only one that will take hold."

The patients remained resting at a hotel, Kaiser-I-Hind on the pastoral outskirts of town. Nine brothers and their wives and children operated the friendly two-story inn. "There was always a long pile of their little comely brown children loosely stacked in its veranda," wrote Twain, "and a detachment of the parents wedged among them, smoking the hookah or the howdah, or whatever they call it."

The group's second-story high-ceilinged, big-windowed rooms allowed for breezes. Twain, bored, once again fell to observing the mischievous

Indian crows, this time tormenting a monkey that lived in a tree across the way and also harassing a cow that lived in their courtyard.

As one patient got well, another relapsed, and their stay would stretch out. The lucrative, large city of Delhi loomed as next on the schedule, but rumors of a smallpox outbreak made them all quite leery. Clara and Livy were inoculated.

So, they rested. Twain made notebook entries for only two days between March 1 and March 15. A new friend, a Mr. Aklom, brought them loads of books from his home. A local high-ranking official, Colonel Jacob, sent oranges and bananas.

After five days of rest, everyone was feeling a bit better, so Smythe made reservations for a Saturday, March 7, departure, and Twain decided to squeeze in some Jeypore sightseeing on Friday. They drove in a carriage to the famed bazaar. Twain saw: "Girls with [Christ]ian skirt on, & naked busts & bellies. Women *clothed* in gold bangles. 2 elephants & plenty tall camels. Huge cloud of pigeons."

He lucked into visiting on the day of a public procession, the gift of a wealthy manufacturer of religious idols, and Twain found the streets crammed with people, and the balconies too. At the famed, enormous "Palace of the Winds," women peered out of some of the 953 windows and arched niches, a kind of human dovecote designed to allow wives and daughters in purdah to look out without being seen.

In a nation known for vibrant color, travelers agreed that Jeypore stood out for its exuberantly vibrant color. The place had a Mardi Gras feel, most days of the year:

> Then the wide street itself, away down and down and down into
> the distance, was alive with gorgeously-clothed people not still, but
> moving, swaying, drifting, eddying, a delirious display of all colors
> and all shades of color, delicate, lovely, pale, soft, strong, stunning,
> vivid, brilliant, a sort of storm of sweetpea blossoms passing on the
> wings of a hurricane; and presently, through this storm of color,
> came swaying and swinging the majestic elephants, clothed in their
> Sunday best of gaudinesses, and the long procession of fanciful
> trucks freighted with their groups of curious and costly images, and
> then the long rearguard of stately camels, with their picturesque
> riders.

Delight Sweetser added some details to Twain's impressionist picture:

The Jeypore costume is the most picturesque of India. The men wind their turbans to one side, jauntily, the women wear a quantity of full colored skirts with tinseled hems, and their heads and arms and ankles are heavy with jewelry. The sole garment of the small boy is usually a gay-colored little [sleeved coat] that should come down to his heels, but it is always button-less, and it floats in the breeze behind him as he runs.

Indian women flocked to the great Four Corners market to buy jewelry of gold, silver, glass and brass, and anklets and nose rings. Bauble hustlers competed for the attention of foreign tourists. "The street juggler looped the torpid python around his body and held the head before him to be photographed, as if the coiling creature were only a garden-hose with fangs in the nozzle," wrote an American visitor. A magician repeatedly showed his empty hands and palms, wiggled them, shook them, then reached down deep in a large bucket of water and pulled his hands up and poured out fine *dry* sand.

Ironically, pink Jeypore, which had such an ancient feel to it, was governed by a maharajah who had attended the Chicago World's Fair of 1893 and had brought back progressive ideas about sanitation and clean water. He also introduced women-only hours for museums and built technical schools for youngsters. His forward thinking, however, did not prevent him from pursuing some traditional hobbies, such as owning 350 fine horses and maintaining a stable of fighting elephants.

The Clemens foursome began packing on March 7, but once again the travel plans to Delhi had to be scuttled. Carlyle Smythe started running a high fever and broke out in sores. The doctor diagnosed smallpox. Smythe was quarantined in a room, the trip on hold. Clara grew sick again. The doctor re-examined Smythe and decided he had German measles and a touch of malarial fever; Clara too had malarial fever.

Since Livy remained the only one in tip-top health, she decided she would brave an outing by herself (with servants driving, of course). She learned that Thursday morning was the women-only time at the art museum, located in a magnificent palace in a park. The collection featured local artifacts, especially fabrics and jewels of bygone maharajahs.

She was also eager to examine the current women of Jeypore, up close. However, she made one miscalculation and her morning turned into a game of hide-and-seek.

> Every part of the museum, even up to the balconies in the second story, & across the roof were packed full of these brilliantly dressed ladies. The only trouble was that I was as great a curiosity to them as they were to me. They crowded about me and chattered & examined me & followed me about. I would get behind cases & get into other rooms to try to get away, but always without success.

The women repeatedly encircled her and jabbered questions in the local dialect. She kept pointing to her mouth, trying to get across that she didn't speak their language: "One lady knew a little English, pressed her way close to me and then asked most politely, pointing to my veil: 'Why do you wear that? It makes black spots on your face.'"

Livy didn't share her retort, but she did note to Clara that she found it amusing to be asked a fashion question by a woman whose "hands were covered with tattoo marks."

Olivia Langdon Clemens, a Victorian-era American, of the free and democratic United States, was certainly more covered, head to toe, than these midriff-baring Indian women. And if Mrs. Clemens wore gloves despite the heat, then not a single square inch of skin would have been exposed to a casual glance.

The week passed in a blur. In the hubbub, someone in Jeypore leaked news of Twain's illness to someone in Bombay, who telegraphed someone in Europe, until it became a Thursday, March 12, squib in a London newspaper, "Mark Twain Seriously Ill," which wound up the following day, Friday, in dozens of American papers.

Twain's illness ran on the front page of the *New York Sun,* and H.H. Rogers sent a worried telegram on Saturday, offering to dispatch his Standard Oil representative in Bombay to rescue Twain.

Twain telegraphed the agent, Major Samuel Comfort, to cable Rogers that he was already healthy again. On Sunday, the *New York Sun* announced that Twain will "get well," with his "condition not as serious as first reported."

Both of the other patients declared themselves ready to travel on Saturday night, March 14. Twain sent a note to the stationmaster asking that their sleeping cars be reserved. Then *he* had to cancel the trip because of a renewed bout of diarrhea, which he blithely confessed to H.H. Rogers in a letter two weeks later. (One guesses Livy didn't proofread that one.)

The group departed the pink city Sunday evening and reached Delhi the next day, to stay one night at the notorious Skinner mansion. They were guests of the current owners, a Bank of Bengal official and his wife, but Twain was more impressed by the building's former occupant.

> It was built by a rich Englishman who had become oriental-
> ized—so much so that he had a zenana. But he was a broadminded
> man, and remained so. To please his harem he built a mosque; to
> please himself he built an English church. That kind of a man will
> arrive, somewhere.

Because smallpox was rumored in Delhi, the Clemens family stayed indoors and didn't sightsee. Twain claimed monkeys invaded his room; one used his hairbrush; others flung things at him; he threw stuff back despite his host's warning. He eventually locked them in the bathroom.

From here, Smythe and Twain squeezed in three last paydays on the subcontinent—two in Lahore and one in far north Rawalpindi (both now in Pakistan)—before everyone took a 1,443-mile train ride back to Calcutta.

Lahore hosted the nation's largest railroad machinery works; Rawal-pindi had the largest military base. The family spent the bulk of the trip as guests in Lahore of yet another high-ranking official, historian/civil servant Herbert C. Fanshawe and his niece. Twain, fading in the heat, left few notes, but he did ride an elephant for the second time. Note-book states: "Lunched with Lieut-Governor of the Punjab. Lent us his elephant—*one* of them."

Twain apparently improved his riding technique, at least in his travel book version.

> It was a fine elephant, affable, gentlemanly, educated, and I was
> not afraid of it. I even rode with confidence through the crowded
> lanes of the native city, where it scared all the horses out of their
> senses, and where children were always just escaping its feet. It
> took the middle of the road in a fine independent way and left it
> to the world to get out of the way or take the consequences. I am

used to being afraid of collisions when I ride or drive, but when one is on top of an elephant, that feeling is absent. I could have ridden in comfort through a regiment of runaway teams. I could easily learn to prefer an elephant to any other vehicle, partly because of that immunity from collisions, and partly because of the fine view one has from up there, and partly because of the dignity one feels in that high place, and partly because one can look in at the windows and see what is going on privately among the family.

A telegram reached them that the departure date of the steamer *Wardha*, which would take them to Africa, had been moved up two days. So, another pair of lectures had to be canceled. The family immediately left for the two-day train trip southeast to Calcutta. Once they reached the Continental Hotel, Clara suffered a relapse of malarial fever. The doctor reluctantly allowed her to travel, hoping the sea breezes would help. Twain found time to observe that residents of Calcutta wore nothing on their head, but the horses there wore a white pith sun protector that resembled a graduation mortarboard. He fervently hoped he could introduce that style for American horses.

They boarded the SS *Wardha* on Thursday, March 26. Ships leaving the famed port of Calcutta traveled out along the wide mouth of the Hoogli River. Twain seems to have gone a bit delirious in the heat. As the ship progressed down the Hoogli, which soon widened to a mile and a half, the author began imagining that he was back on the Mississippi, especially as he occasionally saw a "white-columned European house" with the forest behind. He wondered if it was a Louisiana plantation, and then when he saw thatched native huts, he imagined them slave quarters. "For 6 hours this has been the sugar coast of the Missi[ssi]ppi."

He also revived his curiosity about piloting down a river. He learned that the *Wardha* drew 24 feet of water and that at one shoal point, high tide was 24 feet, 4 inches. He was very impressed that the British recorded daily tide depths down to the inch at key low-water points.

The temperature on deck was roastingly hot by day and bracingly cold and windy by night. Clara discovered monstrous cockroaches in her cabin and refused to sleep there, so she and her mother and her father slept on deck. Livy woke up with wind-chapped cheeks. Twain complained about the mosquitoes.

The ship left the brown river to head 780 miles by the blue waters of the Bay of Bengal to Madras. Then Twain suddenly got sick again with a bad rasping hacking cough. They all found it deliriously hot in the cabins, too breezy out of them, and the food on the ship rotten.

Livy, who had been a pillar, cracked. Throughout the trip, she had ranked as the strongest among them—emotionally and physically—but she confessed all her worst fears in a letter to her sister, written aboard the *Wardha*. She hadn't received any mail in weeks from America. Her husband and daughter were ill. She had tallied up their net profit (after expenses) from three months in India at a mere $1,000 for eighteen performances.

> When . . . I think of the list of creditors, and the money yet to be paid, I feel our going home and inhabiting our own house is far in the distance. Very, *very* far. You know I have a pretty good courage, but sometimes it comes over me like an overwhelming wave, that it is to be bitterness and disappointment to the end.

She said she regretted burdening Sue, but her worries about her husband troubled her.

"Poor old darling, he has been pursued by colds and inabilities of various sorts. Then he is so impressed with the fact that he is *sixty* years old. Naturally I combat that idea all that I can, trying to make him rejoice that he is not *seventy*. . . ."

She said she longed to sip tea on the veranda with her sister. She tried to end on a higher note.

"I realize and appreciate that we have had more than our share of the good things of this life, and I try not to fret, even if we can never get back into our house again, and live in our old way."

The holy grail for Livy was to reunite the whole family in their wonderful home in Hartford, with three daughters and seven servants and two horses and one carriage, and piles of cats and a laughing Papa ringleading it all.

The *Wardha* reached the harbor of Madras down the coast on March 31. A small boat took the Clemens party ashore for breakfast at a downtown hotel, but Twain felt too miserable in the sweltering heat to ride around sightseeing. Livy and Clara continued without him, and he returned to the ship.

He sat alone in a wicker deck chair, reading the newspaper through wire-rimmed spectacles. When a reporter for *Madras Standard* found him, the newspaperman was shocked to find such a tired old man, with "paleness of countenance" and no "vigour of middle manhood." Twain coughed his way through the long interview. The reporter, who must have known shorthand, wrote down a massive stream of consciousness as Twain rambled on about book advances (no, he did not recently receive $50,000), and about India's horrific poverty; he mostly sidestepped a question about Indian independence, praising Indians' command of the English language but lamenting their lack of "inventive genius of the various practical arts." On Venezuela, he opined: "It is absolutely silly to think that America and England would ever fire a shot at each other."

He concluded the interview a bit abruptly and walked to the side of the ship to watch circus equipment and animals, including tigers, being loaded for Harmston's traveling circus. A contemporary review reveals that Harmston's, besides the wild beasts, featured trapeze and tightrope acts with especially attractive female performers, such as Miss Brandon doing a "rainbow dance" in "fairylike drapery" and the Warren sisters on the flying trapeze, who resemble "two elves swinging upon sun beams."

Twain, at the rail, made small talk with a carny man. With his wife and daughter sightseeing in Madras, the conversation somehow veered to the topic of sex.

The circus man told him that in the Dutch settlements in Sumatra, the Dutch government delivered prostitutes to the soldiers' barracks twice a week and that those women were all first inspected for sexual diseases. Twain told the man that he had just been in Rawalpindi, where a British general had told him that "half the soldiers in the hospital" have syphilis or gonorrhea; "they go home and marry healthy girls & disease them."

Twain elaborated in his notebook:

> By all accounts England is the home of pious cant & cant of the most harmful sort. . . . These fine hearty young fellows come here to defend England & England makes no provision for their natural passion—infamously betrays them to their destruction, knowing her treachery (officialdom does) but afraid to go in the face of cant. Then these 70,000 young men go home & marry fresh young English girls & transmit a heritage of disease to their children & grandchildren. Clean women subject to rigid inspection, ought to be kept for these soldiers. Any other course is treachery to the soldiers.

Twain would later decide to keep his thoughts on syphilis and lusty British soldiers to himself, and not include them in his travel book.

That afternoon, after Harmston's circus was loaded, another circus of a much smaller size came aboard as well. An Indian juggler-magician and his sister performed a basket trick that absolutely staggered Twain. He wrote it up in great polished detail, but apparently Livy later decided it was too risqué to include in the travel book.

It seems fitting to add this long-suppressed account here, near the end of Twain's memorable trip to India.

> The juggler was a tall young native, with some clothing but not much—naked arms & naked legs; the usual light rag or so of the country on him. His sister was a well built woman; lithe, trim & graceful. The brother threw a rope netting over her—a netting that had rope fringes to its sides. He tied these fringes together in numerous places & in hard knots; binding the woman in the net in such a way that her nose was between her knees; & so compactly that he could tumble her about as if she were a solid chunk. Then he lifted her up by her bindings & crowded her into a basket. There seemed to be barely enough room to get the upper half of her in.

Twain described the magician cramming his sister into the two-foot-tall woven basket, which sloped outward to a wider base. The brother stood on her shoulders as though she wouldn't fit. He mashed a lid down on her, then draped it all with a sheet. He played on a flute and chatted with his sister to show she was still inside. Then he suddenly flung off the sheet and lid and yanked up the rope netting and cast it in the air. Twain was impressed at how quickly she had untied herself in so small a space.

> Clearly the entire woman was in the basket, now. . . . It did not seem to me that the basket was large enough to hold her, no mat-ter how much shrinkage she applied to herself. Still she was surely there; there was no other place for her to be. The basket stood alone, on the open deck, in the glare of noonday; she could not get out of it without being seen.
> Suddenly the brother threw off the cover & jumped into the

basket with both feet & began to dance—in what was an empty basket, so far as I could see. It was the most astonishing thing I ever saw, the most incredible, the most impossible.

The brother then leaped out and put the lid back on and began poking long swords through the basket.

[He] kept on stabbing through the basket at apparently all angles & from all directions. It seemed to me that if there had been a cat in there it would surely have been spitted. Then he took off the cover & immediately the woman hopped out of the basket. . . . It was far & away ahead of anything I have ever seen any of our experts do.

He was less impressed with the magician's fortune-telling abilities. The loinclothed impresario predicted in broken English that Twain would live to be eighty and be "happy, too, dam happy."

———

The *Wardha* stopped at Colombo in Ceylon to unload the circus and load up some tea. The two-day docking enabled Twain to give his first talk in two weeks; unfortunately, torrential rain fell, flooding the avenues, and the date was April 3, Good Friday. Most of the English-speaking citizens had fled the steamy metropolis for their bungalows in the mountains. Newspapers judged the town "absolutely deserted" and Twain found his hall half empty.

Even Livy and Clara abandoned him to head seventy-five miles to the antiquity-filled higher altitudes of Kandy, where tourists could see temples and a classic relic: Buddha's tooth.

The highlight of the brief wet Ceylon stopover, it turned out, was picking up a stack of American mail, which, as they rounded the globe, seemed to pull them magnetically homeward.

Two of Susy's letters to Clara have survived. They are absolutely shocking. Susy—confused, self-doubting, perhaps secretly lady-lovelorn Susy—was happy!

Half a world away, she transmitted her glow from her three weeks around New Year's in New York City, which she describes as the "most perfectly delightful" time of her life. "I had a 'success fou' [i.e., "wild crazy success"] . . . thanks to mental science and without the help or presence of that mighty power, the grey grenouille [*i.e., gray frog, her nickname for her father*]."

Back in December, she and some friends had performed a play in Orange, New Jersey, for her much-loved former classmate, Louise Brownell, in which Susy sang and played Sarah Bernhardt, and it had dazzled Louise. Then after New Year's, Susy and Louise visited the Bohemian side of New York City, with its artists and writers and musicians. Despite her stints in Europe, Susy had no idea that an *American* city could offer that kind of culture and sophistication.

> I came away from there a full fledged lover of society, at least of N.Y. Society. No city in the world can rival it for brilliancy and interest and *life* and intelligence, and all manner of resources. Yes, the life there *can* be ideal, the sort of life that "Mark Twain" could attract to him. I am sure we would all *love* it.

She had written the letter from Hartford near the end of January, when she was briefly staying in the Clemens home, with the renters, Alice Hooker Day and family. Susy, striving for a newfound upbeat Mental Science positivity, aimed to defy the provincial Hartford debutantes, her supposed friends. She judged Daisy Warner (the queen bee daughter of a Clemens neighbor) and the other twentysomethings crass and dull. "Well, there's no use talking [about them]—they don't *exist*, and it's hard to associate with the dead just yet." (She sometimes sounded like her father.)

But Susy noted that at least the Clemens home on Farmington Avenue looked lovely and the bookshelves did too and the Connecticut sky, and she was convinced she could survive even in Hartford with Mama, Papa and Clara back . . . and the occasional soul-nurturing trip to New York City. But clearly, her dream would be that they would all move to the mecca of the arts, Manhattan!

Also in the Ceylon mailbag, Livy received a letter drawing her back to the United States, from Alice Hooker Day, who painted idyllic Hartford scenes, such as ice-skating on the frozen river by the house, and steaming cocoa held in snow-caked mittens. Alice also raved about the new and improved Susy.

And now Livy began to weave a fantasy of reuniting her family in

Hartford with maybe—dare she dream it?—winters in that expensive wonderful place, New York City.

Livy frankly admitted to envying Alice living in Livy's own Hartford home. She told Alice that their finances would probably make their decision for them, but she held out hope that they could return. She said she cherished her Hartford friends and thought herself too old to make a new set of high-caliber intimates. Livy knew that Alice also was weighing whether to stay in Hartford or set out for a new location. (Husband John Day's dry goods business was staggering a bit in the wake of the 1893 Panic.)

> Oh, Alice, beloved friend, build a pretty place in Hartford some
> where near us, then we will try to put money in our purse and go
> back there & live. Let us remain whales in tubs. Then if we only
> put money enough in our purse we might take a flat in New York
> for two or three months in mid winter.

"Whales in tubs"! What an amazing expression for lording it over society in a provincial city!

CHAPTER 25

Dreams at Sea

S ea voyages often provide meditative interludes, a suspension of travel while traveling.

Mark Twain luxuriated in the respite. They would bob along the calm sea for a full month on their way to South Africa with a stop on the island of Mauritius to change to a larger, finer ship. "The holiday comes very handy for us," Twain wrote to H.H. "I am very glad to have a resting spell; I was getting fagged with platform work."

As with the other voyages, the author seemed to relax and regain a sense of playfulness. He overheard a dirty joke and apparently repeated it to Livy: "They called the old gentleman Sir Priapus, because he was so erect." His next entry is: "You didn't *get* that, *did* you?"

He inspected the ship's library and found it quite worthy—if for one feature only: the shelves contained *no* Jane Austen. He ultimately decided that a ship's library without even a single book deserved high praise because it contained *no* Jane Austen.

His notebooks reveal an almost bizarre range of interests: religious preferences in ant colonies, worst public floggings, the anonymity of executioners, the insecurities of God. Twain deemed it pathetic that "God" in all major religions demands constant praise. "We make fun of poor little vain girls who fish for compliments." He also found yet another rags-to-riches story that thrilled him. Sir Robert Clive, one of Britain's great military heroes in India, had left a warehouse job—where he was called "Bob"—to enlist in the army and had returned home the ruler of kingdoms in India with "all the English world crowding to look at him,

& envy him, & shake him by the hand, & deafen him with the roar & thunder of his name."

Twain recorded in his notebook that the first mate, a Scotsman, could tell the most outrageous lies and be believed by the ladies at the dinner table. The Scot mentioned keeping a pet *flying fish* at his farm and letting it out into the fields to catch birds and frogs. He spoke of once hooking an enormous shark in the Pacific Islands and sharing it with the natives, who sliced open the belly and discovered the possessions of a missionary. The islanders refused to share with him items such as a watch and a hairbrush, but they gave him a crumpled piece of paper that turned out to be a lottery ticket worth . . . half a million francs.

"My own luck has been curious all my literary life," marveled Twain in his notebook, "I never could tell a lie that anybody would doubt, nor a truth that anybody would believe."

The author slipped into a lazy routine: a morning shave on deck, coffee-and-fruit breakfast and then hours of reading and dreaming in the breeze under the awnings on the deck, followed by a convivial evening dinner.

> There is no mail to read and answer; no newspapers to excite you; no telegrams to fret you or fright you—the world is far, far away; it has ceased to exist for you . . . it is gone from your mind with all its businesses and ambitions, its prosperities and disasters, its exultations and despairs . . . they are a storm which has passed and left a deep calm behind.

While Twain was enjoying his deep calm in April 1896, his volunteer business manager, H.H. Rogers, was back in New York trying to negotiate a complete works deal that could save the author. And despite his consummate skills, he was having a hard time making publishers act rationally. Also, lawyer Bainbridge Colby had been busy with other clients and had been neglecting for months to handle Twain's bankruptcy assignment. Fortunately, Twain knew none of this.

The *Wardha* hit its first African port of call. The lush tropical island of Mauritius—so different from the parched plains of India—hardly excited his curiosity. He seemed most concerned that the former French colony, perhaps the "wettest place in the world" beside the ocean, might prove too damp to strike a match to light his cigar.

They transferred to the *Arundel Castle,* which swung around Madagascar and approached the South African coast. Two dozen Afrikaners on board stayed up past midnight singing songs of their homeland that Twain found surprisingly touching. Then someone suggested a "humorous" dirty song about having sex night after night crossing the Atlantic. Despite no one joining in, the man braved it alone. The punch line—that all the supposed sex acts were actually dirty double entendres—failed to rouse even a chuckle. "It was as if the tale had been told to dead men."

Twain was arriving in a South Africa embroiled in a deep political crisis; the conquering whites had largely subdued African tribes such as the Zulus, but now the British government and some wealthy ungovernable British adventurers were fighting against defiant Dutch-and-German-descended Boers in a scramble to gobble up territories glittering with gold and diamonds. The ink rarely dried on maps. The black Africans were lured and attacked by both sides.

On May 6, Twain and his family walked down the gangplank at Durban in Natal, in southern Africa, the start of the final leg of the round-the-world tour. It would not take him long to tell a few jokes and almost spark a major international political incident.

CHAPTER 26

Africa

He wasn't trying to be a crusader, but straight-faced humor is always dangerous. Sarcasm tends to lie flat on the printed page.

The patriotic British press had been straining to portray a bunch of British citizens (and a few Americans) in Boer prison as heroic martyrs, and Twain swiftly turned the whole situation into farce. He also succeeded in deeply irritating the most powerful man in Africa, forty-two-year-old British mining millionaire-politician Cecil Rhodes (best known today for Rhodes scholarships and a place formerly known as Rhodesia). Ironically, Twain repeatedly declared himself baffled by the politics behind it all. It's easy to see why he was baffled.

The map of the southern quarter of the African continent in 1896 looked like a patchwork quilt sewn by someone on hallucinogenic drugs: Orange Free State, Natal, Transvaal, Zululand, Pondoland, Griqualand, Basutoland, British Bechuanaland, Cape Colony. The splintering stemmed from the usual roots: greed and tribal loyalties.

The Dutch had started colonial settlements at the Cape of Good Hope near the tip of Africa in the mid-1600s; the British had arrived 150 years later, and began slicing off more and more choice bits. Descendants of the Dutch, called Boers, battled throughout the nineteenth century to defeat the local African tribes, and also to prevent the British from swallowing the entire region.

To cite one turf war, the Kimberly diamond mines, probably the most valuable square footage on earth, fell near the disputed border of the

Orange Free State (Dutch) and Griqualand (under British control). Bloody skirmishes were fought until the British in 1876 paid £90,000 (about $10 million today) for the acreage. (This turned out to be a world-class bargain, as the mine a couple of decades later would generate that kind of profit *every week*.)

Now, another squabble was brewing. The sixty-seven gold mines in Dutch Transvaal generated 2.265 million ounces of gold in 1894; that's seventy *tons* of gold. Many foreigners, mostly British, some American, lived in Transvaal, and, as Uitlanders (i.e., outsiders), were forced to pay higher taxes and had minimal legal and political rights. Also, the Boer monopoly gouged for necessities such as dynamite. Cecil Rhodes convinced himself that British citizens were at risk—or at least the gold mines were. He claimed a letter begging help had been sent to him.

Around New Year's 1896, Dr. Leander Jameson, along with Cecil's brother, Colonel Frank Rhodes, led a force of 600 armed raiders across the border from the British Cape Colony into Transvaal. Dr. Jameson had expected the outraged foreign citizens to rise up and join him. They didn't. The Boers defeated the raiders in four days; they shipped off some to England but kept prominent local citizen-rebels for trial. Four leaders were sentenced to death (later commuted); by the time Twain arrived in May, about 50 attackers, including American mining engineer John Hays Hammond of San Francisco, were still locked up in a Pretoria prison. British patriots claimed abusive Boer prison guards tortured the men, served them vile food and crammed them into unsanitary cells.

Enter the comedian. Some prominent foreigners living in Transvaal hoped they could entice the visiting world celebrity to go see the prisoners, observe their "frightful sufferings," and then lobby President Paul Kruger, the crusty patriarch of the Boers, for a reprieve or temporary release. That was the plan.

After spending his first week in Africa in pleasant Durban, as the guest of British doctor Robert Campbell, Twain agreed to make the long train trek up north into the higher-elevation Transvaal cities of Johannesburg and Pretoria: to perform but also to meet the prisoners and meddle in geopolitics. He was acclimating himself to the transition from India to Africa. Here, the rickshaw drivers were not scrawny Hindus but magnificently muscled tall Zulu warriors, some with horned headgear and big feathers to attract the tourist trade. Here, he saw black men and women who reminded him of slaves in his pre–Civil War days, but they didn't speak like American blacks. It was unsettling. He was also profoundly tired of mounting the platform.

He convinced Livy and Clara to stay at the coast, and set a plan to meet up in a month at Port Elizabeth. He thought they deserved to enjoy the charms of Dr. Campbell's garden and his circle of warm, gracious friends, and to avoid thirty-hour rickety Boer train rides. Clara had already found partners to join her for horseback riding on the beach. Livy was worried about him. The faithful husband would write his wife almost every day for the next fourteen days.

On the way north, Twain stopped off at the Natal capital of Pietermaritzburg, a bustling town at an elevation of 2,000 feet, and he performed two nights. He tried out tailoring the raft story to have Huck have a long debate with his conscience after he saves Jim.

The author, by the second day on the road, already regretted not bringing his family along. Smythe borrowed the hotel kitten (gray and sociable) to calm him; he also shared a hot Scotch with him. On this wifeless journey, Twain would certainly suffer more foot-in-mouth moments, more double booking of engagements, more dark mood swings. "It's pretty lonesome without you," he wrote that second night. "Dear heart, I miss you all the time."

Livy wrote back: "I miss you sadly, dearheart, but I hope you are having a good & in every way profitable time. But you must continue to miss me & to think that you do not get on as well without me, as you do with."

Twain continued on 300-plus miles more, up to Johannesburg, elevation 5,764 feet, southern Africa's largest noncoastal city, with a growing population of 100,000. Ever since his arrival in Africa, he was coping with a post-India lack of joyous color. He found the Boers dour puritanical people, and he was especially appalled by their wardrobe. "For ugliness of shapes, and miracles of ugly color inharmoniously associated, they were a record." He singled one Boer out.

A gaunt, sickly country lout six feet high, in battered gray slouched hat with wide brim, and old resin-colored breeches, had on a hideous brand-new woolen coat which was imitation tiger skin— wavy broad stripes of dazzling yellow and deep brown. I thought he ought to be hanged, and asked the station-master if it could be

arranged. He said no; and not only that, but said it rudely; said it
with a quite unnecessary show of feeling.

Twain wasn't a huge fan of the tribal fashions either. He found many of
the women wearing a drab "short brown blanket" that made him long for
the Indian women in "vivid deep" colors, "usually silks, soft and filmy."

They reached the bustling decade-old mining mecca of Johannesburg—in transition, moving hovels to the fringes and now packed with
smart carriages, mansions, banks, factories. This picturesque Transvaal
city, however, was still bitterly divided by the angry rift between the
Boers and the gold-seeking foreigners. He performed three successful
nights at the Standard Theatre.

At his hotel, he met with those who were instigating him to meddle: American consul Robert Chapin and Natalie Hammond, the very
pregnant wife of the American engineer sentenced to fifteen years in
prison. Hammond's unmarried "& most picturesquely beautiful" sister
also implored Twain to help. John Hays Hammond, who had worked for
William Randolph Hearst, oversaw Cecil Rhodes's entire gold-mining
operation and was said to be earning the unthinkable salary of $150,000
a year ($4½ million in today's dollars). He might have been the highest-
paid salaried private employee in the world.

Twain's mission-of-mercy delegation took a morning three-hour train
ride forty miles to Pretoria, then drove out that afternoon in a carriage
to the notorious Boer penitentiary that also housed convicted "Kaffirs"
or black Africans. Twain was introduced to the fifty or so prisoners—
most of them wealthy educated British men. "How the hell did you find
your way to this god-forsaken hole?" John Hays Hammond asked him in
greeting. "Getting into jail is easy," Twain replied. "I thought the difficul-
ties arose when it came to getting out." Twain discovered that he had met
the forty-year-old Hammond in New Haven, Connecticut, back when
Hammond was a senior at Yale.

Eyewitness Carlyle Smythe, whom Twain delegated to memorize
everything, later delivered an account:

When we entered the prison quadrangle, it seemed from the
laughter and bright clothing that we were attending some tennis
[party]. This surprise was scarcely lessened when we had been

taken round the dormitories, crowded with clean beds and deco-
rated with photographs of the prisoners' loved ones, as well as of
some attractive actresses. The culmination of our surprise was
reached when we had been introduced to the prisoners' private
larder, stocked with such unusual prison delicacies—unusual, as far
as my experience goes—as Yorkshire hams, Scandinavian sardines
in piles, Bologna sausage, pate-de-foie gras, and French olives.
Then [a toast to] the health of the visitor was proposed in the large
dormitory. The beverage was Scotch served in [tin cups], and two
of the "brutal" prison guards actually joined in the toast. Mark
Twain richly appreciated the situation; and [gave] an impromptu
speech of delicate persiflage.

A guard told Twain that he could speak to the prisoners but he should
not cross a certain white painted strip on the floor: the "death line,"
shouted one prisoner. Twain sat in a chair and earnestly told the prisoners how lucky they were to be in jail and that they would have wound up
there anyway, and "by the look of their countenances" they would probably wind up back in jail someday. He expected that after a few more
months, they would prefer "jail & its luxurious indolence" to the "sordid
struggle for bread outside."

Twain then pointed out what an amazing opportunity prison presented.
Cervantes, while imprisoned, wrote *Don Quixote;* iron bars could not
stop the Spaniard's imagination from wandering off and fighting wind-
mills, chasing knights, "enjoying all the intoxicating delights of glorious
war without its dangers." And John Bunyan penned *Pilgrim's Progress* in
prison. "Never would have been written if Bunyan hadn't been in jail."

Twain's full text is lost, but his concluding remarks are known. "I have
come here today at the invitation of your friends outside who cherish
your welfare and interest beyond all else; and I have arranged to see
President Kruger on your behalf. From this prison, I promise you that I
will go direct to President Kruger, and with all the earnestness of which
I am capable, I mean to urge him, in your interests, to——prolong your
sentences!"

History is silent on how many prisoners laughed. American mining
engineer Thomas Mein shouted that Twain was welcome to stay with
them, perhaps write a book or two. The humorist gracefully declined.

His speech might have irritated some prisoners, but that isn't what set off the furor. On the way out, a reporter asked him about the prisoners' fate, and he joked that he had stayed in many hotels with far worse service. He elaborated on the fine beds, fine foods, fine staff.

The departing remark was picked up in many newspapers, outraging both sides . . . the Boers were appalled at the cushy conditions of these convicted traitors, and the British, accusing the Boers of inhumane treatment, had no outrage to peddle. Cecil Rhodes had apparently hoped that outrage might fuel a British military invasion and rescue.

The humanitarian group returned to the hotel. The articles ran the next day; Carlyle Smythe received a summons from "Miss Rhodes," one of Cecil's two sisters, who had read Twain's speech in the paper. "Can you imagine anything more tactless?" she asked, shrilly. "I do not know Mr. Clemens; I have no desire to know him but I want him to know that I consider him a damned fool."

Smythe relayed the message, which Twain later said came via Miss Rhodes but originated with her brother, Colonel Frank Rhodes, who was one of the four leaders, then under a suspended death sentence.

[She told Smythe] the prisoners were furious because I praised their lodgings & comforts. The colonel said either *he* was a dam fool or I was. He seems to be in doubt. I'm not. We are all fools at times; this is *his* time. The prisoners ought to have had a policy, & stuck to it. But no, [American, Henry A.] Butters & others were for conciliating the Boers (which was wise), Col. Rhodes & others were for *driving* them—which *wasn't*.

After Twain's visit, the Boer wardens apparently cracked down, and the prisoners lost privileges such as booze, cards, actress photos, maybe even smokes.

A few days later, Twain did indeed meet with "Oom Paul" (Uncle Paul) Kruger, fierce seventy-year-old patriarch of the Boers, a bearded, rough-hewn, Old Testament zealot. Not formally educated, he took the Bible literally and defied the British as infidels. He wore plain working-man's clothes, and smoked cheap Boer tobacco. The meeting was brief because Kruger was suffering from a hoarse voice and bad cold. Twain later recorded: "He said he felt friendly toward America & that it was his disposition to be lenient with the American captives."

A jokey press item appeared in numerous British newspapers across the Empire that "Om Paul" Kruger—known for his earthy, pious ways—had added to his current two-book library of the Bible and *Pilgrim's Progress* the *Complete Works of Mark Twain*.

Four days after their meeting, Kruger let all but the four ringleaders out on payment of a hefty £2,000 per man ($300,000 in today's dollars) fine. The leaders, including Hammond, would be fined £25,000 each ($3.75 million today) and freed ten days later. Cecil Rhodes, it was said, paid the fines and paid salaries during the six months in prison.

Twain, surprisingly, didn't take credit for their release. And both sides seem not to have forgiven him even though the prisoners were freed so soon after his supposed screw-up. John Hays Hammond, who became extremely wealthy and returned to America in 1900, held a grudge against Twain that he vented years later to a friend:

> Mark Twain said the food and accommodations were fully equal
> to the Waldorf Astoria in New York, and if John Hays Hammond
> knew what was good for him, he would ask for a life sentence. . . .
> A storm of indignation swept over South Africa, and our situation
> was not improved. Since then I have failed to find anything "funny"
> in anything Mark Twain says or does.

Hammond's extra suffering lasted about two weeks.

Although Twain tried to avoid the Jameson Raid topic in future *public* interviews, he did indulge his *private* curiosity over certain mysteries, such as how the prisoners maintained their plush lifestyle inside the grim Pretoria penitentiary. He interviewed a freed rebel he met on a train: "The women [visitors] hid tins of sardines in their bosoms, vast bolognas in their bustles, cigarettes in their stockings, & bananas between their legs, & watched their chance to deliver them to the prisoners."

The more Twain thought about it, the more he found himself irritated by the behavior of the Rhodes siblings, who were clearly surrogates for their famous Machiavellian brother. Twain would not weigh in while he was in Africa, but he would harshly single out Cecil Rhodes in his later travel book.

> What is the secret of his formidable supremacy? One says it is his
> prodigious wealth . . . ; another says it is his majestic ideas, his vast
> schemes for the territorial aggrandizement of England, his patri-

otic and unselfish ambition to spread her beneficent protection and
her just rule over the pagan wastes of Africa and make luminous
the African darkness with the glory of her name; and another says
he wants the earth and wants it for his own, and that the belief that
he will get it and let his friends in on the ground floor is the secret
that rivets so many eyes upon him and keeps him in the zenith
where the view is unobstructed.

One may take his choice. They are all the same price. One
fact is sure: he keeps his prominence and a vast following, no
matter what he does. . . . He tricks the Reformers into immense
trouble with his Raid, but the most of them believe he meant
well. . . . He raids and robs and slays and enslaves the Matabele
[natives] and gets worlds of Charter-Christian applause for it.
[*The Crown chartered Rhodes's "British South Africa Company"
and allowed it to accumulate and rule vast territories.*] He has
beguiled England into buying Charter waste paper [*i.e., stock
certificates*] for Bank of England notes, ton for ton, and the
ravished still burn incense to him as the Eventual God of Plenty.
He has done everything he could think of to pull himself down
to the ground; he has done more than enough to pull sixteen
common-run great men down; yet there he stands, to this day,
upon his dizzy summit under the dome of the sky, an apparent
permanency, the marvel of the time, the mystery of the age, an
Archangel with wings to half the world, Satan with a tail to the
other half.

I admire him, I frankly confess it; and when his time comes I
shall buy a piece of the rope for a keepsake.

Straight-faced humor *is* dangerous.

Twain would spend two months in Africa and perform thirty times in
fifteen cities, ranging from the largest and oldest, Cape Town (population 85,000), down to tiny Cradock (4,300), known for its wool and
ostrich feather trade. Despite the mining wealth, southern African cities
remained relatively picayune compared to the likes of Sydney or Bombay.
In many African municipalities, white Europeans or their descendants
accounted for about half the population, while the rest were black Afri-

cans or imported East Indian "coolies." A preference for not hiring local black natives, who were characterized in one guidebook as "naked, lazy and polygamous," led to a massive importation of indentured laborers from India. (Mahatma Gandhi was then a twenty-six-year-old London-trained barrister living in Durban, lobbying for improved working and living conditions for Indian people.)

Twain spent another night in Pretoria and performed. "Audience composed, chiefly of Africanders & direct descendants of the old Boers; hard to start, but promptly & abundantly responsive after that."

After the stressful goings-on, Twain looked forward to a good night's sleep at the fine Grand Hotel, not far from Parliament House. He was getting ready for bed and heard the clock strike ten bells. He checked his expensive Waterbury watch, which said 9:30 p.m.

> I supposed that the climate was affecting it. I shoved it half an hour ahead; and took to my book and waited to see what would happen. At 10 the great clock struck ten again. I looked—the Waterbury was marking half-past 10. This was too much speed for the money, and it troubled me. I pushed the hands back a half hour, and waited once more; I had to, for I was vexed and restless now, and my sleepiness was gone. By and by the great clock struck 11. The Waterbury was marking 10.30.

Twain jotted in his notebook that around midnight he took a "man's dose of Scotch" and went to sleep. He found out the Parliament's great clock in the Boer capital had "a peculiarity which exists in no other clock, and would not exist in that one if it had been made by a sane person; on the half-hour it strikes the succeeding hour, then strikes the hour again, at the proper time."

Twain and Smythe left Pretoria for a 650-mile, five-city circuit south to smaller towns, after which he would meet his family on the coast, where they would arrive via boat.

He headed to Krugersdorp, where the Boers had defeated Jameson's raiders five months earlier. He happened to notice a monument to an earlier Boer victory back in 1881, when they had ousted the English. And he was struck yet again by the silliness of any patriotic monument.

Talking of patriotism, what humbug it is; it is a word which always
commemorates a robbery. There isn't a foot of land in the world
which doesn't represent the ousting and re-ousting of a long line of
successive "owners" who each in turn as "patriots" with proud and
swelling hearts, defended it against the next gang of "robbers" who
came to steal it and *did*—and became swelling-hearted patriots in
their turn.

Twain stayed as a guest and dined at the home of a vibrant British
couple, the Seymours. He enjoyed a lively dinner party in a happy home
with a glossy cat. On the next morning, Mrs. Seymour, who had acted as
a nurse to the British wounded, rushed to deliver Twain to catch his train
to Bloemfontein.

She is small & gentle & womanly, but she has abundance of fire
& nerve; drove me to the station 10 am May 28, Thursday with a
pair of horses over a rough & rocky & guttered road—drove like
Satan; how she kept her seat I don't know; it would have been a
hard drive for me, only I was in the air the main part of the time &
the air at Krugersdorp is very thin & soft on account of the great
altitude. Nothing else saved me from having my spine driven out at
the back of [my] head like a flagstaff.

Looking out from his train car heading south, he was awed by the
graceful meadows of southern Africa. He wrote to Livy:

I think the veldt is just as beautiful as Paradise—rolling & swelling,
& rising & subsiding, & sweeping on & on like an ocean toward
the remote horizon & changing its pale brown by delicate shades
to rich orange and finally to purple & crimson where it washes
against the hills at the base of the sky.

Twain, the storyteller, always seemed to want to be Twain the Victorian wordsmith. He wrote to Livy from Bloemfontein, a small market
town nestled in the hills. He knew she would be concerned that he might
be lazy and wear dirty, wrinkled clothes.

I have been 3 hours packing & shaving—7:30 to 10:30; & now I haven't anything left to do but do up two suits of clothes & some soiled linen & cigars & things in the shawl-strap & I'll be ready for the train. I never open the large valise. It is nicely & compactly packed & I leave it just as you left it. If I should take anything out, I couldn't get it back again.

So Twain had been two weeks separated from his wife, and he was basically telling her that he hadn't used any of his main clothes because she had packed the bag so perfectly. He was living out of a shawl-strap, or travel sack. (The couple had perfected some aspects of their marital comedy routine.)

Here he was traveling in the heart of perhaps the most racially divisive place on earth, a place that teased his memory to his childhood amid slavery in the Old South. He listened to the black women speaking near Bloemfontein and heard the "sweet soft musical voice" of blacks in America. "I followed a couple of them a mile to listen to the music of their speech & the happy ripple of their laugh."

As he ventured to King William's Town in Cape Colony, he observed cactuses with fiery red tongues pluming upward like torches amid the veldt; he also saw more scenes that collided with his pre–Civil War memories of blacks. He observed tribal villages, *kraals,* with mud-walled, thatched-roofed round huts.

Grouped about the kraal, picturesque adult savages in long brown blankets & juvenile savages stark naked; grouped at the station, ex-savages in European garb glibly chattering English, the two groups as different as . . . birds & quadrupeds. And here close by on the Sunday afternoon in K[ing] W[illiam]'s town troops of black women drifting churchward elaborately tastefully and expensively clothed in up-to-date European style.

Twain's sympathy for and curiosity about black Africans notwithstanding, he found himself moving through a severely segregated society. *Brown's South Africa,* a respected guidebook that went into many editions, matter-of-factly stated: "The majority of servants in (British) Cape Colony are coloured women, neither very trustworthy nor accomplished and with an absolutely stoical disregard for cleanliness in any shape or form." Over in (Dutch) Transvaal, the law strictly forbade black Africans from legally marrying.

And Twain decided to change his speech repertoire. In Australia, he added remarks on U.S.–British eternal friendship; in India, to spotlight religion, he expanded his bits on Adam and the serpent. Now, here in southern Africa, he altered his opening night and dropped "Huck Saves Jim," which is basically the account of how a white boy defied the law and risked eternal damnation to save his black slave friend. Twain had tried a revised version in Pietermaritzburg, but it apparently had fallen flat. He told the slave/raft story only two or possibly three times out of thirty appearances in Africa. He had dozens of stories to choose from. He wasn't a political crusader; he was a comic in debt.

Twain replaced it on many opening nights by inserting a couple of mock-manly stories, about his less-than-heroic 1,700-mile retreat during the Civil War and his equally unbrave duel in Nevada during his newspaper days. He had called a rival editor a "thief or a body-snatcher or something," and that led Twain to face a "lanky gaspipe" adversary.

But the story he told most often in Africa was a ghost story told by a slave. Instead of celebrating the freeing of a slave, he was celebrating the *art* of a slave, the storytelling art.

"The Golden Arm" had mesmerized him in childhood when his uncle's gray-haired slave Daniel used to tell it, and Twain had spent a lifetime perfecting his own version. He had embarrassed Susy by telling it to her sophisticated classmates at Bryn Mawr. His daughter had fled; her college friends had loved it. He often hauled the tale out at family gatherings and dinner parties. He even wrote about how to tell it.

> On the platform I used to tell a negro ghost story that had a pause in front of the snapper on the end, and that pause was the most important thing in the whole story. If I got it the right length precisely, I could spring the finishing ejaculation with effect enough to make some impressible girl deliver a startled little yelp and jump out of her seat—and that was what I was after.

Twain collected the "yelps" like scalps, and had recorded in his notebook in Pietermaritzburg a few weeks earlier: "Ghost made ⅔ of the house yelp. Wonderful lot of pretty girls & young misses."

On June 8, 1896, in King William's Town (known locally as "King"), to a packed house, he did his new opening repertoire and then concluded with "Golden Arm." He told it in Negro dialect, working in sound effects of moans and wailing winds:

Once 'pon a time dey wuz a montrus mean man, en he live 'way out in de prairie all lone by hisself, 'cep'n he had a wife. En bimeby she died, en he tuck en toted her way out dah in de prairie en buried her. Well, she had a golden arm—all solid gold, fum de shoulder down. He wuz pow'ful mean—pow'ful; en dat night he couldn't sleep, gaze he want dat golden arm so bad.

When it come midnight he couldn't stan' it no mo'; so he git up, he did, en tuck his lantern en shoved out thoo de storm en dug her up en got de golden arm; en he bent his head down 'gin de win', en plowed en plowed en plowed thoo de snow. Den all on a sudden he stop [*make a considerable pause here, and look startled, and take a listening attitude*] en say: "My LAN', what's dat!"

En he listen—en listen—en de win' say [*set your teeth together and imitate the wailing and wheezing singsong of the wind*], "Bzzz-z-zzz"—en den, way back yonder whah de grave is, he hear a voice! he hear a voice all mix' up in de win' can't hardly tell 'em 'part—"Bzzz-zzz—W-h-o—g-o-t—m-y—g-o-l-d-e-n arm?—zzz—zzz—W-h-o g-o-t m-y g-o-l-d-e-n arm!" [*You must begin to shiver violently now.*]

En he begin to shiver en shake, en say, "Oh, my! OH, my lan'!" en de win' blow de lantern out, en de snow en sleet blow in his face en mos' choke him, en he start a-plowin' knee-deep towards home mos' dead, he so sk'yerd—en pooty soon he hear de voice agin, en [*pause*] it 'us comin' after him! "Bzzz—zzz—zzz—W-h-o—g-o-t m-y—g-o-l-d-e-n—arm?"

When he git to de pasture he hear it agin closter now, en a-comin'!—a-comin' back dah in de dark en de storm—[*repeat the wind and the voice*]. When he git to de house he rush up-stairs en jump in de bed en kiver up, head and ears, en lay dah shiverin' en shakin'—en den way out dah he hear it agin!—en a-comin'! En bimeby he hear [*pause—awed, listening attitude*]—pat—pat—pat—hit's acomin' up-stairs! Den he hear de latch, en he know it's in de room!

Den pooty soon he know it's a-stannin' by de bed! [*Pause.*]
Den—he know it's a-bendin' down over him—en he cain't skasely
git his breath! Den—den—he seem to feel someth'n c-o-l-d, right
down 'most agin his head! [*Pause.*]

Den de voice say, right at his year—"W-h-o g-o-t—m-y—g-o-l-
d-e-n arm?" [*You must wail it out very plaintively and accus-
ingly; then you stare steadily and impressively into the face of
the farthest-gone auditor—a girl, preferably—and let that awe-
inspiring pause begin to build itself in the deep hush. When it has
reached exactly the right length, jump suddenly at that girl and
yell,* **"You've got it!"**

*If you've got the pause right, she'll fetch a dear little yelp and
spring right out of her shoes. But you must get the pause right;
and you will find it the most troublesome and aggravating and
uncertain thing you ever undertook.*]

Twain judged that Pratt & Whitney's best machines couldn't calibrate
that pause to the millionth of a second required. Katy Leary, the longtime family maid, remembered the ending slightly differently. She said
Twain would start softly with "Who's got my golden arm?" and keep whis-
pering it softly, then a bit louder and louder, "then very loud and hard
toward the end—when he used to rise right up out of his chair, and lean
way forward over the table, and point his finger straight at somebody,
and cry, 'YOU've got my golden arm!,' in most blood curdling tones" and
"frighten any one almost to death."

The whole story took only six or seven minutes, but it provided a stel-
lar send-off to cap the night. Many South African critics liked that tale
and the Australian poem best.

Now gone three weeks, he was even more burnt out on performing,
and the nuisances of travel were catching up to him:

This little darkey boy came in with a candle & woke me up an hour
before dawn to ask me if I wanted my boots cleaned. At 6, which
is still before dawn, coffee was carried around & delivered in the
rooms. This is simple straightforward insanity.

And his thoughts were swirling darker.

Ask a man of 50, "if you were dead now, what would you give to have your life restored?" He wouldn't give a brass farthing.

Twain missed his wife even more. He knew she and Clara were scheduled to leave Durban on June 6 and travel by boat to Port Elizabeth. Before joining them, he first had to fulfill his engagement to perform a few nights in East London.

> It is no use, Livy dear, I am homesick for you all the time. It is unusually bad yesterday & to-day. If you were here no doubt, I would be reading some book or other, but no matter, I would be *conscious* of you & that is communion & satisfaction. . . . I wish Smythe would come. Maybe we could play cards. But no, he is busy. Lord, it is a tiresome life. What is there so hateful as lecturing! But I've no doubt I've got to cover the whole United States next year.

Without Livy, his imagination ran gloomier. No one had agreed on a U.S. lecture tour for the following year. Twain also began imagining that Harper had neglected to publish *Joan of Arc,* which had recently finished the serialization run. "Is it *possible* that there is a hitch there, and that it hasn't *been* issued in book form?" he wrote. "If so, I don't think it is of any use for me to struggle against my ill luck any longer."

Livy and Clara, who had enjoyed Dr. Campbell's garden and circle of friends, were due to depart Durban on the *Athenian,* and eleven people accompanied them to the pier. Clara pointed out to her mother: "All those people came to see *us* off and not papa." Livy relayed Clara's comment to her husband, who dashed off one last letter before the reunion, which included:

> I am glad you had eleven people on the dock to see you off on your own merits. Sometimes an entire town will turn out in order to get rid of people. (That's for Clara.)

Twain's first "At Home" in the scenic beach town of East London had almost been rained out by thundershowers, causing sparse attendance and a punning local scribe to blame "the in-Clemens-y of the weather." The performer was parked there at the Beach Hotel for a three-day engagement. He now tolerated no rejections from Smythe, and the pair played lots of billiards and cards. Twain loved billiards but wasn't especially good at it. His notebook over the years records numerous losses. His authorized biographer, Albert Bigelow Paine, admitted that the literary lion sometimes felt the need to change the game rules midstream. Twain was losing consistently to Smythe, so he tweaked the rule of "flukes," that is, if someone made an accidental/uncalled shot, he received the point, but he lost his cue stick (i.e., his turn). Twain happily reported all games with Smythe now went down to the last few shots.

Clara and Livy were waiting in charmless, mercantile Port Elizabeth. "It seems to me that Mr. Clemens has been gone a year," Livy vented to her sister. "I hope this will be our last separation." Clara, stuck in a cramped hotel room, hated the place. (Apparently, no local dignitaries had welcomed them.) "I wouldn't live in this bleak town for a million dollars a minute."

Twain was ready to leave East London on Sunday, but a winter storm hit, with "raw and blustery" seas slamming against the breakwater, spewing froth a hundred feet skyward. He played more billiards. Finally, on Tuesday at 6 p.m., the 4,392-ton *Norham Castle* set off for the 150-mile trip to Port Elizabeth.

Twain rejoined his family at the hilltop ocean-view Grand Hotel on Wednesday morning, June 17, after five weeks apart. He was thrilled to see Livy but was completely burnt out on lecturing, which he thought he had been doing for "a thousand years."

The Clemens family knew they had less than a month left in Africa; they began writing about sending the other two daughters to meet them in England. Twain had eight remaining performances, then they would be taking one of the Union Line steamships from Cape Town to Southampton. The next day, a cablegram reached Cape Colony reporting that one of the regular ships that sailed from South Africa to England, the *Drummond Castle*, had just sunk off the north coast of France, with 400 lives lost. (The actual number would turn out to be 243.) About 125 local citizens had died; flags flew at half-mast; one Durban family lost ten relatives. As Twain pointed out in his notebook, when an Atlantic steamer went down, the localities of the casualties were spread out. This "region stands paralysed." His shows were postponed because it seemed wrong to laugh. Clara had to spend another week in her least favorite town.

The maritime disaster spooked the Clemens family. Word soon leaked that the *Drummond Castle* captain, W. W. Pierce, who had drowned, had had two prior accidents—*Doun Castle* and *Courland Maid*—both downplayed. Twain was flabbergasted that the captain's career had weathered the incidents, since passengers and steamship owners usually avoid captains who beach ships, even if it isn't their fault. "[Pierce] was a relative of the owners," wrote Twain in his notebook and in his later travel book.

The hideous news soured everyone's mood and almost silenced the dining room at the Grand Hotel in Port Elizabeth. One voice remained and it wasn't the celebrity author.

> A great long tow-headed spider-legged jackass-voiced American girl. She & 3 young men sit at a small table by themselves, & she gabbles & gabbles & gabbles—all her words audible the length of the dining room. She has an idea that she talks brightly; & she loves to listen to it. The other sixty people present may possibly be enjoying it too, but they do not look it. They are all still. The stillness would amount to solemnity but for this blatherskite's raucous interruptions of it.—There is talk of taking up a collection to have her drowned. She is the very worst sample of the ill-bred American girl astray I have ever seen.

When Twain tried to ignore the girl and opened the local newspaper, he found another source for irritation: the coverage of the war against the Matabele tribe. "The dispatch-writers," he found, "word their accounts [with] grandiloquent military phraseology proper to real war; they see nothing ludicrous in applying it to these mere assassinations." From what he could tell, most battles ended with something like "a great slaughter of helpless natives on the one side; on the other, a horse killed and a man wounded."

Indeed, a sample June news report from Bulawayo backs him up.

> Sir Frederick Carrington . . . ordered Captain Spreckley to start soon after dawn with 97 mounted men, two Maxims, and one Hotchkiss, in order to co-operate with Colonel Beal's column at once attacking the *impi* [*i.e., native war party*] whose presence in the vicinity had been reported. . . .
>   After a short fusillade, the mounted troopers charged and the natives fled in utter rout. The force kept up the pursuit in an

easterly direction until the horses were completely tired out. The rebels' loss was between 100 and 200 while the force had two men seriously wounded and one horse killed.

The *Drummond Castle* tragedy delayed Twain's comedy by a few days, but he performed on June 22. Carlyle Smythe reported that a blind woman laughed so loudly and so relentlessly that she had to be escorted from the theater.

Mail dribbled in at various ports of call, and Twain was surprised to learn that his best friend and adviser, the wealthy widower H.H. Rogers, had remarried, two years after losing his first wife, Abbie. Twain crafted a congratulatory telegram but then decided not to send it. He claimed in a wordy letter that he had sent one too many happy telegrams that had arrived during tragedies, such as when he had cabled wedding congratulations to a bride who had suddenly lost her father. Perhaps a truer reason for not sending the telegram might have been the cost: a fifteen-word telegram from Cape Colony via England to New York (in those pre-Internet days) cost about $20 (about $600 today).

Twain instead wrote a sweet letter, pronouncing himself delighted that H.H. was now married to the forty-nine-year-old society widow Emilie Augusta Randel Hart.

> I would have chosen Mrs. Hart every time, and so it has cost me not a pang to praise you up to her, a blame sight higher than you probably deserve; for I want her to be satisfied with you. I wanted to make her feel restful and easy about her bargain; and at the same time I was determined to earn the million you owe me if it cost the last rag of conscience I had in stock.

Twain added he was shipping via the next available vessel his wedding gifts, which included pairs of elephants, of rhinoceroses, of giraffes and of zebras, also "thirty yards of anacondas" and a flock of ostriches. "The wedding present business is expensive when you work it from Africa."

The family headed for the final circuit: a big swing north to the Kimberley diamond mines and then southwest to the departure port, Cape Town.

The sparkle of Kimberley certainly attracted Twain, and it had for a long time. As far back as the dawn of his literary career in 1871, Twain—

then a newlywed Buffalo newspaper editor—had cooked up a scheme to send a former drinking buddy, writer John Henry Riley, to Kimberley, to take notes for a travel book that Twain could write to follow up his huge hit *Innocents Abroad*. Twain also wanted Riley to buy claims to a mine or two, and acquire a few big gems or a dozen. He bankrolled Riley, but the man apparently bought a claim from a man who didn't own the mine, and Riley died the following year of cancer. Nothing came of the project. Before arriving in the diamond district, Twain had already decided how to play the Kimberley chapter: the rediscovered Riley deeds, when located on a map, would happen to include the world's most lucrative diamond mines.

Twain arrived on Wednesday, July 1, in Kimberley, after twenty-five hours' worth of train rides from Port Elizabeth. The town looked underwhelming considering the wealth; corrugated iron shacks dotted zigzaggy streets amid a handful of low municipal buildings. The main attraction was the heavily guarded "Big Hole." Twain thought you could easily drop the Roman Coliseum in there and have plenty of room to spare.

The author received a tour from a Mr. Robeson, the assistant to the American who was running the place, mining engineer Gardner F. Williams, a native of Michigan. Twain learned his Nevada silver expertise wouldn't help him here, and that diamonds are found in a state quite different from precious metals, which are embedded in rock ledges. Twain compared a diamond mine to a giant well filled up with rubbish that had to be sifted; he said the diamonds floated like raisins in a pudding of bluish mud and rock.

He marveled at the efficiency of the De Beers operation run by Williams, which sifted 12 million pounds of blue rocks and mud *every day* through massive "concentrators" that watered, swirled, and reduced the heap by 99% and delivered the "slush" to "pulsators" that cast off another 75% and turned the remainder into dark-colored sand to be delivered to the sorting tables.

> I . . . saw the men deftly and swiftly spread it out and brush it
> about and seize the diamonds as they showed up. I assisted, and
> once I found a diamond half as large as an almond. It is an exciting kind of fishing, and you feel a fine thrill of pleasure every time
> you detect the glow of one of those limpid pebbles through the veil

of dark sand. I would like to spend my Saturday holidays in that charming sport every now and then. Of course there are disappointments. Sometimes you find a diamond, which is not a diamond; it is only a quartz crystal or some such worthless thing. The expert can generally distinguish it from the precious stone, which it is counterfeiting; but if he is in doubt he lays it on a flatiron and hits it with a sledgehammer. If it is a diamond it holds its own; if it is anything else, it is reduced to powder. I liked that experiment very much, and did not tire of repetitions of it. It was full of enjoyable apprehensions, unmarred by any personal sense of risk. The De Beers concern treats 8,000 carloads—about 6,000 tons—of blue rock per day, and the result is three pounds of diamonds.

Twain spent several days there. He learned that, not surprisingly, a big worry for the managers was theft. He sympathized with the native sorters—usually young girls—who touched fortunes every day and went back every night penniless to sleep in hovels. Native workers were hired for three-month shifts and not allowed off the property; the search on departure was extremely thorough and included days in naked lockup and doses of laxatives, such as "Eno Salts."

Kimberley didn't offer much entertainment for a mining town, but Twain said the natives performed a war dance for them. No doubt exhausted from his travels and his proximity to diamonds, the author didn't bother to describe it, but Gardner Williams left a memoir:

No mining camp on earth before ever held such a motley swarm of every dusky shade, in antelope skins and leopard skins and jackal skins and bare skins, with girdles and armlets of white ox-tails, and black crane plumes and gorgeous bird feathers, and dirty loin cloths, and ragged breeches, and battered hats and tattered coats. With and without the fire of rum they might dash off at any moment into some wildly whirling reel or savage dance, gabbling in a hundred dialects, whooping with weird cries, and chanting plaintive, gay, and passionate strains, now dissonant, now sweet.

He was describing the earlier days when natives did the shoveling for rival claim stakers. But Twain was apparently treated to an authentically costumed performance. In the early days, diggers merely tunneled into the "pudding" and fatal collapses occurred frequently; Gardner Williams brought a new method of systematically hoisting vast slices of "pudding" earth.

Twain concluded with a left-handed compliment. "Nothing is so beautiful as a rose diamond with the light playing through it, except that uncostly thing which is just like it—wavy sea-water with the sunlight playing through it and striking a white-sand bottom."

Twain had clearly departed without a sparkly souvenir. He mentioned how hard it was even for "known and accredited" guests to steal anything.

Home beckoned, or at least a ship to England, and one step closer to home.

CHAPTER 27

Reuniting the Family

Everything was anticlimax. He was ready to stop lecturing. He could barely bring himself to see the famed Table Mountain behind Cape Town. He opted for a balcony view on a cloudless day instead of the three-hour trek. This African part of his endless odyssey concluded with three sold-out performances. He even defiantly added Huck and Jim back into the mix one night.

The Clemens family boarded the luxurious SS *Norman* on July 15 for the two-week 6,000-mile voyage to Southampton, England. Carlyle Smythe joined them; he had some speaker recruiting to do in England.

Since letters took about three weeks to reach the United States, Twain and his wife had already written tentative plans for ferrying the girls to England. Livy had informed her sister that they expected to arrive in England around August 1, and so she expected Susy and Jean (and maid Katy) to take an American Line steamer for the weeklong crossing sometime between August 5 and August 12. "Although I want them *ready* to start on the 5th (not before) or 12th of August *I don't want them really to start until we send a cable saying 'come.'*" She underlined the entire last part of the sentence. Clearly the *Drummond Castle* was playing on her mind. "Because if they started before getting a cable from us they might find us in the bottom of the sea when they reach England, or on our way to America."

She said she now thought her husband would write his book in England and then lecture there to try to speed the debt repayment.

Mr. Clemens feels that he must make all the money that he can for we *long* so to be out of the bondage of debt. It seems as if we should have to work a long, *very* long time yet before we should be free. Forty or fifty thousand dollars is a very large sum of money to try to earn.

Livy had learned in a prior letter from her brother that the Langdon Coal Company was deeply in debt and struggling. The debts would grow to more than $600,000, dwarfing Twain's debacle with Webster, but the family company had assets such as actual coal mines. Perhaps at her husband's urging, Livy now inquired how much she could be liable for if the firm failed. She wrote hopefully: "[I] suppose the 'limited' that the firm have on their name limits the liabilities to what is in the concern." She meant she hoped she couldn't owe more than her stake. Like her husband, she really didn't know the business details.

Once the family was safely tucked aboard the large sleek *Norman,* her husband, as ever, began to enjoy being on a ship, playing cards, watching the waves, reading and *not* performing.

I got horribly tired of the platform toward the last—tired of the slavery of it; tired of having to rest up for it; diet myself for it, take everlasting care of my body and my mind for it; deny myself in a thousand ways in its interest. Why, there *isn't* any slavery that is so exacting and so infernal. I hope I have trodden it for the last time; that bread-and-butter stress will never crowd me onto it again.

No record exists of how much Twain earned in South Africa, but thirty nights should have certainly netted him more than $5,000. He intended to carry that money and use it to live on in England; hence, there's no record of him shipping any of it to H.H. Rogers in New York.

"Father luxuriated in cigars and books all the way from Africa to England," Clara later recalled, "and we thought of nothing but the pleasure of seeing Susy and Jean again."

Twain also had time to ruminate on his financial future; he very much hoped that some publishing house would soon issue a complete edition of his works. While at sea, he wrote: "The *main* thing is to get the books *going* again after a long and calamitous rest."

He pored over the half dozen letters Rogers had sent him chronicling H.H.'s spluttering efforts to reconcile Henry Harper of Manhattan (running a traditional publishing house) and aggressive Frank Bliss of Hartford (overseeing an army of door-to-door salesmen). Bliss and his cohorts were proving more frustrating. "They can talk longer and cover a wider range than anybody I know," H.H. wrote to Twain. "The only mistake those fellows made was going into the publishing business instead of the preaching business."

Harper had submitted a generous written proposal to put out editions, offering Livy (as copyright holder) 15% of list price of the first 5,000 copies, 20% thereafter; they were willing to let American Publishing issue more recent Twain titles, but only as part of an entire set. Bliss was willing to agree to that, but all kinds of other minutiae separated the two sides, such as Harper wanting to create a Uniform Edition with volumes matched exactly in size and shape and therefore expecting to sell to Bliss printing plates or printed copies; such as Bliss refusing to set a precise royalty for Twain; such as Harper wanting Bliss to guarantee not to underprice them.

Negotiations eventually broke off, as H.H. had a day job and had to travel with fellow Standard Oil executive John Archbold for the annual three-week inspection tour of oilfields in Kansas, Kentucky, Tennessee and Virginia. H.H. admitted to Twain that he was exasperated with publishing because as a businessman, he judged that the brand "Mark Twain" was booming thanks to the worldwide lecture tour, and that the books needed to go on sale right away.

> Those Hartford fellows are enough to perplex a saint . . . but the godly qualities I possess I think are quite sufficient for the job, and I can exercise as much patience to the square inch as they can. They get a proposition and then sit back in the traces waiting to tire me out.

H.H. was implying that they expected him to sweeten his offer to get an answer. Instead, H.H. tried a new strategy: he sent a telegram threatening that unless they responded immediately he would assume the deal was dead. He got an instant reply that they would confer the following day. "I have coaxed, pled, bullied and blustered to mighty little purpose with those people but I am not going to give up until we get the job finished."

In the final letter Twain received before embarking for England, H.H. sounded optimistic; the sticking point now was the Harper fee for printing identical editions for Bliss to sell.

The 7,537-ton *Norman,* with its pair of beige smokestacks, streamed northward through calm seas. On another key front, Twain gleaned from H.H.'s letters that the debt repayment process was going slowly. Bainbridge Colby had failed to convince the two largest creditors, Mount Morris Bank and the Barrows, to take the 50% deal. "Colby has dropped into a state of lethargy for the moment, and we are dropping carpet tacks in his way to stimulate his ambition," H.H. had written. "He is a rather spasmodic sort of a cuss."

Colby, amazingly, *after two years,* hadn't yet finished selling off the firm's assets. His latest stumbling block was Fred Grant, son of Ulysses S., who was suing to collect full royalties from his father's memoirs, even though the books were being sold during the liquidation of a defunct firm.

Twain exploded over Grant's greed. Webster & Co. had truly doubled the family's income from the war hero's memoirs, had helped save the family from financial ruin, and they were now nickel-and-diming Twain. "I'm never going to pay *them* a cent *any*how," Twain wrote. H.H., who had discovered that he was a distant relative of the Grant family, told Twain he was dropping his plans to restore the gravestone of the shared ancestor, "since I . . . learn[ed] what a puny little weasly, good-for-nothing, ungrateful kind of man Fred Grant is."

(Grant would wind up as the second-highest-ranking officer in the U.S. Army.)

The H.H. letters also reveal once again the depth of his and Twain's friendship. H.H. confided in Twain his exasperation with his seventeen-year-old son. (The following problems *might* stem from the father's recent gift.)

Harry's yacht is being fitted out and he is about the biggest nuisance there is in the vicinity of 57th Street. He puts on too many airs and it will require the services of a man to take him down. . . . When you come home . . . avoid making any appointments until you have engaged with me to give him a blamed good thrashing. You haven't any idea, Clemens, really how sassy he is.

The yacht was fifty-one feet long, according to the *Fairhaven Star*. H.H. worried that his stamina wouldn't be sufficient for a long fight with a feisty teenager. "I would send for the 'Harlem Coffee Cooler' [*a light-skinned African-American boxer*] but I understand he is under a permanent engagement in London." (Twain and H.H. had seen the "Cooler" box at Madison Square Garden.)

Aboard the *Norman,* Twain found out that the passenger list included several other celebrities. A few freed Jameson raiders were traveling home, as was Barney Barnato, self-made forty-four-year-old fast-talking, ebullient millionaire. Barnato, a London Jew, had risen from East End shop clerk to diamond mogul and had received what was then the world's largest check, for £5 million, in 1888 when Cecil Rhodes had bought him out.

The *Norman* reached Southampton on July 31. Twain sent a telegram telling his two daughters and Katy to pack up and sail on the next ship. He and Livy and Clara checked into the South Western Hotel as a way station, while looking for more permanent lodgings. Twain contacted his British publisher, Chatto & Windus, to send for his accumulated mail.

The stack, which included a fat British royalty check, marked a torrent of good news. H.H. Rogers had written on July 9 from New York that the deal was basically done to sell *two* new editions of Twain's works, one a *complete edition* to be offered by Bliss/American Publishing via door-to-door sales, and the other, featuring the titles since *Huckleberry Finn,* to be sold by Harper in stores. Bliss had also agreed to pay a $10,000 advance for the round-the-world-travel book.

Best of all, and added matter-of-factly at the bottom of the letter: "[Bliss and] the American Publishing Company proposes to make a new contract (destroying the old one) with Mrs. Clemens for their publications, giving her half the profits on all the books or perhaps 15% [royalty] as Mrs. Clemens may elect."

This marked Twain's holy grail for publishing royalties. It would triple the *Innocents Abroad* payout from 5% to 15% of list price, and double the royalty for *Roughing It,* which had lingered at 7½%. It would defy patriarch Elisha Bliss in the grave. Unlike most authors' backlists, Twain's still had major sales potential.

Twain relayed his joy. "It's about time somebody was squeezing that gang—they've robbed me for a quarter of a century; and wherever I catch Bliss's old thief of a father, be it hell or heaven, over the balusters [*i.e., stair railings*] he goes."

Twain informed H.H. that they had found a house for a month in quaint Guildford in Surrey (twenty-five miles from London) and Mrs. Clemens was seeking one for a longer stay. Their new temporary rental house, "Highfield," seemed delightful, perched on a hill with a fine valley view, servants, and, best of all, a billiards table. He also said they had invited Rogers's phenomenal assistant, the towering and brilliant Katherine Harrison, to come visit them in England. A giddy happiness pervades the letter, which Twain signed "With lots of love to all of you, SL. C. M.T."

Also in the stack of mail was a July 3 letter from lecture agent Major Pond informing Twain that Pond had seen Susy in Hartford and she looked well. Pond had attended the funeral of Twain's neighbor Harriet Beecher Stowe, who had died at eighty-five. Charles Dudley Warner, another neighbor, had walked Pond over to the Clemens house, where Susy and Katy Leary were camping out on Farmington Avenue during the days. (Susy was sleeping at the Warners', and caretaker Katy Leary lived in an apartment on Spring Street.)

> [Susy] seems quite happy where she is. She says it seems much like home to her, and she wishes you would come back. The place is beautiful but there is a terrible atmosphere of lonesomeness there. The last time I visited the place you and Mrs. Clemens and a party of Hartford friends were there and it was delightful.

Pond dangled all kinds of speaking tour offers, but Twain—buoyed by publishing optimism, exhausted from his trip—sent back a crisp refusal note, stating he would not lecture in England or America.

The Clemenses were settling into their new temporary home. One happy day, Twain cajoled Clara to play secretary for him and allow him to dictate a letter, citing ludicrous reasons such as a cut on his *left* hand, a walking injury, and hair loss. The dutiful daughter wrote: "These he considers cause enough to be shoving all his affairs onto the shoulders of an other." In the note, Clara wrote to publisher Andrew Chatto that her father would be pleased to have lunch with him in a week, on Monday,

August 17. (The two would become friends, a friendship not hindered by the fact that genial Chatto paid Twain a 20% royalty.)

The family kept expecting any day to receive a cablegram that the girls had departed but instead received only: "Unavoidably delayed." As of Monday, August 10, Twain wrote Pond: "Susy & Jean are not on their way hither, we do not yet know why." Confusion mounted. (No telephone line would connect New York and London until 1926.) Cablegrams cost 25 cents a word, including address, so that a ten-word telegram cost the modern equivalent of $75.

A letter arrived on Friday morning, August 14, informing the family that Susy was slightly ill but not to worry. (That letter had to have been sent before August 7.) They did worry and cabled for details. The response they received was "Wait for cablegram in the morning." They cabled again demanding more information. The hours dragged.

Livy feared the worst and began packing to catch a ship from Southampton with Clara, leaving the next day for New York. Twain was leaning toward waiting. He had scheduled that Monday meeting with his British publisher. He went to the telegraph office and waited till it closed at midnight. He and Livy sat up till 1 a.m., irrationally hoping for some sort of response to arrive.

Livy had sprained her ankle during the house hunting and was limping. She and Clara and Twain boarded the Saturday morning train to Southampton. Twain had informed the local telegraph operator to forward any telegrams to Southhampton. One arrived, stating that "recovery would be long but certain." Twain found hope in that; Livy despair.

Livy and Clara boarded the American steamship *Paris*, which departed Saturday, August 15, for the one-week passage to New York.

Twain, soon afterward, berated himself for how he had behaved at parting.

I am always hiding my feelings; but my heart was wrung yesterday. I could not tell you how deeply I loved you nor how grieved I was for you, nor how I pitied you in this awful trouble that my mistakes have brought upon you. You forgive me, I know, but I shall never forgive myself while the life is in me. If you find our poor little Susie in the state I seem to foresee, your dear head will be grayer when I see it next. (Be good and get well, Susy dear, don't break your mother's heart.)

Probably at Livy's suggestion, Twain gathered up Carlyle Smythe from his hotel and brought him back to Guildford as a companion. Female house servants also attended them there. Twain cabled Livy's brother and sister that Livy and Clara were coming; he also set up a cable address—"Clemens Guildford"—to save words and money.

Twain, anxious, talked Smythe into playing billiards past midnight. He feared disaster but refused to believe it. On Monday, Andrew Chatto—bearded, cigar-smoking bibliophile—showed up with a pile of favorable *Joan of Arc* reviews. (Chatto published elite authors such as H. G. Wells, Aldous Huxley, Samuel Beckett.) The magazine *The Speaker* called *Joan of Arc* "not only the best thing [Twain] has ever done but one of the best things done by anybody in fiction for a long time past." Twain wrote a jaunty note to Livy crowing about the praise, especially because he knew that *Joan* was his wife's favorite among his books. She had encouraged the subject from day one, since the topic represented a shining example of a courageous brilliant young woman to their three daughters. Chatto told him he eagerly awaited Twain's next book.

That Monday night and the following night, Twain and Smythe kidded around and played billiards. Twain was standing in the living room around midnight on Tuesday when the doorbell rang. A messenger delivered a succinct telegram from his brother-in-law: "Susy could not stand brain congestion and meningitis and was peacefully released today."

Twain later wrote: "It is one of the mysteries of our nature that a man, all unprepared, can receive a thunder-stroke like that and live."

He told no one in the house. As his authorized biographer put it:

He had torn his family apart and set out on a weary pilgrimage to pay, for long financial unwisdom, a heavy price—a penance in which all, without complaint, had joined. Now, just when it seemed about ended, when they were ready to unite and be happy once more, when he could hold up his head among his fellows—in this moment of supreme triumph had come the message that Susy's lovely and blameless life was ended. There are not many greater dramas in fiction or in history than this. . . . Mark Twain's life had contained other tragedies, but no other that equaled this one. This time none of the elements were lacking—not the smallest detail. The dead girl had been his heart's pride; it was a year since he had seen her face, and now by this word he knew that he would never see it again. The blow had found him alone—absolutely alone among strangers—those others half-way across the ocean, drawing nearer and nearer to it, and he with no way to warn them, to prepare them, to comfort them.

Clara and Livy were in the middle of the Atlantic Ocean, four days from scheduled arrival in New York Harbor on Saturday, August 22, with no technological means to contact them.

Susy had started acting odd around the beginning of August. After her triumphant December and January in New York, she had found it too dull to return to the farm in Elmira. She had convinced Aunt Sue to allow her to stay in Hartford with the Days, who were renting the Clemens house, and when the Days departed sometime after February, Susy moved in with longtime family friends/neighbors, the Warners. Throughout her stay in Hartford, Susy's chaperone and helper, longtime family maid Katy Leary, lived in an apartment on Spring Street.

Susy did her vocal practice at Katy's, and Katy later recalled that people would line up in the street outside for the afternoon "concert," to listen to her sweet pure voice. Over the months away from Elmira, Susy began trusting Mental Science more to help her overcome bad moods and cure ailments. She also turned to spiritualists who claimed to be able to strengthen her voice.

Katy accompanied her on numerous visits and often took a nap in a back room. One unnamed spiritualist would pass her hand over Susy's throat and tell her things. One time, Katy, gruff and Irish, woke up from dozing and heard the woman tell Susy that she had heard Susy sing during the previous night and so had her husband. Katy knew the woman's husband had been dead for a quarter of a century. "Rats," muttered Katy loudly, and she eventually dragged Susy out of there. Susy called the woman a good healer. "She's a regular pirate," countered Katy. "I had the awfullest feelings . . . sitting there." Susy often met other spiritualists next door at the Beecher house, a receptive hotbed for that fad.

On August 1, Katy received the long-awaited telegram summoning them to England on the next boat. Katy rushed to Elmira to pack up Jean and then, along with Aunt Sue Crane and Uncle Charley Langdon and his wife, Ida, traveled to the departure port of New York. Katy took the train to Hartford around August 4 to pick up Susy.

A horrific heat wave was just hitting the Northeast, with relentless high temperatures in the upper 90s and very high humidity. The muggy air was hard to breathe. In that era before air-conditioning, no sustained relief existed except traveling to the ocean or the mountains.

Katy wanted Susy to come immediately to New York City, but Susy felt too ill to travel and asked to wait till evening when it might be a little cooler. Katy packed the trunks, but by evening and the following morning Susy felt worse; she had a fever.

She didn't want any doctor; she wanted a faith healer, "Miss B.," but Katy refused to listen and had family physician Dr. Porter come. At first he thought it was heatstroke and exhaustion, and he prescribed rest and fluids and isolation. In that era, the rest cure popularized by Dr. Mitchell Weir was in vogue, especially for "hysterical" females. So Dr. Porter had Susy transported over to stay in her bedroom in the empty Clemens home nearby.

It's unclear when exactly she took a turn for the worse. She grew agitated and delirious. She stalked up and down her room, muttering over and over: "Up go the trolley cars for Mark Twain's daughter. Down go the trolley cars for Mark Twain's daughter."

She grew delusional, and thought herself the protégé of the long-dead mezzo-soprano Maria Malibran, who had passed away sixty years earlier after a riding accident. Susy began scribbling incoherent notes in large script on *forty-seven* 9″x 5¼″ lined sheets of paper, writing perpendicular to the lines, words flowing together as though she was having trouble seeing.

> In strength I bow to Mme Malibran Mr Clemens Mr Zola. . . . She must endorse it. There is no appeal from my command. . . . she is not unjust. . . . In me darkness must remain from everlasting to everlasting forever. . . . you will never follow far enough in her footsteps artistically to dominate the artistic world with light.

At some point, longtime family friend Reverend Joseph Twichell ("Uncle Joe") left his summer retreat in the Adirondack Mountains to come down to try to comfort Susy. He spent long hours trying to "still the storms that swept her spirit."

Katy, Aunt Sue and Uncle Charley traveled to Hartford and joined the longtime coachman Patrick McAleer and gardener John O'Neill in tending to her in that sweltering hot room.

She would accept medicine only from Katy's hand. The relatives did not want to send a dire cable to England and kept waiting, hoping. Apparently the doctor did not diagnose spinal meningitis until her very agitated behavior on Sunday, August 16. At one point, Susy reached for one of her mother's gowns in the closet and thought her mother was dead and began to cry. Katy found it heart-wrenching and pitiful to watch her.

Spinal meningitis, a quite dangerous condition, comes in many forms; it occurs when the membranes covering the brain and spinal cord (meninges) become inflamed. Meningitis could be caused by a virus or bacteria, or by fungus, parasites or tumors. Susy's was probably bacterial given the severity; no cure existed in 1896, although doctors were experimenting with lumbar punctures for diagnosis. (In 1907, injections of Flexner's Serum started reducing the meningitis death toll; after 1944, antibiotics such as penicillin could save 85% of infected patients.)

Susy went blind. She told Uncle Charley: "I am blind and you are blind." Katy fed her a few spoonfuls of milk on Sunday, August 16, her last food. The Clemenses' twenty-four-year-old daughter folded her hands across her chest and never moved them again, or regained consciousness.

She died at 7:07 p.m. Tuesday, which was when the telegram was sent to England.

Susy's body was shipped to Elmira for burial. The family returned to New York, stayed at the Waldorf Hotel, and waited for Livy and Clara to arrive.

————

Twain, who did not tell Smythe or the servants for a day, began a period of self-loathing that would last months. This was not his first encounter with the death of a close family member—at age eleven, he had lost his father and at twenty-two his younger brother Henry and in 1872, in his third year of marriage, his sickly son Langdon had died at nineteen months. But past losses didn't ease anything.

He immediately poured out letters to Livy. "Reproaching myself for a million things whereby I have brought misfortune & sorrow to this family." Through grief-stricken leaps of logic, he convinced himself that when he had swayed his sister Pamela to allow her daughter to marry his future business partner Charles Webster back in 1875, that had started the chain of events that led to the Webster bankruptcy and then to the round-the-world tour and this fatal abandonment of Susy. He searched his baggage and couldn't find a scrap of a letter from Susy that he had kept.

He berated himself for not writing his daughter more often. "I neglected her as I neglect everybody in my selfishness. Everybody but you. I have always written to you."

He wished he could have been at the dock to spare Livy when "Charley's tears reveal all . . . I wish I could have spared you this unutterable sorrow."

He kept writing and grew more agitated:

I loved Susy, loved her dearly; but I did not know how deeply, before.

You will see her. Oh, I wish I could see her, and caress the unconscious face & kiss the unresponding lips—but I would not bring her back—no, not for the riches of a thousand worlds. She has found the richest gift that this world can offer; I would not rob her of it.

Be comforted, my darling—we shall have *our* release in time. Be comforted, remembering how much hardship, grief, pain, she is spared; & that her heart can never be broken, now for the loss of a child.

I seem to see her in her coffin—I do not know in which room. In the library, I hope; for there she & Ben [*i.e., Clara*] & I mostly played when we were children together & happy. I wish there were five of the coffins side by side; out of my heart of hearts, I wish it.

[*Twain assumed the funeral would be in Hartford.*]

She died in our house . . . died where she had spent all her life till my crimes made her a pauper & an exile. How good it is that she got home again.

In his next letter he wrote:

I eat—because you wish it; I go on living—because you wish it; I play billiards, and billiards, & billiards, till I am ready to drop—to keep from going mad with grief & with resentful thinkings.

At 8 tomorrow morning, your heart will break, the Lord God knows I am pitying you.

Livy and Clara steamed toward New York. Twain had cablegrammed H.H. to clear the dock of friends and to have Dr. Clarence Rice deliver the news by taking the quarantine boat out first, but that didn't happen. On Friday, as the *Paris* glided along Long Island for arrival the following morning, a small boat delivered some packages to the ship. The captain called Clara into his cabin. He handed her a newspaper, which had a front-page headline: MARK TWAIN'S ELDEST DAUGHTER DIES OF SPINAL MENINGITIS. Clara stood stunned; her eyes brimmed with tears.

There was much more but I could not see the letters. The world stood still. All sounds, all movements ceased. Susy was dead. How could I tell Mother?

Clara walked like a zombie through the metal corridors of the ship.

I went to her stateroom. Nothing was said. A deadly pallor spread over her face and then came a bursting cry, "I don't believe it!" And we never did believe it.

Uncle Charley Langdon and Reverend Joe Twichell boarded the quarantine boat early Saturday morning to break the news, but Livy and Clara already knew. Twain's nephew Sam Moffett, whom Hearst had transferred from the *San Francisco Examiner* to the *New York Journal*, waited on the dock with the rest of the family. "Aunt Livy seems completely crushed," he wrote to his wife.

They took carriages to the Waldorf Hotel for a brief rest before boarding the train to Elmira. Livy wanted to know everything about Susy's illness. Aunt Sue bitterly blamed spiritualists and Mental Science. Katy, who had spent the most time with Susy over the recent months, tried to console Mrs. Clemens, speaking of God's will and other pieties. Then she told her of Susy's last moments of consciousness.

I told her how that last night I was lifting Susy in her bed, how she put her arms around my neck and rubbed down my face with her two little hot hands, and she laid her cheek against mine and said, "Mamma, mamma, mamma!" . . . When I told this, Mrs. Clemens was sitting in a big chair in the Waldorf, leaning back, just crushed with her grief, but when she heard this, she just stretched out her two hands and held mine hard. I was crying then, I was crying so I couldn't speak; so I just held her hands and she held mine . . . it was the only thing we could do for each other.

The family members talked that morning and they talked during the long train ride to Elmira. Livy scavenged for every detail of her daughter's past year. They arrived at 10:30 p.m. on the very same platform on which one year, one month, one week prior, they had tearfully waved good-bye and blown kisses under the glare of the new electric lights as three-fifths of the family headed off around the world.

Once they reached the Langdon house, Katy saw Mrs. Clemens walk immediately to the drawing room, where Susy lay peaceful and immobile in her coffin. Katy recalled: "Such anguish! She didn't speak, only she moaned a little bit, just like a child." Mrs. Clemens refused again and again to leave the room. She wanted to keep looking at her "beautiful" daughter.

The family buried Susy the next day, Sunday, August 23. Death and burial notices ran in many newspapers. Livy and Clara both blamed her death on the "evil influence of spiritualism"; Livy bitterly wondered why no one in Hartford had reached out to her brother and sister in Elmira to come intervene. She believed that spritual agitation had killed the frail girl. The Clemens family always believed that Susy's death could have been prevented. (It's impossible to know how Susy contracted the disease, which is usually spread through exchange of saliva or eating of contaminated food.)

Jean, in her oddly rational way, told her cousin Sam that it was "better" that Susy had died because she would have had to live out her life "permanently insane."

Livy had the news of the burial cabled to her husband. She then cabled the following day, on Monday, August 24, asking about his health. He heard nothing after that for the next four days.

Twain, alone in Guildford except for Smythe, now began to parse the timing of various letters and illness notices. His daughter had died on August 18. Letters take a week. Ten days had passed.

I get a cablegram which I am wholly unprepared for—a message which strikes like a sword [on August 18] . . . & I sit back [now] & try to believe that there are any human beings in the world, friend or foes, civilized or savage, who would close their lips *there*, & leave me these many, many, many days eating my heart out with longings for the tidings that never come.

He took very long walks. He and Smythe occasionally looked for a house, since this Guildford lease ran out soon. He made Smythe play billiards till midnight or 1 a.m., until Smythe was "no longer able to stand up." He castigated himself some more.

My remorse does not deceive me. I know that if she were back I should soon be as neglectful of her as I was before. . . . My selfishness & indolence would resume their power & I should be no better father to her, no more obliging friend and encourager & helper than I was before. If I could call up a single instance where I laid aside my own projects & desires & put myself to real inconvenience to procure a pleasure for her I would forget all things else to remember that.

The following day, he berated others: "Not a line yet, not a single line. It seems as if I cannot bear it. It is a bleak day, cold & silent,—Sundaylike & mournful." He says the Clemens family has entered true Hell, "not the lying invention of the superstitious." He wonders where they will go and hide.

Livy, Clara, Jean and Katy boarded the *St. Louis* in New York Harbor, and H.H. Rogers had upgraded them to a suite of the finest cabins. Livy never left the room, and so was spared encountering "the eyes of either the curious or the compassionate." They reached Guildford September 10 and departed the next day for London.

[We] shall get a house there and shut ourselves up in it and bar the doors and pull down the blinds and then take up the burden of life again. . . . I shall write the book of the voyage—I shall bury myself in it. . . . It kills me to think of the books that Susy would have written and that I shall never read now. The family has lost its prodigy. Others think they know what we have lost—intimates of hers—but only we of the family know the full value of that unminted gold; for only we have seen the flash and play of that imperial intellect at its best.

He would mourn his daughter for long months, but some part of him would gradually heal. In a year or two, he would tell jokes again; he would give funny after-dinner speeches. Livy would never fully recover. "I don't think Mrs. Clemens ever stopped grieving for Susy," said Katy, decades later, looking back.

CHAPTER 28

Alone in London

They found a four-story attached red brick townhouse, full of turret-style bay windows on the corner, in a tranquil part of Chelsea, not far from the north bank of the Thames. They kept the address (23 Tedworth Square) a secret. They wore black; they bought mourning stationery bordered in black. Livy refused all visitors; the Clemens women rarely left the house. Though late-nineteenth-century Chelsea boasted many famous writers and artists, especially down the block on Tite Street, Mark Twain did not seek out any of them.

The family lingered in bitterness over Susy's "un necessary" death; they blamed their Hartford friends such as the Warners for not warning them. Livy refused to take comfort in letters from others who had lost children. She told her husband: "They have lost a daughter, but they have not lost a Susy Clemens."

The damp chill of London did nothing to improve their moods. Twain was so convinced that the heat was failing in the house, he carried a thermometer room to room checking. "It was a long time before anyone laughed in our household," wrote Clara. "Father's passionate nature expressed itself in thunderous outbursts of bitterness shading into rugged grief. . . . there was no drawl in his speech now."

In that testy atmosphere, Twain railed about what had caused Susy's death. He didn't blame spiritualism as much as his wife did; he blamed God or God's absence; he blamed Charles Webster, but he also blamed Livy for her high-minded, no-compromise, righteous sense of honor about debts.

Many years later, Clara tried to re-construct the sort of conversations that she overheard her mother and father having in those first months of grief.

> FATHER: Once the idea of that infernal trip [*to pay debts*] struck us we couldn't shake it. Oh, no! for it was packed with sense of honor—honor—honor—no rest, comfort, joy—but plenty of honor, plenty of ethical glory. And as a reward for our self-castigation and faithfulness to ideals of nobility we were robbed of our greatest treasure, our lovely Susy in the midst of her blooming talents and personal graces. You want me to believe it is a judicious, a charitable God that runs this world. Why, I could run it better myself.
>
> MOTHER: Youth dear, one does not act honorably for the sake of reward or even approbation.
>
> FATHER: I do. I want payment in some coin for everything I do. If I can't get peace and joy in return for propping up my blather-skite of a crumbling soul, then—I'll let her rot and the quicker the better. . . .
>
> MOTHER: Oh, Youth, there must be a reason for such tragedies.
>
> FATHER: Well, I would like just five minutes to understand the plan of the Creator, if He has one.

Soon after his outbursts, he would sidle up to his wife and beg forgiveness and tell her that he loved her, according to Clara.

Starting October 4, Twain plunged into writing his travel book, and he later informed his sister that he worked every day, all day for the next three months. The work distracted him from moping or raging. A strange book it would turn out because at times, he tried to do jaunty *Innocents Abroad* jokes with excessively chiming clocks and collapsing deck chairs, and at other times, he rose up in fierce indignation at imperialism and genocide. He padded the book with long, serious quotations from other travel writers.

Twain aptly later characterized the funny bits as "lying cheerfulness" and he wondered if he had pulled off the ruse. He hadn't set a title yet, but he was considering *Another Innocents Abroad*. He worried, however, that this book might not live up to the high standards set by his debut runaway bestseller.

On Sundays, he took a few hours off from writing to take the two girls on walks through the fog and clouds, often delivering a dark monologue. They could reach fashionable Hyde Park in a little over a mile, or cross the Thames to Battersea Park. Everywhere they turned, Clara recalled they seemed to see a sad homeless woman, a scrawny stray cat.

Livy wrote to a friend in late October:

Now my world is dark. I cannot find Susy & I cannot find the light. No one knows, and only Mr. Clemens and Clara can suspect, what Susy was to me. . . . Always word was sent from Hartford that she was doing so well. It all seems too bitter to be carried.

Money clearly still preoccupied the family. The daughters vaguely knew that lack of money had forced the family to split up for the trip, and so they tried in their small way to help one day by asking for the cheapest seats to a London show. Apparently, the ticket seller was rude, and Twain exploded. He immediately contacted his friend Bram Stoker, the Lyceum Theatre manager (then writing *Dracula* in his spare time), to demand that the "large blonde man with spectacles" be fired immediately. "Perhaps he can imitate a gentleman's gentleman when people apply for boxes, but in any case he is a hog."

Twain also dourly started to make a weekly budget to try to rein in expenses. Their belt tightening still led to a patrician lifestyle. Topping the list were food, rent, clothes and servants; those four entries equaled $15,000 a month in current currency, or $180,000 a year. He then apportioned amply for essentials such as whiskey, beer, claret and cigars, which added another $600 a month in today's dollars. He gave up on the list before filling in the blanks for bicycle rental, Clara's music lessons, or Jean's tutor. Given Twain's poor math and Livy's heiress upbringing, budgets didn't suit the Clemens family much, except to depress them.

The seclusion prevailed. Livy refused to see Alice Hooker Day, then visiting England. (The Days had failed to clear the Hartford house of their stuff, had broken numerous glasses, had failed to warn Livy of Susy's state of mind, hadn't even paid the rent until Twain's local attorney chased them.)

The Tedworth Square house featured an ample thirty windows, but the family kept the curtains mostly drawn. Twain became obsessed with the odd indoor lighting patterns that blended newfangled electric with gas. He found his fifteen-foot-square study had five electric bulbs, two gas burners, and wall sconces for six candles.

Not in any mood to play the clown, Twain decided he would *never* lecture for money again, and so he put all his hopes on the publishing deal to pull them out of debt. And then he quickly lost all hope in that deal, since it wasn't yet signed. He expected "Satan to mix in and spoil everything." He grew confused over how much he still owed on the Webster debts. Was it $40,000 ($1.2 million today) as he first thought, or was it now $80,000 ($2.4 million)? Did the Webster assets cover only 35%? He couldn't master the numbers, and he despised his foot-dragging lawyer. "If Colby were only dead . . . then we could galvanize the corpse and put some energy into it; and what is more, some intelligence."

Sixteen-year-old Jean, who in recent years had been acting odder, started having strange temper tantrums, absence seizures and bodily fits. The family tried not to believe that she suffered from epilepsy, as recently diagnosed by a doctor in New York. "Poor Jean was now subject to epileptic attacks—the second tragedy in our year of absence," later wrote Clara. "These attacks made her life a burden and no doctors were able to help her." The family mentioned her illness to no one.

Clara had wanted to study music at a conservatory in continental Europe with a famous instructor, *away* from the family. Her plans, which would break up the foursome, were put on hold.

Thanksgiving arrived and the family ignored it. Livy's and Twain's birthday arrived without a word spoken.

But around this time of late November, Twain—still heartsick over losing his daughter—tried hard to save someone else's daughter. He would call her the "most marvelous" woman since Joan of Arc; he would predict that her name would be remembered a thousand years in the future. Mark Twain tried to rescue blind-deaf prodigy Helen Keller.

CHAPTER 29

Helen Keller

Mark Twain first met Helen Keller in March 1895, a few months before leaving on his speaking tour.

Fourteen-year-old Helen was displaying such amazing talents for a handicapped person that some people thought her a fraud, some kind of magic act. How could a girl, coffin-blackness blind and stone deaf since contracting scarlet fever at age one and a half, learn to read and write, and understand poetry and literature, do math problems, even pick up German and Latin? How was it possible?

The meeting with Twain occurred at the New York City apartment of Laurence Hutton, a *Harper's* editor and artsy gadabout, and it came at a crucial point in Helen's life. Her father, Colonel Arthur H. Keller, a struggling Alabama businessman, was sinking deeper in debt and threatening to exhibit his daughter, to "show her as you would a monkey," as one of Helen's appalled advocates put it.

As each guest entered at Hutton's A-list Manhattan gathering, Helen shook hands, and then she put her fingers to the lips of her lifelong teacher, Anne Sullivan, to learn the identity of the person. If the name was unfamiliar, Miss Sullivan spelled out the letters on Helen's palm.

Twain brought along H.H. Rogers. H.H. could afford ringside boxes at Madison Square Garden, but it took a certain literary cachet to be invited to the Huttons' for a private viewing of the prodigy. Helen sat on the couch, put her hand to the lips of Mark Twain, sitting next to her. He recounted a long funny episode and was delighted that the attractive young deaf woman laughed at just the right moments.

Then Miss Sullivan put one of Helen's hands against her lips, and spoke against it the question "What is Mr. Clemens distinguished for?" Helen answered in her crippled speech, "For his humor." I spoke up modestly and said, "And for his wisdom." Helen said the same words instantly—"And for his wisdom." I suppose it was a case of mental telegraphy since there was no way for her to know what it was I had said.

After a few hours, as the party was breaking up, someone asked if Helen would be capable of identifying each person from the introductory handshake. Anne Sullivan said she thought she could. One by one, the guests filed out, shook her hand, and Helen said their names correctly. Twain, always a bit subversive, merely patted her on the head lightly as he left.

Helen called out, "Oh, it's Mr. Clemens." He was absolutely flabbergasted. "Perhaps someone can explain this miracle, but I have never been able to do it." He wondered if she could feel the "wrinkles in his hand" through her hair? (Many years later, Helen informed him that she had "smelled" him—Twain smoked on average about twenty cigars a day.)

Helen Keller's main benefactor died in 1896. John Spalding, the "Sugar King" of Boston, who had been very generous, failed to provide for her in his will. The Huttons informed Twain around Thanksgiving— three months after the death of his own "family prodigy" daughter—that they were trying to raise money to put Helen through Radcliffe, the most prestigious women's college in the nation. (College scholarships were rare in the nineteenth century and usually provided by private individuals; Harvard, however, starting in 1874, pioneered the creation of a general beneficiary fund from alumni donations to offer interest-free loans to "young men of ability.")

Twain wrote a remarkable letter to H.H. Rogers's new wife.

Dear Mrs. Rogers,—

Experience has convinced me that when one wishes to set a hard-worked man at something which he mightn't prefer to be bothered with, it is best to move upon him behind his wife. If she can't convince him it isn't worth while for other people to try.

Mr. Rogers will remember our visit with that astonishing girl at Laurence Hutton's house when she was fourteen years old. Last July, in Boston, when she was 16 she underwent the Harvard examination for admission to Radcliffe College. She passed without a single condition. She was allowed only the same amount of time that is granted to other applicants, & this was shortened in her case by the fact that the question-papers had to be *read* to her. Yet she scored an average of 90, as against an average of 78 on the part of the other applicants.

It won't *do* for America to allow this marvelous child to retire from her studies because of poverty. If she can go on with them she will make a fame that will endure in history for centuries. Along her special lines she is the most extraordinary product of all the ages.

Twain informed Mrs. Rogers that Laurence Hutton's wife had contacted him. She had asked him to approach "wealthy Englishmen" to chip in to create a "permanent fund" to support Helen and her teacher, Miss Anne Sullivan, and to pay her fees at Radcliffe, which Harvard had founded for women just two years earlier.

I would gladly try, but my secluded life will not permit it. I see *nobody*. Nobody knows my address. Nothing but the strictest hiding can enable me to write my book in time.

So I thought of this scheme: Beg you to lay siege to your husband & get him to interest himself and Messrs. John D. & William Rockefeller & the other Standard Oil chiefs in Helen's case; get them to subscribe an annual aggregate of six or seven hundred or a thousand dollars—& agree to continue this for three or four years, until she has completed her college course. I'm not trying to *limit* their generosity—indeed no; they may pile that Standard Oil Helen Keller College Fund as high as they please; they have *my* consent.

Twain pushed Mrs. Rogers to lobby just for an annual sum of money, as opposed to Mrs. Hutton's idea to raise a huge sum and then have Helen live off the 4% interest.

No, for immediate and sound effectiveness, the thing is for you to plead with Mr. Rogers for this hampered wonder of your sex,

& send him clothed with plenary powers to plead with the other chiefs—they have spent mountains of money upon the worthiest benevolences, & I think that the same spirit which moved them to put their hands down through their hearts into their pockets in those cases will answer "Here!" when its name is called in this one.

There—I don't need to apologize to you or to H.H. for this appeal that I am making; I know you too well for that.

Good-bye, with love to all of you—
SL Clemens

H.H. Rogers agreed. (He was also approached by Hutton at a Lotos Club dinner.) Rogers paid for years, at least a decade. This mostly forgotten tycoon is best known—outside Fairhaven, Massachusetts—for helping both Mark Twain and Helen Keller.

Helen would later reminisce in her memoirs about H.H. Rogers and Twain. She loved that Rogers gave the financial aid with no strings attached, and often invited her and her tutor to his palatial 57th Street mansion. They once took a day trip aboard his magnificent yacht *Kanawha*. The sea spray and the rhythm of the boat bouncing on the waves enchanted the blind girl. "I had to pinch myself every little while to see if I was awake or dreaming."

She idolized Twain as a great writer, but she perceptively conceded that she occasionally found his outraged tirades—both the funny ones and the serious ones—a bit over the top. "Sometimes it seemed as if he let loose all the artillery of Heaven against an intruding mouse."

She and her teacher would visit him years later at his new home in Connecticut. Twain gave her a tour, then invited the blind girl to play billiards, which she declined, stating the obvious. And he replied that a blind person could probably beat him and most of his friends. The author showed her to her room and said if she needed anything during the night, that cigars and a flask of bourbon were in the bathroom.

Helen Keller, often as independent minded as Twain, a crusader for the handicapped, for women, and for living wages, would eventually try to ease herself away from the charity of capitalists such as Rogers. She turned down Andrew Carnegie face-to-face. "I hope to enlarge my life and work by my own efforts," she told him. Ironically, that decision would force her—like Twain—to mount the platform to pay the rent.

Three days before Christmas, 1896, Twain wrote a heartfelt thank-you note to Mrs. Rogers for helping Helen.

It is superb! And I am beyond measure grateful to you both. I knew you would be interested in that wonderful girl, and that Mr. Rogers was already interested in her and touched by her, and I was sure if nobody else helped her you two *would;* but you have gone far and away above the sum I expected—may your lines fall in pleasant places here and Hereafter for it!

While Twain found himself in the thanking business, he added another bit of gratitude. "I want to thank Mr. Rogers for crucifying himself again on the same old cross between [publishers] Bliss and Harper; and, goodness knows, I hope he will come to enjoy it above all other dissipations yet, seeing that it has about it the elements of stability and permanency."

Since Twain refused to return to America while still in debt and at risk of further legal humiliation, H.H.'s deal making would determine whether America's most famous author would ever reside in the United States again.

CHAPTER 30

A London Revival

The Clemens family ignored Christmas. Pious carolers might parade through the streets, Harrods might stock the latest mechanical wind-up toys, but the family would have none of it. Twain dubbed it the first time in a quarter century of marriage that they hadn't exchanged presents. "The day came and went without mention," he wrote to H.H.

Susy's absence eclipsed all. "I did not know that she could go away, and take our lives with her, yet leave our dull bodies behind."

Twain in his letters often struck a forlorn melodramatic note, but he actually seemed the first of the family members to start recovering—except, perhaps, for Jean, who was emotionally off-cue. Twain was immersing himself in writing his yet unnamed travel book and very rarely seeing the occasional friend.

On January 4, 1897, some very good news arrived. Husband and wife signed the new publishing contract, worked out by H.H. Rogers after two years of negotiations, creating a "Uniform Edition" of Twain's work. (Livy's fountain pen failed—or her hand—and Twain felt it necessary to vouch in the margin for the authenticity of her signature.)

The fine print had slowed H.H., who observed he would certainly be dead by now if he had spent his entire career negotiating only publishing contracts. Each publisher had drawn blood where it could. Harper had demanded that Bliss use copies identical to theirs for its door-to-door sales, sell them only in complete editions, and produce them on Harper's printing plates, rented for a large fee. Bliss, for its eye gouge, withheld

Twain's six early bestsellers from Harper, denying them a complete set for store sales, and Bliss refused to let Harper have Twain's upcoming travel book, even after a five-year wait. And Bliss, to continue his father's traditional torment, reneged on giving the author 15%; Frank, son of Elisha, settled on 12½%, which seemed to have miffed H.H. Rogers, who then compelled Bliss to guarantee he would compensate Twain enough to ensure 50% "gross profits" after each year. H.H., with admirable idealism for the accounting profession, even went so far as to try to define Bliss's "gross profits" and disallow expenses such as shipping fees, advertising, bookkeeping and office overhead.

One strongly senses that only Twain's presence in India and overseas had made this complex deal possible. In fact, back around Thanksgiving Twain had tried to weigh in with three radical new formulas. He had asked H.H. to turn them into succinct business propositions so that Twain could personally negotiate them with both publishers, who would come visit him in England. H.H. didn't reply for a month and instead presented Twain with this finished contract.

The deal was finally done, or was it? Frank Bliss and Henry Harper did not sign it immediately. Both sides continued to haggle over who would publish future Twain books.

After a month of waiting for the signatures, Twain, as prolific as any writer, suffered writer's block—just for one week, but it shocked him. Toward the end of February, he wasn't sleeping: "I am grown so nervous about the contracts that such sleep as I get doesn't do much good, and so my work drags badly and lacks life. I should think that if Bliss meant to sign at all he would get at it. . . . If he wants concessions, let's grant them."

And Twain was staggered at Colby's slowness over the Webster debts, now approaching the third-year anniversary of the April 1894 bankruptcy/voluntary assignment. "The nights that Bliss lets me sleep, *Colby* interferes." Twain was worried that if Bliss—who sold books door-to-door—backed out, that would turn the hundreds of pages Twain had already written into wastepaper.

Harper publishes very high-class books and they go to people who are accustomed to read. That class are surfeited with travel-books. But there is a vast class that isn't—the factory hands and the farmers. *They* never go to a bookstore; they have to be hunted down by the canvasser. When a subscription book of mine sells 60,000, I always think I know whither 50,000 of them went. They went to people who don't visit bookstores.

Twain, despite not wanting to play the clown, still clearly had fears about luring a sophisticated audience. His track record to date proved his door-to-door releases were vastly more *financially* successful than the likes of *Connecticut Yankee* or *Joan of Arc*.

His fears mounted. "I am ashamed to seem so nervous and scared, but by gracious it's just the way I feel." Henry Harper signed on February 26 after some last-minute concessions about printing-plate insurance and contract viability, but nothing was resolved about future books. Frank Bliss signed on March 4, 1897. The next day, H.H. paid transatlantic rates to rush the good news. Twain responded:

5:30 pm . . . The cable "Signed" has just arrived, I can't tell you how glad I am. It is like a new start in life. It takes a great deal to stir me up now, but this has done it. I am ever, *ever* so much obliged to you. You are the best friend a man ever had and the surest.

Twain would call the charming ruthless robber baron his "best friend" for the rest of his life. H.H. Rogers unquestionably ranked as one of the great deal makers of his Gilded Age generation; this Twain contract marked a mere trifle compared to his gargantuan consolidation of warring mining interests to create Amalgamated Copper.

The buoyed author raced to finish his travel book and collect his $10,000 advance ($300,000 in today's currency) from Bliss.

Twain wrote the book over seven months from October 4 to May 18 in a small room in a grieving household in London, while often wracked by business anxiety *and* dealing with a near-comatose wife who usually doubled as his front-line editor. "I wrote my last travel book in hell, but I let on, the best I could, that it was an excursion through heaven." Twain would later confess to William Dean Howells, "Some day I will read it, & if its lying cheerfulness fools me, then I shall believe it fooled the reader."

For instance, Twain changed his favorite Indian servant's name to

"Satan" (*after* the trip) and then had him say: "**God** want to see you," when showing in Ismaeli sect leader Mohammed Agha Khan. (No matter that Muslims believe there is no god but Allah, and that this young Khan was a holy prince.) "When he rose to say good-bye, the door swung open and I caught the red flash of a red fez, and heard these words, reverently said—'Satan see God out?'"

Twain decided to top each chapter with a Pudd'nhead Wilson maxim. He was repeating a popular feature from his recent novella, *The Tragedy of Pudd'nhead Wilson*, a switched-at-birth mystery that hinges on fingerprinting. The creative decision might seem odd, since these witty maxims have *absolutely nothing* to do with the chapters that follow, but many of them represent Twain's most famous sayings. (The cash-poor author was also harboring the idea of collecting them into a money-making calendar or selling them as sets of postcards.)

Classic: A book which people praise & don't read.

The very ink with which all history is written is merely fluid prejudice.

It was the schoolboy who said: "Faith is believing what you know ain't so."

So many of these are vintage Twain at his irreverent best. He jotted them down on scraps of paper as they occurred to him, or clustered them on the last pages of an 1897 notebook.

These maxims also capture his dark mood, and many didn't make the final book. When he felt at his bleakest over the loss of Susy, he wrote the following unused maxims:

Favored above Kings & Emperors is the stillborn child.

No real estate is permanently valuable but the grave.

He crossed the following one out. Though pithy, it might have cut too close to home, even for self-mocking Twain:

Debt makes a man a coward.

Several others appear to have been deemed immoral, perhaps by Livy:

> If Christ were here now, there is one thing he would <u>not</u> be—A
> Christian.

> Be happy & you will not be virtuous.

His wife played a large role in the editing of Twain's works throughout his career. She certainly wasn't a copy editor. Her spelling and punctuation are erratic, and she is often blamed for prissifying her husband. Huck Finn slipped through mostly unscathed, but her influence seems to have grown over the years as he sought New England literary respect. (Another factor: Twain also began reading aloud most of his works to his family of four Victorian-era females; his content needed to be suitable for three daughters.) In London, Twain told a reporter about Livy's role: "I don't always know just where to draw the lines in matters of taste. Mrs. Clemens has kept a lot of things from getting into print that might have given me a reputation I wouldn't care to have."

Twain clearly now also wanted to busy his wife with editing his latest book:

> She has nothing in the world to turn to; nothing but housekeeping,
> and doing things for the children and me. She does not see
> people, and cannot; books have lost their interest for her. She sits
> solitary; and all the day, and all the days, wonders how it all happened, and why.

He was trying to lift her out of her doldrums. Although they ignored their twenty-seventh wedding anniversary on February 2 out of respect for Susy and did not exchange gifts, Twain secretly rededicated future editions of her favorite book of his, *Joan of Arc:* "To My Wife Olivia Langdon Clemens this is tendered on our wedding anniversary, in grateful recognition of her 25 years of valued service as my literary adviser & editor, 1870–1895."

She edited the entire travel manuscript twice. Sixty-two slips of paper from one edit have survived, with scribbled notes and rebuttals. At times, they reveal the marital comedy at its best and . . . worst.

Livy edited out "stench," informing him: "You have used that pretty often." Twain countered: "But can't I get it in *any*where? You've knocked it out every time. Out it goes again . . . and yet stench is a noble good word." (Actually, it made the final book three times.)

Twain had originally described more vividly the overcrowded *Flora* steamship caught in high seas.

LIVY: Retching and gagging and heaving . . . is *too* vulgar.

TWAIN: All right, it comes out.

FINAL VERSION: The [passengers] became immediately seasick and then the peculiar results . . . ensued.

LIVY: Change breech-clout. It's a word that you love and I abominate. I would take that and "offal" out of the language.

TWAIN: You are steadily weakening the English tongue, Livy.

Many of the edits involved questions of propriety, Victorian-style.

LIVY: I don't like the "shady-principled cat that has a family in every port."

TWAIN: Then I'll modify it just a little.

FINAL VERSION: One of these cats goes ashore . . . to see how his various families are getting along.

Twain and his wife played a bit of cat-and-mouse over the naughty bits. He tried to slip a few by her, sometimes succeeding, sometimes failing.

Twain was writing about the human stampede to Ballarat when gold was first discovered in Australia. He strung together a Whitmanesque catalog of the arriving horde: "the editors, the lawyers, the clients, the barkeepers, the bummers, the blacklegs, the thieves, the loose women, the tight women, the grocers, the butchers, the bakers . . ."

Livy caught "the loose women, the tight women." Twain compromised and removed only the sly bit: "the tight women." (The adjective *tight* also meant "drunk" in that era; perhaps Livy missed the sexual joke entirely.)

In one passage, Twain wanted to have fun with the misuse of the English language by foreigners such as Hindus.

I have a foreign neighbor in this quiet corner of London. . . . He boldly talks the English language just as if he were acquainted with it. . . . It became known around the neighborhood that this gentleman's family wanted another servant. Some said it was a maid that was wanted, some said it was a cook. Yesterday a fine strapping grenadier of an Irish woman called, in the hope that it was a cook that was wanted. She stood grand and monumental and smiled down upon the little man and said:

"What kind of servant is it you want, Sor?"

The word "maid" had slipped out of his mind for the moment but he remembered a word, which meant the same thing and would answer:

"I want a virgin."

"You want a what?"

"I want a virgin. Are you a virgin? You do not look like a virgin?"

At this point the neighbors flocked to his rescue and he was removed to the hospital.

Livy lopped out the entire scene. Clearly, the joke had been simmering in Twain's brain since he had finished his book about Joan of Arc, who is often referred to as the "Maid of Orleans" (*La Pucelle d'Orléans*); "Maid" is short for "maiden," which is synonymous with "virgin." A doctor actually examined her virginity during her final imprisonment.

A little bit of risqué matter that eluded Livy perhaps did so only because Twain used a very obscure word. When the RMS *Warrimoo* reached the Pacific island of Suva, Twain described the demi-clad inhabitants.

And there we saw more natives: Wrinkled old women, with their flat **mammals** flung over their shoulders, or hanging down in front like the cold-weather drip from the molasses-faucet; plump and smily young girls, blithe and content, easy and graceful, a pleasure to look at.

That word *mammals* was waved onward by Livy, as well as by British publisher Andrew Chatto and a proofreader. The unabridged *Oxford English Dictionary* cites *mammals* as an anglicized form of the Latin *mammalia,* meaning "breasts," but far more commonly it serves as a noun describing animals, such as zebras. Sometimes, a man will strain to slip in a little nudity.

One bit of religious irreverence didn't make it in, either. Twain had wanted to use the sale of Ganges water as a springboard to revive an unused anecdote from his 1867 *Innocents Abroad* trip to the Holy Land. He said the sailors aboard the *Quaker City* so resented the behavior of the pilgrim passengers that they went below deck and poured out the "holy water" from the River Jordan and replaced it with ship's water.

> A trick was privately played; the bottles reached America full
> of water but not a drop of it was holy. It was decanted into little
> phials, about two score precious drops in each & these phials
> were distributed far & wide over the Union. The water was used
> exclusively for baptising babies. I have met millions of young men
> & women who were christened with it in those long gone days &
> every one of them was humbly trying to live up to that water. They
> supposed they had a difficult task but really it wasn't anything. I
> could have lived up to it myself.

On April 14, 1897, Twain wrote to H.H. that he had finished writing the book. He also informed him that he was dedicating it to H.H.'s seventeen-year-old son Harry.

> THIS BOOK is affectionately inscribed to my young friend HARRY
> ROGERS with recognition of what he is, and apprehension of what
> he may become unless he form himself a little more closely upon
> the model of . . . THE AUTHOR.
> But if you think he wouldn't like it, just suppress it when the
> manuscript reaches you.

The last two years weren't shaping up too shabbily for Harry: he received a yacht and a dedication from Mark Twain.

Twain had decided to leave out any mention of visiting South Africa. "A successful book is not made of what is *in* it, but what is left *out* of it," he wrote to H.H., sounding like many a red-pencil-happy book editor. "I have left out South Africa and saved the book's life." Despite the maxim-like phrasing, both Livy and H.H. thought Twain should cover that political hot spot of Boer versus Brit. Twain grumbled, swore that the newsy material would be stale, but he eventually relented.

Twain spent three grumpy weeks adding 20,000-plus words. The passages, at times, read as though written at gunpoint. He skimped on observation and devoted most pages to twitting Cecil Rhodes and damning the botched Jameson Raid. His foul mood led him to create his memorable line about keeping a piece of the rope used to hang Cecil Rhodes. On the whole, Twain's book was virulently anti-imperialist, except for the pass Twain gave England for modernizing India.

———

Twain had sent early pages to Frank Bliss, his American publisher; he had expected an enthusiastic response. He received no response for weeks. Then he received his royalty statement from American Publishing, and his six bestselling books, including *Innocents Abroad* and *Tom Sawyer*, had generated only $260 in three months. Maybe Twain's backlist—despite H.H.'s brilliant contract—wouldn't be worth all that much if no one wanted to buy his books.

Bliss's silence also meant that maybe the publisher couldn't raise the $10,000 advance or had hated the pages and wanted to back out.

With gloomy financial prospects clouding his mood, the author learned that reports had been surfacing in various American newspapers that Mark Twain was dying alone and impoverished in a shabby rooming house in London. The *Cincinnati Inquirer* stated on June 1, 1897: "Utterly broken down, mentally and physically, his once brilliant mind incapable of further effort and almost penniless, his life is drawing to a close."

The *New York Herald* elaborated: "Bravely and sturdily he fought up to the last endeavouring to regain some portion of his lost fortune, and now it seems his indomitable energy has at last left him, and that we are not likely to have any of those flashes of genius."

Quite a few newspapers ran pre-obituary pieces to stay ahead of the news cycle. The *New York Evening Journal* crowned him the "greatest humorist of the century" but added: "He coined money by being funny, often at the expense of reverence. He was the court jester of literature up to the time he undertook to be serious and meddled with Joan of Arc."

The *Herald* added a cheap shot of its own in its pre-obit: "Had he been less of a humorist, he might have been more of a business man."

To get at the truth of Twain's situation, the *New York Journal*, owned by Hearst, cabled an assignment to its London bureau. The bureau chief, Frank M. White, sent a cub reporter over on the morning of June 2 to Twain's rented house in Chelsea. Twain was still in bed; he refused to come down; the naive reporter sent up the printed cablegram.

If Mark Twain dying in poverty, in London, send 500 words.
If Mark Twain has died in poverty, send 1000 words.

Twain scribbled out a quick reply full of cross-outs.

James Ross Clemens, a cousin of mine, was seriously ill two or three weeks ago in London, but is well now. The report of my illness grew out of his illness. The report of my death was an exaggeration.

Over time and retelling, the phrase morphed to: "The reports of my death are greatly exaggerated."

Frank M. White, who had met Twain and would go on to an illustrious career in journalism, showed up in the afternoon to interview Twain. "Of course, I am dying," he told White, "but I'm not dying faster than anybody else." The author said he found the report of his poverty "harder to deal with" than his death. White obligingly reported that Twain was living in a "handsomely furnished house in a beautiful square."

White later clarified how that phrase might have changed to the present tense. Newspapermen sending cables often dropped small obvious words and all punctuation to save transatlantic fees. When the Twain article ran, the phrase turned up: "The report of my death is an exaggeration."

In fact, the poverty charge did gall him mightily, and it came just after he had received that anemic royalty payment from Bliss, who wasn't rushing to pay the $10,000 advance.

Mark Twain, ever the schemer, ever the overgrown boy who didn't whitewash *much* of that fence, saw an opportunity in the widespread reports of his bleak poverty and discomfort: launch a Mark Twain newspaper charity and also create an outrageously priced Mark Twain benefit lecture series. He did not consult Livy or H.H. with either plan.

CHAPTER 31

Charitable Schemes

The *New York Herald* had run one of the most damning pieces about Twain's dire poverty; they seemed a ripe candidate to undo the wrong.

On June 13, 1897, on the front page of the fourth section of the fat popular Sunday newspaper, the *Herald* kicked off a charity drive . . . for someone who was living in an elegant townhouse, employing a full-time maid and cook.

Twain had earlier allowed an unnamed friend to try to talk the *Herald* into doing this. Officially, for the record, Twain knew nothing of the campaign and was surprised by it. (The *Herald* didn't mention the full-time maid and cook, or expensive turreted townhouse.)

The headline and subheads ran:

MARK TWAIN SMILING Through His Tears,
BUT IN SORE STRAITS.
Celebrated American Humorist Tells of His Affairs,
and the Herald Starts a Subscription for Him.
LIST IS OPENED WITH $1,000.

The plea began:

He who has lightened the load of life for an entire generation is now himself bowed down by care. Mark Twain is more than a mere jester. His fun is of the superior kind that is based on truth. He has a hatred of sham and humbug. . . . He is above all an American, imbued with the American spirit. All good Americans should therefore lend him a helping hand.

A *Herald* reporter had sought out Twain for an interview; amusingly enough, Twain repeatedly denied being sick, sad, friendless or penniless, and the reporter repeatedly chalked it up to Twain heroically putting on a brave face.

"I could not help thinking there was something forced in his careless tone," wrote the reporter. "I learned . . . in spite of Mr. Clemens' sturdy disclaimer, he is overwhelmed with financial embarrassments." He quoted Twain telling a meandering story about a missionary who painted the ills of the world at such great length that Twain no longer wanted to contribute. He also quoted Twain delivering a long rambling story about French courts. Both stories seemed to show him as a dotard who had lost his snap. Then the *Herald* ran its pre-obit. "Those who know him well will tell you that at times he can be very serious but after such a spell he is certain to surprise and startle you by suddenly confronting you with some grotesque and irresistible master stroke." The paper praised every aspect of Twain's career and then built to a quote by William Dean Howells, who predicted Mark Twain's humor "would live forever."

After two days the $1,000 *Herald* fund stood at $1,006, not exactly a stampede of support. Nonetheless, the paper declared: "The Herald's movement to provide a fund to relieve the needs of genial Mark Twain has met with an instant and hearty endorsement." Celebrities and editors around the country were quoted. "One relief expedition to London to rescue Mark Twain from his cheap English boarding house is worth a hundred sent in search of the North Pole." Another supporter: "If every man who has had the cobwebs swept out of his brain and his view of life made brighter by a roaring laugh over the pages of the American humorist would contribute a dollar, Mark would become a multi-millionaire." "Honor the man now; he'll enjoy it more than under a monument."

On June 16, 1897—three days into the drive—H.H. sent a cablegram that cost more than the contributions raised so far from outsiders: "All think Herald movement mistake withdraw graciously Langdon approves this. Rogers."

Twain replied to H.H. *by letter,* which would take a week to arrive and allow the fund to continue a while.

He stated: "I can't retire gracefully from the matter." Twain claimed that a friend (not named) had approached him three months earlier when he was "down in the depths" and "everything looking black and hopeless." He told H.H. he had promised not to repudiate it. "The project may end in humiliating failure, and show me that I am not very popular after all, but no matter, I am used to humiliations these years."

He admitted that he never told Livy about it because she would have objected. Twain mentions somewhat ominously the famous recent suicide of ruined South African mining millionaire Barney Barnato, who had jumped off a ship mid-ocean. "Nobody ever gets the courage till he goes crazy."

Twain signed off melodramatically: "Good-bye and don't ever get as low-spirited as I am. It isn't healthy." The suicide hint seemed to stem from the limbo state of his debts, his next book, his Uniform Edition. Also, he was filling his notebook with every scrap of memory of Susy. "In the matter of the *talking* gift, I know myself that she was not merely remarkable, she was extraordinary."

Livy and Twain were quite the pair. She too mentioned suicide in letters, but hers stemmed directly and only from her daughter. She wrote: "I cannot reconcile myself to going on in this world with Susy gone out of it. . . . I loved that child peculiarly because she needed me peculiarly. Then I went and left her."

On June 17, the day after H.H.'s cablegram, *Town Topics*, whose arch "Saunterings" column helped inspire *The New Yorker*'s "Talk of the Town," ran some satire and critiques of the Twain charity campaign.

> Neither the *World* nor the *Journal* in the moments of deepest and most desperate degradation have been guilty of anything half so vile and vicious as the *Herald*'s abominable assault on the dignity and proud name of "Mark Twain." [Owner James Gordon] Bennett's impudent attempt to represent one of the foremost of American authors as a pauper in need of a charity fund to keep him from the poorhouse is a condemnable outrage.

Town Topics, a culture and gossip weekly for high society, pointed out that if Bennett cared so much about Twain, he could pay off Twain's debts from his million-dollar-a-year income or give Twain an easy high-salary job at the *Herald*. "The whole affair smacks of malice and petty vengeance."

Town Topics satirized the scene at what it called the *Daily Lunatic:* "Thousands of persons called to express their sympathy with the worthy cause that we have so gloriously championed." A hired fund-raiser got a contribution from the "738th citizen" he approached. A caller who wanted to remain anonymous offered a five-cent streetcar "transfer ticket—not good after 3 p.m." The caustic weekly ran a poem:

> *But just remember Mark is tired*
> *   And wants to take a rest,*
> *And hence has haply been inspired*
> *   To make this little jest.*
>
> *So though you may not see the point,*
> *   Just laugh away a lot*
> *Laugh till your bones are out of joint.*
> *   Then send him all you've got.*

The *Herald*, apparently not attempting satire, recorded a dime contributed by a newsboy, also ten poor people in Brooklyn banding together to muster a dollar. The *Herald* soon recognized an inherent problem in launching a charity for a man with debts and issued a clarifying statement. "The Herald Fund is designed to meet the personal wants of the writer, not for the creditors." Each contributor got his name in the paper; after six days, the list had only twenty-four names, including some suspect ones such as "Cash" and "Fern M. Wood" (a dead mayor of New York).

On Saturday, June 19, tight-fisted Frank Bliss sent a cablegram: "Herald Fund hurting you. Will you cable us disapproval?"

That same day, Twain, finally realizing that this scheme was imploding, dashed off a letter to *Herald* publisher James Gordon Bennett, then in Paris.

I concealed this matter from my family, & hoped that when they found it out I could persuade them to be reconciled to it, but I have been disappointed in that, & have failed, after three days of

strenuous effort. I hoped & believed & I still believe that a sufficient fund could be raised to lighten my debt very greatly & possibly even discharge it but the family are not willing & convinced me
that I have no right to take your money & other men's to smooth
my road with.

He asked Bennett to end the Fund. "I am already grateful to you for
wanting to help me out of my slavery of debt."

Bennett, fifty-six-year-old bon vivant, yacht racer and aging international "bad boy," had exiled himself to Paris after he had drunkenly peed
into the grand piano at his wealthy fiancée's home during an 1876 New
Year's Eve party. Though erratic and lordly, he had built the *Herald* into an
ever more profitable newspaper by keeping the solid reporting mandated
by his famous father but adding in more personal ads, crime and sports.
He also liked gimmicks, such as sending Henry M. Stanley to Africa.

The letter somehow miscarried or Bennett ignored it because the
Twain fund continued day after day, heralding the *Herald* and humiliating Twain.

Andrew Carnegie, a longtime friend of Twain, sent $1,000, so the fund
now swelled to $2,225. Twain—desperate to end it—contacted the local
Herald man in London, who replied that Bennett was traveling and that
neither he nor Bennett had seen Twain's first letter.

On Monday, June 21, an increasingly alarmed H.H. cablegrammed:
"Twenty two hundred [dollars] looked upon as Herald fake."

The *Herald* editors in New York kept blithely running what certainly
seemed like fake contributions. Wednesday, June 23: "To Deny Himself
Cigars Selberry Mullers Dispenses with a luxury to send $1 weekly to
help the humorist." (Twain's lead character in *The Gilded Age* was called
Mulberry Sellers.)

Twain—even more desperate to end this thing—drafted a note to give
to the rival *New York Journal* (where his nephew worked), but Livy nixed
it since it drew attention to the fact that the *Herald* fund had failed and
because Twain lashed out at friends for not contributing. Livy wanted
him to bow out very gracefully *on the high road* at the *Herald* by refusing
to accept charity and thanking everyone.

Twain claimed to be willing, but he still had yet another ruse up his
sleeve. He asked H.H. Rogers to *pretend* to give $40,000. "I wish you
would collect $40,000 privately for me from yourself, then pay it back to

yourself, and have somebody tell the press it was collected, but that by Mrs. Clemens' desire I asked that it be returned."

He realized he wasn't certain that H.H.'s conscience could handle that kind of subterfuge, but he explained: "It will reverse things and give me a handsome boom, and nobody will ever be the wiser. I like the idea. I don't see any harm in it."

H.H. mulled it over. Twain clearly still didn't fully accept Livy's concepts of honor and self-respect. His inner riverboat gambler still did daily battles with his inner Joan of Arc. While all this newspaper charity inched forward, with embarrassing results, Twain was cultivating a second scheme. Twain claimed that certain *unnamed* people had approached him about doing one benefit lecture performance in several cities at astronomical ticket prices. He claimed he had at first scoffed at the idea, but now with the book finished, he wrote a letter to his old friend Frank Fuller resurrecting it.

Fuller, eight years older than Twain, was a charismatic wealthy former doctor who had once been acting governor of Nevada, and had supervised Twain's first failed (but packed) lecture at Cooper Union in New York at the start of Twain's career. Fuller had made a fortune selling odorless India rubber cloth for buggy tops (and condoms) and he now operated a thriving health food business, based out of his gadget-filled New Jersey farm.

Twain's idea, or rather the unnamed endorser's idea, was that ten very wealthy men would pitch in $1,000 each for all the tickets to one performance. These would be auctioned off, reducing the burden to the millionaires. Twain even made a list of plutocrats who liked him. He informed Fuller that he could stomach a handful of $10,000-a-night, record-breaking lectures to allow the Clemens clan to return to Hartford, but he couldn't face a long tour, given his health and his family tragedy.

He was quite precise with Fuller about weaving a tangled web. "In writing to me or in talking with people don't indicate that *I* know anything about it." He told Fuller that his family knew nothing about it. "They plan to fool around till about Sept. 1, then go to Vienna for fall and winter for Clara's piano lessons." He sounded a tad irritated over which family member's desires were guiding the family.

Twain now became almost frantic to end the newspaper charity campaign.

Town Topics ran another satire, this time full of fake fund endorsements by people seeking self-advertisement:

> Enclosed please find ten cents for the Twain Fund . . . for the great American humorist . . . now denied the luxuries to which he has so long been accustomed.
>
> —PROPRIETOR OF PINKEY'S PATENT PINK PALLIATIVE PELLETS

> If Mr. Twain will come to Asbury Park and deliver a humorous address to the sea-serpent from the boardwalk for, say, four hours a day, I'll see that he doesn't want for anything.
>
> —JAMES BRADLEY

> Say, I know a good ting wot's dead easy. I'll let Marky in on the ground floor while I work de upstairs.
>
> —BOWERY BILL

Former world champion boxer "Gentleman Jim" Corbett proposed a ten-round boxing match "if Twain is really as sick as the papers make him out." He guaranteed they would split the "gate receipts" and also "kinetoscope privileges."

Twain reached out again on Thursday, June 24, to Percy Mitchell, *Herald* correspondent, and demanded his statement be cabled at once to the New York office. Mitchell agreed. (This opt-out recusal, long delayed, smacks of heavy input from Livy.)

> I made no revelation to my family of your generous undertaking in my behalf and for my relief from debt, and in that I was wrong. Now that they know all about the matter they contend I have no right to allow my friends to help me while my health is good and my ability to work remains, that it is not fair to my friends and not justifiable, and that it will be time enough to accept help when it shall be proved that I am no longer able to work.

He requested that all contributions be immediately returned. "I was glad when you initiated that movement, for I was tired of the fact and worry of debt, but I recognize that it is not permissible for a man whose case is not hopeless to shift his burden to other men's shoulders."

The item ran on Sunday, June 27, under the headline MARK TWAIN DECLINES HELP, stopping the campaign two long weeks after it began. Twain also dropped a thank-you note to the Scottish steelmaker Carnegie, and promised someday to "call at your house and drink a right gude willie waught wi' you."

The benefit lecture series was still percolating, but Twain soon wrote to Fuller, who had sent optimistic reports: "Livy refuses her consent and we've got to drop it. She says that if I can go on the platform again I must go in the old way and at ordinary prices, and she won't let me diverge from that."

Twain was still being force-fed honor. "I see that I have got to stick to the legitimate," wrote the author, sounding like one of his own scheming *Gilded Age* characters, "and I never liked the legitimate much."

CHAPTER 32

Joys of Payback

Contrary to Twain's fears, Frank Bliss within a month, in July 1897, delivered the sizable book-advance check of $10,000 to H.H. Rogers's office on Wall Street, and Mr. and Mrs. Clemens began to see daylight on the three-year-old debts.

The author, for whom charities had recently been canceled, departed with his family for a summer vacation in a villa overlooking Lake Lucerne in Switzerland. Joining them from the States were Livy's sister, Sue Crane, her manservant Ernst, and niece Julia Langdon; all seven of them would stay in a quiet hillside retreat in Weggis (pronounced "Vegas"). They could row on the lake, bicycle, walk amid the wildflowers, read or pass lazy hours on the porch. "Sunday in heaven is noisy compared to this quietness," Twain would write. He hoped to spend every summer there for the rest of his life.

In a series of letters, H.H. Rogers informed Twain that he now held the remarkable sum of $27,000 (almost $1 million today) for the author. He had this mighty sum even though H.H.'s assistant Katherine Harrison had already paid $7,000 to the forty-four creditors who had requested the 50% settlement.

Twain's surprisingly large accumulation came mostly from the new $10,000 and from Harper's book and magazine payments (*Joan of Arc*), stage royalties (*Pudd'nhead Wilson*) and from Twain's net lecture earnings from Australia and India of about $8,500.

Twain, clearly pleased, began crafting a reply, plotting strategy, and meanwhile Livy started adding up the Clemens family savings; she tallied the $27,000 in H.H.'s hands and the £2,400 she held in a London bank account (British book royalties and South African platform fees), and some income, which she had received from her brother Charley from one of her flusher-time investments. While Livy "ciphered," Twain calculated too.

Lo, three years into his bankruptcy, he was still trying to figure out how much he owed. Pen-dragging lawyer Bainbridge Colby had finally completed the sale of Webster assets and paid out a total of $22,075 (27.7%) to the 101 creditors for their $79,705 in approved claims.

So, after Colby's payment, that left Twain—according to Livy's full repayment code of honor—still on the hook for the $57,630 balance. Twain juggled the figures from a progress sheet supplied by H.H.'s assistant, Katherine Harrison, and realized that he and brother-in-law Charley Langdon had already paid about $10,000, so that left him owing $47,000. Livy finished her arithmetic and triumphantly informed him that they now had $49,000 and were capable of repaying the entire debt. Twain immediately wrote the proud words into the letter he was drafting to H.H., and from this point on, Twain starts to sound a bit giddy about his future.

"I will write [another] book, maybe a couple; and a year from now I will prepare for the platform—a farewell shout—and then retire on what's left, and stop worrying." He added sarcastically it would be a "pity" if the troubled Mount Morris Bank, to whom he still owed $21,112, went bankrupt before he could fully repay them. Twain also daydreamed a bit about issuing an expensive signed deluxe edition of his complete works bound in various leathers, and the letter concluded with a heartfelt hope that Mrs. Rogers, who had been ill, would recover quickly. He signed his "SLC" with a flourish. The restoration of his pride seemed imminent.

But before he could mail the letter, he was forced to add a postscript. "Alas! Mrs. C's addition was defective—the accumulation is $39,000, not $49,000."

(Her error, $10,000 in 1897, would be worth about $300,000 today.)

Nonetheless, the mere glimpsing of the shore of possible repayment, the brief sighting, boosted Twain's mood enormously. His playfulness starts to return to his notebooks and to his daily life.

Livy's sister Sue wrote to nephew Sam Moffett, now an editor at the *New York Journal*:

I find your uncle Sam looking well and seeming quite himself. He is cheerful & full of work, and never more gentle and lovely. It is a joy to see him and hear him talk. This moment I hear him singing, always a sweet sound.

Aunt Sue described the villa as delightfully situated on a lush hillside with the Rigi Alps looming behind and the lake below, a "soothing and most restful place." She told Sam she expected her brother-in-law would write well here; she had especially enjoyed a recent "scrap" he had read aloud.

Twain was now cocky enough (and concerned enough about his health and sanity) to turn down Major Pond's offer of $50,000 for a 125-night U.S. tour. He fired off a telegram, and then eased into a newspaper-free, kick-around-writing-projects summer before heading off to Vienna for Clara's piano lessons.

The family, feeling a bit richer, ordered a rental piano to be hauled up the hillside for Clara, who would soon be auditioning for one of the world's premier music teachers: "Piano hired from Lucerne, it got wedged in the front door & stayed so 2 hours & blocked the way—the family on the inside, I on the outside; they anxious to get out, merely because they couldn't, I burning to get in for the same reason."

The summer drifted along with the next big career event for Twain, the late-fall release of his travel book in both the United States and United Kingdom.

His newfound chipperness revealed itself also in reaming out a British proofreader, always a sign of high spirits.

Conceive of this "tumble-bug" interesting himself in my punctuation which is none of his business . . . and then instead of correcting mis-spelling which *is* in his degraded line, striking up a mark under the word & silently confessing that he doesn't know what the hell to do with it! The damned half-developed foetus! But this is the Sabbath day and I must not continue in this worldly vein.

Has a man ever sounded happier?

The family also met a Byron-like young man, "ethereally pale and pensive," who rambled on about his plans to establish a utopian *nudist* colony in Africa . . . to live on "nuts, apples and the love of God, without raiments or noteworthy occupations."

As Clara put it, "the long-haired dreamy maniac" asked her father if the Clemens family would join him in Africa and help create a lofty example to the world. Twain puffed on his pipe, deliberated, and then drawled that his "misfortunes" had not quite brought him to the point of "living in the jungle."

The "Jubilee Singers," a tour group of six black Americans—three of them former slaves—arrived in the Lake Lucerne region to perform gospel and Negro spirituals. He adored that kind of American music, and this chance occurrence thrilled him and clearly revived his prodigious observation skills, capturing European surprise at this troop of formally dressed African Americans.

How charming they were—in spirit, manner, language, pronunciation, enunciation, grammar, phrasing, matter, carriage, clothes—in every detail that goes to make the real lady and gentleman, and welcome guest. We went down to the village hotel and bought our tickets and entered the beer-hall, where a crowd of German and Swiss men and women sat grouped at round tables with their beer mugs in front of them—self-contained and unimpressionable looking people, an indifferent . . . and disheartened audience—and up at the far end of the room sat the Jubilees in a row. The Singers got up and stood—the talking and glass jingling went on. Then rose and swelled out above those common earthly sounds one of those rich chords the secret of whose make only the Jubilees possess, and a spell fell upon that house. It was fine to see the faces light up with the pleased wonder and surprise of it. No one was indifferent any more; and when the singers finished, the camp was theirs. It was a triumph. It reminded me of Launcelot riding in Sir Kay's armor and astonishing complacent Knights who thought they had struck a soft thing. The Jubilees sang a lot of pieces. Arduous and painstaking cultivation has not diminished or artificialized their music, but on the contrary—to my surprise—has mightily reinforced its eloquence and beauty. Away back in the beginning—to my mind— their music made all other vocal music cheap; and that early notion is emphasized now. It is utterly beautiful, to me; and it moves me infinitely more than any other music can. I think that in the Jubilees and their songs America has produced the perfectest flower of the ages; and I wish it were a foreign product, so that she would worship it and lavish money on it and go properly crazy over it.

He was perhaps thinking of the craze for Polish pianist Paderewski, or the reception of Swedish singer Jenny Lind.

August 18 marked the anniversary of Susy's death. Livy woke early, told no one her plans and left the house by herself. She boarded a lake steamer and spent the day alone at various distant inns. Twain sat by himself under a tree on a nearby hillside and wrote an allegorical poem, which was later published in *Harper's*.

Heartfelt it might be, but a poet he is not. The best lines tackle sudden loss and the hopes for reuniting someday.

> *And none was prophesying harm—*
> *The vast disaster fell:*
> *Where stood the temple when the sun went down,*
> *Was vacant desert when it rose again!*
>
> . . .
>
> *They stand, yet, where erst they stood*
> *Speechless in that dim morning long ago;*
> *And still they gaze, as then they gazed,*
> *And murmur, "It will come again;*
> *It knows our pain—it knows—it knows—*
> *Ah surely it will come again."*

Twain's best shot at finishing paying off his debts and maybe even restoring his fortune lay in his upcoming travel book. The author, after trying to couple *Innocent Abroad* with *The Latest* and *The Last* and *The Surviving*, finally settled on *Following the Equator*. (The British version would be *More Tramps Abroad*, piggybacking on his most popular British book, *A Tramp Abroad*.) He loaded Frank Bliss down with suggestions for a so-called "canvassing book" that the door-to-door salesmen and saleswomen would use to get preorders. Nineteenth-century subscription publishing resembled a kind of print-to-order business.

Readers got their first glimpse of the new book in an excerpt in the nation's largest-circulation newspaper, Joseph Pulitzer's *New York World*, whose half-million circulation was rivaled only by Hearst's *New York Journal*.

The *World* headline on October 10, 1897, ran in script: "Be Good and you will be lonesome—Mark Twain." Two photos were turned into illustrations. Major Pond's playful snapshot showed Twain, Livy and Clara at the rail of the ship, leaning over a sign that read: ALL STOWAWAYS WILL BE PROSECUTED AT HONOLULU. That wild roller-coaster ride down the mountain in India dominated the text.

Copies of the book would not arrive for two months, but the excerpt would help the traveling salesmen. Bliss—who clearly worried about the unevenness of Twain's writing—had spent heavily to create a lavish 712-page American edition, with a royal blue cloth binding and a gilded, embossed elephant design on the cover. He was charging a hefty $3.50, which equaled two days' wages for most Americans. (That's about $100 nowadays.) While books were proportionately far more expensive in that era of nickel beer and twenty-five-cent meals, *Following the Equator* was an especially expensive book, costing more than double the British six-shilling edition.

Bliss ran ads to find commission salesmen; Frank N. Doubleday, who sold the excerpt, pitched his company to handle the New York market. Suddenly, an unexpected glitch threatened to slow preorders. Newspaper reports surfaced widely in early November that Mark Twain had paid off his debts and was quite wealthy with $82,000 in the bank. The American Publishing Company's marketing plan called for stressing Twain's need. Bliss cabled Twain about the news; he cabled back: "Lie. Wrote no such letter. Still deeply in debt." His denial appeared in the *New York Times* and elsewhere.

Twain's stance was narrowly correct; even though he had almost amassed enough money to pay his debts, he had not yet paid them.

Twain, on the same day, wrote an exasperated but amused letter to Bliss:

Be patient; you have but a little while to wait; the possible reports are nearly all in. It has been reported that I was seriously ill—it was another man; dying—it was another man; dead—the other man again. It has been reported that I have received a legacy—it was another man; that I am out of debt—it was another man; and now comes this $82,000—still another man. . . . Therefore, don't worry, Bliss—the long night is breaking. As far as I can see, nothing remains to be reported, except that I have become a foreigner. When you hear it, don't you believe it. And don't take the trouble to deny it. Merely just raise the American flag on our house in Hartford, and let it talk.

With Twain's public poverty reestablished, salesmen returned to the field. The incident sparked Twain to request that H.H. wait till right *after* the book release to begin repaying the creditors. He would soon write that he was "getting a little tired of being traded on as the only real living, unrivaled, genuwyne [*sic*] marketable pauper."

By now, the family had moved on to elegant Vienna, then the glittering Old World cultural capital of Teutonic Europe, with its elegant Ringstrasse, its Hapsburg emperor, Mahler helming the opera, Klimt painting gilded canvases, Freud researching, and seventy-two-year-old Strauss still guiding waltzes. Clara was accepted into the class of one of the world's most accomplished piano teachers, Theodor Leschetizky, who had taught Paderewski, whose worldwide popularity verged on a cult. (The pianist's luxuriant tangled hair resembled Twain's, but his ticket prices dwarfed the writer's.) The Clemenses moved into seven airy rooms at the Hotel Metropole, where even after Twain negotiated a 40% discount for lodging, food and maid service, that still left the family paying $460 per *month*, which nearly equaled an American workman's average wages *for a year*.

Over time, Twain became a magnet, a second embassy, for all Americans visiting Vienna and a recognizable celebrity to Austrians. When he entered the hotel dining room or ballrooms or theaters, heads swiveled; he was invited to aristocratic soirees at palaces and mansions; a certain playful decadence ruled, and Twain enjoyed the fad that had high-born Austrian women smoking pipes and even strangely long cigars. (Clara thought they looked like they were playing the flute.) The Clemens family all spoke German with greater (Livy) and lesser (Twain) efficiency; they eventually accepted callers in their parlor at 5 p.m. several days a week. Clara recalled policemen parting the crowds for "Herr Mark Twain."

The no-frills British edition, with just four illustrations, debuted on November 12, 1897. (To secure British copyright protection, it had to be published at least a day *before* the American edition.) Bliss would not deliver American books for another month.

The first British reviews were the kindest—"keenly enjoyable," "a humorist without rival," etc.—but a consensus of "disappointment" began to build. (Fortunately for Twain, few, if any, of the negative reviews reached him in Vienna.)

Reviewers complained about the excessive padding of extracts, of cheap jokes aimed at Cecil Rhodes and Jane Austen. Most craved more of Twain's original observations. (In Twain's defense, ill health and his lecturing schedule curtailed his chances for sightseeing to approximately forty days out of a year on the road.)

The reader who is looking for passages to arouse his laughter will have to plod through much sand before he comes across an oasis.
—*LITERARY WORLD*

The travel reminiscences have no longer the fresh fun of youth.
—*BOOKMAN*

But they *all* adored his Pudd'nhead maxims. And they *all* padded their own book reviews by extensively quoting them. "Man is the only animal that blushes. Or needs to." Ultimately, some English critics plunged the knife: "If the fooling were good, there would not be so much reason to complain; but unfortunately the signs of the author's labour are only too evident."

Despite the reviews, Andrew Chatto went back to press four times after his initial pessimistic 5,000-copy first print run. (Recent Twain books *Joan of Arc* and *Tom Sawyer, Detective* had both topped out at about 6,000 copies.) Chatto would print 23,000 in half a year. Thanks to friend and theater manager Bram Stoker negotiating a staggering 25% royalty for Twain, the author would earn a solid £1,745 ($8,725, or $261,750 today). This would almost single-handedly wipe out Livy's math error.

The American edition reached readers in early December. The handsome book weighed four pounds and was printed entirely on glossy "plate" paper to set off 193 illustrations and photos from top illustrators such as Dan Beard and A. B. Frost. Publisher Bliss had clearly steered the artists toward humor, exoticness, and nudity. (Nudity among so-called uncivilized races seemed permissible to staid nineteenth-century Victorians, not unlike the color photos in *National Geographic* magazine to most twentieth-century Americans.) Also, Livy had no control over the art.

One pretty East Indian woman with a nose ring and bared midriff is identified in the caption as: "A Road Decoration." Photographs of semi-clad "nautch" dancers stand pages away from nude Maori natives "bathing and cooking in the springs." (Bliss knew his market: those winters can be long in Nebraska.)

In the raciest (and maybe darkest) drawing Dan Beard depicted a group of naked statuesque female and muscular male natives writhing in agony after just having been fed a poisoned Christmas pudding by an Australian rancher. Out of the rancher's pipe, in the trail of smoke, are the words: "Wishing you a Merry Christmas."

Besides the nudity, the photos delivered the far corners of the world: photos of prayer ghats on the Ganges and of warring elephants, and of bustling crowds in ancient markets in Jeypore. Numerous drawings depicted Twain in comic situations: smoking a baseball-bat-sized cigar, battling Indian crows, being carried up a mountain.

Twain did not oversee the art, either; he didn't even get to see the final edit of the American edition. Bliss cavalierly made late cuts, apparently to accommodate illustrations and to smooth the placement of chapter endings.

Reviews in America starting in early December seemed to follow the pattern in England, celebrating at first, then deflating over time. But the first handful rated as absolute Valentines. The *New York Sun* called it Twain's "best book," an opportunity "to look at countries and strange peoples through shrewdly observant eyes." The *Boston Herald:* "funny as ever." The *San Francisco Chronicle* opined "few living writers can rival Mark Twain in the use of vigorous English."

Twain specified that free copies go to his closest friends. H.H. Rogers reported liking the book but added:

I can appreciate under what trials you wrote your book and I think it a remarkable production when we consider the fact. The book is spoken of most pleasantly by every body. The people in New York, of course, do not get hold of your book promptly by reason of the fact that it is sold only by subscription. . . . I enclose a criticism from Harper's Magazine, which you will probably see before this reaches you.

Twain's friend Laurence Hutton, who had introduced him to Helen Keller, wrote the review, which was a squib in "Literary Notes" and, though gracious, had to hurt. Hutton started with an almost formulaic compliment that the book "interests and amuses," but he then judged it "not so funny" as *Innocents* or *Tramp Abroad* and explained the shortcoming by reminding the reader that it was "undertaken to raise the burden of a business debt . . . and concluded in the midst of an almost overwhelming domestic sorrow." He assessed it as more "grave than gay," more "severe" than "lively." (Interestingly, Harper's publishing arm—at the time—did not have distribution rights to this book.)

Life magazine found it "a strange conglomerate of philosophical reflection, travel notes, stories picked up by the way, Pudd'nhead Wilson maxims, and elaborate and more or less tenuous satire." The critic added helpfully: "Anyone who has acquired the art of judicious skipping can get a great deal of fun out of the book."

Another reviewer, also helpful, observed: "If Jack Sprat were fond of sociology and his wife preferred humor, they might alternately enjoy reading Mark Twain's new book aloud."

Again, Twain seems to have seen very few of the negative reviews, British or American; he sensed he would be exiting debt soon. His mood was generally good.

In early December, H.H.'s assistant in New York mailed out a round of preliminary checks to ninety-seven creditors. Unlike Livy, Miss Harrison could certainly cipher and she issued checks for odd amounts, such as $926.42, to get them leveled up at 75% of their approved claims paid. (She did, however, forget about the Thomas Russell lawsuit settlement and mistakenly sent a check for $2,540 to the binders, who returned the "donation," as they called it.)

Those debt repayment checks went out and received better reviews than the book.

H.H. forwarded an early batch of favorable thank-you notes:

We have read of examples of such sterling integrity but this is the first time where a similar thing has occurred to us in our business experience.

—GILL ENGRAVING ($50.57)

I appreciate Mr. Clemens manliness no less than his incomparable humor.

—SALES AGENT THEODORE H. HILL, RALEIGH N.C. ($3.27)

"For the first time in my life I am getting more pleasure out of paying money out than pulling it in," Twain wrote to Rogers.

His notebooks brim with story and book ideas—"Dukes for Sale—Orders Filled by Cable" "Buried Treasure in Missouri Village" "Satan & his little devils at dinner—'Papa, papa, gimme a Christian.'" However, he was actually having trouble starting another book that he wanted to continue writing. He dabbled in writing plays (*Is He Dead?*) and translating plays from German.

The home stretch of paying the debt colored everything and perhaps distracted him. He wrote to William Dean Howells:

> Of course, a good deal of friskiness comes of my being in sight of land—on the Webster & Co. debts, I mean. . . . I hope you will never get the like of the load saddled onto you that was saddled onto me three years ago. And yet, there is such a solid pleasure in *paying* the things that I reckon maybe it is worth while to get into that kind of a hobble, after all. Mrs. Clemens gets millions of delight out of it; & the children have never uttered one complaint about the scrimping, from the beginning.

Two obstacles remained to *full* repayment: Mount Morris Bank and the Barrow family. Twain was still convinced that the bank, with the connivance of Twain's former partner Fred Hall, and Hall's friend on the board of the bank, Daniel Whitford, had committed fraud and doctored up $9,000 in nonexistent loans. He wanted an investigation before paying them.

But H.H. Rogers abruptly solved that. He succeeded in convincing crusty bank president William Payne to accept a flat 50% settlement of the original amount, with no interest and no promise to pay any more.

In effect, H.H., in one stroke, just saved Twain one-quarter of his total debts, lopping $14,371 off the ultimate $57,630 due from Twain after the sale of Webster assets. Twain wrote H.H.:

"You've crucified the Bank, sure enough! I shake your hand! and am your obligedest and humblest servant. *Now* it's plain sailing."

Twain elsewhere would succinctly and *very perceptively* sum up their relationship: "You and I are a team: you are the most useful man I know, and I am the most ornamental."

H.H. had been a guiding force behind the Standard Oil empire; he would soon try to corner the copper and steel markets; he had recently earned $3 million from a Boston gas deal he did in his spare time. He brought his mechanical brilliance to shipbuilding and railroad design. His ferocious knack for organization and efficiency bolstered him in everything from building factories to business deals. As Twain later put it: "He was not disturbed by the complications and perplexities that were driving me toward insanity." And while some biographers praise H.H.'s sense of humor, he seems to have been a better audience than performer, if his letters to Twain are any indication. The few attempts at humor fall flat; what emerges is a constant need for precision, an inability to waffle.

Katherine Harrison sent out the final Twain repayment checks in February 1898 to everyone but the Barrow family, which was still owed $11,147. (George Barrow, a sharp upstate New York lawyer, was holding out for 6% interest payments; he would cave four months later, and, in any case, Twain had enough money now to pay him.) "I wish I could shout it across the water to you so that you would get it ten days ahead of this letter but I'm afraid my lungs are not strong enough."

The U.S. Postal Service delivered the checks for the final 25% payment, and the thank-you notes started pouring into H.H.'s office. Astonishment and amazement on one business letterhead after another doesn't begin to capture it: a bankrupted author was repaying in full in 1898 a debt stemming from the business crash of 1893.

> Goodness knows, we would have signed a receipt at any time if the receipt had been sent to us whether the money was or not. . . . We cannot tell you how much admiration we have for Mr. Clemens in undertaking to liquidate the obligations of his unfortunate firm. Kindly say to him for us that he is a credit to his country, and we

dare say he will be used as an example to American youth of all time to come, of clear grit and thorough honesty.

—CARSON HARPER CO. (ENGRAVERS, DENVER COLORADO, $48)

No words can express the good feeling towards him that I have to know that there is some honest people left that have a principle and my best wishes for success goes forth for Mr. Clemens.

—DANIEL G.F. CLASS (WOODCUT PRINTER, 23 CITY HALL PLACE, NEW YORK, $3.35)

We were deeply grieved when his hard times came, and were only too happy to do what we could at the time in relieving him of further obligation to us. He has really only done what we always knew he would do, but in accomplishing it has added tenfold to his past reputation for integrity, and has given the world an example which shows the high honor of an American gentleman.

—CROCKER BURBANK & CO. (PAPER MANUFACTURERS, FITCHBURG, MASSACHUSETTS, $1,147.35)

Livy and Twain and the whole family sat in their ornate rooms in Vienna and read and re-read the creditors' letters. "I am as cheerful as anybody now I have got my self respect back," Twain wrote. "He was so happy when all them debts was paid," later recalled housemaid Katy Leary, "that he said he felt just like a boy again—free and out of school."

Over in England, Dr. J. Y. W. McAlister, Twain's occasional drinking pal, editor of *Library*, member of the Savage Club, wrote a note to the *London Daily News* proclaiming Mark Twain out of debt. He compared his friend to Sir Walter Scott. The notice would get picked up extensively by newspapers in the United States, including the *New York Times* (March 12, 1898).

Twain wrote to H.H.: "Mrs. Clemens has been reading the creditors' letters over and over again, and thanks you deeply for sending them, and says this is the only really happy day she has had since Susy died."

CHAPTER 33

Back in the Game

After spending almost four years to escape debt, Mark Twain waited ten days before exploring a major new investment. "I've landed a big fish to-day," he wrote excitedly to H.H. Rogers on Thursday, March 17, 1898. "He is a costly one, but he is worth the money—worth it because America has *got* to buy him whether she wants to or not; it isn't a type-setter, which people may take or leave as they choose."

A newspaperwoman at tea with Livy on Tuesday had mentioned in passing that she had recently interviewed a young inventor who she thought stood poised to revolutionize the world's carpet and garment industries. Twenty-five-year-old wunderkind Jan Szczepanik had invented a "Designing Machine" that could electrically copy images and patterns directly onto cloth and carpets, a kind of photocopier for Jacquard looms. (Szczepanik had already patented the "telectroscope," a rudimentary closed-circuit TV.)

Twain eagerly spent the next day at the U.S. embassy gathering statistics on American looms and factories (even though the most recent reference books there were eighteen years old), and he arrived at a hastily arranged meeting with the inventor and his Austrian financial manager on Wednesday at 9 p.m., carrying eleven pages of questions. "My extraordinary familiarity with the subject paralyzed the banker for a while," Twain wrote to H.H. Rogers, "for he was merely expecting to find a humorist, not a commercial cyclopedia—but he recovered presently."

The money man, Ludwig Kleinberg, told Twain after the interrogation that Twain could earn a living as a "financier" if the writing career ever dried up—"a very nice compliment and quite true, though you probably don't believe it."

(H.H., reading the letter, must have felt like he was watching his friend speed-skate toward the edge of a cliff.)

By morning, Twain had decided to take a two-month option—for an undisclosed sum—to buy U.S. rights to the Designing Machine *for $1½ million*.

The author once again needed investors, just as he had for the Paige typesetter. And just as he had dubbed Paige the "Shakespeare of mechanical invention," he would soon christen handsome wax-mustachioed Szczepanik "the Austrian Edison" in the pages of *Century* magazine. He bragged in his letter to editor Richard Watson Gilder that Szczepanik has "inventions enough in his head to fill [his four-story laboratory] to the roof."

Twain bombarded H.H. with statistics. He made assumptions that must have made the logical Rogers's skin crawl. The aching-to-invest writer assumed that since half the Austrian factories used Jacquard looms, then half the American factories must use those looms. Twain figured that if each of the 2,000 U.S. textile factories employed ten designers at an annual salary of $600 each, the Szczepanik machine could save the industry $10 million a year, which would make it extraordinarily valuable. Dollars signs, followed by complicated, optimistic calculations, speckled the pages.

Twain advised H.H. to rush to Cheney Silk Mills in Manchester, Connecticut, and gather some "fresh" statistics, and then to sail to Europe immediately and take this "big fish" off his hands. He wrote: "You remember the negro's prayer, time of the Charleston earthquake? Come down, Lord, come *quick!* Come down, yo' own self, *don't send yo' Son—* dis ain't no time for chillun!"

He forecast that the $1½ million invested would float a company worth $5 million or $10 million. "And *I* think the Standard Oil should take the *whole* of it. You can make it pay 200 per cent a year on that capital."

And Twain's deal also called for him to receive a commission on every dollar raised, but he informed Rogers that he wanted to plow back almost all of his potential $180,000 commission into buying stock shares for himself.

The author's biggest fear was that he might sell off his option and miss out, since an American businessman named William Wood, representing the carpet industry, had arrived in Vienna a day late and wanted to know Twain's price. Twain refused to reveal one and explained his thought process in his notebook: "I was afraid he would offer me half a million dollars for it. I should have been obliged to take it. But I was born with the speculative instinct & I did not want that temptation put in my way."

Twain's follow-up letter to H.H. on Szczepanik's invention a week later began with the parenthetical "I feel like Colonel Sellers." Nonetheless, Twain flooded Rogers with pages of pie-in-the-sky projections until H.H. finally—after two more weeks—forwarded a testimonial from an actual executive in the textile industry, of Arlington Mills in Boston, who had examined the Szczepanik brochure, "Photography in Weaving." William Whitman pointed out that only a "limited" number of American companies used Jacquard looms, and he placed "no very high value on the invention."

Twain, who didn't have $1½ million in pocket change, was forced to abandon the project, but he didn't leave empty-handed: the inventor gave him a hand-towel-sized cloth instantly stamped on a Jacquard loom with a caricature of Twain. Financier Kleinberg also pitched him on a Dutchman's project to make blankets out of wool and peat moss.

Twain would stay in Vienna (excluding summer sojourns) from September 1897 to May 1899; he became a bright light, a desirable catch, in the salon circuit of Old World aristocrats and foreign politicians.

Vienna proved immensely hospitable to the legendary American writer; the Austrian newspapers repeatedly referred to him as "unser berühmter Gast," that is, "our famous guest." (Stephen Crane, passing through, grouchily called him a "society clown.") Twain could read German (though he hated the Gothic script) and could speak it painstakingly, but the uphill sledding of expressing himself often left him lapsing into English.

The author—distracted for so many years by business woes and health issues—had trouble gaining traction to write a new long-form novel. But he did cobble together eight magazine articles there, including two quite fine ones: "Stirring Times in Austria" (about unrest in the Reichsrath) and "Concerning the Jews" (defending the "Chosen People" while acknowledging their talent for moneymaking).

His "Stirring Times" (*Harper's,* March 1898) had captured the ethnic hatreds of this Eastern European empire larger than France or Germany whose government had encouraged anti-Semitism to distract the various other ethnicities—Serbs, Croats, Czechs, Hungarians—from killing each other. "In all cases, the Jew had to roast," wrote Twain in what cultural historians consider one of the first pieces on forces leading to the rise of the Nazi movement.

That Jew-roasting observation sparked controversy and led Twain to clarify his views on Jews in *Harper's* the following year. He argued—provocatively—that it was the Jew's honesty that infuriated people, not his cheating, and that the hatred stemmed from simple jealousy of wealth. He did lambast Jews for shirking military duty, abandoning Dreyfus, and dominating world commerce. He expected both Christian and Jew to hate his piece.

Twain, however, confessed in a letter to H.H. Rogers a certain bias in favor of Jews. He almost took that view a step further, but then crossed out the following lines: "There is one thing I'd like to say but I dasn't.—Christianity has deluged the world with blood and tears—Judaism has caused neither for religion's sake."

And in an earlier letter to Reverend Joseph Twichell, he had written:

> Land, Joe, what chance would the Christian have in a country
> where there were 3 Jews to 10 Christians! Oh, not the shadow of a
> chance. . . . It's a marvelous race—by long odds the most marvel-
> ous that the world has produced, I suppose.

Twain clearly sought out Viennese Jews to discuss this serious topic of persecution. The humorist, however, chose to include in his notebook a joke he had heard:

> TEACHER: Who was Moses's mother?
> BOY: Pharaoh's daughter.
> TEACHER: No-no—she *found* him in the bulrushes.
> BOY: Yes—that's what *she* said.

The famous guest dabbled in playwriting yet again, shipped his output to London and New York, and yet again failed to sell any plays, or even any translations of hit Austrian plays. A London stage manager called one effort "all jabber and no play." Twain ordered H.H. Rogers to burn his unsold *Is He Dead?* (Numerous *other* authors had successfully adapted Twain's own works to the stage.)

He also wrote near this time what some consider a late-in-life gem of a short story: "The Man That Corrupted Hadleyburg."

One doesn't need Vienna's Freud to see the subconscious motivation here. Twain felt immensely guilty that his greed had split the family, and, in his distorted view, caused Susy's death. His point in the short story is that even the very best Americans in the very best small town of Hadley-burg will degrade themselves to lust after money. He followed the same theme in "The $30,000 Bequest." In a way, he was damning the whole human race so that his behavior was no worse than his peers.

Clara was thriving in Vienna as part of Leschetizky's prestigious clique, often leading the family to classical musical performances. Her father attended a recital and marveled at her seventy-year-old professor's astounding vitality and virtuosity.

She was also besieged by gentleman callers; the *New York World* wrongly married her off to an Austrian count. (She would meet her future husband, Jewish piano prodigy Ossip Gabrilowitsch, in Austria.) Poor Jean sank further into epilepsy; one of the world's preeminent specialists in Vienna informed Twain that "in some cases the disease had been outgrown, but he knew of no authentic case of its cure by physicians." Twain refused to believe him, cursed the medical profession and began seeking alternative healers.

Twain's life in Vienna turned into daily writing binges followed by rounds among the highest levels of Viennese society. Countess Misa Wydenbruck-Esterhazy adopted the Clemens clan, as did salon-hostess Madame von Dutschka. Introductions snowballed, filling their calendar.

The famous American did enjoy the aristocratic soirees in Twain fashion. He had the breadth of personality to mock the nobility and crave to be a prince—all at the same time. (He contended that any election-loving democrat who denied wanting to be a prince was fibbing.)

Twain, who had refused all Pond's lecture offers, agreed to do a charity benefit in the ornate Bösendorfer-Saal for a favorite hospital of the royal family. The 800-seat theater was sold out at benefit-inflated prices. Twain performed some classic pieces and finished with "Golden Arm":

We had a staving good time. Many of the seats were $4 each.
Packed house, and lots of 'standees.' Six members of the Imperial

family present and four princes of lesser degree, and I taught the whole of them how to steal watermelons.

Forty-one-year-old Sigmund Freud attended, even though he had to miss a speech that night by the personal physician of Chancellor Otto von Bismarck. "I treated myself to listening to our old friend Mark Twain in person, which was a sheer delight," associate professor Freud later wrote to Dr. Wilhelm Fliess.

Afterwards, one Countess de Laszowska introduced Twain to the petite, beautiful, thirty-nine-year-old Countess von Bardi, a Portuguese princess.

A few days after the charity performance, Twain decided he and Livy should call at the imperial palace where the countess was staying with her archduchess sister and sign the guest book, akin to leaving a card. (In Vienna, in that era before ubiquitous telephones, protocol demanded the dropping off of cards by the lower-ranking family to explore the possibility of a visit.)

Livy, always agog at royalty, agreed. They arrived at the palace just past noon and asked for the guest book. The royal doorkeeper, standing in the marble portico, asked: "You are Americans?" They replied "Yes." He said, "You are expected."

The ensuing misunderstanding would absolutely delight Twain. The liveried servant told them her royal highness would return soon, and he requested that they follow him upstairs. Livy politely demurred and again requested the guest book. He refused.

Livy was convinced he meant some *other* Americans. She repeatedly explained, but her nervous German failed to convince him. Twain later logged each exquisite moment of Livy's discomfort in his notebook:

There can be no mistake, gnädige Frau; her Royal Highness left particular orders that her absence must be explained & that you must be shown upstairs. It is but a few minutes—she will come almost at once.

The other servant also insisted—& beguiled us upstairs; but when we found that he was taking us to a drawing room, Livy drew the line—she would go no further—let us have the visitor's book & get away; & down she went again. There was no book—would we write on a piece of paper? Yes, that would do. So the portier was commanded to furnish paper & a pen. But he was going to obey the higher orders or die at his post. He would hear none of these arrangements; we *must* go upstairs & wait. The sentinels were close by, with their guns. I am a prudent man. I said we would obey.

So we went up again, laid off our wraps, & were conducted through one drawing-room (saw a gown scurrying out a door) & left alone in another. Livy was in a great fright; & made the servant promise to inquire, & if it was a mistake come back & tell us & give us a chance to fly before being ordered out.

Twain reported himself "charmed" by the situation; he knew that only a stage princess would order the guards to humiliate them and frog-march the peasant intruders out the back. He was convinced a *real* princess would try to smooth over any mix-up over visiting Americans. Livy squirmed. Twain observed.

The princess eventually arrived with the archduchess and a pack of little princes and princesses, and they all had a delightful twenty-minute visit. Twain later learned that the Clemenses were indeed the "Americans" expected, but at 2 p.m., not 12:30 p.m. He must have mentioned at the hotel that he intended to go to the palace, and someone had apparently informed the royal family.

Vienna was wunderbar, and so was hobnobbing with Hapsburgs, but the author—with his debts paid—now began to weigh returning to the United States. Livy dashed that thought, demanding the family stay together in Europe for Clara's musical training and (secretly) for Jean's cure. (They had not shared Jean's illness with anyone outside the family circle.) Twain explained—not entirely convincingly—to H.H.: "I robbed the family to feed my speculations, and so I am willing to accommodate myself to their preferences."

Livy booked them for cold-water spa therapy for the summer at Kaltenleutgeben. Patients plunged every morning into an icy stream cascading out of the mountains (water temperature below fifty degrees), then jogged up a steep hill into the woods to a meadow for calisthenics and then back down for another frigid plunge, then a hot bath, then breakfast. It is hard to picture Mr. or Mrs. Clemens following such a regime, but they cheered on their daughters.

The prestigious doctor of the *Wasserheilanstalt* required a six-week minimum stay. The family rented secluded Villa Paulhof. Even though Twain was out of debt, he had no idea if his travel book or uniform edition would sell. So he surreptitiously hatched yet another moneymaking scheme. (Livy, not knowing about the somewhat bawdy scheme, would note to her sister how eagerly her husband wrote that summer.)

He counted *The Rubáiyát of Omar Khayyám* (playful, lyrical translation of Victorian poet Edward Fitzgerald) among his favorite poems, with quatrains such as:

Come, fill the Cup, and in the fire of Spring
Your Winter-garment of Repentance fling:
> *The Bird of Time has but a little way*
To fly—and lo, the Bird is on the Wing.
> . . .

Ah, make the most of what we yet may spend,
Before we too into the Dust descend;
> *Dust into Dust, and under Dust to lie*
Sans Wine, sans Song, sans Singer, and—sans End!

Twain spent the late summer at Kaltenleutgeben amusing himself and penning a spoof to be called "Omar's Old Age"; he hoped to market it in a decadently high-priced, very limited edition. Twain modeled his verses after Fitzgerald's but made his naughtier, and he graphically focused on the frustrations of age instead of the pleasures of youth.

Khayyam/Fitzgerald:

Myself when young did eagerly frequent
Doctor and Saint, and heard great argument
> *About it and about: but evermore*
Came out by the same door where in I went.

With them the Seed of Wisdom did I sow,
And with my own hand labour'd it to grow:
> *And this was all the Harvest that I reap'd—*
"I came like Water, and like Wind I go."

Twain:

Myself when Young did eagerly frequent
Some shady Houses, & heard Argument
*   About It & about; but evermore*
I liked It well, & in I went.

Into this Bawdy House, & Why, well knowing,
But Whence, for Wisdom's sake not showing,
*   And out of it, the Wine exalting me,*
I knew not Whither, windy went, a-blowing.

Fitzgerald bathes it all in a soft romanticism; not frank Twain. Some of the American author's other quatrains perhaps reveal a lot about his health and sexuality at the unripe calendar-turn of sixty-two:

Ah, now in Age a feeble stream we Piss,
And maunder feebly over That & This,
*   Thinking we Think—alas, we do but Dream—*
And wonder why our Moonings go amiss.

Our sphincters growing lax in their dear Art,
Their Grip relinquishing, in Whole or Part,
*   We fall a Prey to confidence misplaced,*
And fart in places where we should not fart.

Behold—the Penis mightier than the Sword,
That leapt from Sheath at any heating Word
*   So Long ago—is peaceful now and calm,*
And dreams unmoved of ancient Conquests scored.

A Weaver's Beam—Handle of a Hoe—
Or Bowsprit, then—now Thing of Dough:
*   A sorry Change, lamented oft with Tears*
At Midnight by the Master of the Show.

Twain wrote to his British publisher, Andrew Chatto, in November 1898, enclosing the quatrains and marking the envelope "Confidential." He claimed a wealthy American friend had suggested to him that he should release *Omar's Old Age* as "a rare book for collectors" at either 500 copies at $50 each or else 30 copies at $1,000 each. The unnamed friend promised to buy one at $1,000 and place five more. "Come—is it a wild & vicious scheme? . . . Read them, then *burn* them at once; don't let any see them or hear about them."

He directed that Chatto should refer to *Omar's Old Age* in all future correspondence in code as "ABC," presumably to evade Livy.

Chatto replied that he respected the verses as "scathing satire" and as a "work of genius," but he worried that one day Twain would "regret" printing them. He agreed a limited edition was feasible, but he estimated they could charge at most $100 a copy, not a $1,000. He also conjectured that the newspapers would eventually get hold of it.

Twain immediately sent a postcard to Chatto, agreeing to the "unwisdom" of releasing it "in any form, at any figure." (The author would use twenty of the tamer quatrains for a piece a year later, called "My Boyhood Dreams" for *McClure's;* the naughtier ones remain hard to find, in very limited editions.)

The swiftness with which Twain dropped the project can be explained beyond matters of taste. He had hoped that *Omar's Old Age* would make him big money fast.

H.H. Rogers was suddenly doing that for him.

Twain's nest egg in New York was growing thanks to the summer book royalty payments from the continued release of *Following the Equator* and *More Tramps Abroad* in the first half of 1898. (Although the first print run of *Equator* had tallied a "disappointing" 20,000 copies, Bliss sent out salesmen again, and the figure was now approaching a respectable 40,000 that would earn Twain almost another $10,000 beyond his advance.)

H.H. Rogers, J. P. Morgan, and others were conspiring in 1898 to create a steel monopoly by buying and combining four companies. Rogers was elected to the board of directors of Federal Steel in October 1898, and late that month, he put Twain's surprisingly sizable nest egg of $17,139 into Federal Steel. He bought him $201^{7}/10$ shares of preferred stock at $69 and $249^{3}/10$ shares of common stock at $28, and the shares had a face value of $45,000.

("Insider trading" was not firmly established as illegal until the Securities Exchange Act of 1934. Many great American fortunes hinged on investments based on company information not known to the public; these "insider" deals were then considered a fine perk for managers, owners and their friends.)

Twain was absolutely overjoyed. He wrote to H.H. on Nov. 2, 1898: "That is immense news. For 24 hours I have been trying to calm down and cool off and get sane over it, but I don't succeed very well. I would rather have that stock than be free from sin."

Within four days, by November 6, he wanted to mortgage their Hartford house and rustle up a big advance on his autobiography so that H.H. could buy him double the number of shares. He barely talked himself out of seeking any new debts; he remained absolutely giddy over the shares he owned.

> It just occurs to me; am I a Vice President, or a Director in the
> Steel Company, or only a General Manager? . . . What is the
> wages? And will I get anything for advice? . . . do you think I had
> better go on with literature for a while, or begin to run the com-
> pany *now*?

In a month, Rogers sold the steel stock for a solid 33% profit of $5,750; he then timed buying back in and purchased a fresh 712 shares of Federal Steel common stock at 32, which after *only a week*—just as Christmas approached—showed a 44% paper profit of $10,000 on Twain's $22,889. He asked Twain whether to sell. Twain cabled back just after New Year's: "Follow your judgment whatever it is. I take the risk. Clemens." Rogers held on to it.

Twain couldn't keep his good news all to himself. Even though he knew his friend William Dean Howells was struggling financially and was weighing lecturing to pay the rent, Twain shared the splashy fanfare of his newfound wealth with him. He claimed that Livy had tallied up their bank accounts and discovered $107,000 (the math and/or Twain's strict veracity seem suspect), and he expected his British and American copyrights, as part of the new Uniform Edition, would deliver another $200,000. "I have been out & bought a box of six-cent cigars; I was smoking 4½ [cent] before."

Twain sometimes seemed jealous of Howells's reputation as both a *witty* and a *serious* writer/editor/critic. A poll was running in *Literature* picking out American "Immortals" and Howells was placing first, while Twain was second.

> Jean has been in here with a copy of *Literature,* complaining that I am *again* behind you in the election of the 10 consecrated members; & seems troubled about it & not quite able to understand it. But I have explained to her that you are right there on the ground, inside the poll-booth, keeping game—& that that makes a large difference in these things.

On January 21, 1899, Rogers sold the stock and cabled the results: "Profit $16,000." Twain was thrilled. The new total was about $38,000. *Rogers had more than doubled the nest egg in less than two months.* (Rogers probably hoped that he would never have to hear the name Szczepanik again . . . and he wouldn't.) Twain wrote him some typically cheeky notes:

> It was a gaudy trip that that $17,000 made when it went lecturing for half a semester under your able management. I wish to retain your services, sir, and it is my intention to raise your salary. (Jan. 24, 1899)

> Now that I am prospering at such a rate, thanks to you, I am feeling pretty young and very comfortable. I wish I were there, to sit in the office and see you bet, and then watch the hen perform; it would give life a new zest. (Feb. 2, 1899)

The "hen" is Twain's pet name for the stock purchase; instead of a goose laying golden eggs, it's a "hen," which also happens to be a pun on Henry H. Rogers's boyhood nickname.

Twain ordered Bliss at American Publishing to send his royalty check for about $5,000 over to H.H. Twain craved more action. He told his broker–robber baron, "I hope you will see a safe chance to bet and will bet the whole pile." *Bet the whole pile!* Twain positively cackles when comparing H.H.'s rocketing investment returns to those of Livy's brother Charley, who years ago had put her money in safe investments paying 5% a year.

Twain can't contain his joy at his financial rebirth; he can't resist toying with the man who made it possible. (Rogers now held about $50,000 for Twain.)

Oh, look here! you are just like everybody; merely because I am literary, you think I am a commercial somnambulist, and am not watching you with all that money in your hands. Bless you, I've got a description of you and a photograph in every police office in Christendom, with the remark appended: "Look out for a handsome tall slender young man with a gray moustache and courtly manners and an address well calculated to deceive, calling himself by the name of Smith."

Howells had written Twain telling him Twain could now afford to live in style in Manhattan. The famed literary critic, for his part, was renting an affordable house in New England for seven months and then renting at the San Remo on the west edge of Central Park, which offered apartments starting at $75 a month, with full board for another $12 a week.

By mid-March, after six months, H.H. Rogers had *almost tripled* his friend's nest egg. He then pulled everything but left a mere $5,000 investment in American Smelting.

While H.H. often helped Twain with his portfolio, he never again performed such a frenzied service. One reason might have been Twain's inability not to second-guess; Federal Steel continued to skyrocket after the sale in January, and his 712 shares became worth $60,000 more! Twain wrote to Howells, "I feel just as if I had been spending $20,000 a month & I feel reproached for this showy & unbecoming extravagance." And Twain once drafted a little tribute to H.H. in which he slyly mentioned that H.H. was not a cutthroat businessman because he was willing to sell a stock on the way up, giving the other man a chance. Comments like that don't generally make a robber baron want to run your portfolio.

Since H.H. wasn't actively trading, Twain—needing action—found a British executive to invest for him in South African mining stocks. One trade shows Twain buying sixty shares of Roodeport Central Deep at £2⅞. (By 1910, the stock would drop 83% to £½, with Twain still owning it.)

Around this time, he discovered Plasmon, a milk powder extract.

The American ambassador in Vienna, Charlemagne Tower, had recommended it to him. It was a protein powder. Twain soon decided it had cured him of lifelong indigestion, could solve world hunger since it was cheap (delivering the nutriment of half a pound of steak *a day* for 25 cents *a month*), and (in a vintage Twain-Sellers delusion) was a panacea for all ills. A German company manufactured it from leftover waste milk that usually got fed to the pigs; entrepreneurs were forming a Plasmon company for England and afterward the United States. And Twain wanted in. Paperwork slowed his investment.

––––––––

With debts paid, a new nest egg growing, and Clara done with piano lessons, Twain once again looked to return to America, in the fall of 1899. But first, Livy still wanted to "cure" Jean of her epilepsy. Writer friend Poultney Bigelow had heard that Dr. Jonas Kellgren, with an office in the fashionable Belgravia section of London, was working miracles with his new "Swedish Movement Cure." Basically, Kellgren's version of osteopathy theorized that all illnesses except cancers could be cured through a realignment of the bones, especially the spine. The doctors kneaded and pounded and drill-sergeanted patients through aerobics. (Current medical science now judges it absurd to hope to massage and manipulate away epilepsy.)

The family left Vienna on May 26, 1899—twenty-seven high-born well-wishers overfilled their railroad carriage with bouquets of roses and forget-me-nots. The little Countess Bardi wept. Twain accepted his wife's suggestion to squeeze in a visit—en route to London—to the estate of the "great Bohemian" nobleman, Prince von Thurn und Taxis. As the horse-drawn rig carried them from the station, Livy tucked her feet into the fur foot muff. "All along the way, the peasantry lifted their hats to us, that of course being because we were in the Prince's carriage," wrote Livy to her sister. They drank tea at the fireside, and the noble couple and their son recited Twain to Twain, teasing him, "Don't you remember?"

In London Dr. Kellgren examined Jean and earnestly "promised" Mr. and Mrs. Clemens that he could cure their daughter in "two or three years." He cited examples of two English ladies cured of epilepsy in five years.

The family, in hopes of speeding up the cure, agreed to go to Kellgren's clinic in Sanna, Sweden. Before leaving, Twain—out of mourning, feeling flush—agreed in June to attend dinners at four prestigious London private clubs, including the Authors' Club and the Whitefriars Club.

In one speech, he reminisced about his 1872 visit to England: "In those days, you could have carried Kipling around in a lunch basket; now he fills the world. I was young and foolish then; now I am old and foolisher."

Every appearance added to his fame. But the big international celebrity found himself marooned at yet another health cure. At Sanna, white-suited attendants commandeered patients (and *some* of their relatives—Clara had somehow talked her way out of it) to live in rustic cabins in the middle of a grassy plain. After a fine first week of improvement, Jean suffered one of her worst epileptic seizures. "Jean fell in a spasm striking her head on the slop jar," Twain wrote in his notebook. "A bad convulsion; she lay as if dead—face purple & no light in her eyes."

Twain ran for the attendants. Jean eventually regained consciousness. Doctors warned the family that Jean might have to get worse before improving. They took her off all medicine. And the three family members settled into a routine at this strange no-frills health spa.

Clara, who had switched from piano to voice, claimed to be sick in London and was recuperating from catarrh in her chest. Twain—sort of—invited her to come join them in Sweden. (One senses that Livy had asked her husband to invite their daughter and this was the result.)

Dear Spider:

This is the daily itinerary.

8 to 10 a.m. Inferior London coffee for the damned.

10 to 12. "Treatment" for the damned.

12 to 2. Pant and gasp & fight the flies

2. Dinner for the damned.

3, till 8 p.m. Pant & gasp & fight the flies.

8. Supper & flies for the damned.

9 till 11. Flies, fans & profanity.

11 p.m. Bed. Tallow candles. Flies. No night—dim, pale-blue daylight all night (lat. 58 N.) Cool, & might be pleasant, but the flies stand watch-&-watch, and persecute the damned all night. No nettings for protection.

Rooms—the size of a tiger's cage.

Earth-closet [*i.e., composting toilet contraption, dropping soil into a bucket of feces*]

Not a bath-room in the whole settlement.

A great lake, but not near by.

Open fields all around the damned—no woods.

Row-boats on a simmering puddle—none on the lake.

It's 4:30 p.m., & too blazing hot to write.

Make your peace with Satan, & come along. Leave your clothes behind: fly-paper is the only wear.

Twain was reserving some of his best humorous writing for family and friends. Jean was seizure free for a long stretch in August, and so he and Livy were finally sleeping through the night. The family decided that the Kellgren treatments were working and must be continued.

Twain was still longing to return home, so he assigned friends to explore high-quality osteopaths in New York. Since he didn't reveal that Jean suffered from epilepsy, he didn't get enough information for the family to plan an immediate return. He eventually confided in his nephew Sam Moffett and H.H. Rogers, and assigned them the research.

The family left Sweden after three months, then lingered in London, with Jean going to Dr. Kellgren. Twain socialized. H.H. Rogers had given him a nest egg, but his long-term income still depended on his Uniform Edition. He heard through friends the shocking news that his publisher, Harper, was sinking. Twain—with Livy's strong backing—had staked his future on the more prestigious house of Harper over Bliss's door-to-door American Publishing.

During the fall of 1899, after a botched sale to McClure's, Harper failed, under the burden of $2 million in debt.

This would eventually turn out to be a break for Twain when brash thirty-five-year-old Colonel George M. Harvey took over, cleaned out the sleepy Harper cousins, revitalized the house, and singled out Twain and Howells as twin pillars of the new company.

His luck, at least financially, had changed. Twain was even more ready to return home. "I am tired to death of this everlasting exile," he wrote H.H. Rogers.

However, Livy, certainly since Susy's death and maybe before, controlled the schedule. She had profoundly conflicted feelings about returning to American and perhaps to their Hartford home. Jean loudly craved it; Clara waffled, since she was thriving in Europe, but Livy—simply put—dreaded seeing Hartford with Susy gone. She also worried about being able to afford to live in Manhattan in a style befitting them. What if her husband lost all his money on Plasmon or some other scheme? What if the books didn't sell?

Then, something amazing happened, a kind of blindside miracle, a comic-opera third-act windfall that sped up their plans. Livy learned she could return to America with *her* own money restored.

Charley Langdon, Livy's depressed and often inept brother, who had run the family coal business to the verge of ruin, stumbled onto a too-good-to-be-true deal that turned out to be indeed true, and it had saved the company.

Langdon Coal owed the enormous sum of $672,000; its primary creditor, the sixty-six-year-old reclusive bachelor, Elmira banker Matthias Arnot, after immense patience, was weighing legal action to recover more than $200,000. A decade earlier, Charley had bought and expanded a new mine, Neilsen Colliery, that had suffered fires and strikes and, as Twain once put it, "produced debt only."

Langdon, on the brink of despair, having several times contemplated suicide, approached Pennsylvania Railroad, then one of the world's largest corporations, which was owed significant freight fees for carrying the Langdon coal (647,000 tons of coal in 1899). The railroad company turned down Charley's offer to sell Langdon Coal, with the rude send-off: "not at any price." He persisted and returned to plead his case and was reluctantly granted a final courtesy meeting with the financial department. It happened to be with a "Captain John P. Green."

Charley Langdon, twenty years earlier, had been appointed by Governor Alonzo Cornell to be Brigadier-General of the Commissary for the New York State Militia, a largely ceremonial position. Langdon used the title of "General," especially in business transactions, for the rest of his life.

As Charley wrote in his celebratory letter to his sister: "Captain Green was very glad to see 'General' Langdon." Charley, thinking himself bold, offered to sell Langdon Coal to Pennsylvania Railroad if it would take over the company's debts, and, to sweeten the deal, he pledged that the Langdon siblings would not seek to be reimbursed for thousands of dollars they had lent the company over the years. (This sale—on these terms—would save Charley, Sue, and Livy from being liable for the massive debts to banker Arnot, the railroad, and any other creditors.) Captain Green replied, "General, your proposition isn't fair to you and your sisters."

Pennsylvania Railroad structured a deal whereby *all creditors* would be repaid in full in exchange for 60% of the company stock. The family and Arnot would retain 40%. Charley wrote Livy that he had never even allowed himself to dream of such good terms. He consulted the railroad company, and he expected her stock to be worth about $100,000 and to start paying dividends again. "I get nervous with delight as I write."

Twain relayed the glorious, surprising news to H.H. Rogers on March 11, 1900, then drew a distinctly Twainian/Colonel Sellers conclusion:

In view of these facts it has seemed to me that it was about time for me to look around and buy something. So I looked around and bought. Therefore, please send me $12,500 so that it will reach me mid-April. Pretty soon I will tell you what it is that I have bought; then you will see that I am thoughtful and wise.

Twain clearly didn't want H.H. puncturing his optimism. (The Szczepanik episode had lasted a mere five weeks.) The investment was Plasmon. Twain would become a founding partner of the British syndicate. He fantasized that the British government would use Plasmon to cure the famine in India; he ciphered phantasmagorically large numbers; he salivated at the prospect of combining forces with meat extract Bovril. A railroad and mining magnate named Henry A. Butters (whom he had heard about in South Africa) would be launching Plasmon USA; the author clamored for a piece of that as well.

Twain crowed to H.H. that one pound of Plasmon (i.e., albumen powder) contained the "nutriment" of sixteen pounds of the best beef. (This British investment would turn out reasonably well and would pay regular dividends; the American company, however, would fulfill Twain's uncanny knack for finding fraudsters and con men.)

The author wrote a shameless letter to lure Carnegie to invest in Plasmon. He addressed the letter to the sixty-four-year-old Carnegie's *three-year-old daughter,* Margaret. (The mogul had married late in life for the first time.) Twain advised the little girl to make sure her mother was not looking and then to pour "five or six fingers of Scotch" for her father.

> This will mellow him up and enlarge his views, and before he
> solidifies again you will *have* him. That is, to say, you will have
> his cheque for £500 drawn to order of "Plasmon Syndicate, Ltd"
> which you will send to me, and you and I will be personally respon-
> sible that the money is back in his hands in six months, and along
> with it 500 shares in the Plasmon Company, all paid up.

(One suspects that Livy did not proofread this letter.) Around this time, in late spring of 1900, Dr. Kellgren informed Twain that Jean had turned a corner and would get well. The family rejoiced. Twain found a highly recommended New York osteopath, Dr. George Hellmer on Madison Avenue.

Livy's profoundly mixed feelings on returning to Hartford still slowed her decision making about returning to America. She confided in her good friend Grace King:

> We must either sell the [Hartford] place or go back & live in it. We
> cannot afford to keep it and not live in it. . . . My own affairs are
> looking a little better now & we hope this year to get something
> from them. Of course we could not live in our old expensive way
> but I think with care & if we kept no horses that we could live
> there with our present income. . . . I think at any rate we shall try
> it for a year.

Livy changed her mind yet again and thought maybe they should stay in a residential hotel in New York. After canceling a June 16, 1900, departure, she rescheduled.

Debt free and an international celebrity from all that far-flung cover-age, Mark Twain, after five years abroad, was finally heading home to America. On October 6, 1900, he, Livy, Clara, Jean and Katy boarded the SS *Minnehaha*.

CHAPTER 34

Homecoming

The ship docked at the West Houston Street pier on the Hudson River at 9 p.m. on Monday, October 15. Twain, the showman, let the riffraff exit first, and then he ambled down the gangplank into a swarm of reporters representing almost two dozen newspapers, including Pulitzer's *New York World*, Hearst's *New York Journal*, Reid's *New York Tribune*, Bennett's *New York Herald*, Ochs's rejuvenated *New York Times*. Each of the reporters wanted the honor of shaking Twain's hand. Their reverential, near idolatrous coverage of the return of "the bravest author in all literature" would be picked up by newspapers all across the country, from the *Salt Lake Tribune* to the Portland *Oregonian* to Baltimore's German-language paper *Der Deutsche Correspondent*.

His first words to the long-lingering mob were: "No, I didn't get off on the wrong side of the boat." *New York World:* "There was the familiar bushy hair, the twinkling semi-mysterious eyes, the peculiar drawling voice, half Yankee, half Southern, the low-turn collar of the West, and the immaculate shining silk hat and long frock coat of the effete East."

Twain, famous for his deadpan, was unable to suppress several smiles as he talked for half an hour. "The halest, ruddiest, heartiest, most cheerful passenger was Mark Twain."

The newspapermen generously observed that he appeared much younger now than he did when he departed a half decade earlier; they all retold the story of his debts. Many papers, following the *New York Sun*, doubled the amount owed to a mountainous $200,000. His nephew's chivalrous words echoed as his own, as reporters dug up yellowed clips from August 1895: "The law recognizes no mortgage on a man's brain. . . . Honor is a harder master than the law. It cannot compromise for less than 100 cents on the dollar."

Pulitzer's widely read *New York World* found his conduct inspirational and compared him to . . . Sir Walter Scott: "Now he returns, his labors ended and his object accomplished: free from debt and a thoroughly happy man. . . . The American man with a conscience is not yet an extinct type."

Twain recounted many of the stops on his itinerary. He guessed that owing money must have made him funnier because the "English people laughed at all my stories." The author vowed not to lecture for a payday ever again, and announced that he had turned down $50,000 for 100 nights across the South. (Twain's affection for big numbers never ceased.)

With the election looming in three weeks, reporters asked him whether he planned on voting for McKinley-Roosevelt (Republican) or Bryan-Stevenson (Democrat); he said he wasn't sure, but then again he might run himself. MARK TWAIN WANTS TO BE PRESIDENT promptly bannered the *New York Press*.

He even warned the reporters not to believe him:

Now I have lied so much, in a genial, good-natured way, of course, that people won't believe me when I speak the truth. I may add that I have stopped speaking the truth. It is no longer appreciated—in me.

The only discordant note struck was Twain's apparent opposition to America's military involvement in the Philippines, which he presciently called a "quagmire"—a term that would be resurrected for Vietnam. "Mr. Clemens startled some of his listeners when he said in answer to a question that he was on general principles an anti-imperialist," stated the *New York Sun*, which added, "It was remembered afterwards he was also a humorist."

For the next two months, Twain would be feted, quoted, pampered, lionized on a scale rarely ever accorded to any American celebrity or politician, let alone a writer.

He would be the guest of honor at the city's elite clubs; he would speak to various prestigious societies at various impressive venues such as Carnegie Hall, Delmonico's, Sherry's; wealthy hosts vied to invite him to private dinners. He would soon brag to a London friend of turning down three invitations a day on average, with seven rejections occurring occasionally.

On day two, the *World* offered him an unprecedented $500 for half an hour's work if he would briefly attend a William Jennings Bryan political rally and dictate some comments. (He turned it down.) On day three, he spoke at a Waldorf-Astoria fund-raiser for the orphans of the Galveston hurricane; he told an anecdote about being mistaken for Mark Twain on the elevated train eight years earlier. After he agreed with the stranger that he did indeed resemble "Mark Twain . . . that symbol of all virtue and purity," the fellow started having second thoughts. Twain received big laughs and thunderous applause.

His distinctive bushy looks made him recognizable in the streets in an era before the widespread appearance of photos in newspapers and magazines.

The family moved into the respectable but not fancy Hotel Earlington on 27th Street, off Broadway. Neither he nor Livy had any intention of going to Hartford right away, but on day four of the homecoming, Charles Dudley Warner, Twain's coauthor and longtime neighbor, died suddenly while taking an afternoon walk. This would mark the funeral of yet another member of the Clemens inner circle in Hartford, the so-called Monday Evening Club, the convivial twice-a-month A-list gathering for opinions and cocktails. Twain said the guest list was shifting to the cemetery.

Jean was told she would be left in New York so that the other family members could have an excuse to leave Hartford quickly and not spend the night. (A more likely reason was the fear of Jean embarrassing them by having a fit in public.) Then Livy decided she couldn't bear to go. Twain and Clara rode the train to Connecticut together.

The Clemens family relationship with the Warners, though outwardly fine, was troubled. Livy privately blamed them for not helping Susy. And Warner himself, six years older than Twain, had over the years confessed to friends that he regretted coauthoring *The Gilded Age,* which had been savaged by critics. Twain compounded Warner's irritation when he bought out Warner's share in dramatic rights and then reaped all the rewards when John Raymond scored a massive hit, playing Colonel Sellers.

Twain and Clara attended the 2 p.m. funeral at the Asylum Avenue

Church. Reporters gathered around Twain, who, besides other comments, found time to slip in a plug for Plasmon, which he credited with curing eight years of indigestion. He failed to mention his ownership stake, or that he had agreed to try to sell British company shares to wealthy Americans.

After the funeral, Twain couldn't resist stopping by the family home on Farmington Avenue and entering the charming turreted abode for the first time in five years. He found the experience disturbing. "I realized that if we ever enter the house again to live, our hearts will break," he wrote a friend. Clara had long crying jags during the entire trip.

Twain returned to New York to resume his hectic schedule. They ate dinner at the home of portly Dr. Rice. Then the Clemenses had an exquisite meal at the 57th Street mansion of H.H. Rogers, with seventeen guests, mostly H.H.'s family, seated at a magnificent large round table, with the center section overflowing with a profusion of American Beauty roses in elevated vases. Twain clearly failed to thrash twenty-year-old Harry, the recipient of the book dedication, because Harry persisted in defying his parents and had set a November wedding date. Jean, who briefly kept a therapeutic diary, recorded all the gossip. And as for H.H.'s daughter, twenty-five-year-old May, Jean overheard that H.H. Rogers had paid $50,000 to make her first husband, with whom she had eloped, disappear four years ago. Twain continued to pitch H.H. on Plasmon and hoped to have him set up a meeting with John D. Rockefeller. At 11 p.m., "we drove home in [Rogers's carriage which] looked like a private vehicle of state and not in a shabby cable car." (Unfortunate Jean seems to have inherited her mother's snobbiness and her father's grouchiness—without too many redeeming qualities.)

After a week at the middle-class Hotel Earlington, Livy started searching for a suitable residence in Manhattan; she feared their budget wouldn't match their needs. Once burned, Livy seemed to fear financial setbacks, and it took some convincing to make her believe in the impending Langdon Coal money and in her husband's future book royalties.

Publisher Frank N. Doubleday, who very much hoped someday to handle Twain's Uniform Edition, found a real estate agent, brought along Mrs. Doubleday, and showed the Clemenses several furnished houses, coincidentally not too far from Doubleday's home on 16th Street and Union Square.

The family, after considering a toney Washington Square Park place that was dark, chose a fine four-story red-brick Greek Revival townhouse (14 West 10th Street) with light airy rooms and an extraordinary pair of eight-foot-tall windows on the parlor floor. Jean liked the choice because it had many soft couches for her to lie down on if she felt faint or "absent-minded," as the family euphemistically described her seizures. They moved in on November 1. According to Katy:

> Mr. Clemens . . . didn't bother to sign no lease, but we all went and just moved right into the house! Mr. Doubleday was away for a few days, it seems, and when he come back and went to hunt up Mr. Clemens at the hotel and found that he'd moved over to this new house without even signing the lease or seeing the agent, why, poor Mr. Doubleday, he nearly fainted!
>
> Doubleday: "You can't move into a house until you've signed the lease!"
>
> Twain: "Well, I *have* moved in, haven't I? and that's all there is to it. But bring along your lease, Doubleday. I'll sign it *now*!"

Twain's authorized biographer, Albert Paine, recounted that Twain treated Doubleday as surrogate superintendent and sent him notes about leaky boilers and drafty windows . . . "whatever he thought might lend interest to Doubleday's life."

The Clemenses had agreed to pay $200 a month for the furnished house. To get some idea of how expensive that was, the *World* real estate classifieds offered a seven-room apartment off Central Park on 63rd Street for $70 a month. The family—feeling flush—had two rental pianos delivered; they hired, in addition to Katy Leary, four new full-time servants—a maid, a laundress, a cook from H.H. Rogers and a French-speaking butler, Sherman.

(Twain in his autobiography would trace Livy's declining health to the strain of "housekeeping" in Manhattan; apparently, he was referring to managing the staff or, maybe, managing the flow of guests.)

Jean noted that Anna, the new maid, would have to be taught a few things "such as not . . . remaining seated when we are standing talking to her." The first cook had to be shifted to laundress when they hired the "third cook" from H.H. Rogers.

Katy reported that once newspapers printed the address, the house became a tourist attraction. Unfortunately for the stockbroker who lived at 14 *East* 10th Street, that house also drew fifty wrong knocks a month. Boys who had read Tom Sawyer clustered near the Twain doorway until the neighbors complained. Twain wrote half an apology note: "My family try to get me to stop the boys from holding conventions on the front steps, but I basely shirk out of it, because I think the boys enjoy it. And I believe *I* enjoy it a little, too, because it pesters the family."

Reporters knocked for a comment on every topic. Clara later recalled:

Once settled, Father was overwhelmed by an exhibition of the most sensational kind of cordiality from the public, press and friends. One could never begin to describe in words the atmosphere of adulation that swept across his threshold. Every day was like some great festive occasion. One felt that a large party was going on and that by and by the guests would be leaving. But there was no leaving. More and more came. And the telephone rang so steadily that the butler got no time for other work.

Loyal housemaid Katy Leary also remembered all the hoopla:

It was wonderful how glad everybody was in America to have Mark Twain back again. The newspapers was just full of it. They couldn't say enough. They admired him so for all the fine things he'd done, goin' round the world on that lecture tour and payin' back all his debts and everything like that. My! He was a real hero, I tell you. And they couldn't do enough for him—the people as well as the newspapers. They couldn't have done more if he'd been royalty.

Once Twain moved into the new townhouse, he started a streak of *carpe diem/carpe noctem* truly astounding for a man turning sixty-five. "Strangely enough . . . Father did not seem to weary easily," recalled Clara. "There was so much excitement in his daily life that he felt constantly stimulated as if by wine."

The hosting honors for the first weekend of November fell to *Harper's* book critic, theater reviewer, travel writer Laurence Hutton in Princeton, New Jersey. (Twain had apparently forgiven him for his left-handed-compliment review of *Following the Equator*.) More than fifty people crowded in on Sunday to welcome Twain home. "Never knew him so well and happy," Hutton wrote to a friend. Twain told Hutton that he would not accept any other out-of-town invitations, but then when he heard about the Yale–Princeton football game in two weeks, he simply told Hutton that he was returning for it and noted it in his memorandum book. Chagrined, Livy informed Hutton "she had never known him to do such a thing."

The tribute and adulation clearly revitalized Twain. William Dean Howells wrote to fellow writer Thomas Aldrich after observing Twain for about two weeks:

> Clemens is here, settled down for the winter in West 10th Street, and looking younger and jollier than I've seen him for ten years. He says it is all Plasmon, a new German food-drug he's been taking, but I think it's partly prosperity. He has distinctly the air of a man who unloaded.

Clara, also swept up in the parade, decided she would try to launch her professional singing career, and, with a talent agent, orchestrated a low-key debut for November 9. She wanted to be known as Clara Clemens with no mention of her father. Twain teased her that it would be impossible, and, of course, he was right (although maybe he helped fulfill his own prophecy). Within days, *Concert Goer* and dozens of newspapers, such as the *San Francisco Call,* described "Mark Twain's daughter" as having a rich mezzo-soprano voice, a facility for singing in foreign languages, and a ready wit inherited from her father. (She would perform a few times, then bronchitis would derail her debut.)

Livy and Jean seem to be the two family members less swept up in the goodwill. Jean's seizures increased. Osteopath Dr. Hellmer told the family not to worry because his bone manipulations were clearly working. He compared Jean's situation to a "darky's dog" barking up the *right tree,* which will set the raccoon to moving and yelping. He warned of one patient having thirteen seizures in a day.

Dr. Hellmer also treated Livy, who was not feeling well. Jean recorded his early November diagnosis: her mother's "acid centers" had caused her gout to flare up; her goiter was bad, but "Dr. Hellmer had cured larger ones"; her low collar bones needed adjustment; the tear duct in her left eye, despite operations, still didn't function correctly. Livy agreed to start twice-a-week treatment, the same as Jean, but not on the same days. (No one seems to have noticed that Livy's health was best when untreated during the yearlong trip.)

Invitations fluttered in but often not for awkward Jean. Mama Livy made every effort to have the girl included. On election night, Tuesday, November 6, Jean joined the group, led by the children of Richard Watson Gilder of *Century* magazine:

> We left here about ten and walking to Fourth Ave. took a car
> went up towards Union and Madison Squares through packs and
> jams of noisy men and women. Nearly everyone had a tin horn,
> which they were blowing loudly in each other's ears. It was per-
> fectly horrible.

Free theater tickets showered down like confetti; someone sent a "motor coupe" to carry Livy and Jean to the Harlem Opera House to see handsome Hartford star William Gillette on November 10. Twain was impressed by his wife's bravery in riding in it. Unfortunately, Jean had two seizures en route and then later had a temper tantrum at the dinner table. In her diary she sadly recorded:

> It is dreadful to feel as I so often do. To have no real friends, no
> talent of any kind, no love, no home or at least not to live at home
> and no health or truly an abominable health. If I could only have a
> real love, a real talent & a decent sort of health. . . . Clara seems to
> me to have so much; she has two great talents, many true friends
> and more than enough devoted lovers.

That same night, her father was once again the toast of the town. The prestigious Lotos Club for performers and admirers of the arts honored him at a testimonial dinner. More tables than ever in the club's history crowded the first floor; plate decorations included papier-mâché jumping frogs. New York State governor-elect Benjamin Odell showed up, as did U.S. senator Chauncey Depew and former House speaker Thomas B. Reed and Civil War general George McClellan and African American reformer Booker T. Washington. Clustered around Twain at the guest of honor's table were H.H. Rogers, Dr. Rice and nephew Sam Moffett.

Club president Frank Lawrence delivered more of a coronation than an introduction, as did numerous other speakers.

> We hail him . . . as the possessor of the quaint and peculiar genius, which has discovered unsuspected possibilities of language and of thought . . . whose works have always commanded the widest audience and been received the world over with unbounded applause.

Lawrence, a respected lawyer, also seized on Twain's "manliness and courage" in bearing great burdens of debt and grief. Some speakers chose banter over bowing.

William Dean Howells said: "I am glad to have Mr. Clemens among us again, because for one thing I hated to see him having such a good time abroad." Senator Chauncey Depew was pretty certain Twain returned because of a bounced check in England. A banker named Joseph Hendrix heard that Twain regretted not being motivated by debt anymore and offered to lend him some money. These fat cats were having a good time.

When Twain stood up, the applause lasted almost three minutes, as measured by the pocket watch of the *New York Times* reporter. Twain replied to the excessive praise with one of his mock-modest responses: "It is not for me to say whether these praises were deserved or not. I prefer to accept them just as they stand, without concerning myself with the statistics upon which they have been built."

Twain said he was pleased the host had mentioned his debts, because he wanted to thank ninety-five of his ninety-six creditors. "I was not personally acquainted with ten of them, and yet they said, 'Don't you worry, and don't you hurry.' I know that phrase by heart, and if all the other music should perish out of the world it would still sing to me."

(Twain, in this very happy moment, chose to forget the troublesome Mount Morris Bank, the Barrows, the Grants, to whom he had owed almost two-thirds of the $79,705 debt.)

Twain did a riff on the recent election, which had put William McKinley and Theodore Roosevelt in the White House, and he brilliantly used his patented slow delivery-and-pause to skewer publicity-happy "Rough Rider" Roosevelt.

And now, for a while anyway, we shall not be stammering and embarrassed when a stranger asks us, "What is the name of the vice-president?" [*general laughter*]. This one is known, this one is pretty well known [*pause*], pretty widely known [*longer pause*], and in some quarters [*pause*] favorably [*much laughter over that last*].

Twain kept his speech relatively short and concluded:

Seven years ago, when I was your guest here, when I was old and despondent, you gave me the grip and the word that lift a man up and make him glad to be alive.

And now I come back from my exile young again, fresh and alive, and ready to begin life once more, and your welcome puts the finishing touch upon my restored youth and makes it real to me, and not a gracious dream that must vanish with the morning.

I thank you.

The *New York Sun* judged: "Nobody enjoyed the evening, if appearances mean anything, more than the snowy-headed guest of honor." Major Pond wrote Livy that the club's enthusiastic welcome "eclipsed" all prior tributes.

The *New York Journal* assigned a reporter to shadow the author for a "A Day with Mark Twain/Funniest Man in the World." The piece lay flat on the page, and Twain vowed to do no more newspaper interviews. Twain met with backers to try to set up a Plasmon factory in Briarcliff, New York. Laurence Hutton, who had started taking it, said Twain told him Plasmon cured everything from dandruff to corns.

Twain went to Carnegie Hall on November 12 for a piano recital, as family friend Ossip Gabrilowitsch ("Gabi" to them from Vienna) gave them a box. (Of course, Twain was applauded as he entered.) Twain, Jean, Livy, Clara, Dr. and Mrs. Rice, and William Dean Howells's son, John, sat together. Gabi's bravura performance drew three encores. "The applause was like a tornado," wrote Jean, whose hand ached from clapping. Twain sent a welcome-to-America bouquet onstage. Jean's day was spoiled slightly by Mrs. Rice's bonnet, which featured an entire stuffed parrot. "I would as soon go out with a skull & bones on my breast as wear such murderous ornaments."

That same night marked yet another Twain tribute. The Press Club dinner started off with the usual extravagant praise from the club president, Colonel William Brown. Twain responded: "And must I always begin with a regret—that I have left my gun behind?" The author had promised to shoot the next host who fulsomely introduced him. Twain then launched into a roast of sixty-year-old Colonel Brown, former publisher of the *New York Daily News,* calling him "dead to all honorable impulses" and saying his face revealed "marks of unimaginable crimes." (Twain apparently didn't know that Brown had recently been forced into sudden retirement by his managing partner's widow.)

A few days later, the Society of American Authors honored him at Delmonico's. He was already starting to weary of tributes. Jean must have overheard him say: "Most of the members are people who have written insignificant little articles either in some rather poor magazine or monthly or weekly paper and consequently desire to be considered authors."

Twain defused the excessive praise that night in yet another way. "Everybody believes that I am just a monument of all the virtues, but it is nothing of the sort," he said. "I am leading two lives, and it keeps me pretty busy." He claimed to be full of "interior sin." (This seems a classic example of him not being believed when he *was* telling the truth.)

That weekend he returned to New Jersey to witness his first football game, sitting on the Princeton side, hearing the raucous fight songs. (Again, the crowd applauded when they spotted him.) The Missouri boy who had attended far too many operas and piano recitals enjoyed the gridiron battle. Favored Yale won, 29–5. The author dropped comments throughout: "I should think they'd break every bone they ever had." "That Yale team could lick a Spanish army!" "This beats croquet.")

A few days later, the Nineteenth Century Club invited him to a dinner at Sherry's. A pair of long-winded speakers bloviated on "The Disappearance of Literature," never once mentioning Twain's works, yea or nay. They predicted few current books would survive as long as Sir Walter Scott's works or John Milton's. Their snobbery brought out a feisty side of Twain, who dared them to place his works side by side with any classics and see which sold more.

Professor Winchester also said something about there being no modern epics like *Paradise Lost*. I guess he's right. He talked as if he was pretty familiar with that piece of literary work, and nobody would suppose that he had never read it. I don't believe any of you have ever read *Paradise Lost,* and you don't want to. That's something that you just want to take on trust.

The family was settling into the new townhouse on 10th Street. Katy, the least neurotic member of the entourage, was especially enjoying it.

Oh I could fill a book with just the doings that winter. It was like a fairy story, and it was just as exciting to me to hear about them things as it was to the rest of the family. . . . Everybody was so glad to have Mark Twain back again, they was just chasin' him everywhere. He was flooded with invitations from the highest and grandest in the town. . . .

    You see, people was crazier about him than ever, and every magazine and newspaper in the world was after him to write for 'em. They'd pay him anything he wanted. Why, I heard that one time he was offered as much as a dollar a word from one magazine if he'd give them an article.

Livy found herself entertaining small dinner parties and hosting teas and she craved some of her fine silverware from the Hartford home, so she sent Katy to go fetch it. The loyal housemaid, with several bundles, hired a night hack carriage from Grand Central at 42nd Street, and the large strapping Irish cabby charged her $1.50 (about $45 in today's dollars) to go a mile and a half. Twain came out and argued that the fare sheet stated 50 cents the first mile, and 25 cents each additional mile, which made it 75 cents. Twain paid him $1; the nighthawk called him "a damned old fool."

Twain decided to press charges, and he instantly became a hero to workaday New Yorkers for standing up to a cabby. Many of them were large men who charged according to whim. "I am doing this just as any citizen who is worthy of the name of citizen should do," soap-boxed Twain. The driver, twenty-four-year-old William Beck, was fined and had his license suspended.

    A few days later, Beck came to Twain's home to plead for his job back; he claimed he supported his large Irish family—Katy didn't believe him, saying "an Irishman could muddle anyone"—but Twain accepted the apology and agreed to sign off on his reinstatement. Twain's mercy won him more favor.

These five weeks of nonstop parties, dinners, tributes, Plasmon huckstering, were finally taking their toll. Around Thanksgiving Twain's gout flared up; he also developed a bronchial cough and a toothache. Twain limped to the Aldine Association and St. Nicholas Society banquets.

Twain wrote to a friend on December 12: "I am dead, *dead* tired of talking & feeding. I have crept out of all my engagements except one tonight & one in the middle of January."

That night he would introduce young war correspondent Winston Churchill at the Waldorf-Astoria. Leading writers had refused to attend in protest of England's land-grabbing battles in South Africa. Twain judged it better to show up and air his contrarian views to the 1,200 attendees. He would stress his anti-imperialist sentiments: "Mr. Churchill and I do not agree on the righteousness of the South African war, but that is of no consequence. There is no place where people all think alike—well, there is heaven; there they do but let us hope it won't be so always."

Twain lambasted imperialism around the globe, singling out the major powers, including the United States in the Philippines. He concluded of Churchill:

> By his father he is English, by his mother [*Jeanette Jerome of Brooklyn*] he is American—to my mind the blend which makes the perfect man. We are now on the friendliest terms with England. Mainly through my missionary efforts I suppose; and I am glad. We have always been kin: kin in blood, kin in religion, kin in representative government, kin in ideas, kin in just and lofty purposes; and now we are kin in sin [*British war in South Africa, American war in the Philippines*], the harmony is complete, the blend is perfect, like Mr. Churchill himself, whom I now have the honor to present to you.

———

Twain met repeatedly with Colonel Harvey at Harper and came away convinced Harvey could sell his backlist of books. *Harper's Weekly* did its share to build the brand. It commissioned a double-page illustration of Twain meeting his fictional characters for the December 15 issue. He

saw Frank Bliss of American Publishing. He tendered offers from Frank
Doubleday.

The Lotos Club promised twenty-three-year-old budding artist James
Montgomery Flagg a lifetime membership if he would paint a portrait
of Twain. The author first said he would "rather have smallpox than sit
for his picture," but he finally consented. So Flagg spent several Sunday
mornings at 14 West 10th Street. "He told me stories in his drawl and I
got laughing so I couldn't paint."

Twain sat in the back room; his wife sewed in the parlor. He would
bait Livy. "My wife cusses too, not the same words. *She* says 'Sugar!' and
the Recording Angel will give her just as black marks as he does me!"

Twain was pleased with the work of Flagg, who would go on to create
that famous "Uncle Sam Wants You" poster for World War I. Twain liked
that the artist did not give him genteel "society" eyebrows but left him a
woolly thicket.

Mark Twain was no one's clown. He was easing away from his stand-
up comedy act. He would never do it again for money, despite Major
Pond offering $1,000 a night. But he would reprise his act . . . for free . . .
for a friend.

On January 7, he did his full classic stage routine—"Stealing a Watermelon," "Corpse," "Mexican Plug," "Australian Poem," "Christening"—at
H.H. Rogers's mansion on 57th Street; the guests sat in camp chairs
throughout the ballroom. Twain stood by a roaring fire.

Once again, he evoked his outrage at discovering that unripe watermelon; he shared his fear of the dead body in the moonlight. He recalled
when the Mexican horse bucked him up higher than the church steeple.
"But when I got back," [*pause . . . wait for it . . . wait for it . . .*] "the
horse was gone." [*Laughter.*] The audience had heard the stories before
but still loved them. Only he could tell them.

Twain performed, by way of saying thanks to the man who had helped
save his copyrights and helped save his family from the "poorhouse"; he
was honoring the man who had helped save *him,* Samuel Langhorne
Clemens, helped restore his spirits.

Twain had left in disgrace in 1895 and returned triumphant in 1900.
The tag-team combination of H.H. Rogers with his pragmatism and
Livy with her high honor had worked well for him. The push-pull on
his soul refined his humor. Thanks to newspaper coverage of his per-

formances, his name was spread around the world. He was financially secure.

Mark Twain had chased the last laugh and had caught it. Ovations certainly awaited him during his final decade, but it would be pretty hard for anything to top these weeks of adulation when the American author came back home.

Postscript

Olivia Clemens was not certain the family's honor had been fully restored. She requested that H.H. Rogers investigate the Mount Morris accounts. "There is a little settlement that Mr. C. will make with the bank when it's proved what he owes them," she had written to a friend.

Dated April 26, 1901, the bank's detailed accounting—loan by loan—appears accurate and shows Twain still owing $14,370. It does, however, reveal that Mount Morris collected about $9,000 in interest charges over five years. Also, by matching the loan dates to letters sent by Fred Hall, one discovers not fraud, but a lack of clarity by the novice executive and an almost childish downplaying of any new loans to make Webster appear viable. Livy's health began to decline around this time, and there's no record that Twain paid any more money to Mount Morris. (Almost all biographers have stated that Twain paid his debts in full.)

The doting mother, Livy never fully recovered from Susy's death. Doctors treating her thyroid and heart problems and neurasthenia soon prescribed an isolation cure—not unlike posh solitary confinement, with brief visits by nurses and family members. Twain was forbidden to see his wife for months at a stretch, from 1902 onward. On December 30, 1902, he saw her *for five minutes* and again on their thirty-third anniversary in February 1903. He sent her sweet loving notes most mornings, but she bristled at what she perceived as his increasingly acerbic humor in his published pieces.

Where is the mind that wrote the Prince & P[auper], Jeanne
d'Arc? the Yankee &c. Bring it back! You can if you will—if you
wish to. Think of the side I know, the sweet dear, tender side—that
I love so. . . . Does it help the world to always rail at it?

(Note the books that she chose.) The dream of any kind of reunion in
Hartford vanished in May 1903, when the family sold the Farmington
Avenue home—having kept it for a dozen years without ever living in
it again. The couple, who had pegged its cost at $150,000, sold it for
$28,800 to Richard Bissell, an insurance executive.

The family tried Europe yet again as a rest cure, but Livy kept fading.
Twain mounted a heroic lie and told her—despite his abandonment of
formal Christianity—that he believed in "immortality" and an afterlife.
Livy, who dreaded death, died at age fifty-eight on June 5, 1904, in Florence, Italy. She was no longer around to tame his tantrums, to lighten
his moods.

———

Daughter **Jean** also went on a downhill slide, with brief respites from
her "absent-mindedness" (seizures), her severe depression and occasional violent behavior. She tried to kill Katy Leary twice, and after
her mother's death was institutionalized. Twain lacked the patience to
care for her. Awkward Jean envied her sister Clara's numerous admirers and her talents at both piano and voice. She had written in her brief
diary: "Is it going to be my miserable lot never to really love and be
loved? That would be too dreadful & would offer another fair reason for
suicide."

In 1909, Twain, now living in Redding, Connecticut, experimented
with having Jean move back to live with him. The twenty-nine-year-old
seemed to be thriving, happily preparing for the holiday season, decorat-
ing the tree, buying presents. She took a bath on Christmas eve morning, had a seizure and died in the tub. Twain wrote bittersweet fumbling
words to Clara, then in Europe: "You can't imagine what a darling she
was that last two or three days; and how fine and good and sweet and
noble—and joyful, thank Heaven!—and how intellectually brilliant. I
had never been acquainted with Jean before. I recognized that."

———

Clara, despite putting on a good face for the public, avoided spending long stretches with her father. In 1909, internationally renowned pianist Ossip Grabilowitsch, along with a male singer and Clara, agreed to do a fund-raiser for a library in Redding. Twain introduced Clara, with more edge than grace: "My daughter has not been singing long before the public and is not as famous as either of these gentlemen, but I am sure you will agree with me that she is much better-looking."

She married Ossip soon after, and Twain attended the wedding, wearing his red gown from his honorary degree at Oxford, no doubt drawing attention away from the bride. She lived into the 1960s, almost outliving her only child, her troubled daughter, Nina.

––––––––

In the opening years of the new century, **Twain** remained the most sought-after guest of honor, the man in white, the celebrity.

That first winter, he wrote his most strident published piece of anti-imperialism, "To the Person Sitting in Darkness," which *Harper's* chose not to publish and Twain would place in the *North American Review*.

"The Blessings-of-Civilization Trust, wisely and cautiously administered, is a Daisy. There is more money in it, more territory, more sovereignty, and other kinds of emolument, than there is in any other game that is played."

He wrote *King Leopold's Soliloquy* and *Eve's Diary* and others—some published only posthumously. He dictated what he claimed would be a brutally honest autobiography—with sections embargoed for a century—but the book turned out disjointed, often inaccurate, but occasionally wildly entertaining.

While Mark Twain's published writings turned darker for the last decade of his life, his mischievousness in his private life did not disappear, and his friendship with **H.H. Rogers** deepened.

The tycoon bought an elegant 227-foot steam yacht that rivaled J. P. Morgan's *Corsair*, and he took the gray-haired boys—Twain, ex-speaker Reed, Dr. Rice, gadabout Hutton, among others—for several long cruises: all male, full of alcohol, cards and practical jokes.

On the first voyage, in August 1901, they threw Twain's prized umbrella overboard, lashed to a cannonball, and watched him spend days cursing and searching for it. When they returned, Twain placed a classified ad in the *New York Sun* advertising a reward for a lost 97-cent umbrella and directing all finders to deliver the goods to Dr. Rice's office. Within a week, Dr. Rice, caretaker of the throats of the Metropolitan Opera, had 117 umbrellas.

For the next year's cruise to Cuba in 1902, Twain was having trouble shaking free of houseguests. He wrote H.H.:

> I am anxious to come, and shall if it be possible. May the Lord bless you and keep you and watch over you. You are too wicked to die and too good to live. I *do* want to go on that excursion; I want to play poker once again before I die, and to breathe the salt air out of the mouth of a champagne bottle and be wicked. I have been good too long.

Twain missed the first leg of the voyage (and had to take a train to Florida) but made up for it by sending to H.H. a speech to help kick off the trip from Boston. He advised reading it to a "half drunk" audience.

Rogers had dubbed the guests of the expedition "The Mammoth Cod Club." The "Mammoth" might have been a nod to 250-pound ex–House speaker Reed or to fishing. In any case, Twain decided that the title actually meant that Rogers would accept into his Mammoth Cod Club only men whom "nature has endowed with private organs of a size superior to common mortals."

Twain protested this discrimination. "I fail to see any special merit in penises of more than usual size." He found no history books claiming that the fathers of Washington, Napoleon or Caesar were exceptionally well endowed.

He quoted Matthew in the New Testament about God making man. "Can any of you by taking thought add one cubit to his stature?" Twain noted that he at times "by taking thought" had added "inches" but it wasn't a "permanency."

He argued that monumental size came from frequently exercising the limb, like the well-muscled arm of a blacksmith. "Membership in your Society is a confession of immorality." The author professed that he was dedicating his life to pious study and meditation.

Twain might have advised Rogers to have the audience more like two-thirds drunk.

Off Cuba, the yacht ran into a storm. Rogers loved teasing Twain, the river pilot, about his seasickness. Twain stood alone clutching at the rail, heaving, as the ship plunged between the waves. Rogers sent a crewman who asked, "Mr. Clemens, can I get you something?" "Yes," he replied in that drawl, "yes,—get me a little island."

Twain and Rogers kept up the hijinks in New York. One running joke was that every time Twain visited H.H., he "accidentally" stole something, such as Rogers's "brown slippers" or a "ham."

Other millionaires got in on the fun. Twain was once ill with a bad chest cold and decided that he needed a finer brand of whiskey to shake it off. He had Katy telephone Andrew Carnegie and demand that two bottles of his best Scotch be sent before 6 p.m. or Twain would give him "down the banks" (an old Irish expression for ruining somebody).

As Katy tells the story, Carnegie's butler couldn't believe the message, so he put Mr. Carnegie on the line and Katy repeated it word for word. Carnegie roared with laughter and said, after he got his breath, he'd attend to it. He sent over two bottles by messenger; then the next week he sent Twain a dozen bottles of whiskey, and then the following week he sent a barrel of whiskey. A few hours later, Carnegie showed up at the door of Twain's place at 21 Fifth Avenue. Katy answered and acknowledged receiving the barrel of whiskey. Carnegie laughed hard and said, "Well, now, I hope that *barrel* of whiskey will keep his mouth shut, at last!"

Twain, in these years, never wrote any anti-capitalist essays. He even helped organize a meeting of the harshly criticized, monopolist Rockefellers with fifty magazine publishers at the Aldine Club.

His financial problems completely disappeared in 1903 when H.H. Rogers struck a new publishing deal for him. Harper and Twain bought out Bliss/American Publishing's rights to the six early Twain books, as well as *Pudd'nhead Wilson* and *Following the Equator* for $50,000, and now Harper would issue the Uniform Edition and pay Twain a 20% royalty and a minimum of $25,000 a year. (Most American workers still earned $500 a year or less.) Twain had achieved his coveted 50% net profit with a publisher.

The author that year plunged $25,000 into Plasmon USA and $16,000 into American Mechanical Cashier and would lose the entire sums. Twain under oath, trying to get his money back, complained about being swindled by a man named "Butters," who was paid $12,000 a year and should have been paid "$3 a century." Twain said he was promised to be let in on the ground floor, only there wasn't any ground floor. Henry A. Butters, a smooth-talking onetime railroad millionaire temporarily short on funds, joined James W. Paige and Charles L. Webster in Twain's select rogues' gallery. Twain, whose thoughts sometimes drifted to lingams, described Butters as a "stallion in intention, eunuch in performance."

Under oath in court on December 20, 1907, he was asked if this was the first time that he had been swindled. "No, I have been swindled out of more money than there is on the planet," he told the judge. Then Twain thought about it a few moments and added: "I oughtn't to say I was swindled out of all the money. Most of it was lost through bad business. I was always bad in business."

H.H. Rogers, on the other hand, continued to thrive financially. He even risked a vast portion of his $50 million fortune on privately funding an ambitious railroad project in mountainous Virginia and West Virginia. At the April 3, 1909, dedication dinner in Norfolk, Twain spoke: "I would take this opportunity to tell something that I have never been allowed to tell by Mr. Rogers, either by my mouth or in print, and if I don't look at him I can tell it now." (Clearly, Twain's emotions were choking him up.)

> He saved my copyrights, and saved me from financial ruin. He it was who arranged with my creditors to allow me to roam the face of the earth for four years and persecute the nations thereof with lectures, promising that at the end of four years I would pay dollar for dollar. That arrangement was made; otherwise I would now be living out-of-doors under an umbrella, and a borrowed one at that. You see his white mustache and his head trying to get white. He is always trying to look like me—I don't blame him for that.

Rogers's 442-mile coal-transport railroad would quickly start raking in ever larger profits.

On Wednesday, May 19, 1909, Twain took the train alone from Connecticut to New York City. By minutes, he had missed a telegram sent from the home of H.H. Rogers. Clara, then staying in Manhattan, met him at Grand Central Station and told him that his good friend had died early that morning. Reporters clustered around him. "This is terrible, terrible," he said. "I cannot talk about it." Deeply upset, he leaned heavily on his daughter and walked very slowly toward the exit. He rested a few minutes in the waiting room, trying to compose himself.

Days later, Twain stood shoulder-to-shoulder with William Rockefeller and E. H. Harriman as pall-bearers at Rogers's burial. The *New York Times* placed Rogers in the same sentence with John D. Rockefeller, crediting him with creating Standard Oil.

Mark Twain—Samuel Langhorne Clemens—died eleven months later on April 21, 1910, at age seventy-four.

Front-page obituaries around the world hailed his meteoric career—as humorist, as novelist, and as a world-traveling public speaker who had paid his debts. His words and sayings echoed that week and would continue to echo.

Twain left an estate valued the following year at a hefty $471,136, placing him among the top 1% or 2% of wealthiest Americans. (That sum equals about $15 million today.)

In his will written in 1909, he bequeathed his entire fortune to his two daughters but only Clara was alive to claim it. Tucked away in the legal document was Twain's final comment on his financial misadventures. He stipulated that the gift to his daughter be "free from any control or interference on the part of any husband she may have."

Acknowledgments

A nyone who tackles Twain must offer deep salaams to the Mark Twain Project at University of California, Berkeley. The bright quiet airy room in Bancroft Library offers one-stop shopping for almost all Twain letters, notebooks, photos (either in copies or originals). The scope is staggering and daunting, and sparked a very long stay for me at the Rodeway Inn a mile away. All that's missing at MTP is what Twain ate for breakfast on September 28, 1873. And that might be there too, for all I know.

My deepest thanks to *all* the scholars and potentates there, especially Victor Fischer and Sharon Goetz and former do-all assistant Neda Salem. Welcome to new assistant Melissa Martin.

The Clifton Waller Barrett collection at the University of Virginia also packs a very large and fine array of key Twain material. And the websites of both collections make leaving home most days (or getting dressed) optional.

Speaking of the Internet, Barbara Schmidt delivers encyclopedic lively pages on dozens upon dozens of eclectic Twain topics. She is a fount at www.twainquotes.com.

One of the hardest parts of writing this book revolved around sorting out Twain's finances. Did the great author skirt the law with his asset transfer to Livy? University of Pennsylvania professor David A. Skeel tolerated my e-mails and taught me much about 1890s bankruptcy practices. As did Jim Millstein, a corporate and sovereign debt expert, and so did Leon Bayer, veteran bankruptcy lawyer in Los Angeles. They helped; any mistakes are mine (or maybe Twain's).

I want to extend sincere gratitude to Nathaniel Ball at Elmira College and Kevin MacDonnell, rare book dealer, for the Pond photographs; to printer Richard L. Hopkins for the Paige typesetter answers; to Professor Jay Cook of the University of Michigan for insights about round-the-world performers; and to Debra Charpentier of the H.H. Rogers Collection at the Millicent Library. Thanks also to Ann Causey at the University of Virginia; David Flegg at State Library of Victoria, Australia; Natalie Russell at the Huntington Library in Santa Barbara; Jean Rose at Random House UK (which bought Chatto & Windus); Cindy Lovell, executive director at the Mark Twain House; and to Anna Petersen at the Hocken Collection in New Zealand.

Grazie to my family, as always. At least you had Twain quotes to listen to . . . along with the Webster balance sheets.

Ultimate thanks to Esther Newberg and to my editor and friend, Bill Thomas. He highlighted, in the margin of my manuscript, Twain's quote: "A successful book is not made of what is *in* it, but of what is left *out* of it." I think he would like me to convey that message to his other authors and to the rest of the world.

Readers, you can reach me at rzacks@forbiddenknowledge.com or via www.richardzacks.com.

Appendix

MARK TWAIN'S ASSIGNMENT PROCEEDINGS FOR CHARLES L. WEBSTER & CO.
For the math-minded, here are exact *detailed* debt and repayment figures, numbers
that Mark Twain never fully grasped.

DEBT

Charles L. Webster & Co. debts approved by assignee Bainbridge Colby: $79,704.80

REPAYMENT

Pd. from Webster assets by Colby (20% of debt) to 101 creditors	$15,940.96	May 16, 1895
Pd. by C. Langdon to Russell & Sons (balance of 80%)	$4,295.85	July 14–20, 1895
Pd. by Twain (30% of debt) to 44 creditors who accepted 50% assignment plan	$7,354.43	before Oct. 1896
Pd. by Colby to Mt. Morris Bank	$250.00	Dec. 18, 1896
Pd. by Colby (7.696% of debt) to 56 creditors[1]	$3,824.18	April 3, 1897
Pd. by Twain (installment to level 97[2] creditors at 75% of debt)	$7,653.00	Dec. 6, 1897
Pd. by Twain to 97 creditors (final 25% installment of debt)	$6,648.33	Feb. 9, 1898
Pd. by Twain to Mt. Morris Bank (22.4%) to put bank at $15,000 pd.	$6,612.46	Feb. 24–26, 1898
Pd. from Fred Hall's acct. to Mt. Morris Bank	$136.18	Feb. 24–26, 1898
Forgiven by Mt. Morris Bank (via H.H. Rogers)	$14,370.82	Feb. 24–26, 1898
Pd. by Twain to Barrows (72.304% balance)	$11,147.04	July 9, 1898
Balance owed to Mrs. Grant and apparently forgiven	$1,471.55	

---

[1] Forty-four creditors had received a 50% settlement, and Russell had been paid in full. So Colby gave $2,309.09 (the 7.696% due to these forty-five creditors) to Charles Langdon, presumably to reimburse him for some of the money he had paid to settle with Russell. (This sum should not be included in the totals above.) Colby's handling confused even Katherine Harrison, H.H.'s nimble assistant.

[2] Four others—Thomas Russell, Mount Morris Bank, Barrow family and Julia D. Grant—were not included.

Notes

ABBREVIATIONS

FE	Mark Twain, *Following the Equator: A Journey Around the World*
HH	H.H. Rogers
Lifetime with MT	Katy Leary and Mary Lawton, *A Lifetime with Mark Twain: The Memories of Katy Leary, for Thirty Years His Faithful and Devoted Servant*
LL	Dixon Wecter, editor, *Love Letters of Mark Twain*
MT	Mark Twain
MT–Howells	Henry Smith and William Gibson, editors, *Mark Twain–Howells Letters: The Correspondence of Samuel L. Clemens and William Dean Howells, 1872–1910*
MT–HH	Lewis Leary, editor, *Mark Twain's Correspondence with Henry Huttleston Rogers, 1893–1909*
MT-Int	Gary, Scharnhorst, *Mark Twain: The Complete Interviews*
MTP	Mark Twain Papers & Project, University of California, Berkeley
My Father	Clara Clemens, *My Father, Mark Twain*
NB	Typed notebook transcript, MTP
UVA	Barrett Collection, University of Virginia

PROLOGUE

1   "Think of it. George Washington": NB, 35:55.

1   "corkscrewing in and out": All quotes about the Darjeeling rail trip are taken from *FE*, 535–43.

3   "Jean, darling, look on the map": Olivia Clemens (hereafter Livy) to Jean Clemens, Feb. 16, 1896, MTP.

4   "I have a perfect *horror*": Livy to Susan Crane, Apr. 22, 1894, MTP.

CHAPTER 1: JOYS OF SELF-PUBLISHING

5   "[He] and I always meet": *Autobiography of Mark Twain* (ed. Harriet Elinor Smith), 1:106.

6   "I have never felt so desperate in my life": MT to Fred Hall, July 19 and 30, 1893, MTP.

6   "not be called upon": Contract between MT, Charles Webster, and all, Apr. 1, 1887, MTP.

7   "daily issue of un-medicated closet": MT to Webster, May 10, 1885, Samuel C. Webster, *Mark Twain, Business Man*, 323.

7   "no words in which to paint": Quoted in Scharnhorst, *Twain in His Own Time*, 152.

7   "guesswork" with "brains": MT to Hall, Jan. 11, 1889, Clemens Papers, Berg Collection.

8   "The faster installment": Hall to A. B. Paine, Jan. 14, 1909, quoted in *Twainian* (1947) 6:2.

8   "lingering suicide": Autobiographical dictation, June 2, 1906, MTP.

8   "I want to sell": MT to Hall, June 26, 1893, Clemens Papers, Berg Collection.

9   "the billows of hell": MT to Livy, Sept. 17, 1893, *LL*, 270.

9   "they were not moved": MT to Livy, Feb. 15, 1894, MTP.

10   "[Dr. Rice] told me": MT to Livy, Sept. 17, 1893, MTP.

10   "six minutes": Ibid.

11   "mutual envy": Conversation with Debra Charpentier, archivist, Henry H. Rogers Collection, Millicent Library, Fairhaven, MA.

11   "I didn't care if he was an Archangel": MT to Livy, Sept. 21, 1893, *LL*, 273.

12   "A child should have seen it": MT to Livy, Sept. 28, 1893, *LL*, 274.

12   "I am horribly homesick": MT to Clara, Sept. 30, 1893, MTP.

12   "Sometimes I seem to foresee": MT to Livy, Sept. 28, 1893, *LL*, 274.

12   "He detested the thought": *My Father*, 139.

12   "It was not purely perdition for him": W. D. Howells, quoted in Scharnhorst, *Twain in His Own Time*, 229.

CHAPTER 2: PRINTING MOGUL

13   "the Shakespeare of mechanical invention": *Autobiography of Mark Twain* (ed. Harriet Elinor Smith), 1:124.

13   "He visited me every few days": *Autobiography of Mark Twain* (ed. Charles Neider), 230.

14   "ever look at a stock report again": MT to Webster, Apr. 25, 1884, Webster, *Mark Twain, Business Man*, 251.

14   "Let Marsh send me a statement": MT to Webster, Aug. 9, 1882, Ibid., 193.

14   "I was only about half as big": Albert B. Paine, *Mark Twain: A Biography*, 76.

14   **"EUREKA!"**: *Mark Twain's Notebooks & Journals*, vol. 3:441.

15   "At 12:20 this afternoon": MT to Orion Clemens, Jan. 5, 1889, MTP.

16   "And there in Kentucky": Twain, *The Gilded Age*, 14.

16   longest patent application: Paige's three linked patent applications yield this page total. His single application (No. 547,860) nicknamed "The Whale" was the longest at 218 pages, in an era when many applications, such as Mark Twain's Scrapbook (No. 140,245), tallied less than 10 pages.

16   "small, plump and well-formed": *Boston Daily Globe*, June 10, 1892.

17   "What a talker he is": Apr. 23, 1893, NB, 33:10.

17   "handsome": Ibid., 9.

18   "Well, Livy darling": MT to Livy, Dec. 9, 1893, *LL*, 282.

18   "darling back porch": MT to Livy, Dec. 25, 1893, MTP.

19   "Merry Xmas! Promising progress": MT to Livy, telegram, Dec. 25, 1893, MTP.

20   "Now I tell you": MT to Livy, Dec. 28–29,1893, MTP.

20 "courteous but firm": MT to Livy, Jan. 12, 1894, *LL*, 290.

20 "I came up to my room": MT to Livy, Jan. 15, 1894, Ibid., 293.

20 "There are people who": Jan. 15, 1894, NB, 33:48.

20 "Wedding-news": Feb. 2, 1894, NB, 33:51.

CHAPTER 3: SAFE EGGS AND BROKEN EGGS

21 "Put all your eggs": NB, 33:8.

21 "Familiarity breeds": Ibid., 33:55, 33:59.

21 "It nearly killed the fifteen": MT to Livy, Feb. 7, 1894, MTP.

22 "I intend that some of the things": Livy to HH, Feb. 14, 1894, quoted in *MT–HH*, 39.

22 "He was as shy": MT to Livy, Feb. 11–13, 1894, MTP.

24 "hereby sell, assign, transfer": March 9, 1894, MT asset transfer to Livy, signed by HH, UVA. David Skeel, a corporate law professor at the University of Pennsylvania who specializes in debt, called Twain's maneuver a classic "fraudulent transfer"; James Millstein, who handled the AIG bankruptcy, concurred, as did bankruptcy attorney Leon Bayer, who studied the Twain case. Although Webster & Co. owed Livy $70,000, she was not entitled to what lawyers call "preferred" status over the claims of other creditors, such as the Barrow family, owed $15,000. These experts stated that the creditors would have had solid grounds under 1895 law for going to court to try to claw back the assets from Twain's wife. Most Twain biographers, however, have stated that this shady maneuver (orchestrated by H.H. Rogers) occurred within normal bankruptcy proceedings with the blessing of the creditors. Curiously, Twain's notebook covering this time period is missing.

25 "electrical treatment": MT to HH, Aug. 25, 1894, *MT–HH*, 71.

25 "The world looks so attractive": Susy to Clara, Aug. 10, 1894, MTP.

26 "He told me the other day": Susy Clemens, *Papa*, 101.

26 "How I hate that name": Grace King quoting Susy in Scharnhorst, *Twain in His Own Time*, 180.

26 "an angel's visit": Livy to MT, Apr. 10, 1894, MTP.

27 "[Hall] could hardly keep": MT to Livy, Apr. 20, 1894, *LL*, 299.

28 "The assignment was": *New York Tribune*, Apr. 19, 1894, 1.

28 "Such property as Mr. Clemens has": *New York Times*, Apr. 20, 1894; *New York Herald*, Apr. 19, 1894, 1.

28 "Mark Twain's latest is not a joke": *Brooklyn Eagle*, Apr. 19, 1894, 4.

29 "But I have a perfect *horror*": Livy to Susan Crane, Apr. 22, 1894, MTP.

30 "Don't let it disturb": MT to Livy, Apr. 22, 1894. MTP

30 "I hope your business": James Pond to MT, Apr. 19, 1894, MTP.

30 "Except when I think of you": MT to Livy, Apr. 22, 1894, MTP.

31 "Nobody finds the slightest": MT to Livy, May 4, 1894, *LL*, 301.

31 "My darling, I note": MT to Livy, July 23, 1894, *LL*, 305–6.

31 "Hard conditions": MT to Livy, May 4, 1894, *LL*, 301.

31 "commercial matters": Fred Hall to A. B. Paine, Jan. 14, 1909, quoted *Twainian* (1947) 6:2.

32 "It was confoundedly difficult": MT to Livy, May 4, 1894, *LL*, 301.

32 "Thank you for being glad": Livy to Alice H. Day, May 23, 1894, MTP.

32 "Mr. Rogers tried to tell me": MT to Livy, July 17, 1894, *LL*.

33 "If I were over there": Livy to MT, July 31, 1894, *LL*, 308–9.

34 "Suppose father had been": MT to Livy, July 23, 1894, *LL*, 306.

34 "a tall, lean, skinny": Autobiographical dictation, Feb. 21, 1906, MTP.

CHAPTER 4: THE TRIALS OF PAIGE AND JOAN OF ARC

36 "such an incredibly small coop": MT to HH, Aug. 25, 1894, *MT–HH*, 71.

36 "This is a book which writes itself": MT to HH, Sept. 2–3, 1894, Ibid., 73.

37 "congestion of the right lung": MT to HH, Oct. 5, 1894, Ibid., 80.

37 "Would you think a person": MT to HH, Oct. 7, 1894, Ibid., 81–82.

39 "When the machine": MT to HH, Nov. 2, 1894, Ibid., 89.

39 "large, rambling, quaint": Albert B. Paine, *Mark Twain: A Biography*, 989–90.

40 "With a *concealed* machine": MT to HH, Nov. 7, 1894, *MT–HH*, 92.

40 "I am putting in these dull hours": MT to HH, Nov. 21, 1894, Ibid., 97.

40 "That would have been *fore*sight": MT to HH, Nov. 28, 1894, Ibid., 98.

41 "The sight of Joan": Twain, *Personal Recollections of Joan of Arc*, 212.

41 "I *seemed* to be entirely expecting": MT to HH, Dec. 22, 1894, *MT–HH*, 108.

43 "I am 59 years old": MT to HH, Dec. 27, 1894, Ibid., 112.

43 "Certainly it was a marvelous invention": Paine, *Mark Twain: A Biography*, 991.

44 "Nothing daunts Mrs. Clemens": MT to HH, Dec. 27, 1894, *MT–HH*, 114.

44 "Meantime the thing for me": MT to HH, Jan. 21, 1895, Ibid., 118–19.

44 "No man can say aught": *Alta California* (San Francisco), July 21, 1867.

45 "Man will do many things": *FE*, 206.

45 "Don't disappoint us": MT to HH, Feb. 8–9, 1895, *MT–HH*, 129.

CHAPTER 5: AN ODD HOMECOMING

46 "cyclonic blasts": *Harper's Weekly*, Feb. 23, 1895, 174.

47 "kiss you *hard* on that little": Susy Clemens, *Papa*, 15.

48 "It was decided": *My Father*, 136.

48 "There is more artistic feeling": Max O'Rell, "Mark Twain and Paul Bourget," 307.

49 "The Americans are lions": Max O'Rell, *A Frenchman in America*, 86.

49 "one love which a Frenchman places": NB, 42:70.

49 "There is a moral sense": Ibid., 39:8.

49 "The population of the world": Ibid., 39:21.

50 "Livy, darling when I arrived": MT to Livy, March 20, 1895, *LL*, 312.

51 "Don't Know": *My Father*, 4.

51 "Hartford is resounding": MT to Livy, March 21, 1895, *LL*, 313.

52 "a number of people": MT to HH, Apr. 7, 1895, *MT–HH*, 138.

52 "We were to have stopped": MT to HH, Apr. 14, 1895, Ibid., 141.

52 "At first I thought": MT to Franklin Whitmore, March 27, 1895, Ibid., 134.

54 "Mr. C[lemens] looks": George Warner to Lilly Warner, May 21, 1895, MTP.

55 "as big as a turkey's egg": MT to Robert U. Johnson, May 30, 1895, MTP.

CHAPTER 6: NOT ENOUGH TIME TO CURSE

56 "tedious, witless": Autobiographical fragment, "Something about Doctors," MTP.

57 "sloughed out": MT to James Pond, June 19, 1895, Clemens Papers, Berg Collection.

57 "We are determining": MT to HH, June 4, 1895, *MT–HH*, 150.

57 "Always obey your parents": "Advice to Youth," Apr. 15, 1882, *Mark Twain Speaking* (ed. Fatout), 169.

58 "I guess I am out of the field": MT to James Redpath, May 10, 1870, MTP.

58 "Oh, Cable": Quoted in Fred W. Lorch, *The Trouble Begins at Eight*, 171.

59   "All of which": Twain, "How to Tell a Story," *Best Short Stories of Mark Twain* (ed. Berkove), 340.

59   "To be good is noble": *FE*, frontispiece.

60   "The chief feature": MT to James Pond, June 11, 1895, Clemens Papers, Berg Collection.

60   "Mark Twain is to-day": MT's tour promotional pamphlet, 1895.

61   "The Century people": MT to HH, June 15, 1895, *MT–HH*, 152.

61   "To be virile": MT to Frank H. Scott, June 18, 1895, Ibid., 153.

61   "Try as you may": Twain, Mark. "Taming the Bicycle," MTP.

61   "flat": Robert Johnson to Richard W. Gilder, July 9, 1895, MTP.

61   "careless servants": Livy to Franklin Whitmore, June 18, 1895, MTP.

62   "I have found it": MT to Frank Fuller, July 6, 1895, MTP.

62   asked whether he must "obey": MT to HH, June 26, 1895, *MT–HH*, 157.

63   "I know that Mr. Clemens": Livy to HH, June 27, 1895, Ibid., 158–59.

63   "If Colby had": MT to HH, June 29, 1895, Ibid., 159.

64   "Mrs. C. is dead-set": MT to HH, June 30, 1895, Ibid., 161.

64   "telephone message from town": MT to HH, July 8, 1895, Ibid., 164.

64   "It is mighty good": MT to HH, July 5, 1895, Ibid., 163.

64   "I shan't be able": MT to HH, July 8, 1895, Ibid., 165.

CHAPTER 7: TWAIN GRILLED, LIVY BURNT

65   "would not permit": Quotes from *New York Herald, New York Sun, New York Times,* and *New York Tribune,* July 12–13, 1895.

68   "[Mark Twain] was supposed": *Publishers Weekly,* July 27, 1895.

69   wide-ranging subpoena: Subpoena to Olivia Clemens, Clemens papers, Box 7, UVA.

69   "comical defeat": MT to HH, July 14, 1895, *MT–HH,* 167.

69   "It may have been a mistake": HH to MT, July 16, 1895, Ibid., 169.

69   "Mr. Rushmore thinks": MT to HH, July 14, 1895, Ibid., 166.

70   "I shall do everything": HH to MT, July 16, 1895, Ibid., 168, quoting July 15 telegram.

71   "I can't make any more": MT to Pamela Moffett, July 14, 1895, MTP.

71   "The maid certainly has": Clara to Pamela Moffett, July 6, 1895, MTP.

71   "badly fatigued": Major James L. Pond's observations in July and August are all taken from his calendar entries in *Eccentricities of Genius*.

72   "a jumble of vulgar compliments": *Autobiography of Mark Twain* (ed. Neider), 165.

73   "I was solicited": *Cleveland Plain Dealer,* July 19, 1895, quoted in *Mark Twain Speaking* (ed. Fatout), 279.

73   "Why, with their scufflings": MT to HH, July 16, 1895, *MT–HH,* 171.

73   "I shan't attempt to go": *Mark Twain Speaking* (ed. Fatout), 286.

74   "Pond never deals": MT to Charles L. Webster, Jan. 4, 1887, *Mark Twain's Letters to His Publishers* (ed. Hill), 212.

74   "Pond is not an interesting liar": MT to William D. Howells, July 3, 1899, *Mark Twain–Howells Letters,* 704.

75   "sunny, balmy, perfectly delicious": Twain's travel observations, NB, 35:9.

76   lawsuit had been "silenced": MT to HH, July 20, 1895, *MT–HH,* 172.

76   "They never made a prophecy": MT to HH, July 29, 1895, Ibid., 176.

77   "head idiot of this century": MT to HH, Oct. 20, 1896, Ibid., 242.

CHAPTER 8: AMERICA: DRY RUN FOR THE WORLD

79   "poor little modest mama": Susy to Clara Clemens, July 30, 1895, MTP.

79   "best Hungarian fancy brands": Karl Baedeker, *United States*, 329.

80   "There it is": *Mark Twain Speaking*, 516.

80   "You do not recognize": Ibid., 167–68.

80   "I know who wrote *Tom Sawyer*": *Minneapolis Journal*, July 23, 1895; *MT-Int*, 155.

80   "His talk—I encountered him": Quoted in Rodney, *Mark Twain Overseas*, 238.

80   "Why, I was in": *Minneapolis Penny Press*, July 23, 1895; *MT-Int*, 159.

81   "The trouble begins": Fred Lorch, *The Trouble Begins at Eight*, frontispiece.

81   "swallow-tail": *Minneapolis Times*, July 24, 1895. 1–2. Includes performance text.

84   "And that brings me by the same process": *Minneapolis Times*'s version of speech, combined with Twain's edits for public reading in *Adventures of Huckleberry Finn* (ed. Walter Blair and Victor Fischer), Appendix D.

87   "In a crucial moral emergency": NB, 35:34.

87   "I am getting": MT to HH, July 24, 1895, *MT–HH*, 174.

87   "I can stand considerable petting": MT to Livy, Jan. 4, 1894, MTP.

CHAPTER 9: TRAVELING WITH A VOLCANO

88   "It is impossible": Livy to Annie Trumbull, Aug. 19, 1895, MTP.

88   "There is the peace": NB, 35:17.

89   "a little unreasonable": James Pond, *Overland with Mark Twain*, 7.

90   "A single crying infant": Karl Baedeker, *The United States*, xx.

90   "the crystal-clear atmosphere": NB, 35:18.

90   "The horse fell on him": Ibid., 35:19.

91   "[Butte] is a fearful place": "The Story of Copper" by Charles F. Speare in *American Monthly Review of Reviews* 34 (1906): 566.

91   "compact, intellectual": NB, 35:20.

92   "Crab Town": *The Official Northern Pacific Railroad Guide*, 247.

92   "Parties of 50": NB, 35:22.

93   "colored": Ibid., 35:23; Pond, *Overland*, 9.

94   "Now you are to come": MT to HH, July 5, 1895, *MT–HH*, 163.

95   "Splendid big negro": NB, 35:23.

95   "Lovely & oft majestic": Ibid., 35:24.

96   "buildings ten stories high": Pond, *Overland*, 10.

96   "As we passed": James B. Pond, *Eccentricities of Genius*, 217.

97   "perpetual smoker": Ibid., 219.

98   "Uncle Sam is still": Samuel Moffett to Mary Moffett, Aug. 9, 1895, MTP.

98   "She was a beautiful woman": Pond, *Overland*, 12.

99   "Splendid house": NB, 35:27.

99   "overflowing with": Samuel Moffett to Mary Moffett, Aug. 11, 1895, MTP.

100   "Such a fearful": NB, 35:328.

100   "Never mind": *San Francisco Examiner*, Aug. 24, 1895; *MT-Int*, 190–92.

104   "cannot permit 'an' hospital": MT to Andrew Chatto, July 22, 1897, MTP.

104   "I am idle until": *San Francisco Examiner*, Aug. 17, 1895; *MT-Int*, 185–86.

106   "too grave": MT to Sam Moffett, Nov. 10, 1895, MTP.

106   "We all like so much": Clara Clemens to Sam Moffett, Aug. 17, 1895, MTP.

107   "I've signed a lot": MT to HH, June 4, 1895, *MT–HH*, 149.

108   "that paltering ass": MT to HH, Sept. 27, 1896, Ibid., 237.

108 "Prosperity is the best": Pudd'nhead maxims from *FE*.
109 "It may seem strange": Pamela Moffett to Samuel Moffett, Sept. 6, 1895, MTP.

CHAPTER 10: SEPARATION

111 "he could easily develop": MT to HH, Aug. 17, 1895, *MT-HH*, 183.
111 "Your conscience": Kipling in *New York Herald*, Aug 17, 1890; *MT-Int*, 117–26.
112 "Hydrophobia, seamanship & agriculture": NB, 35:29.
112 "He was a constant surprise": Clara Clemens, "My Father," 21.
113 "The smoke is so dense": MT to HH, Aug. 19, 1895, *MT–HH*, 186.
114 "I wish they would always": NB, 35:32.
115 "Pond is superannuated": MT to HH, Sept. 13–15, 1895, *MT–HH*, 188.
115 "She looked dingy": James Pond to Samuel Moffett, Aug. 27, 1895, MTP.
115 "Dear little spider": Susy to Clara Clemens, Aug. 10, 1895, MTP.

CHAPTER 11: AT SEA

117 "Father was like": *My Father*, 142.
118 "He did not smoke or chew tobacco": *FE*, 27.
118 "When I was a youth": Ibid., 33.
118 "Notice has been put": NB, 35:42, 43, 46.
119 "A SPLENDID ORCHESTRA": Fred Lorch, *The Trouble Begins at Eight*, frontispiece.
119 "In other cities": Lorch, *Trouble*, 277, 279–80.
120 "When these islands": Ibid., 277.
120 "He told the truth": *Pacific Commercial Advertiser*, Sept. 2, 1895.
121 "Honolulu lights were": Livy to Susy Clemens, Aug. 30–31, 1895, MTP.
121 "Oahu just as silky": NB, 35:39.
121 "Ain't there *any*body": Ibid., 35:46.
122 "Kodak fiend": *Pacific Commercial Advertiser*, Sept. 4, 1895.
122 "I was rather afraid": Livy to Susy Clemens, Aug. 30–31, 1895, MTP.
122 "brain-fever" nightmares: Clara Clemens to Sam Moffett, Nov. 12, 1895, MTP.
122 "Aunt Rachel": NB, 35:7.
123 "Fifty years from now": Ibid., 35:54.
123 "I think it unlikely": *FE*, 71.
124 "I used to remember": Charles Webster, *Mark Twain, Business Man*, 397.
124 "They were there eating": *FE*, 75.
124 "Was it possible": *My Father*, 142.
124 "cannibal fork": NB, 35:48.
124 "is pretty cheerful": Livy to Susan Crane, Sept. 5, 1895, MTP.
125 "Why, look at England": *Tom Sawyer Abroad*, 144.

CHAPTER 12: GREETINGS, MATE

126 "Don't forget my soulful": *Sydney Morning Herald*, Sept. 16, 1895.
126 "labyrinth of bays and channels": William J. Galloway, *Advanced Australia*, 70.
126 "Do you think": *Sydney Evening News*, Sept. 16, 1895.
127 "No shyness": NB, 34:15.
128 "undersized": *Melbourne Argus* and *Sydney Morning Herald*, Sept. 17, 1895.

129   "with a rakish curl": *Sydney Daily Telegraph*, Sept. 17, 1895.

129   "rattle and bustle": *Melbourne Australasian*, Sept. 21, 1895.

129   "My instinct teaches": *Sydney Daily Telegraph*, Sept. 17, 1895.

130   "Glory of my life": Herbert Low, *Worker*, Apr. 2, 1908, quoted in Shillingsburg, *At Home Abroad*, 28.

131   "The surroundings are made": *Melbourne Australasian*, Sept. 21, 1895.

131   "picturesque little figure stole out": *Sydney Morning Herald* and *Sydney Evening News*, Sept. 20, 1895.

132   all five stories: "Corpse" had appeared in *Innocents Abroad* (chap. 18); "Mexican Plug" in *Roughing It* (chap. 24); "Grandfather's Old Ram" also in *Roughing It* (chap. 53); Huck and Jim on the raft in *Huckleberry Finn* (chap. 16); and "Terrors of the German Language" in *A Tramp Abroad* (Appendix D).

132   "And next I should feel": NB, 35:33; Twain, *Roughing It*, chap. 53; *Autobiography of Mark Twain* (ed. Smith), 3:167; *Minneapolis Times*, July 24, 1895.

136   "[The] dog [is] an instrument": *Autobiography* (ed. Smith), 3:171.

137   "If [the] Viennese ladies": *My Father*, 192–93.

138   "awkward utterer": MT to Thomas B. Aldrich, Jan. 28, 1871, MTP.

138   "I detest him because": *Melbourne Argus*, Sept. 17, 1895.

139   "I suppose life can never": O'Rell, "MT and Paul Bourget," *North American Review*, March 1895, 304–5.

140   "large subject": *Melbourne Evening News*, Sept. 26, 1895.

140   "I hope it was nothing critical": *Sydney Sunday Times*, Sept. 22, 1895.

140   "We have had a darling": MT to HH, Sept. 25, 1895, *MT–HH*, 188.

CHAPTER 13: CASHING IN ON THE PLATYPUS

141   "the biting cold": *FE*, 152–53.

141   "I believe in early rising": *Melbourne Herald Standard*, Sept. 26, 1895.

142   "Convictoria": NB, 35:56.

142   "The Pope invites us": *Melbourne Argus*, Sept. 24, 1895.

144   "at a bad stage": NB, 34:20.

144   "Let one of us be far": *Mark Twain Speaking* (ed. Fatout), 295; *Wellington Post* [NZ], Nov. 9, 1895.

145   "I felt that sort of feeling": Gathered from the *Melbourne Argus*, Oct. 1, 1895, *Queenslander*, Oct. 19, 1895, and *Hobart Mercury*, Nov. 2, 1895; Shillingsburg, *At Home Abroad*, 45–46; NB, 35:32–33; MT to Jack Harrington, Aug. 28, 1895, MTP; Parsons, "Mark Twain in Australia," *Antioch Review* (Winter 1961): 462–64.

148   "idiotic" advertising mix-up: NB, 35:55.

149   "It is the loftiest": Ibid., 35:56.

149   grateful to Dr. Fitzgerald: By the time Twain dictated his autobiography, he convinced himself Dr. Fitzgerald had cured him in a day.

149   "The Lidy will be down": Livy to Susan Crane, Nov. 3, 1895, MTP.

150   "One is not required": NB, 35:57.

150   "Stanley of Africa": NB, 40:19.

150   "wretched American women": *Mark Twain's Notebook* (ed. Albert Paine), 209.

150   "The ladies": NB, 35:57.

151   a single dark-skinned aboriginal: Twain, *FE*, 155.

151   "It was an excursion": Ibid., 181.

152   "When the curtain rose": *Adelaide South Australian Register*, Monday, Oct. 14, 1895. (No Sunday newspaper allowed.)

153   "The coat of wool": *FE*, 227.

153   "Bidders like barking dogs": NB, 34:23–24.

154   "I think papa": Livy to Susy Clemens, Oct. 20, 1895, MTP.

154   "I wouldn't go": *My Father*, 128, 147–48.

155   "patriarchal and grave": *FE*, 232.

155   "By and by I was smitten": Twain, *Roughing It*, chap. 26.

156   "No, I've been down on the blankets": *Ballarat Courier*, Oct. 21, 1895.

157   "They will fumigate": NB, 34:19.

157   "Everything runs smoothly": Clara Clemens to Martha Pond, Feb. 18, 1896, MTP.

157   "sedate savant": Carlyle Smythe, "The Real Mark Twain," 30.

159   "The RR is the only": NB, 34:23.

159   "We have come": *Melbourne Age*, Oct. 28, 1895; *Mark Twain Speaking* (ed. Fatout), 300.

160   "He has the mind": Susy Clemens, *Papa*, 89.

160   "saveloys": Shillingsburg, *At Home Abroad*, 118.

160   "He is a very wealthy man": Livy to Susan Crane, Nov. 3, 1895, MTP.

160   "snatching a visit": MT to Henry Harper, Oct. 28, 1895, MTP.

161   "In German, a young lady": *A Tramp Abroad*, 273.

161   "eternal life of goodbyes": Clara Clemens to Sam Moffett, Nov. 12, 1895, MTP.

CHAPTER 14: MAORILAND

162   "All people think": *FE*, 251–52.

163   "No celebrity can": Michael Davitt, *Life and Progress in Australasia*, 337.

164   "And it was in this paradise": *FE*, 281.

164   "glimpse of any convicts": Livy to Susan Crane, Nov. 3, 1895, MTP.

165   "seen men's backs flogged": NB, 34:25.

165   "Convicts were 'assigned'": Ibid., 34:28.

166   "bush-covered hills": Ibid., 34:27.

166   "one of the most interesting": Davitt, *Life and Progress,* 338.

166   "great deal of creaking": Livy to Susan Crane, Nov. 3, 1895, MTP.

167   "whistling woman": Haweis, *Travel and Talk*, 138–39.

167   "vast level green": *FE*, 287.

168   "Everybody rode horseback": From *Mark Twain Speaking* (ed. Fatout), 51–52; *Otago Times*, Nov. 7, 1895; *Wellington Evening Post*, Dec. 11, 1895; *My Father*, 139.

171   "The tattooing": *FE*, 287–88.

172   "peremptory big frowsy": NB, 34:34.

172   "a beautiful bathing beach": Ibid., 34:37.

172   "[Twain] could certainly": Shillingsburg, *At Home Abroad*, 139–40.

172   "undignified work": Smythe, "The Real Mark Twain," 34.

173   "It is the strangest": NB, 34:34–35.

173   "The fact that man invented imprisonment": NB, 34:35.

173   "you have dropped down": Davitt, *Life and Progress,* 353.

174   "an English dude": Denton and Dillingham, *Incidents of a Collector's Rambles*, 67–68.

174   "Plenty dogs": NB, 34:49.

175   "The lauded chamois": Twain, *A Tramp Abroad*, 233.

175   "There are very few halls": *Queanbeyan Age*, Nov. 16, 1895.

176   "If a person had": *FE*, 298.

176   "As stupid as a Moa": Haweis, *Travel and Talk*, 113.

177   "In our country": *Christchurch Weekly Press*, Nov. 21, 1895; *Bonfort's Wine Circular*, March 25, 1896. The earliest version had "druggist," which the British press changed to "apothecary."

177 "Mr. Clemens does not allow": Livy to Joseph Kinsey, Nov. 21, 1895, MTP.
178 "No towels to wipe with": *My Father,* 151.
178 "I had a cattle-stall": *FE,* 302.
179 "like a telegram": Ibid., 304.
179 "only shipwreck": *My Father,* 152.
180 "Traveling and lecturing": *New Zealand Herald* (Auckland), Nov. 21, 1895. *MT-Int,* 257.
180 "Naturally that makes him": Livy to Susan Crane, Nov. 21, 1895, MTP.

CHAPTER 15: BIRTHDAYS AND LONGING

181 "Nothing could be daintier": *FE,* 311.
182 "I claimed that her": NB, 34:42.
182 "My friend on the right": *Australasian* (Melbourne), Oct. 5, 1895, 43.
183 "the solemn deep": NB, 34:43.
183 "Away down here": MT to Joseph Twichell, Nov. 29, 1895, MTP.
185 "We have enjoyed": Susy to Clara Clemens, Sept. 16, 1895, MTP.
188 "stunning Queen-of-Sheba": NB, 34:45.
188 "Early in the morning": Ibid., 34:46.
189 "had saved so many": *FE,* 321.
189 "Tonight when Mark Twain": *My Father,* 146.
189 "Plenty Maoris here": NB 34:47.
190 "When we got back": Livy to Susy Clemens, Dec. 2, 1895, MTP.
190 "When the white man": NB, 34:52.
190 "Now let us have a storm": NB, 36:2–5.
191 "He said he wished to express": *Barrier Miner* (Broken Hill), Dec. 21, 1895.
191 "By their insane howlings": *Clarence & Richmond Examiner* (Grafton), Dec. 24, 1895.
192 "very large, very wide": Livy to Susan Crane, Dec. 26, 1895, MTP.
192 "bidding Australia good bye": *Sydney Evening News,* Dec. 31, 1895.
192 "One must say it": NB, 36:17–18.
193 paying off his debts: This tally includes lecture income *and* accumulated magazine fees, as well as book royalties.

CHAPTER 16: TO INDIA

194 "an easy flowing tale": Twain shipboard incidents from NB, 37:1–8.
195 "such an oven": Clara Clemens to Jack [no last name cited on letter], Jan. 13, 1896, MTP.
195 "hell-fired cold": MT to HH, Jan. 12, 1896, *MT–HH,* 190.
196 "tortoise shell shoe horn": *Ceylon Observer,* Jan. 14, 1895.
196 "incurable stupidity of man": NB, 36:22
197 "He makes good speed": *FE,* 339.
197 "The most amazing varieties": NB, 36:18.
197 "What a dream": *FE,* 340.
198 "most fascinating": Livy to Susan Crane, January 17–24, 1896, MTP.

CHAPTER 17: BOMBAY!

199 "Father seemed like a young": *My Father,* 153.
200 "The lobbies and halls": *FE,* 348.
201 "The hotel noises": NB, 36:21 (differs from *FE*).
202 "They would sit there": *FE,* 353.
202 "A good travelling servant": *A Handbook for Travellers in India, Burma, and Ceylon,* xv.
202 "well-equipped": NB, 36:24.
202 "something new to play with": *FE,* 359–68. Twain calls him "Pedro" in the notebook and "Manuel" in *FE.*
203 "Had to decline": NB, 36:24.
203 "a capacious briar-root": *Times of India* (Bombay), Jan. 23, 1896; *MT-Int,* 275.
203 "Absolutely, the *most*": Livy to Susan Crane, Jan. 17–24, 1896, MTP.
203 "[Pedro] was a failure": *FE,* 364–65.
204 they called him "Mauzie": Twain called the new servant "Mauzie" in his notebook but "Mousa" and then "Satan" in *FE.*
205 "The ninety minutes": *Times of India,* Jan. 25, 1896, MTP.

CHAPTER 18: EYES WIDE

206 "The barbaric gorgeousnesses": *FE,* 357.
207 "Slambang": NB, 36:23.
207 "Every year the Empress": *FE,* 380.
208 "You have also your demi-gods": Mutalik, *Mark Twain in India,* 107.
208 "These children": *FE,* 383.
208 "The dining room": Livy to Susy Clemens, [undated] quoted in *My Father,* 157.
209 "All right, I'll make it emeralds": NB, 36:25; Carter, "Olivia Clemens Edits Following the Equator," 204.
209 "with the quiet elegancies": *FE,* 369.
210 "When the iron gate": NB, 36:26.
211 "It seemed horrible": Pennefather, *A Visit to India,* 142.
211 "One marvels to see": *Madras Times,* Jan. 31, 1896, MTP.
211 "This is the drive": *FE,* 346.
213 "boy's toes": NB, 36:26.
213 "A club should not": Ibid., 36:25.
214 "trim & comely": Ibid., 36:27–28; *FE,* 386–89.
215 "Father was touched": *My Father,* 156.
215 "a wee brown sprite": *FE,* 369. Twain's notebook and *FE* disagree over the date of the meeting.
216 "Sells indulgences": NB, 36:34.
216 "captivated the serious-minded lad": Khan, *Memoirs of Aga Khan,* 54.
216 "When I had drunk nine cups": Mutalik, *Mark Twain in India,* 129–31; Carter, "Olivia Clemens Edits," 205.

CHAPTER 19: RAILS, RICHES AND ELEPHANTS

218 "We named him": *FE,* 404.
219 "It was a very large": Ibid., 400–403.
219 "Such rows as went": *My Father,* 159.

220 "These silent crowds": *FE,* 403.
221 "drawn by picture-book horses": *My Father,* 159.
221 "intensely Indian": *FE,* 407.
221 "I took a ride": Ibid., 411.
222 "Father seated": *My Father,* 154.
222 "We were never free": Ibid., 161.
223 "mixed modern": *FE,* 412.
223 "Some of the little": *My Father,* 155.
224 "When we came back": *FE,* 448.
224 "Slept all the way": NB, 36:33.

CHAPTER 20: HOLY CITIES

225 "a mistake somewhere": MT to Dr. Sidney Smith, Feb. 1, 1896, MTP.
226 "I missed": *FE,* 459.
226 "Should have had": NB, 36:38.
226 "A loin-cloth": *FE,* 460.
226 "[Satan] got out of the train": Ibid., 587–90.
228 "Kindly forward": NB, 36:35.
228 "Apparently the European": Ibid., 36:37.
228 "For the forbidden fruit": Ibid., 36:35; the last line is quoted from the *Times of India,* Jan. 25, 1896, MTP.
229 "It was a curious": *FE,* 467.
229 "with a pair of dead": NB, 36:36.
230 "beyond imagination": *FE,* 469.
230 "The sand is literally": Gordon-Cumming, *In the Himalayas and on the Indian Plains,* 83.
230 "a man who hasn't": NB, 36:38.
231 "horrible dwarf": Caine, *Picturesque India,* 375.
231 "fakeers in plenty": *FE,* 473.
231 "gave him a wild and demonish": Carpenter, *From Adam's Peak to Elephanta,* 266.
232 "We could have found": *FE,* 475.
232 "It is not worth": Ibid., 482.
234 "'Very fine looking cattle'": *Calcutta Englishman,* Feb. 8, 1896, MTP.
234 "I think one would": *FE,* 497.
235 "There is hardly": Ricalton, *India Through the Stereoscope,* 189.
235 "Sometimes they hoisted": *FE,* 502.
236 "I see a Hindu": *Calcutta Englishman,* Feb. 8, 1896; *MT-Int,* 286.
236 "He got me so nervous": *FE,* 504.
237 "Go to **The Well of Fate**": Twain's pilgrim guide: *FE,* 484–94.
239 "Dying man couldn't make": *Mark Twain's Notebooks & Journals,* 3:538.
239 "much study": "Living god": *FE,* 507–13.
240 "toothless": Delight Sweetser, *One Way Round the World,* 191–92.
240 "The Hindoo has a childish": *FE,* 493–94.
241 "a sedate savant": Smythe, "The Real Mark Twain," 30.
241 "In 2 years": NB, 36:57.

CHAPTER 21: THE HEART OF THE BRITISH RAJ

243 "exasperating colds": MT to Susy Clemens, Feb. 7, 1896, MTP, quoted in H. Ahluwalia, "Mark Twain's Lecture Tour in India," 13.

244 "That will be my first": MT to HH, Feb. 8, 1896, *MT–HH*, 193–94.

244 "The electric light": *A Handbook for Travellers in India, Burma, and Ceylon*, 60.

245 "When one considers": *Calcutta Englishman*, Feb. 8, 1896; *MT-Int*, 286–87.

246 "My courage has been tested": *Calcutta Englishman*, Feb. 11, 1896, quoted in Ahluwalia, "Mark Twain's Lecture Tour in India," 24. (Pronouns shifted to first person, and pauses inserted.)

247 "proud or ashamed": "Our Note Book," *Bengal Tiger*, Feb. 29, 1896, 1–2. Coverage of Twain and the tournament.

249 "What is a crusade?" Version from *Mark Twain Speaking* (ed. Fatout), 285–86.

250 "Several had to": NB, 36:44.

251 "It is a fluted candlestick": *FE*, 517.

251 "Sir David Ochterlony": Biography, Massachusetts Historical Society, http://www
.masshist.org/database/822.

251 "The last thing": NB, 41:15.

CHAPTER 22: HIMALAYAN JOY RIDE

252 "easy chairs, sofas": Livy to Jean Clemens, Feb. 16, 1896, MTP.

252 "Sound sleep": NB, 36:44, 48–49.

253 "All day long": Sweetser, *One Way Round the World*, 179.

253 "a snake": Gordon-Cumming, *In the Himalayas and on the Indian Plains*, 544.

253 "on special occasions": *Murray's*, 270.

254 "a man who conversed": MT to Charles Webb, Feb. 16, 1896, MTP.

254 "The [rail]road is infinitely": *FE*, 529.

255 "prepared for grand emotions": Chevrillon, *Dans L'Inde*, 81, 83.

255 "lost its head entirely": NB, 36:39.

255 "You surely can't": *Calcutta Englishman*, Feb. 19, 1896, MTP.

256 "Throngs of Hill people": Caine, *Picturesque India*, 345–56. (Darjeeling).

256 "chaffering": O'Brien, *Darjeeling: The Sanitarium of Bengal*, 36.

257 "I stayed at home": *More Tramps Abroad*, 369.

257 "We did not regret": *My Father*, 162.

257 "We . . . then changed": *FE*, 535–43. (Rail trip).

258 bizarre diagram: NB, 36:49.

259 "We started in rugs": MT to HH, Feb. 17, 1896, *MT–HH*, 195.

CHAPTER 23: MUTINY ON THE GANGES

261 "I went out": Clara Clemens to Martha Pond, Feb. 18, 1896, MTP.

261 "dazzling yellows": Clara Clemens to Pamela Moffett, Feb. 18, 1896, MTP.

262 "One has rather": Eliza Scidmore, *Winter India*, 179.

262 "The military history": *FE*, 550.

263 "policy of unjust": *A Handbook for Travellers in India, Burma, and Ceylon*, lxxii.

263 "Owing to the fire": Ibid., 243.

264 "The last eight or ten": *FE*, 562.

264 "I feel all thro'": NB, 36:51–52.

265   "I said it was a fever": *FE*, 590.
266   "the blackest crime": Ricalton, *India Through the Stereoscope*, 354.
266   "The worst rider": *A Handbook for Travellers in India*, 261.
266   "If they surrendered": Pennefather, *A Visit to India*, 59.
268   "The [Indian people] have acknowledged": Mowbray Thomson, *The Story of Cawn-pore* (London, 1859), 262.
268   "The English see the Hindu": Chevrillon, *Dans L'Inde*, 459.
268   "The color bar[rier]": Khan, *Memoirs of Aga Khan*, 52.
268   "At that moment": NB, 36:53.
269   "You cannot keep": *FE*, 507.
270   "A gust of wind": Ibid., 579–80.
270   "lovely interesting man": Livy to Susan Crane, Feb. 28, 1896, MTP.
271   "The cringing salaam": NB, 36:52.
271   "I offered to depose a Rajah": Ibid., 36:53.
272   "So he had to go": *FE*, 590–91.

CHAPTER 24: FEVERISH IN THE PINK CITY

273   "immediately ordered": NB, 36:54.
273   "soft rich tint": *FE*, 594.
273   "There was always": Ibid., 584–85.
274   "Girls with [Christ]ian": NB, 36:56.
274   "Then the wide street": *FE*, 596.
275   "The Jeypore costume": Sweetser, *One Way Round the World*, 224.
275   "The street juggler looped": Scidmore, *Winter India*, 355.
276   "Every part of the museum": Livy to Jean Clemens, March 10, 1896, MTP.
277   "It was built": *FE*, 583. The "Englishman" part is a bit loose; Colonel James Skinner (1778–1841) was the son of a Rajputana princess, captured at age fourteen, and of a *Scottish* military officer of the East India Company. He spoke Persian and English, founded a famed light cavalry, and had fourteen wives.
277   "It was a fine elephant": *FE*, 582.
278   "For 6 hours": NB, 36:60.
279   "When . . . I think of the list": Livy to Susan Crane, March 30, 1896, MTP.
280   "paleness of countenance": *Madras Standard*, Apr. 1, 1896; *Mark Twain Speaking*, 291–92.
280   "By all accounts": NB, 36:57–58.
281   "The juggler": Mutalik, *Mark Twain in India*, 132–34; NB, 37:19–21.
282   "most perfectly delightful": Susy to Clara Clemens [undated, probably late Jan. or early Feb.], 1896, Hartford (despite "1895" scrawled near top; the events described clearly occurred after Dec. 30, 1895), MTP.

CHAPTER 25: DREAMS AT SEA

285   "The holiday comes": MT to HH, Apr. 24, 1896, *MT–HH*, 209–10.
285   "They called the old": NB, 37:34.
285   "We make fun of poor": Ibid., 37:47.
285   "all the English": Ibid., 37:37.
286   "My own luck": Ibid., 37:11.
286   "There is no mail": *FE*, 616.

286   "wettest place": MT to HH, Apr. 24, 1896, *MT–HH*, 210.
287   "It was as if": *FE*, 635.

CHAPTER 26: AFRICA

289   "sufferings": Smythe, "A Dealer in Brains," *Adelaide Register,* Sept. 28, 1920.
290   "It's pretty lonesome": MT to Livy, May 15, 1896, MTP.
290   "I miss you sadly": Livy to MT, May 19, 1896, MTP.
290   "A gaunt, sickly": *FE,* 664, 667.
291   "short brown blanket": NB, 38:5.
291   "most picturesquely beautiful": MT to Clara Clemens, May 22, 1896, MTP.
291   "How the hell did you": Hammond, *Autobiography of John Hays Hammond,* quoted in Scharnhorst, *Twain in His Own Time,* 207.
291   "When we entered": Smythe, "Dealer in Brains."
292   "death line": NB, 38:12; MT to Livy, May 23–24, 1896, MTP.
292   "enjoying all the intoxicating": *Yorkshire Evening Post,* June 29, 1896.
292   "I have come here": Smythe, "Dealer in Brains."
293   "Can you imagine": Ibid.
293   "the prisoners were furious": NB, 38:33.
293   "He said he felt friendly": Ibid., 38:17.
294   "Mark Twain said the food": Parsons, "Mark Twain: Clubman in South Africa," 248.
294   "hid tins of sardines": NB, 38:23.
294   "What is the secret": *FE,* 709–10.
296   "naked, lazy and polygamous": Brown, *Brown's South Africa,* 73.
296   "Audience composed": NB, 38:11.
296   "I supposed that the climate": *FE,* 72.
296   "man's dose": NB, 38:14.
297   "Talking of patriotism": Ibid., 38:19.
297   "She is small": Ibid., 38:18.
297   "I think the veldt": MT to Livy, June 1, 1896, MTP.
298   "I have been 3 hours": MT to Livy, June 3, 1896, MTP.
298   "I followed a couple": NB, 38:31.
298   "Grouped about the kraal": NB, 38:39.
298   "majority of servants": Brown, *Brown's South Africa,* 23.
299   "thief or a body-snatcher": Twain, "How I Escaped Being Killed in a Duel" in *Every Saturday,* Dec. 21, 1872.
299   "lanky gaspipe": *Bombay Gazette,* Jan. 28, 1896.
299   "On the platform": Twain, "How to Tell a Story," in *How to Tell a Story & Other Essays.*
299   "Ghost made ⅔ of the house": NB, 38:9.
300   "Once 'pon a time": Twain, "How to Tell a Story."
301   "Who's got my golden arm?" *Lifetime with MT,* 22.
301   "This little darkey boy": NB, 38:37.
302   "Ask a man of 50": Ibid., 38:37.
302   "It is no use": MT to Livy, June 10, 1896, MTP.
302   "Is it *possible*": MT to HH, June 6, 1896, *MT–HH,* 216.
302   "All those people": Parsons, "Mark Twain: Traveler in South Africa," 10.
302   "I am glad": *My Father,* 167.
302   "in-Clemens-y of the weather": Parsons, "Mark Twain: Traveler in South Africa," 27.
303   "It seems to me": Livy to Susan Crane, June 16, 1895, MTP.

303 "I wouldn't live": Parsons, "Mark Twain: Traveler," 11.
303 "raw and blustery": Ibid., 27.
303 "a thousand years": *FE,* 712.
303 "region stands paralysed": NB, 38:50.
304 "A great long tow-headed": Ibid., 38:48–49.
304 "The dispatch-writers": Ibid., 38:49.
304 "Sir Frederick Carrington": *Sheffield Independent,* June 8, 1896.
305 "I would have chosen": MT to HH, June 18, 1896, *MT–HH,* 217.
306 "I . . . saw the men deftly": *FE,* 703.
307 "No mining camp": Williams, *The Diamond Mines of South Africa,* 218.
308 "Nothing is so beautiful": *FE,* 708.

CHAPTER 27: REUNITING THE FAMILY

309 "Although I want them": Livy to Susan Crane, June 21, 1896, MTP.
310 "Mr. Clemens feels": Livy to Susan Crane, June 19, 1896, MTP.
310 "I got horribly tired": MT to HH, July [22], 1896, *MT–HH,* 227.
310 "Father luxuriated": *My Father,* 170.
310 "The *main* thing": MT to HH, July [22], 1896, *MT–HH,* 227.
311 "They can talk longer": HH to MT, Apr. 10, 1896, Ibid., 203.
311 "Those Hartford fellows": HH to MT, June 18, 1896, Ibid., 219.
312 "Colby has dropped": HH to MT, March 6, 1896, Ibid., 198.
312 "I'm never going": MT to HH, June 19, 1896, Ibid., 222.
312 "what a puny little weasly": HH to MT, Apr. 10, 1896, Ibid., 206.
312 "Harry's yacht": HH to MT, May 22, 1896, Ibid., 214.
314 "It's about time somebody": MT to HH, Aug. 12, 1896, Ibid., 229.
314 "These he considers": Clara/MT to Andrew Chatto, Aug. [n.d.], 1896, MTP.
315 "Unavoidably delayed": *Lifetime with MT,* 136.
315 "Wait for cablegram": Susy Clemens, *Papa,* 52 (Neider's commentary).
315 "recovery would be long": Ibid.
315 "I am always hiding": MT to Livy, Aug. 16, 1896, MTP.
316 "Susy could not stand": MT to Livy, Aug. 28, 1896, MTP.
316 "It is one of the mysteries": *Autobiography of Mark Twain* (ed. Neider), 323.
316 "He had torn his family": Paine, *Mark Twain: A Biography,* 1021–22.
317 "Rats": *Lifetime with MT,* 134.
318 "Up go the trolley": *Mark Twain's Notebook* (ed. Paine), 319.
318 "In strength I bow": Susy Clemens, *Papa,* 44–47.
319 "I am blind": NB, 39:55.
319 "Reproaching myself": MT to Livy, Aug. 19, 1896, MTP.
321 "There was much more": *My Father,* 171.
321 "Aunt Livy": Samuel Moffett to Mary Moffett, Aug. 23, 1896, MTP.
321 "I told her": *Lifetime with MT,* 138–39.
322 "evil influence of spiritualism": Livy to Alice H. Day, Oct. 22, 1896, MTP.
322 "permanently insane": Samuel Moffett to Mary Moffett, Aug. 20, 1896,
323 "I get a cablegram": MT to Livy, Aug. 28, 1896, MTP.
323 "My remorse does not": MT to Livy, Aug. 29, 1896, MTP.
323 "the eyes of either": MT to HH, Sept. 10, 1896, *MT–HH,* 235.
324 "I don't think": *Lifetime with MT,* 140.

CHAPTER 28: ALONE IN LONDON

325 "un necessary": MT to HH, Dec. 18, 1896, *MT–HH,* 255.

325 "They have lost": MT to William D. Howells, Sept. 24, 1896, *MT-Howells,* 662–63.

325 "It was a long time": *My Father,* 179.

326 "Once the idea": Ibid., 179–80.

326 "lying cheerfulness": MT to William D. Howells, Apr. 2, 1899, *MT-Howells,* 690.

327 "Now my world is dark": Livy to Alice H. Day, Oct., 22, 1896, MTP.

327 "large blonde man": MT to Bram Stoker, Nov. 2, 1896, MTP.

328 "Satan to mix in": MT to HH, Sept. 20, 1896, *MT–HH,* 236.

328 "Poor Jean": *My Father,* 177.

328 "most marvelous": Speech, Apr. 3, 1909, Norfolk, VA; *Mark Twain Speaking* (ed. Fatout), 642.

CHAPTER 29: HELEN KELLER

329 "a monkey": Quoted in Nielsen, *Beyond the Miracle Worker,* 140.

330 "Then Miss Sullivan put": Autobiographical dictation, 1:133, MTP.

330 "Dear Mrs. Rogers": MT to Emilie Rogers, Nov. 26, 1896, *MT–HH,* 253.

332 "I had to pinch": Helen Keller, *Midstream: My Later Life,* 289.

332 "Sometimes it seemed": Ibid., 49.

332 "I hope to enlarge": Dorothy Herrmann, *Helen Keller: A Life,* 168.

333 "It is superb!" MT to Emilie Rogers. Dec. 22, 1896, *MT–HH,* 255–56.

CHAPTER 30: A LONDON REVIVAL

334 "The day came": MT to HH, Jan. 4, 1897, *MT–HH,* 259.

334 "I did not know": MT to Joseph Twichell, Jan. 19, 1897, Ibid., 262.

335 "I am grown so nervous": MT to HH, Feb. 26, 1897, Ibid., 265.

335 "Harper publishes very high-class": MT to HH, Nov. [20], 1896, Ibid.,249.

336 "I am ashamed": MT to HH, Feb. 26, 1897, Ibid., 266.

336 "5:30 pm . . .": MT to HH, March 5, 1897, Ibid., 266.

336 "best friend": Ibid.; MT to HH, March 4, 1894; photo inscription, Nov. 21, 1900, in Messent, *Mark Twain and Male Friendship,* 8; Dias, *Mark Twain and Henry Huttleston Rogers,* 160.

336 "I wrote my last travel book": MT to Howells, Apr. 2, 1899, *MT–Howells,* 690.

337 "**God** want to see you": *FE,* 366.

337 "Classic": *FE,* 241, 699, 132.

337 "Favored above Kings": NB, 42:67, 42:68, 42:68, 41:43, 42:70.

338 "I don't always know": Frank M. White, "Mark Twain as a Newspaper Reporter," 962.

338 "She has nothing": MT to Twichell, Jan. 19, 1897, MTP.

338 "To My Wife Olivia": NB, 41:19.

339 "stench": Carter, "Olivia Clemens Edits," 201.

340 "I have a foreign neighbor": Mutalik, *Mark Twain in India,* 137–38; NB, 41:18.

340 "And there we saw": *FE,* 94.

341 "A trick was": Manuscript of *More Tramps Abroad,* 1230, Berg Collection.

341 "THIS BOOK is": NB, 41:20; MT to HH, Apr. 14, 1897, *MT–HH,* 270.

341 "A successful book": MT to HH, Apr. 26–28, 1897, Ibid., 274.

343 "If Mark Twain dying in poverty": NB, 41:27–28.

343   "James Ross Clemens": White, "Mark Twain as a Newspaper Reporter," 965.

343   "Of course, I am dying": Ibid., 966.

CHAPTER 31: CHARITABLE SCHEMES

344   "Mark Twain Smiling": *New York Herald* coverage, June 13–27, 1897.

346   "I can't retire gracefully": MT to HH, June 16, 1897, *MT–HH*, 283.

346   "In the matter of the *talking* gift": NB, 39:56.

346   "I cannot reconcile": Livy to Grace King, June 27, 1897, MTP.

346   "Neither the *World*": *Town Topics*, June 17, 1897, 13.

347   "I concealed": MT to James G. Bennet, June 19, 1897, MTP.

348   "I wish you": MT to HH, June 23, 1897, *MT–HH*, 286.

349   "In writing to me": MT to Frank Fuller, June 3, 1897, MTP.

350   "Enclosed please": *Town Topics*, June 24, 1897, 14.

351   "call at your house": MT to Andrew Carnegie, July 7, 1897, MTP.

351   "Livy refuses her consent": MT to Frank Fuller, July 2, 1897, MTP.

CHAPTER 32: JOYS OF PAYBACK

352   "Sunday in heaven": MT to HH, Aug. [13], 1897, *MT–HH*, 299.

353   "I will write": MT to HH, Aug. 6, 1897, Ibid., 298.

354   "I find your uncle": Susan Crane to Samuel Moffett, July 22, 1897, MTP.

354   "Piano hired from Lucerne": NB, 41:56.

354   "Conceive of this 'tumble-bug'": MT to Andrew Chatto, July 25, 1897, MTP.

354   "ethereally pale and pensive": *My Father*, 186–87.

355   "How charming they were": MT to Twichell, Aug. 22, 1897, MTP.

356   "And none was prophesying": *Harper's New Monthly Magazine*, Nov. 1897, 930.

357   "Be patient": MT to Frank Bliss, Nov. 4, 1897, MTP.

358   "getting a little tired": MT to HH, Dec. 29, 1897, *MT–HH*, 311.

359   "keenly enjoyable": *London Mail*, Nov. 30, 1897; reviews from Louis J. Budd, *Mark Twain: The Contemporary Reviews*.

359   "a humorist without rival": *Pall Mall Gazette*, Dec. 1, 1897.

359   "If the fooling were good": *The Spectator*, May 21, 1898.

360   "A Road Decoration": *FE*, 347.

360   "best book": *New York Sun*, Dec. 11, 1897; reviews from Budd, *Contemporary Reviews*.

360   "I can appreciate": HH to MT, Jan. 6, 1898, *MT–HH*, 312.

361   "interests and amuses": *Harper's Lost Reviews: The Literary Notes, 1886–1899* (Millwood, 1976), 588.

361   "If Jack Sprat": *Critic*, Feb. 5, 1898; Budd, *Contemporary Reviews*, 476.

362   "We have read of examples": Creditor thank-you notes to MT, UVA.

362   "For the first time in my life": MT to HH, Dec. 29, 1897, *MT–HH*, 310.

362   "Dukes for Sale": NB, 42:52–53.

362   "Of course, a good deal": MT to William Dean Howells, Jan. 22, 1898, *MT–Howells*, 670.

363   "You've crucified the Bank": MT to HH, Feb. 6, 1898, *MT–HH*, 319.

363   "You and I are a team": MT to HH, Dec. 21, 1897, Ibid., 310.

363   "He was not disturbed": Autobiographical dictation, Aug. 6, 1906, MTP.

363   "I wish I could": Katherine Harrison to MT, Feb. 11, 1898, *MT–HH*, 322.

363   "Goodness knows": Creditors' letters to MT, UVA.

364   "I am as cheerful": MT to John Y. McAlister, March 12, 1898, MTP.

364   "He was so happy": *Lifetime with MT,* 167.

364   "Mrs. Clemens has been reading": MT to HH, March 7, 1898, *MT–HH,* 325.

CHAPTER 33: BACK IN THE GAME

365   "I've landed a big": MT to HH, March 17–20, 1898, *MT–HH,* 327.

365   "My extraordinary familiarity": NB, 40:13.

365   "financier": MT to HH, March 17–20, 1898, *MT–HH,* 328.

366   "inventions enough": MT to Richard W. Gilder, Apr. 2, 1898, MTP.

366   "You remember": MT to HH, March 22, 1898, *MT–HH,* 334.

366   "And *I* think": MT to HH, March 17, 1898, Ibid., 330.

367   "I was afraid": NB, 40:14.

367   "I feel like Colonel Sellers": MT to HH, March 24, 1898, *MT–HH,* 337.

367   "limited": William Whitman, report on the Designing Machine, Apr. 5, 1898 (forwarded to MT by HH), Ibid., 344.

367   "unser berühmter Gast": Dolmetsch, *Our Famous Guest,* 9.

367   "society clown": Ibid., 140.

368   "There is one thing": MT to HH, July 26, 1898, *MT–HH,* 354.

368   "Land, Joe, what chance": MT to Twichell, Oct. 23, 1897, MTP.

368   "Who was Moses's mother?" NB, 40:30.

368   "all jabber and no play": MT to HH, July 26, 1898, *MT–HH,* 353.

369   "in some cases": MT to HH, Feb. 5, 1900, recapping, Ibid., 430.

369   "We had a staving": MT to HH, Feb. 5–6, 1898, Ibid., 318.

370   "I treated myself": Dolmetsch, *Our Famous Guest,* 266.

370   "You are Americans?" NB, 40:8–11. (Entire anecdote.)

371   "I robbed the family": MT to HH, July 10, 1898, *MT–HH,* 352.

373   "shady Houses": MT to Andrew Chatto, Nov. 16, 1898, Chatto & Windus Papers.

373   "Behold—the Penis": Gershon Legman, *Mark Twain: The Mammoth Cod, and Address to the Stomach Club,* 11.

374   "Come—is it": MT to Andrew Chatto, Nov. 13, 1898, Chatto & Windus Papers.

374   "scathing satire": Welland, *Mark Twain in England,* 196.

374   "in any form, at any figure": MT to Andrew Chatto, Nov. 19, 1898, MTP.

374   "disappointing": MT to Frank Bliss, Feb. 11, 1898, MTP.

375   "It just occurs to me": MT to HH, Nov. 6–7, 1898, *MT–HH,* 375.

375   "I have been out": MT to Howells, Dec. 30, 1898, *MT–Howells,* 684.

376   "Jean has been": MT to Howells, Apr. 12, 1899, Ibid., 691.

376   "I hope you will": MT to HH, Feb. 2, 1899, *MT–HH,* 387.

377   "Oh, look here!" MT to HH, Feb. 19, 1899, Ibid., 389.

377   "I feel just as if": MT to Howells, Apr. 2, 1899, *MT–Howells,* 690.

378   "All along the way": Livy to Susan Crane, June 2–4, 1899, MTP.

379   "In those days": MT, Savage Club speech, June 9, 1899; *Mark Twain Speaking* (ed. Fatout), 322.

379   "Jean fell in a spasm": NB, 40:60.

379   "Dear Spider": MT to Clara (dateline: "Hell, July 12/99"), MTP.

380   "I am tired to death": MT to HH, January 8, 1900, *MT–HH,* 424.

381   "produced debt only": MT to HH, Apr. 8–9, 1900, Ibid., 441.

381   "not at any price": Charles Langdon to Livy, Jan. 4, 1900, MTP.

383   "five or six fingers of Scotch": MT to Margaret Carnegie, May 28, 1900, MTP.

383   "We must either sell": Livy to Grace King, n.d., 1900, MTP.

CHAPTER 34: HOMECOMING

387   "I realized": MT to Sylvester Baxter, Oct. 26, 1900, MTP.
387   "we drove home": Jean Clemens diary, Oct. 25, 1900, Huntington Library.
388   "Mr. Clemens . . . didn't bother": *Lifetime with MT,* 192–93.
388   "whatever he thought": Paine, *Mark Twain: A Biography,* 1113.
388   "such as not": Jean Clemens, diary, Oct. 27, 1900, Huntington Library.
389   "My family try to get me": MT to [unidentified], Nov. 30, 1900, MTP.
389   "Once settled": *My Father,* 217.
389   "It was wonderful": *Lifetime with MT,* 191–92.
389   "Strangely enough": *My Father,* 217–18.
390   "Never knew him so well": L. Hutton to Edwin Evans, Nov. 9, 1900, MTP.
390   "Clemens is here": Howells to Thomas B. Aldrich, Nov. 4, 1900, MTP.
390   "darky's dog": Ibid., Nov. 12, 1900.
392   "We hail him": John Elderkin, Chester S. Lord, and Charles W. Price (eds.), *After-Dinner Speeches at the Lotos Club* (New York: privately printed, 1911), 372–73; newspaper coverage, Nov. 11, 1900.
393   "And now": McFarland, *Mark Twain and the Colonel,* 65.
394   "dead to all honorable": *Mark Twain Speaking* (ed. Fatout), 353.
394   "Everybody believes": Ibid., 357.
394   "I should think": *New York World,* Nov. 18, 1900; *MT-Int,* 376.
394   "Professor Winchester": *Mark Twain Speaking* (ed. Fatout), 358–59.
395   "Oh I could fill a book": *Lifetime with MT,* 194.
395   "I am doing this": *New York World,* Nov. 23 and 30, 1900.
396   "I am dead, *dead* tired": MT to Edmund C. Stedman, Dec. 12, 1900, MTP.
396   "Mr. Churchill and I": *Mark Twain Speaking* (ed. Fatout), 367.
397   "rather have smallpox": Flagg, "Roses and Buckshot," 168–70, from Scharnhorst, ed., *Mark Twain in His Own Time.*

POSTSCRIPT

399   "There is a little settlement": Livy to Grace E. King, n.d., 1900, MTP.
399   detailed accounting: Box 5, UVA.
400   "Where is the mind": Livy to MT, n.d., *LL,* 333.
400   "Is it going to be": Jean Clemens, diary, Oct. 27, 1900, Huntington Library.
401   "My daughter has not": *My Father,* 280.
401   "The Blessings-of-Civilization Trust": *North American Review,* Jan. 1901.
402   "I am anxious to come": Legman, *The Mammoth Cod, and Address to the Stomach Club,* 22.
402   "I fail to see": Ibid., 18–21.
403   "brown slippers": Paine, *Mark Twain: A Biography,* 1314.
403   "Well, now, I hope": *Lifetime with MT,* 267–68.
404   "stallion in intention": "Plasmon Food Stock" trial transcript (15 pp.), UVA.
404   "I oughtn't to say": *New York American,* Dec. 21, 1907; *MT-Int,* 660.
404   "I would take this opportunity": *Mark Twain Speaking* (ed. Fatout), 642.
404   "This is terrible": "Mark Twain Grief-Stricken," *New York Times,* May 20, 1910.
405   "free from any control": Mark Twain's will, Probate Court, Redding, CT.

Bibliography

———————

MANUSCRIPT COLLECTIONS

Berg Collection, New York Public Library. Webster & Co. and James B. Pond papers. *More Tramps Abroad/Following the Equator* manuscript.

Chatto & Windus Papers. University of Reading, England. Special Collections. Includes *Omar's Old Age*.

Henry H. Rogers Collection. Millicent Library, Fairhaven, Massachusetts.

Huntington Library, San Marino, California. Jean Clemens diary, Langdon and Clemens family papers.

Langdon family wills. Surrogate's Court, Chemung County. Elmira, New York.

Mark Twain Collection, Clifton Waller Barrett Library of American Literature, University of Virginia.

Mark Twain Papers & Project. Unpublished notebooks and letters, newspaper clippings, and photographs. Bancroft Library, University of California, Berkeley.

William Evarts Benjamin Papers. Butler Library, Columbia University.

MAGAZINE ARTICLES

Ahluwalia, H. "Mark Twain's Lecture Tour in India." *Mark Twain Journal* 34, no. 1 (Spring, 1996): 3–49.

Anderson, Frank, and Hamlin Hill. "How Samuel Clemens Became Mark Twain's Publisher: A Study of the James R. Osgood Contracts." *Proof* 2 (1972): 117–43.

Budd, Louis J. "A Listing and Selection from Newspaper and Magazine Interviews with Samuel L. Clemens, 1874–1910." *American Literary Realism* 10 (Winter 1977): 1–30.

Burnet, Ruth A. "Mark Twain in the Northwest, 1895." *Pacific Northwest Quarterly* 42 (July 1951): 187–202.

Carson, Gerald. "Get the Prospect Seated . . . and Keep Talking." *American Heritage* 9, no. 5 (1958): 38–41. (On subscription publishing.)

Carter, Paul. "Olivia Clemens Edits Following the Equator." *American Literature* 30, no. 2 (1958): 194–209.

Clemens, Clara. "My Father." *Mentor* 12, no. 4 (May 1924): 21–22.

O'Rell, Max. "Mark Twain and Paul Bourget." *North American Review* 160 (March 1895): 302–11.

Parsons, Coleman. "Mark Twain: Clubman in South Africa." *New England Quarterly* 50, no. 2 (1977): 234–54.

———"Mark Twain in Australia." *Antioch Review* 21, no. 4 (1961): 455–68.

———"Mark Twain in Ceylon." *The Twainian* 22, no. 1 (1963): 3–4.

———"Mark Twain in New Zealand." *South Atlantic Quarterly* 61, no. 1 (1962): 51–76.

———"Mark Twain: Paid Performer in South Africa." *Mark Twain Journal* 19, no. 2 (1978): 2–11.

———"Mark Twain: Sightseer in India." *Mississippi Quarterly* 16, no. 2 (Spring 1963): 76–93.

———"Mark Twain: Traveler in South Africa." *Mississippi Quarterly* 29, no. 1 (1975–76): 3–41.

Richter, F. Ernest. "The Amalgamated Copper Company: A Closed Chapter in Corporation Finance." *Quarterly Journal of Economics* 30 (1915–16): 387–407.

Schmidt, Barbara. "A History of and Guide to Uniform Editions of Mark Twain's Works." Retrieved from www.twainquotes.com. (Numerous excellent Twain articles on this site.)

Shillingsburg, Miriam. "Down Under Day by Day with Mark Twain." *Mark Twain Journal* 33, no. 3 (Fall 1995): 1–41.

Smythe, Carlyle. "The Real Mark Twain." *Pall Mall Magazine* 16, no. 65 (1898): 29–36.

Weir, Rob. "Vagabond Abroad: Mark Twain's 1895 Visit to New Zealand." *Journal of the Gilded Age and Progressive Era* 8, no. 4 (2009): 487–514.

Welland, Dennis. "Mark Twain's Last Travel Book." *Bulletin of the New York Public Library* 69 (1965): 35–48.

White, Frank M. "Mark Twain as a Newspaper Reporter." *Outlook* 24 (1910): 961–67.

WRITINGS OF MARK TWAIN

Adventures of Huckleberry Finn. Edited by Walter Blair and Victor Fischer. Berkeley: University of California Press, 1988. (1885).

Adventures of Tom Sawyer, The. Hartford, CT: American Publishing, 1876.

Autobiography of Mark Twain. Edited by Charles Neider. New York: Harper & Row, 1966.

Autobiography of Mark Twain. Edited by Harriet Elinor Smith and Benjamin Griffin, with associate editors Victor Fischer, Michael B. Frank, Amanda Gagel, Sharon K. Goetz, Leslie D. Myrick, and Christopher M. Oghe. 3 vols. Berkeley: University of California Press, 2010, 2013, 2105.

Best Short Stories of Mark Twain. Edited by Lawrence Berkove. New York: Modern Library, 2004.

Following the Equator: A Journey Around the World. (Hartford, CT, 1898).

Following the Equator and Anti-imperialist Essays. New York: Oxford University Press, 1996.

Gilded Age, The. (With Charles Dudley Warner.) Hartford, CT: American Publishing, 1873.

How to Tell a Story & Other Essays (New York: Harper, 1897).

The Innocents Abroad. Hartford, CT: American Publishing, 1869.

Love Letters of Mark Twain. Edited by Dixon Wecter. New York, Harper, 1949.

Mark Twain–Howells Letters: The Correspondence of Samuel L. Clemens and William Dean Howells, 1872–1910. Edited by Henry Smith and William Gibson. Cambridge, MA: Harvard University Press, 1960.

Mark Twain in Eruption: Hitherto Unpublished Pages about Men and Events. Edited by Bernard DeVoto. New York: Harper & Brothers, 1922.

Mark Twain Speaking. Edited by Paul Fatout. Iowa City: University of Iowa Press, 1976.

Mark Twain's Autobiography. Edited by Albert B. Paine. New York: Harper, 1924.

Mark Twain Speaks for Himself. Edited by Paul Fatout. West Lafayette, IN: Purdue University Press, 1978.

Mark Twain's Correspondence with Henry Huttleston Rogers, 1893–1909. Edited by Lewis Leary. Berkeley: University of California Press, 1969.

Mark Twain's Letters. Edited by Albert B. Paine. New York: Harper, 1917.

Mark Twain's Letters to His Publishers. Edited by Hamlin Hill. Berkeley: University of California Press, 1967.

Mark Twain's Library of Humor. Edited by Steve Martin. New York: Modern Library, 2000.

Mark Twain's Notebook. Edited by Albert B. Paine. New York: Harper, 1935.

Mark Twain's Notebooks & Journals, Volume 1 (1855–1873). Edited by Frederick Anderson, Michael Frank, and Kenneth Sanderson. Berkeley: University of California Press, 1975.

Mark Twain's Notebooks & Journals, Volume 2 (1877–1883). Edited by Frederick Anderson, Lin Salamo, and Bernard Stein. Berkeley: University of California Press, 1975.

Mark Twain's Notebooks & Journals, Volume 3 (1883–1891). Edited by Robert P. Browning, Michael Frank, and Lin Salamo. Berkeley: University of California Press, 1979.

Mark Twain's Rubaiyat. Edited by Alan Gribben and Kevin MacDonnell. Austin, TX: Jenkins Publishing, 1983.

Mark Twain's Speeches. Edited by William D. Howells. New York: Harper, 1910.

Mark Twain: The Mammoth Cod and Address to the Stomach Club. Edited by Gershon Legman. Milwaukee, WI: Maledicta, 1976.

More Tramps Abroad. London: Chatto & Windus, 1900.

Personal Recollections of Joan of Arc. New York: Harper, 1896.

Tom Sawyer Abroad. New York: Harper, 1894.

Tragedy of Pudd'nhead Wilson, The. Hartford, CT: American Publishing, 1894.

Tramp Abroad, A. Hartford, CT: American Publishing, 1880.

BOOKS

Ahrle, Fred. *Darjeeling Himalayan Railway: Illustrated Guide for Tourists.* London: McCorquodale, 1896.

Allen, Frederick Lewis. *The Lords of Creation.* New York: Harper & Bros., 1935.

Andrews, Kenneth R. *Nook Farm: Mark Twain's Hartford Circle.* Cambridge, MA: Harvard University Press, 1950.

Baedeker, Karl. *The United States with an Excursion into Mexico: Handbook for Travellers.* Leipzig: Karl Baedeker, 1899.

Baetzhold, Howard. *Mark Twain and John Bull: The British Connection.* Bloomington: Indiana University Press, 1970.

Brown, A. Samler. *Brown's South Africa: A Practical and Complete Guide for the Use of Tourists, Sportsmen, Invalids and Settlers.* London: Sampson, Low, Marston, & Company, 1893.

Budd, Louis J. *Mark Twain: The Contemporary Reviews.* Cambridge, UK: Cambridge University Press, 1999.

Caine, W. S. *Picturesque India: A Handbook for European Travellers.* London: G. Routledge, 1891.

Carpenter, Edward. *From Adam's Peak to Elephanta, Sketches in Ceylon and India.* London: S. Sonnenschein, 1892.

Chevrillon, Andre. *Dans l'Inde.* Paris: Hachette, 1891.

Clemens, Clara. *My Father, Mark Twain.* New York: Harper & Bros., 1931.

Clemens, Susy. *Papa: An Intimate Biography of Mark Twain.* Edited by Charles Neider. Garden City, NY: Doubleday, 1985.

Cooper, Robert. *Around the World with Mark Twain.* New York: Arcade Publishing, 2000.

Courtney, Steve. *The Loveliest Home That Ever Was: The Story of the Mark Twain House in Hartford.* Mineola, NY: Dover Publications, 2011.

Davitt, Michael. *Life and Progress in Australasia.* London: Methuen, 1898.

Denton, Sherman F. *Incidents of a Collector's Rambles in Australia, New Zealand, and New Guinea.* Boston: Lee and Shepard, 1889.

DeVoto, Bernard. *Mark Twain's America.* Cambridge, MA: Houghton Mifflin, 1932.

Dias, Earl J. *Henry Huttleston Rogers: Portrait of a "Capitalist."* Fairhaven, MA: Millicent Library, 1974.

———. *Mark Twain and Henry Huttleston Rogers: An Odd Couple.* Fairhaven, MA: Millicent Library, 1984.

Dolmetsch, Carl. *Our Famous Guest: Mark Twain in Vienna.* Athens: University of Georgia Press, 1992.

Doubleday, Frank N. *Memoirs of a Publisher.* New York: Doubleday, 1972.

Elderkin, John, Chester S. Lord, and Charles W. Price. (Eds.) *After-Dinner Speeches at the Lotos Club.* New York: Privately printed, 1911.

Exman, Eugene. *House of Harper: The Making of a Modern Publisher.* New York: Harper Perennial, 2010. Reprint of the 1967 edition.

Fatout, Paul. *Mark Twain on the Lecture Circuit.* Bloomington: Indiana University Press, 1960.

Galloway, William J. *Advanced Australia: A Short Account of Australia on the Eve of Federation.* London: Methuen, 1899.

Gold, Charles. *Hatching Ruin, or Mark Twain's Road to Bankruptcy.* Columbia: University of Missouri Press, 2003.

Gordon-Cumming, Constance. *In the Himalayas and on the Indian Plains.* London: Chatto & Windus, 1884.

Gribben, Alan and Nick Karanovich. *Overland with Mark Twain: James B. Pond's Photographs and Journal of the North American Lecture Tour of 1895.* Elmira, NY: Center for Mark Twain Studies at Quarry Farm, Elmira College, 1992.

Hammond, John H. *The Autobiography of John Hays Hammond.* New York: Farrar & Rinehart, 1935.

A Handbook for Travellers in India, Burma, and Ceylon. 3rd ed. London: John Murray, 1898.

Harnsberger, Caroline. *Family Letters of Mark Twain.* Unpublished typescript, Mark Twain Papers, Bancroft Library, Berkeley, CA.

Haweis, Hugh R. *Travel and Talk: My Hundred Thousand Miles of Travel Through America, Australia, Tasmania, Canada, New Zealand, Ceylon and the Paradises of the Pacific.* London: Chatto & Windus, 1896.

Headley, Russel. *The Law of Voluntary Assignments for the Benefit of Creditors Under the New York Statutes.* Albany, NY: M. Bender, 1896.

Herrmann, Dorothy. *Helen Keller: A Life.* New York: Knopf, 1998.

Hill, Hamlin. *Mark Twain: God's Fool.* New York: Harper & Row, 1973.

———. *Mark Twain and Elisha Bliss.* Columbia: University of Missouri Press, 1964.

Hopkins, Richard L. *The Tragic Saga of James W. Paige's Marvelous Typesetting Machine.* Terra Alta, WV: Hill & Dale Private Press and Type Foundry, 2014.

Hutton, Laurence, John Kendrick Bangs, and Clayton L. Eichelberger. *Harper's Lost Reviews: The Literary Notes.* Millwood, NY: Kraus-Thompson Organization, 1976.

Ingram, J. Forsyth. *The Colony of Natal: An Official Illustrated Handbook and Railway Guide.* London: J. Causton & Sons, 1895.

Jacolliot, Louis. *Voyage au pays des fakirs charmeurs.* Paris: E. Dentu, 1881.

Kahan, Basil. *Ottmar Mergenthaler: The Man and His Machine.* New Castle, DE: Oak Knoll Press, 2000.

Kaplan, Justin. *Mr. Clemens and Mark Twain: A Biography.* New York: Simon & Schuster, 1966.

Keller, Helen. *The Story of My Life.* New York: Doubleday, Page, 1903.

Khan, Mohammed Aga. *Memoirs of Aga Khan: World Enough and Time.* London: Cassell, 1954.

Knox, Thomas. *How to Travel: Hints, Advice, and Suggestions to Travelers by Land and Sea All over the Globe.* New York: C. T. Dillingham, 1881.

Koelbel, Lenora. *Missoula The Way It Was: "A Portrait of an Early Western Town."* Missoula, MT: Gateway Print and Litho, 1972.

Krass, Peter. *Ignorance, Confidence, and Filthy Rich Friends: The Business Adventures of Mark Twain, Chronic Speculator and Entrepreneur.* Hoboken, NJ: Wiley, 2007.

Lawson, Thomas. *Frenzied Finance: The Crime of Amalgamated.* New York: Ridgway-Thayer, 1905.

Leary, Katy, and Mary Lawton. *A Lifetime with Mark Twain: The Memories of Katy Leary, for Thirty Years His Faithful and Devoted Servant.* New York: Harcourt, Brace, 1925.

Legman, Gershon. *Mark Twain: The Mammoth Cod, and Address to the Stomach Club.* Milwaukee, WI: Maledicta, 1976.

Lorch, Fred W. *The Trouble Begins at Eight: Mark Twain's Lecture Tours.* Ames: Iowa State University Press, IA, 1968.

McFarland, Philip. *Mark Twain and the Colonel: Samuel Clemens, Theodore Roosevelt, and the Arrival of a New Century.* Lanham, MD: Rowman & Littlefield, 2012.

Messent, Peter. *Mark Twain and Male Friendship: The Twichell, Howells, and Rogers Friendships.* New York: Oxford University Press, 2009.

Michelson, Bruce. *Printer's Devil: Mark Twain and the Publishing Revolution.* Berkeley: University of California Press, 2006.

Mukerji, Chandra. *Traveller's Guide to Agra.* Delhi: Sen & Co., 1892.

Mutalik, Keshav. *Mark Twain in India.* Bombay: Noble Publishing House, 1978.

Naparsteck, Martin (with Michelle Cardulla). *Mrs. Mark Twain: The Life of Olivia Langdon Clemens, 1845–1904.* Jefferson, NC: McFarland & Co., 2014.

Nielsen, Kim E. *Beyond the Miracle Worker: The Remarkable Life of Anne Sullivan Macy and Her Extraordinary Friendship with Helen Keller.* Boston: Beacon Press, 2009.

Ober, K. Patrick. *Mark Twain and Medicine: "Any Mummery Will Cure."* Columbia: University of Missouri Press, 2003.

The Official Northern Pacific Railroad Guide for the Use of Tourists and Travelers. St. Paul, MN: W. C. Riley, 1893.

O'Rell, Max. *A Frenchman in America.* New York: Cassell Publishing, 1891.

Paine, Albert B. *Mark Twain: A Biography,* 3 vols. New York: Harper & Brothers, 1912.

Parker, Arthur. *A Hand-book of Benares.* Benares: E. J. Lazarus, 1895.

Pennefather, F.W. *A Visit to India.* Adelaide: Bonython, 1894.

Plate, A. G. *The "Lloyd" Guide to Australasia, Illustrated.* London: E. Stanford, 1906.

Pond, James B. *Eccentricities of Genius: Memories of Famous Men and Women of the Platform and Stage.* London: Chatto & Windus, 1901.

Powers, Ron. *Mark Twain: A Life.* New York: Free Press, 2005.

Rasmussen, R. Kent. *Mark Twain A to Z: The Essential Reference to His Life and Writings.* New York: Facts on File, 1995.

Ricalton, James. *India Through the Stereoscope.* New York: Underwood & Underwood, 1900.

Rodney, Robert M. *Mark Twain Overseas: A Biographical Account of His Voyages, Travels, and Reception in Foreign Lands, 1866–1910.* Washington, DC: Three Continents Press, 1993.

Salsbury, Edith C. *Susy and Mark Twain: Family Dialogues.* New York: Harper & Row, 1965.

Salter-Whiter, James. *A Trip to South Africa.* London: William Pile, 1892.

Scharnhorst, Gary, ed. *Mark Twain: The Complete Interviews.* Tuscaloosa: University of Alabama Press, 2006.

———. *Twain in His Own Time: A Biographical Chronicle of His Life, Drawn from Recollections, Interviews, and Memoirs by Family, Friends, and Associates.* Iowa City: University of Iowa Press, 2010.

Scidmore, Eliza. *Winter India.* New York: The Century Company, 1903.

Scott, Arthur. *Mark Twain at Large.* New York: Henry Regnery, 1969.

Shillingsburg, Miriam. *At Home Abroad: Mark Twain in Australasia.* Jackson: University Press of Mississippi, 1988.

Stevenson, Robert Louis. *Across the Plains.* London: Chatto & Windus, 1892.

Strathcarron, Ian. *The Indian Equator: Mark Twain's India Revisited.* Mineola, NY: Dover Publications, 2013.

Sweetser, Delight. *One Way Round the World.* 2nd ed. Indianapolis: Bowen-Merrill, 1898.

Tarbell, Ida. *The History of the Standard Oil Company.* New York: Macmillan, 1904.

Ward, Geoffrey C. and Dayton Duncan and Ken Burns. *Mark Twain: An Illustrated Biography.* New York: Knopf, 2001.

Webster, Samuel C. *Mark Twain, Business Man.* Boston: Little, Brown, 1946.

Welland, Dennis. *Mark Twain in England.* Atlantic Highlands, NJ: Humanities Press, 1978.

Williams, Gardner F. *The Diamond Mines of South Africa.* New York: Macmillan, 1902.

Willis, Resa. *Mark and Livy: The Love Story of Mark Twain and the Woman Who Almost Tamed Him.* New York: Atheneum, 1992.

Illustration Credits

PAGE 8

TOP: *Old Picture Book of Christchurch*

BOTTOM: Courtesy of the Mark Twain Project, the Bancroft Library, University of California, Berkeley

PAGE 9

ALL: *Hamburg-Amerika Linie: Nordland Fahrten* (1910)

PAGE 10

TOP: Library of Congress

BOTTOM: James Ricalton's *India Through the Stereoscope* (1900)

PAGE 11

ALL: James Ricalton's *India Through the Stereoscope* (1900)

PAGE 12

TOP: National Portrait Gallery, London (1889)

CENTER: Baroda views, c.1890, courtesy of the British Library Board

BOTTOM: *Following the Equator* (1898)

PAGE 13

Library of Congress

PAGE 14

TOP AND BOTTOM: Library of Congress

CENTER: Samuel Bourne, 1865. Courtesy of the British Library Board

PAGE 15

ALL: Mark Twain Archive, Elmira College. Courtesy of Kevin Mac Donnell

PAGE 16

Courtesy of the Mark Twain Project, the Bancroft Library, University of California, Berkeley

Index

Richard Zacks is the bestselling author of *Island of Vice: Theodore Roosevelt's Quest to Clean Up Sin-Loving New York; Pirate Coast: Thomas Jefferson, the First Marines, and the Secret Mission of 1805; Pirate Hunter: The True Story of Captain Kidd; History Laid Bare* and *An Underground Education*. His writing has been featured in *The New York Times, The Atlantic, Harper's Magazine* and many other publications. He attended the University of Michigan and the Graduate School of Journalism at Columbia University. He was born in Savannah, Georgia, and now lives in New York City.